AFTERMATH

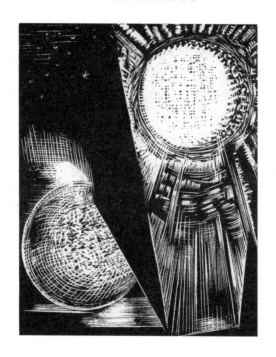

RONALD BLYTHE

First published in England 2010, Black Dog Books,
104 Trinity Street, Norwich, Norfolk, NR2 2BJ,
www.blackdogbooks.co.uk

Text © Ronald Blythe, Foreword © Richard Mabey

A CIP record of this book is available from the British Library.

ISBN 978-0-9549286-9-8

Printed in Great Britain by HSW Print, South Wales

Illustrations by Paul Nash: The Sun and Moon, 1924, woodcut, frontispiece; Joe
Pentifer and Son, 1921, woodcut, p.13; The Bay, 1923, woodcut, p.89; Still Life
No.1, 1924, woodcut, p.135; Meeting Place, 1922, woodcut, p.213; Void of War,
1918, lithograph, p.277; Bouquet, 1927, woodcut, p.337; Angels, 1927, woodcut,
p.385; Sorrow, illustration for Sir Thomas Browne's Urn Buriall and The Garden
of Cyrus, 1922, p. 429

AFTERMATH

SELECTED WRITINGS 1960–2010

ED. PETER TOLHURST

IN MEMORIAM
TONY GLOVER

BLACK DOG
BOOKS

CONTENTS

FROM THE HEADLANDS

FOREWORD
Richard Mabey

I first met Ronnie, as he graciously allows us to call him, in 1969, just after the publication of *Akenfield*. I was working for his publishers, Penguin, at the time, and used this slim connection as a way of getting to meet a person whose luminous evocation of rural life had knocked me for six. I'd conjured up the idea of a school text-book version of *Akenfield* as a pretext, but what I really wanted, dreaming of becoming a writer myself, was to touch his hem, receive some kind of literary benediction, find out how on earth he had done it.

I hadn't needed an excuse, as it turned out. When I arrived at his cottage he was as generous as he has always been to the legions of admirers, invited or not, who have made the pilgrimage to his Suffolk motherlode. He had just come in from clearing out the garden pond, but had found time to make me a cake. The conversation, as I recall, ranged dizzyingly through the vernacular archaeology of ponds, the student revolts of the previous year, the ominous threat of Dutch elm disease, and the edition of Hazlitt he had just been working on. I asked how he had so perfectly caught the voices of *Akenfield*. Had he used a tape-recorder, was the editing difficult? He sounded courteously surprised. There was no technology involved. He simply listened. And then wrote down what he remembered. What he was far too modest to mention, of course, was that these rememberings were acts of imaginative reconstruction, underpinned by a lifetime of exploring the local landscape, of hearing and absorbing the subtle rhythms of local talk, and above all of reading – everything from the Song of Solomon to village signposts.

In the four decades that I've been privileged to know him as a friend, Ronnie has not lost one jot of that intense curiosity and unselfconscious sense of connectivity between life's elements. It's not just that his 'ordinary' life – talking to cats, preaching sermons, chastening the nettles – is seamlessly connected to his writing life, but that they are the same life. Writing (and reading) for Ronnie is simply conversation, a form of extended gossip about the stream of one's consciousness and activities. There's a passage in his Wormingford Trilogy where he describes how a dragonfly settles on a hymnal he's reading in the garden. 'The dragonfly's wings are colourless and translucent, and I can read Winchester and Yattendon through them'. The flesh becomes word.

So though this new collection of his occasional writing consists chiefly of book reviews and introductions to other writers' work, it is not in any sense 'bookish'. The writers featured in it are, so to speak, friends at a distance, and their own everyday lives and emotions are revealed to be as connected with their books as Ronnie's are. It is as if he is able to dowse a whole person from their writings. It's no surprise that *Aftermath* begins with reflections on journals, the literary form in which the bits and pieces of the diarist's life are most intimately entwined. Nor that Ronnie's own journal is no mundane account of his daily round (those details are indelibly recorded in an extraordinary memory bank) but a writer's Day-book, in which he sets down his responses to the day's reading and reflection. 'Put everything down', a poet friend once advised him. 'The total will surprise you.' And surprise us too. Here are his thoughts on the journals not just of literary heavyweights like Dorothy Wordsworth and Samuel Johnson, but of another Johnson, William, the Eton schoolmaster who wrote the Boating Song, and a cryptic confessional about abandoning teaching and the transcendental attraction of boys. Much more down to earth are the diaries (or perhaps they should be called workbooks) of William Dowsing, sent by Lord Manchester to 'cleanse' the churches of Suffolk in the 1640s. Incredibly, Dowsing was a local farmer from Laxfield, which only partly explains why his daily record of wrecking brasses and windows and carved angels is as chillingly matter-of-fact as an inventory of cattle sent for slaughter.

Ronnie tellingly quotes Virginia Woolf, whose view of a journal was that it should be like 'some old desk. . . in which one flings a mass of odds & ends without looking them through. I should like to come back, after a year or two, & find that the collection had sorted itself out & refined itself & coalesced, as such deposits so mysteriously do, into a mould, transparent enough to reflect the light of our life . . .' In one sense this is how Ronnie's essays and excursions seem to have been organised, except one knows a very writerly sub-conscious is working away behind them.

It is bewitching to trace how the narratives wind effortlessly this way and that, joining reading and first-hand experience, compressing past and present so that an event or an insight from a thousand years ago is as real as yesterday's evening's Bluebell Party at Tiger Hill, when, incidentally – except that nothing is incidental in Ronnie's stories – a stone-age axehead punctured the tyre of the Range Rover he was riding in. These kind of synchronicities happen to him – or are just acutely perceived – repeatedly. The section on country life ('From the Headlands') contains an essay that is eventually about writers such as Henry Rider Haggard, and the literature of the great agricultural depression in East Anglia. But the route by which Ronnie arrives at this theme is his unique stylistic signature. It begins with the vicarage children bringing armfuls of newspapers down from the loft. He sits down with them to read 'the juicy bits'. Stanley is emerging from the black depths of Africa. Magic lanterns are £7.17. Three thousand acres of top-quality farmland near Beccles are to be let for shooting. The letters columns complain about 'irregular marriages'. Ronnie remembers that his own grandmother would have been getting wed just about the time the builder's apprentice was heaving all this newsprint into the loft to spread between the joists, and was on her way to live in Cuckoo Tye. His grandfather died when Ronnie was six, but he remembers him as a 'quizzical authoritarian with sky blue eyes'. Grandmother born in 1860, ('years before Hardy had written a word' – a classic Blythean exactitude), and lived long enough 'to glimpse our first television set, a sturdy affair with the lines of a fruit machine' (another). Her longevity fascinated him, and led eventually to the writing of a classic book on old age (a subject covered movingly and challengingly in the final section of this book). And so we move to another nonagerian, Major Bush (alias the writer Michael

Home) who lived in the Breckland, once East Anglia's great heath, where there were always gypsies about. Grandmother had once seen one of their vardoes burnt after a death. Moving about so much, had the Romanies noticed the Victorian 'flight from the land'? – and at last we have arrived at the notional subject of the essay. But this overture – not much more than a thousand words long – has taken us across East Anglia, through Ronnie's family, deep into the sources of his inspiration, and graphically sketched in the tone of Victorian country life.

If you were to make a map of this serpentine narrative it would look like the excited scamperings of a spaniel, darting about after every intriguing scent and sign. It would make teachers of creative writing, with their structural analyses and critical path diagrams, despair. But it is not random rambling, nor, as associations go, 'free'. This – and not in organised, logically unfolding patterns – is how real lives and thoughts move. Ronnie's genius is to so faithfully reflect this wonderfully connected muddle that what is some of the most beautiful and precise prose in modern English reads like conversation.

It is hard to credit that one lifetime can contain so many books read, so many writers understood and remembered (Bunyan, Clare and Wodehouse are all here, and give an idea of *Aftermath's* diversity), such 'a mass of odds & ends' knitted together. But his work has grown like an ecosystem, with every part in some way connected with all the others. A journal entry from the Great War years by Virginia Woolf (who lurks throughout Ronnie's work like a dangerously seductive shadow), expressing her incomprehension that 'this preposterous masculine fiction keeps going a day longer', is echoed in his moving and often angry writing about the poems and letters that came out the two World Wars. The 20th century's casual sacrifice of its young (and old) is one of his greatest pains. He deplores brutality of all kinds, especially that which lurks under that deferential rural cap, 'the way we do things here': the hanging of poor 19th century fieldworkers for the sake of the pheasant; the militaristic frenzy of women from the 20th century Big Houses; the callous indifference to nature of modern industrial farmers. He continuously gives the lie to the idea that a country person must, ipso facto, be a conservative. The rural idyll, he says 'slips in blood'. And though he applauds the way in which East Anglian writers such as Rider Haggard, George Crabbe and the novelist Mary Mann exposed the stark facts about the desperate lives of the rural poor, he will not dismiss them as 'units of the brutish, measureless, human undergrowth'. He celebrates instead their knowledge and skill, their survival instincts. Mary Mann, paradoxically, catches their 'actual voice, thus undermining her sense of their hopelessness, for it comes through witty and strong'.

Which brings us to William Hazlitt. The essay on the 18th century radical essayist is perhaps the finest in this collection, and it shows Hazlitt not so much as Ronnie's hero, as his alter ego. The two have so much in common: they are self-educated countrymen – 'village intellectuals', passionate liberals, Romantics in love with language and with their fellow humans, of whatever station. But Hazlitt was burdened with baggage Ronnie has mercifully escaped. He was bitter, subject to mood-swings and outbursts of violence, intemperate in just about every possible way and incapable of not wearing his heart on his sleeve.

By contrast, Ronnie's work, though deeply personal and often autobiographical, is intensely private. Do not expect disclosures or revelations. The man who has written so sensitively about others' travails and illnesses and loves, is silent about his own. If you were to ask him why, the answer might well be that robust East Anglian response to nosiness, 'Never you mind!' Time enough for that when the biographies are written. But I sense civic courtesy as well behind this diffidence. Over the past half century we have been slavered with self-indulgent memoirs and egotistical confessionals, the literature of the 'me' generation. Ronnie's personal writing offers something far more valuable and noble: the literature of 'us', where the 'I', so to speak, becomes the eye, fascinated with the world beyond itself.

Coleridge once recommended that introspective writers would be better off going for a tramp through the woods than contemplating their tortured egos. This collection is, in a metaphorical sense, like a good tramp with Ronnie Blythe, an exhilarating and expansive exploration of how landscapes, humans and words interact, touched with great humanity and expressed in exquisite but sturdy English: the beat of the feet and hands is there as well as the heart. He is our tribal story-teller, plugged into the common stream of inquisitive conversation that joins us as a species.

PRIVATE WORDS

READING OTHER PEOPLE'S DIARIES

From The Headlands, 1982

There was once a group of poets which William Aytoun dubbed the 'Spasmodic School' on account of its intermittent bursts of creativity, and if there happened to be a similar school for a certain type of diarist, then I should belong to it. My diary-keeping comes into the New Year's resolution, brief Lenten resolve, temporary cutting-down on this or that class of activity, and is no more than a sincere but short- lived attempt to do what I feel I should do. The true diarist never writes against the grain of his own inclination, but rushes along with it. He is pulled to the daily page, however late the hour. The one thing of which I have never had any doubt is that when I am reading a diary I am able to feel the relief of the diarist as he settles to his task. Anyone reading my broken fragments would feel at once that I had been driven to write them by forces that were a compound of duty and experiment. No pleasure there in my own dailiness, only a pronounced struggle to set it all down. All the same, I am addicted to what the natural diarist sets down and have, over the years, read an enormous quantity of, 'January 7th. Took Edward to the station. Returned home the back way and saw the sea through the bare wood . . .' and so on for thirty or forty years. Sometimes it is the full works and no holds barred, sometimes it is nothing very much at all, yet still I read on. 'It is April 1878 and there is late snow and Mr Williams has called . . .' It is enough.

All-out or discreet, natural diarists exhibit the pathetic principle to a naked degree, and even Parson Woodforde isn't quite hidden behind his food mountain. The only diaries I can't read are those by British and American politicians and militarists. So much consciously and artfully putting the record straight puts me off, this and the sound of manoeuvres for outsize publishers' advances. Although the natural diarist would seem to write for himself alone, and even in some

15

instances – Pepys, Beatrix Potter – invents codes to ensure that posterity will not alter this personal condition, there is something very strange in telling oneself everything that one did and is. Vanity? Taken all in all, vanity is at a low ebb in diaries. Natural diarists are compulsively self-staring, self-prying, self-explaining and self-presenting, but without being actually narcissistic. Self-bragging occasionally (Boswell) but rarely self-enamoured. The opposite, in fact. Evelyn Waugh's diary is thick with self-disgust. But whether a diarist is in the 'dead secret' category or simply a person who is compelled to put his day down before he sleeps, oblivious to such considerations as for whose eyes or for what purpose, there is little doubt that diary writing has much to do with turning what is transitory into what is permanent. Without a diary, our talk and actions, and our dreams and current notions, slide down a shute into a vague experience labelled 'last Summer' or 'when I was twenty-four' or 'in the office' or an address or 'work'. *In* a diary everything is held – the verb reflects a safekeeping and a security – in place and in sequence. It is holding in place of the detail of life which makes diaries so riveting.

Here are a few favourite diarists. First that of the boy King Edward VI, which he kept from March 1549 to his death at sixteen. I never read this without feeling as though the Reformation air is raising the leaves in the garden below. Among English monarchs, only Edward and Victoria kept diaries which have been published. Hers is a masterpiece of its kind, his stiff, bright and sharp, like a pennon. All in his own hand, it proclaims most eloquently the precocious education which he, his sister Elizabeth, Lady Jane Grey and similarly learned high born children received in the sixteenth century. The tone of Edward's diary is part innocent and part rather overwhelming. The King's Highnesse in these edgy pages is never the sickly majesty of history. A contemporary commenting on a poem which Edward had written said, 'This young Prince became a perfect schoole maister unto old erroneous men,' and after reading the diary one can believe it. It is not the work of a runtish interruption of the succession list. I was here, I was king, it proclaims, as intelligently and promisingly as Elizabeth herself. A child of his time, he describes with equanimity a hideous glimpse of the festivities surrounding the nuptials of Robert Dudley, his sister's future lover, and

Amy Robsart. A goose has been strung up to make a fluttering, difficult target. It is June 1550 and the diarist is thirteen.

Sir Robert Dudley, third sonne to th'erle of Warwic, maried sir John Robsartes daughter, after wich mariage there were certain gentlemen that did strive who shuld take away a gose's heade, which was hanged alive on two crose postes. Ther was tilt and tornay on foot with as great staves as they run withal on horsbake.

When it comes to the execution of his uncles, Edward is as casual as the White Queen, and glacial in his account of how the members of his first council grabbed great titles for themselves.

I think that the first youthful diary I read was Denton Welch's. Although thirty-three when he died, there is a fretful quality in Welch's *Journals*, due to illness and pain, and a kind of thudding reality which was constantly informing the writer of a death sentence, which has always made him seem perpetually late-adolescent. Or as if time had stopped for him, as with a fine watch crushed by a car, on the day of his accident, 7 June 1935. A woman driver had knocked him off his bicycle and there had been a terrible fracturing of his lower spine, with subsequent constant bleeding, tuberculosis and agony. It was not that he projected himself back to the years before this disaster, when his body was perfect, but that, by some inner strength of will, and by using art and literature as preserving agents, he was able to bring forward much of the poise of his healthy, uninjured being of the pre-1935 period to enable him to lead what was a remarkable literary and social life by any standards, crippled though he was. And then there was the war, and Welch's unique position as a badly wounded young writer whose injuries had nothing to do with the fighting or the bombing, and yet whose work became a correct part of the anti-heroic literature of the hour. Thus it was that Maurice Denton Welch, born in Shanghai in 1915, the year of the Battle of Mons, became an authentic voice of the Second World War and indeed became a cult almost during the late 1940s.

Everything about him focussed an extreme attention. He in his turn seemed to understand this and to accept its implications, although he occasionally defended himself with a kind of malice, or appeared ingenuously incapable of knowing what it was that made people write to him or to try and seek him out. 'I keep on wondering if I'm producing semi-demi A.E.Housman', he wrote in his *Journal*. Certainly the two generations which had responded to Housman (and Forster) would be practised in reading between the lines. The peculiarly English climate which raises art and moral courage from such disparate ingredients as hyper-sensitivity, bourgeois cultural standards and homosexual love was familiar enough, but Welch added an irresistible – at the time – quality to it.

Perhaps the best known photograph of him can partly explain his fascination. It shows a young man seated at a chequer-board on which are arranged a pretty monstrance, three candles burning in cut glass holders and a patch-box, or maybe a counter-box. Behind him swirls a detail from a large painting, a bare arm thrusting its way out of the surrounding chiaroscuro. The young man wears an open necked shirt with the collar turned up. His arms rest on the board and his face, mask-like in the candlelight, is nervous and tense. It is the face of the perennial sick poet, and the candles with their short butts and tall flames tell one that his days are numbered. For those who felt his spell, there was no effeteness in the portrait, simply brilliance and doom. In fact, as a recent critic has pointed out, in the classic pathos of genius being allowed only a brief life to give of itself, 'we touch upon one of the most potent, and seductive factors in the whole Denton Welch case. His life as such forms an almost irresistible paradigm of what Mario Praz labelled the Romantic Agony – 'a desperate creative race against time.' Cyril Connolly placed him with Katherine Mansfield and Barbellion. Pain excused this category of writers their preoccupation with either the minutiae of their introspection or their possessions. When Denton Welch wrote preciously about his bric-à-brac he was given a mandate for doing so which was outside that given to other writers of the period. His obsessive descriptions of healthy soldiers and farm workers, usually stripping to wash or swim, appeared neither wholly self-indulgent nor silly, but oddly elegiac. Both they and the toys with which Welch surrounded himself, the class-consciousness and the banishment of all politics and wider social issues, were all part of a 'civilised structure' whose standards were well-known and admired during the Forties.

Welch wrote and drew (and still rode his bicycle) through the decade and through increasing pain. At one time he considered suicide and went so far as destroying some of his diaries. Those that remain begin with a bounce:

10 July, Friday
And then we all met at Penshurst; I and Maurice and Filthy Freddie, RAF. And first we had tea (I found them waiting for me with scones and butter on the table, when I came in from the rain) . . .

One of the things which had brought him in from the rain, as it were, had been an enthusiastic acceptance by Connolly of Welch's article on Sicker '. . . Being ill made me think of being great and famous. They are always linked together in my mind. I must not be so ill that I cannot be famous.' Now that he had begun to be published all the things which had wrecked his boyhood, his loathing of Repton, from which he had run away at sixteen, his chilly family life, and even the accident itself, retreated. 'Now that is all gone. Broken away, lost and forgotten.' Curiously enough, the war atmosphere actually helped Welch, who was the kind of man, as Jocelyn Brooke said, who would hardly have found life easy in any circumstances. It left him isolated. Besides, others were soon to die as well as he.

Airmen flashed by on bicycles. They all wore that intent look of people who are grimly determined to enjoy themselves for their few free hours from slavery. It's an almost fanatical look. The anxious eyes seem to say, I *must* drink, copulate or what you will. I must, I must, I must, or I am nothing and my leave is wasted. O tomorrow and tomorrow and tomorrow; they'll all pile up until I die.

Unexpectedly, since it is preoccupied with the restoration of dolls' houses, kissing brass crusaders, picnics with ducks' eggs and cherry jam, and elaborate little treats and outings of all kinds, his *Journal* contains the very flavour of the war and its aftermath. Victory Day actually presented problems. Welch captures its peculiar ennui:

19

Aftermath

11 June, Tuesday. 10.15 pm

On Saturday, the Victory Celebration night, Eric suddenly suggested that we should go out to see the beacons and bonfires.

We had just heard that Evie had lost her job in Cornwall and might be coming back to us, and the upset had made us restless.

We drove in the car through the dark up the hill to Plaxtol, and there was a fire in the grounds of Fairlawne, huge, sullen, flat to the ground, with great boughs crumbling. A few people were gathered round it, staring into the flames, and some boys on a bench were singing sadly 'Oh my darling Clementine'. They were nervous of their voices, joking about them. The people stared, there was a great weight of emptiness. I felt that everybody was shamefaced and deadened – dumb, watching, waiting-for-death people.

We went on to Shipbourne Common and there was another larger bonfire with even fewer people about it. From the 'New Inn', several hundred yards away, the most extraordinary jig and blur of music was coming – demoniac in its clanging smashing smudge with the crooner's whisper frighteningly magnified.

Over the long bending grass it ran, through the blackness. It was sadder and more damned than a black monkey or a man in a stone cell clawing at the bars. The great voice was mourning and jigging and weeping all over the world. The blurs and atmospherics were like stabbing sparks. Eric and I watched the flames and the black shapes of the children running against them. There was a moping man too, who seemed to be searching in the grass, shoulders hunched, head sunk.

When rolls and plumes of sparks swept up out of the fire, then showered themselves down on the moping man and the dancing children, it was a medieval devil scene. The loud mechanical wailing, the sullen torpor, the life of the flames were all part of a hell picture.

When we drove on past the 'New Inn', we saw coloured umbrellas, drinkers and singers on the flood-lit grass. It was the only pub that had seemed gay. But its gaiety was like the deafening voice; merciless, made of tin, and mad.

I thought the whole night scene was a gaunt display of desperate failure. The people, for so short a time on the earth, watching their lives' hopelessness, as they stared into the flames . . .

During 1948, the year of his death, the snugness which the war had perversely allowed had quite gone and Welch no longer minded. Instead, the success of his books and the remarkable reputation he had made in such a short time caused him a great longing to be out in the world. It came over him suddenly 'that my life is really too limited to bear . . . Frustration like this has never come to me before. There is so much sensible, obvious reason for feeling it that I am made helpless . . . There should be many new words for what I mean, words that don't whine and pity.' On 10 August he wrote, 'Death seems so far away; it recedes and becomes more and more impossible as one grows iller.' Three weeks later he added his last entry, a very long one about a visit to Sissinghurst – 'Taste which is not one's own is a sort of holiday'. The last unfinished sentence reads, 'Even now, as I write, I . . .' He died on 30 December, all his energy during the final few weeks going into completing a novel called *A Voice Through a Cloud*.

Denton Welch wrote his diary in nineteen ordinary school exercise books, and in an old fashioned schoolboyish script. He wrote quickly and did not correct. 'In Gide's Journal I have just read again how he does not wish to write his pages slowly as he would the pages of a novel . . . It is just what I have always felt about this journal of mine. Don't ponder, don't grope . . .'

No one can read Samuel Johnson's diary without pity, for here, most humbly set out, is the pathology of a virtuous and brilliant man. The famous definition in his *Dictionary* that a diary should be 'an account of the transactions, accidents, and observations of every day; a journal' implies something less profound than that which he made stabs at with his pen after his day's toil or sloth. But no one heeded the advice he gave to friends more when he urged them to keep diaries in which 'the great thing to be recorded is the state of your mind'. Pre-eminently and tragically, Johnson's diary is the troubled record of a troubled state of mind. 'A man loves to review his own mind', he would say. But did he? Could he? If so, it was a penitential love. He wrote his diary in order to learn from his own experiences, to become reconciled to the disparity between his discoveries and his hopes, as he told Boswell, and he also wrote it in what he believed was the full view of the eye of God. The result is awesome, and at the same time childishly intimate, like a Cowper hymn. He can never accept himself. He can never say, I am the kind of man who can't get up in the morning and who likes drink and women. These things weigh him down to such a degree that he can no longer see the eminence of his natural goodness and gifts. As the years pass and we find him still making New Year's resolutions, 'To rise early, to lose no time', etc, and we know by many confessions such as, 'I do not remember that since I left Oxford I ever rose early by mere choice, but . . . two or three times for the *Rambler*', we marvel at this inability to take himself as he is. And his guilt is terrible. 'I have now spent fifty years in resolving, having from the earliest time almost that I can remember been forming schemes of a better life. I have done nothing . . .'

It was not true, of course. Johnson's diary, though episodic and incomplete, reveals a great deal of activity. It is in one respect a stern and powerful meditation on the progress of the orthodox Anglican soul. In other ways it is a key to work in progress and a record of morbidity. Only now and then, as in the delightful account of his visit to France, does he actually spread himself in full and elaborate description. Eventually, with a horror unequalled by anything to be found in any other diary, Johnson moves from his habitual hypochondria into a monstrous medical account of his cumbersome journey to the grave, writing it chiefly in Latin and setting down all the pain and emotion of one who lies 'under dread of death'. Johnson's modern editors, in the Yale edition of his works, comment on the surprising fact that in August 1774 he reveals that he had been reading Robert Southwell, the thirty-four year-old poet-priest who was executed in 1595, and a writer practically unknown in the eighteenth century. Southwell had written,

> *Before my face the picture hangs,*
> *That daily should put me in mind,*
> *Of those cold names and bitter pangs,*
> *That shortly I am like to find:*
> *But yet alas full little I*
> *Do thinke here on that I must die.*

Like Southwell, like all men, Johnson finds it hard to contemplate his own death. His Christian faith seems to have simply intensified his terror of mortality. The diary shows a devout man with a graveyard view of the end which he longs to correct but cannot. Throughout his life he was depressed by his failure to achieve spiritual transcendence. On 21 April 1764, when he was sixty-eight, he wrote:

My indolence, since my last reception of the Sacrament, has sunk into gross sluggishness, and my dissipation spread into wilder negligence. My thoughts have been clouded with sensuality, and, except that from the beginning of this year I have in some measure forborn excess of Strong Drink my appetites have predominated over my reason. A kind of strange oblivion has overspread me, so that I know not what has become of the last year, and perceive incidents and intelligence pass over me without leaving any impression . . . This is not the life to which Heaven is promised.

But whatever the depth of his melancholic despair, nothing finally unsettled the majestic balance of Johnson's mind and it is his sanity and honesty which causes the reader's heart to go out to him in his predicament.

The diary also contains a moving tribute to 'dear poor Tetty', the middle-aged widow whom Johnson had married when he was only twenty-seven and whom he loved most tenderly until her death in 1752 in spite of her addiction to drink and drugs, and much evidence of incompatibility in their two personalities. The entries concerning her memory are a study in remorse, but only thirteen months after her death, whilst on a pilgrimage to her grave at Bromley, he couples a wonderful commendation of her to God with the news that he is thinking of marrying again – a fact which Boswell suppressed in his *Life*.

Apr 23. Easter Monday. Yesterday as I purposed I went to Bromley where dear Tetty lies buried & received the sacrament, first praying before I went to the altar according to the prayer precomposed for Tetty and a prayer which I made against unchastity, idleness, & neglect of publick worship. I made it during a sermon which I could not perfectly hear. I repeated mentally the commendation of her with the utmost fervour *larme à l'oei* before the reception of each element at the altar. I repeated it again in the pew, in the garden before dinner, in the garden before departure, at home at night. I hope I did not sin. *Fluunt lacrymae.* I likewise ardently applied to her the prayer for the Church militant where the dead are mentioned and commended her gain to Eternal Mercy, as in coming I approached her grave. During the whole service I was never once distracted by any thoughts of any other woman or with my design of a new wife which freedom of mind I remembered in the Garden. God guide me.

Eighteen years later he is still mourning her, wishing that when he saw the sea at Brighton she could have seen it with him and making his self-reforming resolutions over her name as others might do at a shrine. He constantly wonders what 'she would have said or done' and ten years later, while at the Palais Bourbon, he is once more regretting that Tetty was not with him to share its wonders. His love for her was frankly unbelievable to many of his acquaintances, and Garrick's cruel but probably truthful picture of her as 'very fat, with a bosom of more than ordinary protuberance, with swelled cheeks of a florid red, produced by thick painting, and increased by the liberal use of cordials; flaring and fantastic in her dress, and affected both in her speech and her general behaviour' made Johnson's lifelong sorrow at her death scarcely credible. Yet the diary exposes a real and poignant love, and a grief quite outside conventional mourning. The fact that she died about Easter became intertwined with his religious concept of renewal, and as time passed, Tetty, who had proved almost impossible to live with, became for Johnson an advocate in heaven. The older he got, the more he sensed their marriage to have had scandalous attributes for which they were equally to blame. Thirty years after he had buried her in the churchyard at Bromley he wrote, 'On what we did amiss, and our faults were great, I have thought of late with more regret than at any former time. She was I think very penitent. May God accept her repentance: may he accept mine' and that night he suffered 'a night of great disturbance and solicitude, such as I do not remember.'

Johnson's diary is a dignified confessional in which the frailties of both body and soul are set down with great severity. The judgement of

24

posterity is that the Doctor was too hard on himself. His practical kindness alone makes him a remarkable figure, for his philanthropy was not one of the adding his name to cheques and petitions' sort, but belonged to that rarer category which puts up with lifelong difficulty and inconvenience because of its need to exercise love towards its fellow creatures. Boswell found it hard to stay in the same room whilst Mrs Williams fed. She was blind and ate with her fingers but, as Tetty's old friend, Johnson took her into his house and looked after her until the end. And he treated his black servant with the total affection and dignity which a good father would treat a son. He was profoundly religious, but Christianity appeared to afflict him more with fear than with joy, acerbating his highly developed sense of guilt and enveloping him in worry. Also, throughout his days he was burdened with disease, badly disfigured even in the eyes of his contemporaries, accustomed as they were to physical ruin. It is little wonder that *The Anatomy of Melancholy* should be the only book that – according to Boswell – 'ever took him out of bed two hours sooner than he wished to rise'. So his diary is the account of the inner life of a great depressive and, as it unwinds in phrases of ponderous Augustan solemnity, the acute difference between the grand language and the privacy it describes is deeply affecting. It is little wonder that to those who knew him Johnson was like a modern Socrates in the Strand and the touchstone of all debate. That he himself frequently hated this role is revealed in those comic instances when he 'roared them off', as it were, Boswell often getting a goring for going too far, or coming too close. But if ever doubts about the essential humility and goodness of the Doctor should arise they are at once corrected by seeing his sad diary.

Some of Johnson's diaries were used by Boswell, two large quartos of them were burnt by the Doctor just before his death, and others only came to light among the vast haul of papers discovered at Malahide Castle just before the last war. While staying with Johnson on 5 May 1776, Boswell managed to copy some of the large diary which Johnson was later to destroy. Two diaries, that describing Johnson's visit to Wales in the summer of 1774 and his visit to France the following year, are filled out with descriptions, the Welsh diary so much so that the editors of the Yale edition of *Diaries, Prayers, Annals* believe that it might have been the intention to write a companion work to *Journey to the Western Islands*. Otherwise, in many respects, Dr Johnson's daily record is terse, full of gaps and fragmentary. In 1783 he had a stroke and began to send Mrs Thrale a day-to-day account begging her to 'forgive the gross images which disease must necessarily present. Dr Laurence said that medical treatises should always be in Latin.' And on 6 July Johnson began his 'Sick Man's Journal', the solemn description of his own dissolution, writing it in Latin and maintaining it to the last detail until within a month or so of his death on 13 December 1784. He prepared methodically for this, burning his papers, sending his works to Pembroke College, arranging to have all the prayers he had composed published by a clergyman friend, George Strahan, and making his will. The 'Sick Man's Journal' is a mixture of savage self-doctoring and heroism in the face of physical misery. It reminds one of how heartfelt were those prayers for an 'easy end' made by those who lived before the age of pain-killers and trustworthy sedatives.

A very different Johnson was William Johnson, an Eton master and author of the famous *Boating Song*, who maintained that he kept a diary during the school holidays for the benefit of 'about three readers'. He was correct when he called it 'a genuine, original book' but revealed more a lack of confidence than a pompous nineteenth century morality when he described his activity as 'more wholesome than cooking novels'. That he should have, in the creative sense, cooked a great deal more than the faintly teasing fragments which have come down to us is all too plain. Friends must have said, 'You should write', immediately recognising Johnson's literary nature, and maybe its suppression, for every now and then, both in his journal and his letters, he gives defensive reasons for not doing so.

He began to write his holiday journal during the summer of 1863, beginning it with the strange statement, 'I am halfway through a long vacation, which may be my last'. He had taught at Eton for eighteen of his forty years and been a pupil at the school before this. It is true that at the start the barbarity of the school filled him with despair and that sometimes he would turn from trying to keep 'my mob in a state of quiet attentiveness when their blood is warm' to watch 'the plasterers and carpenters now working here, and envy them their weekly wages; for all my shoutings and questionings and mortifications, and all the ill-will I have to contract by punishing, I have not received a farthing.' The medieval chapel was being renovated in the midst of the uproar. Johnson battled with the disorder, noting with emotions which he himself called complex that the individual pupils who responded to his teaching were 'as virtuous as men, without men's pride and knowingness, as interesting as women, without women's timorousness and artifice'.

It had been saying goodbye to these favourites of the 1863 class which had temporarily decided him to give up teaching, not the earlier rowdyism. It was all too heart-breaking. One had no sooner acquired the perfect circle of friends and the most useful degree of discipleship than the whole thing was broken up by Oxford or the army. He felt that 'age has for youth a natural priesthood'. The creed he taught contained a nervous Hellenism and a kind of patrician freedom. Then, wherever they might happen to be in the future, in Anglican rectories or in politics, or worshipping 'the Union jack in those famous but fetid towns of the gorgeous East', their duty was *Ephphatha* – 'utter thyself', 'cast thy bread upon the waters'. Johnson was reserved at first in showing that he intended to maintain a priestly role towards special pupils but later, convinced that his vocation was to transmit exciting and radical ideas to people who would one day form a new kind of aristocracy, he grew more reckless. 'I don't mind flooding you with this transcendental stuff about boys: you know it has been for a quarter of a century characteristic of me, and it is no use to *vielilize* . . .' he wrote to a friend.

But in 1863, when the special friendships had become so important that Johnson could not bear to relinquish them even for the winter and summer hols, thus maintaining contact by his journal, he was less easy. Could it have been his activities as 'guerillero' within the education system were attracting crossfire, or was it simply that letters like the following told the full tale?

. . . he was always ready and glad to come to me, lunch, dine, breakfast, tea, sup, walk, drive with me: he was my comforter when I was ill (in Cambridge) nearly three years ago. When he left school I gave him all the volumes then published of the Cambridge Shakespeare, in perfect binding . . . His face in a dozen forms is with me; his innocent, rich, infantine voice, unchanged for fourteen happy years, is with me: I miss him still, though busy and not friendless.

It was to be a bereavement oft repeated, particularly during the summer.

I told M. to-night that tragic heartrending story of the two brothers who crossed and met and touched hands in the dark, going by train across Egypt, the one to India, the other from India, after years of separation. No Greek, no Arab could imagine the heroic flush and throb of such an exchange of Christian names in the midnight. Will they in ages to come say of us, 'Those poor Englishmen whom Newman stirred so deeply could not conceive our emotions? Love and part. Is it for this we are made? Strain tight then, whilst you may yet embrace, poor mortals. . . .

A few months before he started keeping his holiday diary, Johnson was in Torquay, his head full of ideas about his duty to help create a marvellous band of individuals worthy to serve imperial England, and about Eton. Reading Edwin Arnold's *Dalhousie's Administration*, a description of how one man had brought about speedy and excellent reforms in the Punjab, Johnson regretted that the growing practice of consultation held back natural leaders from getting things done. Lying in bed on the 9th of January, he was unable to get to sleep because of thoughts about the 4th of June. 'A half-humorous, half-sentimental boating song' was 'burning to be written out'. The tunes which ran through his brain as he composed his song were 'Waiting for the Waggon' and 'A Health to the Outward Bound'. Years later he was still fiddling with it, saying that it lacked fusion and was a failure, and that he was too old for verse. 'The little slender vein is worked out. But I have my readers, like better men . . .' These readers, generations of them, would know William Johnson as William Cory, author of a much-anthologised poem entitled *Heraclitus*, eight unforgettable lines which summed up that mystical permanency which Johnson longed to discover in his close relationships. Like the Greek poet Mimnermus, he intended to fill his elegies with so much love that he would make them amorous instead of mournful. In *Mimnermus in Church* he challenges Christian transcendentalism.

> *You say there is no substance here,*
>   *One great reality above:*
> *Back from that void I shrink in fear,*
>   *And child-like hide myself in love:*
> *Show me what angels feel. Till then*
> *I cling, a mere weak man, to men.*

He found the conventional worship in the school chapel increasingly odious and a major element in the destruction of the boys' spiritual nature:

Sunday, July 26. (1868) In desk at 3 p.m. Hateful service. A steaming crowd, a most lugubrious, wearisome anthem. When will this absurd sort of worship come to an end; this holocaust, this human incense, this Moloch- squeezing of innocents?

On 4 April 1872 Johnson left Eton suddenly, and in the October of that year he resigned his Fellowship at King's and changed his name to Cory. He had a little house in Halsdon, Devonshire and he retreated there. The reasons for the transformation are officially opaque. To one of his elite he wrote, 'Now the time is come for thinking where you will go, for I am gone – I have just resigned – "turned out to grass" – writing formal letters till I tire, and now getting a change by writing more at ease to you, whom I love and trust and long to see again . . . I am too sad and ill to write any more.' Ephphatha, he tells the master who succeeds him. Don't scold, don't grumble, never be sarcastic, don't be dry, never use a vituperative word like 'idle', tell boys outright what you like and what you hate, what you think about things and make yourself known to the shy and uncouth as well as to the engaging . . . To another of the elite he wrote, 'I have undergone a very strange wounding' . . . 'I go under a tunnel . . .' 'I break my heart every day.'

The tragedy is neither blacked-out nor floodlit. A luminous interest plays over it. Halsdon turns out to be a fine retreat and 'phots' are a rare

29

comfort. They are all over the place, Lyttelton's (in cricket dress), Brett's, Wood's, Luxmoore's, Pollock's – all those beautiful, charming, assured, Victorian proconsular faces. And not only phots but, during the holidays, the still devoted originals, smiling and gay, and happy to accept inscribed copies of *Nuces* or *Iophon*. Johnson/Cory's intention was to direct all that was best in Eton youth to a highly personal form of Whiggery – 'If I were a Tory I should go to bed or to church, as it is I go to work . . .' He abhors what he calls 'kinks' in people. He is often desperate and ever in search of his beloved euphrasy – the mystic flower which clears the mind's eye.

William Cory's own phot shows a pale, rather formidable person. He has big thin ears like the emperor Augustus. Behind the marble brow one can almost hear the struggle between Plato and Christ. He might have made a good university representative, or a tortured don. His literary views were bizarre but somehow reminiscent of the *outré* opinions later to be held by characters in Wilde or Saki. 'Tea is mentioned too often in Turgenev.' 'Young Henry James goes a trifle far in Bret Hartery.' 'Ever since I found Ouida charming in French I fancy French would make me relish . . . Goethe's epigrams or his *Selective Affinities*.' 'As a poet Shakespeare moves me; as a dramatist less. I once saw *Hamlet* acted – I had rather not see it again.' 'I think *Othello* nearly as good as it was possible for anything to be before the human mind had by evolution become capable of *Kenilworth* . . .' Scott indeed is Johnson's hero and a yardstick for measuring everything. His novels are the direct descendant of the *Aeneid* and worth all the Lake poets put together.

On 26 March 1878 Johnson wrote from Madeira to his old friend Warre Cornish,'. . . I may as well now tell you . . . that I have a reasonable expectation of being married. It is a thing I cannot quite justify . . . "A new start" – possibly.' Earlier he had written, 'I am slowly exploring the headlands and bays of that *terra incognita*, girlhood . . .' The girl was the daughter of a Devonshire clergyman, the Reverend George de Carteret Guille. In August she became Mrs William Cory. The following July she gave birth to a son, Andrew. The family lived in Madeira until 1882 and the final decade was weathered at Hampstead. Johnson/Cory died on 11 June 1892 in his seventieth year and shortly afterwards the group of Eton disciples, most of whom were

30

now key figures in Victoria's establishment, published the holiday journals and letters he had devised for them.

There is a certain kind of diarist who writes with no thought of actual publication but who half hopes that his diary will be found. On 3 November 1874 Francis Kilvert wrote,

Why do I keep this voluminous journal? I can hardly tell. Partly because life appears to me such a curious and wonderful thing that it almost seems a pity that even such a humble and uneventful life as mine should pass altogether away without some such record as this, and partly too because I think the record may amuse and interest some who come after me.

He was thirty-three and the curious and wonderful thing, life, was already near its end. And although Kilvert was just under forty when he died, his marvellous diary is really that of an impassioned youth rather than that of a mature man. Its sensuous vision of nature, Anglicanism and society is not dissimilar to that of John Constable, and Kilvert's shimmering landscapes remind one of Constable's glittering statements of transient light and dewiness. His country is that of the Welsh border, Radnorshire and Herefordshire, and the artless account which Kilvert gives of its perfections and complexities is unequalled. He began his diary in 1870 and ended it abruptly in March 1879, the same month during which he had published an exquisite threnody on a little boy who had died and whom he had buried on the previous Christmas Day. Kilvert had gone to see the dead child, who was the shepherd's son, and had kissed him – 'I had not touched death for more than thirty years' – and in his poem he makes the boy request that the village stream, Clyro Water, should be his remembrancer. On 20 August, Kilvert married. A month later he died suddenly of peritonitis, and was buried within sound of the same stream. His diary was discovered just before the last war and selections from it, edited by William Plomer, were first published between 1938 and 1940. Since then it has become recognised as having a place among the few really great English diaries. Reading it casts an irresistible spell and the freshness of the writing permanently carries the freshness of girls, flowers, meals, games, prayers, creatures and sounds of a village of just a century ago.

Francis Kilvert was born at Hardenhuish, Wiltshire on 3 December 1840, the son of the rector. His father ran a prep school at the rectory and Kilvert was three when the nine year old Augustus Hare was admitted to it. Hare's horrific account of his experiences at the hands of Mr Kilvert and his pupils in *The Story of My Life,* his rape by the boys on his first night 'At nine years old, I was compelled to eat Eve's apple quite up – indeed, the Tree of Knowledge of Good and Evil was stripped absolutely bare; there was no fruit left to gather,' – and the floggings he received from the rector, throws a disconcerting light on the exquisite Christian background to his life which is portrayed by the diarist. William Plomer believed that 'certain peculiarities' of Kilvert's character derived from what he had seen at his father's school. Yet, such is his art – and, indeed, his erotic heart – that even when he confesses those desires into his notebooks which should make the modern reader uncomfortable, if not outright condemning, he loses nothing in the process. His life remains that 'curious and wonderful thing'; it is all of a piece. It is, comparatively speaking, minutiae that fill it, the deepest, remotest, richest provincialism that speaks, yet the voice is neither quaint nor old-maidish but young, direct and vital. The only other writer who can equal him on the realities of country life is Hardy. Like Wessex, Clyro and Langley Burrell, Bredwardine and the Wye Valley are now the recognised landscape of genius. Although Francis Kilvert never flinched from mentioning the cruelties of existence and frequently demonstrates a Georgian – rather than a mid-Victorian – robustness towards the difficulties of his day, his diary generally is a convincing testimony to pleasure and happiness. Its tone is unselfconsciously antipuritan, and Kilvert's treatment of his neighbours, whom he divides between 'gentle' and 'simple', provides an unparalleled account of the parish during the nineteenth century. Here is one of my favourite entries from a book which has always been for me a directly open door on to the still and heavy mid-Victorian afternoon.

Friday, 28 June 1872
I promised Mr. Venables in answer to his request that I would stay here

through August till September 1st inclusive and go home for July if my father wants me. I hope this will be the last of the many changes and postponements that have been made in our plans. Going down the village I fell in with old James Jones the sawyer. 'I hear you are going away,' he said in a broken trembling voice. And he walked down the village with me weeping as he went.

Saturday, 29 June

Called at Hay Castle and went with the four pretty girl archers to shoot and pick up their arrows in the field opposite the Castle.

This evening I went out visiting the village people. The sinking sun shone along the Churchyard and threw long shadows of the Church and the tomb-stones over the high waving grass. All round the lychgate and the churchyard wall the tall purple mallows are in flower and the banks and hedges about the village are full of them. Old Hannah Whitney was sitting in her cottage door at work as usual with her high cap and her little red shawl pinned over her breast, her thin grey-bearded nutcracker face bent earnestly upon her knitting till she glanced sharply up over her spectacles to see who it was that was passing.

Wednesday, 3 July

Tom Williams of Llowes and I had long been talking of going up to Llanbedr Hill to pay a visit to the eccentric solitary, the Vicar, and we arranged to go this morning. The day promised to be fine and after school at 10.30 I walked over to Llowes. When the postman, who followed me closely, had arrived we started up a steep stony narrow lane so overgrown and overarched with wild roses that it was difficult for a horseman to pass, but a lane most beautiful and picturesque with its wild luxuriant growth of fern and wild roses and foxgloves. The foxgloves were wonderful. They grew on both sides of the lane, multitudes, multitudes in long and deep array.

Tom Williams was on horseback, I on foot. As we mounted the hill, beautiful views of mountains and valley opened gleaming behind us, and Tom Williams pointed out to me some of the Llowes farmhouses scattered over the hills. The road seemed deserted as we went on our pilgrimage. All folk were busy in their hay fields. Here and there my fellow pilgrim from his point of vantage in the saddle spoke to a labourer or small farmer over the hedge.

As we went up the steep hill to Painscastle the huge green Castle mound towered above us. A carpenter came down the hill from the village. I asked him where the grave of Tom Tobacco lay on the moor, but he shook his head. He did not know.

In the village, a Post Office had been established since I was last here and the village well, the only one, which was formerly common and open to ducks and cattle had been neatly walled and railed round.

Society's need for villains being no less urgent than its demand for heroes, now and then one welcomes a monster-diarist. Villain – extraordinary for all of us in Suffolk – is a seventeenth century farmer from Laxfield named William Dowsing. In 1643 this strange man, then aged about fifty, accepted a commission from Lord Manchester to 'cleanse' the local churches. It was a task which turned out to be not only a duty but a pleasure, as they say, and its highly personalised completion has made Dowsing's name a byword for infamy ever since. So much so that any loss or dilapidation of the county's five hundred or more celebrated churches is now popularly attributed to him. The fact that his 'cleansing' was comparatively slight to what happened to these beautiful buildings under Thomas Cromwell, Elizabeth and Victoria is either unknown or ignored. Dowsing's mistake was to keep a diary. It is Suffolk's 'black book'. As one reads it, the de-mystification of Christianity which occurred under the Tudors and the architectural restoration which took place in the nineteenth century, both of which did untold damage to many an exquisite medieval structure, seem positively enlightened in comparison. Perhaps it is the sound of smashed glass which makes them so, and the crash of hundreds of 'mighty angels' from roofs and windows. Or did that careful and conscientious day by day account of wilful destruction reveal all too plainly the madness of zealots? Whatever it was, the diary which William Dowsing kept from 6 January 1643 to 1 October 1644 has been regarded since 1786 – when it was first published – as an appalling and shameful document. It was reprinted in 1818 and again in 1885, and few – not even those whose allegiance to East Anglia's inherent puritanism has been strict – have been able to read it without rage.

The order for removing scandalous 'pictures' – in other words, stained glass out of churches – was published in 1641. Soon afterwards regional committees were set up to implement the new law, and the Earl of Manchester put in charge of seven eastern counties. The Earl wrote to Dowsing and 'to such as hee shall appoint', that they were to put 'the said Ordinance in execution'. This was that 'all Crucifixes, Crosses, & all Images of any one or more persons of the Trinity, or of the Virgin Marye, & all other Images & pictures of Saints and superstitions inscriptions in or upon all and every ye said Churches or Cappeles . . . shall be taken away and defaced . . .' Dowsing employed the assistance of a man named Francis Jessop from Beccles and for the next year and a half the pair of them, with half a dozen or so ignorant assistants, set to with a will.

A book published in Oxford only three years after Dowsing's visit to Cambridge, *Querela Cantabrigiensis* describes his arrival at the latter university.

And one who calls himself John (William) Dowsing, and by vertue of a pretended Commission goes about the Country like a Bedlam breaking glasse windowes, having battered and beaten downe all our painted glasse, not only in our Chapples but (contrary to order) in our publique Schooles, Colledge Halls, Libraryes, and Chambers, mistaking perhaps the liberall Arts for Saints (which they intend in time to pul down too) and having (against an Order) defaced and digged up the floors of our Chappels, many of which had lein so for tow or three hundred yeares together, not regarding the dust of our founders and predecessors, who likely were buried there; compelled us by armed Souldiers to pay forty shillings a colledge for not mending what he had spoyled and defaced, or forthwith to go to Prison . . .

But the indignation of those who witnessed Dowsing at work pales before the unease and disgust which can still overcome one as one turns the pages of his diary. It is devoid of spirituality. Here is simply the overthrow of one superstition by another. It is Dowsing's total lack of hesitancy which shocks. Also his henchmanship, his blind carrying out of orders. As the rich dark glass shivers and splinters, it never occurs to their destroyer to claim that he is letting in a better light. All he seems to understand is Lord Manchester's letter in his pocket. Generally speaking, the 1641 Order for further iconoclasm was not obeyed with any urgency or completeness by the country as a whole. The last – and most drastic – cleansing of the temples had taken place almost a century before, and ever since the death of Queen Elizabeth people had grown accustomed to a quiet and dignified repairing of their parish churches. So Dowsing's outrages on their fabric seemed ignorant and terrifying – incomprehensible to Christians for whom the stone and wood carvings and painted glass still remaining had largely ceased to be relics of the old religion and had become illustrations to the stories now being read to them from the new official Bible. No wonder the braver among them discovered that they had lost the Church key when Dowsing called.

His activities in other ways have puzzled historians. Why did he only tackle about a third of Suffolk's churches? Why did he miss out or pass over certain buildings? And why doesn't he mention the visit to Cambridge? Was the diary really an inventory written for Lord Manchester's benefit? Evelyn in his *Diary* describes the plundering of monumental brasses at Lincoln in 1654:

The souldiers had lately knocked off most of the brasses from the gravestones (in the Cathedral) so as few inscriptions were left; they told us that these men went in with axes and hammers, and shut themselves in, till they had rent and torn off some large loads of metal, not sparing even the monuments of the dead, so hellish an averice possessed them.

Dowsing lived to be eighty-five, a long time after those eighteen or so months when, at the head of a gang of villagers carrying staves, he wrecked some 150 churches. What did Suffolk say to him when the dust had settled? He was buried among his ancestors in the church at Laxfield on whose tomb the brasses remained intact. He had cleansed this church personally on 17 July 1644 and had taken up 'many superstitious Inscriptions in Brass . . .' He had also defaced the font in which he had been baptised.

His diary opens on Twelfth Night, 1643, at Haverhill, his first church.

We broke down about an hundred superstitious Pictures and seven Fryars hugging a Nun; and the Picture of God and Christ; and diverse others very superstitious; and 200 had been broke down before I came. We took away two popish Inscriptions with *ora pro nobis*; and we beat down a great stoneing Cross on the top of the Church.

At CLARE, Jan. the 6th. We brake down 1000 Pictures superstitious; I brake down 200; 3 of God the Father, and 3 of Christ, and the Holy Lamb, and 3 of the Holy Ghost like a Dove with Wings; and the 12 Apostles were carved in Wood, on the top of the Roof, which we gave orders to take down; and the Sun and the Moon in the East Window, by the King's Arms, to be taken down.

HUNDEN, Jan. the 6th. We brake down 30 superstitious Pictures; and we took up 3 popish Inscriptions in brass, *ora pro nobis*, on them; and we gave order for the levelling of the Steps.

WIXO, Jan. the 6th. We brake a Picture; and gave order for the levelling the Steps.

WHITHERSFIELD, Jan the 6th. We brake down a Crucifix, and 60 superstitious Pictures; and gave order for the levelling the Steps in the Chancel.

SUDBURY, Suffolk. *Peter's* Parish. Jan. the 9th 1643. We brake down a Picture of God the Father, 2 Crucifix's, and Pictures of Christ, about an hundred in all; and gave orders to take down a Cross off the Steeple; and diverse Angels, 20 at least, on the Roof of the Church.

SUDBURY, *Gregory* Parish. Jan. the 9th. We brake down 10 mighty great Angels in Glass, in all 80.
BARHAM, Jan the 22nd. We brake down the Twelve Apostles in the Chancel, and 6 superstitious more there; and 8 in the Church, one a Lamb with a Cross X on the back; and digged down the Steps; and took up 4 superstitious Inscriptions in Brass, one of them *Jesu, Fili Dei, miserere mei*, and *O mater Dei, memento mei – O mother of God have mercy on me!*

ALDBOR0UGH, Jan the 24th. We gave order for taking down 20 Cherubims, and 38 Pictures; which their Lecturer Mr *Swayne* (a godly man) undertook, and their Captain Mr *Johnson*.

IPSWICH. At *Peter's*, was on the Porch, the Crown of Thorns, the Spunge and Nails, and the Trinity in Stone; and the Rails were there, which I gave order to brake in pieces.

IPSWICH *Margarett's*, Jan the 30th. There was 12 Apostles in Stone taken down; and between 20 and 30 superstitious Pictures to be taken down, which a (godly man) a Churchwarden promised to do.

Feb. the 3d. WENHAM *Magna*. There was Nothing to reform.

Feb. the 3d. We were at the Lady Bruce's House, and in Chapell, there was a Picture of God the Father, of the Trinity, of Christ, and the Holy Ghost, the Cloven Tongues; which we gave order to take down, and the Lady promised to do it.

COMEARTH *Magna* (Great Cornard) Feb. the 20th. I took up 2 Inscriptions, pray for our souls; and gave orders to take down a Cross on the Steeple; and to level the Steps. *John Pain*, Churchwarden, for not paying, and doing his duty injoyned by the Ordinance, I charged *Henry Turner*, the Constable, to carry before the Earl of *Manchester*.

Feb. the 23rd. At Mr Capt. Waldegrave's Chappel, in BUERS, there was a Picture of God the Father, and divers other superstitious Pictures, 20 at least, which they promised to break, his Daughter and Servants; he himself was not at home, neither could they find the key of the Chappel. I had not the 6s. 8d. yet promised it. And gave order to take down a Cross.

HELMINGHAM, Feb. the 29th. Adam and Eve to be beaten down.

FROSTENDEN, April the 8th . . . And Mr *Ellis*, an High Constable, of the Town, told me 'he saw an *Irish* man, within 2 months, bow to the Cross on the Steeple, and put off his hat to it.'

BLYTHBOROUGH, April the 9th. There was 20 superstitious Pictures; one on the Outside of the Church; 2 Crosses, one on the Porch; and another on the Steeple; and 20 Cherubims to be taken down in the Church, and Chancel; and I brake down 3 *orate pro animabus*; and gave order to take down 200 more

Pictures, within 8 days. (The Blythburgh angels defeated Dowsing, being unreachable. He tried to shoot them down with musket balls and some of these can still be seen lodged in the ceiling.)

UFFORD, Aug. 31st. See No 26 Where it set down what we did, Jan. the 27th. (Dowsing had destroyed about half of the glass and had given orders for the rest to be broken. But apparently this was not done, and so, eight months later, 'some of them we brake down now') . . . And we brake down the Organ Cases, and gave them to the Poor. – In the Church, there was on the Roof, above a 100 JESUS and MARY, in great Capital Letters; and a Crosier Staff to be broken down, in Glass; and above 20 Stars on the Roof. There is a glorious (Vainglorious) Cover over the Font, like a Pope's Tripple Crown, with a Pelican on the Top, picking its Breast, all gilt over with Gold. And we were kept out of the Church above 2 hours, and neither Churchwardens, *William Brown*, nor *Roger Small*, that were enjoined these things above three months afore, had not done them in May, and I sent one of them to see it done, and they would not let him have the key. And now, neither the Churchwardens, nor *William Brown*, nor the Constable *James Tokelove*, and *William Gardener*, the Sexton, would not let us have the key in 2 hours time. New Churchwardens, *Thomas Stanard, Thomas Stroud*. And *Samuel Canham*, of the same Town, said 'I sent men to rifle the Church' and *Will. Brown*, old Churchwarden, said 'I went about to pull down the Church, and carried away part of the Church.'

ELMSETT, Aug. the 22d. *Crow*, a Deputy, had done before we came. We rent apieces there the Hood and Surplice.

The chilling thing about William Dowsing is not his radical approach to what remained of the symbolism of the old religion but his lack of love, feeling and understanding of the faith which was supplanting it. His orders were to deface and this he did with mindless obedience. He shows indifference to the sheer mess and expense left in his wake, and no consideration at all towards his neighbours. He lacks reverence for anything or anybody. How amazed he would be to know that he now occupies the place of devilishness in the imagination of his home county once occupied by those carved or painted demonic warnings which he obliterated.

Our other Suffolk diarist, George Crabbe, might be said to also have somewhat lacerated his native haunts, though in a very different manner. His sudden flight as a young man from the Suffolk coast to London, and what happened when, at the end of his tether, he begged Edmund Burke to help him, is one of literature's classic examples of fortuitousness. But the incident could not have its unique fascination among the annals of patronage had it not been supported by the brief but detailed diary which the poet kept at this period. Crabbe was not what one might call a natural diarist, and his later journalisings, as his son said, were often little more than lists of names. But his account of the few months covering his arrival in the capital, a near-destitute countryman of twenty-six, and the swift recognition of his genius, makes this three months' diary peculiarly exciting. It shows a young man taking the most important step in his life, the rejection of his background for a place where his intelligence and his personality both told him he naturally belonged. In Crabbe's case it was a step entirely without conceit, and it was taken as much with an East Anglian practicality as with visionary daring. As the odd-man-out son of the little, rough-speaking Aldeburgh saltmaster and as a self-educated, semi qualified rural physician, Crabbe knew, long before he made his famous journey to Westminster, that he had been born into a kind of damnation and that he had a duty to somehow put the whole tragic inheritance behind him. He did so with such thoroughness that his son said that

no one so humbly born and bred, ever retained so few traces of his origin. His person and countenance peculiarly led the mind from the suspicion of any, but a highly cultivated and polished education; venerable, clerical, intellectual – it seemed a strange inconsistency to imagine him, even in early youth, occupied as a warehouseman . . .

Not that Crabbe repudiated either his parentage or his birthplace. What he burst free from was the limitation which his 'condition' imposed. Before he did so, as an apprentice physician and an expert psychologist, he had already taken a deeper look into the real nature of English rural society than any writer had done before. Its myths, strengths, multifarious sexual drives and circumstantial influences were an open book to him, and his knowledge of the heart of things made the conventional social patterns of little account. He never set out to destroy them and, as a Church of England parson, he correctly observed many of them, yet, as Edmund Blunden says, 'the poet prevailed over the professional man', and to the end of his life the man and his work 'remain majestically themselves'. Not only did Crabbe remain the acute spectator of things which happen to other people, adds Blunden, 'he was very willing to have them happen to himself. Literary success and fame did not affect him as genuine experience.'

At the beginning of the winter of 1799, clearly aware that he was a poet and must make up his mind either to fully live and work as one or to abandon such an overwhelming plan and force himself to practice medicine – something he was beginning to dislike – Crabbe walked to a dreary sheet of water known as the Leech pond, stared into it, and 'determined to go to London and venture all'. The pond was on a cliff and 'venal' Aldeburgh lay below him, half-ruined by floods and inhabited by violence and ignorance. Calling God 'the Fountain of Happiness', the young poet begged that the new year should not hold for him the torment of the one which was ending. Part of the torment derived from the borough and part from his not having enough money to marry a girl named Sarah Elmy. Soon afterwards, with a box of clothes, his surgical instruments and three pounds, he sailed from Slaughden, the Aldeburgh quay where he had often been forced to work as a labourer.

In London, Crabbe lodged with a Suffolk acquaintance and her draper husband, and concealed from them as best he could his dilemma. But for Sarah Elmy he kept a factual account of all that happened to him until that amazing day when Burke suddenly removed every obstacle from his path. Crabbe had attached a number of verses to his letter; Burke read both, immediately summoned the poet to his house and transformed the situation. Crabbe's son wrote, 'He went into Mr Burke's room, a poor young adventurer, spurned by the opulent, and rejected by the publishers, his last shilling gone, and all but his last hope with it; he came out virtually secure of almost all the good fortune that, by successive steps, afterwards fell to his lot . . .'

Crabbe's diary has always drawn a special response from me because

41

he never managed to sustain it beyond the three most worried months of his lifetime, when starvation and even prison threatened to destroy him. He addressed it to 'Mira', his sweetheart Sarah, back home in Suffolk, hoping that it would afford her 'some amusement'. It is a lugubrious letter-journal to a girl, devised to elicit sympathy for a penniless and bewildered countryman at the mercy of a violent city. It is not surprising that his family were to know nothing about it until after his death in the light of what was so soon to occur, his rescue by Burke, the patronage of a duke, the justified fame, the return home of a celebrity. The diary is, in fact, a fearful little overture to the full recognition of early genius – not that it was the kind of genius which was to endear him to Aldeburgh. But there Crabbe is, most desperately, if temporarily, knocking on doors for work in a London made quite terrifying by anti-Catholic riots and a total indifference to what happened to any poor creature trapped in its streets, and his note of semi-controlled panic is one which I and probably most would-be writers and artists have felt when young. Diaries, often more so than novels, present an unadorned statement of their readers' as well as their creators' feelings.

May 12th, 1786 . . . I'm dull and heavy, nor can go on with my work. The head and heart are like children, who being praised for their good behaviour, will overact themselves; and so is the case with me. Oh, Sally, how I want you! . . . It is the vilest thing in the world to have but one coat. My only one has happened with a mischance, and how to manage it is some difficulty. A confounded stove's modish ornament caught its elbow, and rent it halfway. Pinioned to the side, it came home, and I ran deploring to my loft. In the dilemma, it occurred to me to turn tailor myself; but how to get materials to work with puzzled me. At last I went running down in a hurry, with three or four sheets of paper in my hand, and begged for a needle, &c., to sew them together. This finished my job, but that it is somewhat thicker, the elbow is a good one yet. These are foolish things, Mira, to write or speak, and we may laugh at them; but I'll be bound to say that they are much more likely to make a man cry . . .

Crabbe may have been a chilly provincial realist but he was never a cold fish. John Evelyn has always struck me as being near-Arctic, yet

I read him avidly. No one knows why he felt a compunction to record what was going on all around him when he was only eleven years old and continued to do so, with various degrees of irregularity, until within three weeks of his death at the age of eighty-six. Like his near-contemporary and frequent companion Samuel Pepys, he wrote out of some deep inner need to put things down and yet with no intention of publishing. There is no sign that either man knew that the other was keeping a diary. Nor could there have been two more contrasting natures exposed in what they secretly stowed away at their desks. The two diaries remained hidden until the early nineteenth century and were then published within only seven years of each other, Pepys's – severely censored – in 1825, and Evelyn's in 1818. The light which they threw on the revolutionary seventeenth century continues to fascinate every kind of reader from the historian to anyone intrigued by the quirks and satisfactions of human nature.

John Evelyn was born on 31 October 1620 at Wotton, Surrey, the son of a country gentleman of whom we learn on page one that he was a stocky, prematurely white haired, taciturn person with the tastes and outlook of a typical English squire. His mother was 'of a proper personage, well timber'd, of a browne complexion; her eyes and haire of a lovely black . . . for Oeconomiq prudence esteem'd one of the most conspicuous in her Country'. These opening pages, formal and yet capable of revealing intimacy through a kind of stylistic splendour, contain the essence of Evelyn's fascination. He keeps the reader at arm's length and yet, at the same time, he is courteously conducting him towards the heart of his existence insofar as he, a strictly orthodox and stiffly repressed individual, can approach it.

After three years at Balliol, and arriving at youthful independence by the death of his father, Evelyn set out on what was an early version of the Grand Tour of Europe. For seven years, until his marriage to a baronet's daughter in a chapel in Paris in the summer of 1647, he wandered leisurely through Holland, Belgium, France and Italy, describing what he saw in splendidly ornate language. He had a passion for spectacle, for gorgeous processions, architecture, gardens, paintings, delicious fruit, jewels, sculpture and customs, though the rich cataloguing of such things already contrasts with a primly observing, but not indulging, personality. And although scandalised by the unrestrained Mediterranean myth and fantasy encrusting the unreformed Church, his sedate Anglican temperament was frequently awed and overwhelmed by the sheer pomp of the Papacy. Nevertheless, it was at this time that Evelyn began to write 'perverted' for converted when he heard of English Protestants returning to Rome, a description which was to become very popular during the late nineteenth century when many High Churchmen followed Newman's example and became, in the eyes of their contemporaries, 'perverts'. During his travels, Evelyn's attitude towards Roman Catholicism is a mixture of bemused contempt and gentlemanly tolerance; it would be a different matter when, late in life, he was to catch James II and his Court hearing Mass in Whitehall 'with the doors wide open'. Similarly, while being inquisitively drawn to hospitals, torture chambers, operating theatres, executions and cruel sensations of all kinds, including watching the circumcision of a Jewish boy which he describes with exquisite indecency, Evelyn remains icy where sexual love is concerned and, so far as his *Diary* is concerned, we have to accept that he was chaste until his marriage to Mary Browne – whose Christian name he never even mentions – and faithful ever after.

The young couple walked from the altar into a Paris gaudy with banners and strewn with flowers. It was Corpus Christi. Unlike Elizabeth Pepys, that delightful, lazy girl who was to enchant and exasperate her husband in a fashion which makes his portrait of her one of the best accounts which we have of a true marriage, Mary Evelyn makes no real entrance into her spouse's diary. Although they were to be together for nearly sixty years and although there are countless references to 'my wife', Mary stays in the shadows. So do all their many sons and daughters. Even the daughter who, incomprehensibly, according to her father, eloped. In fact, the only occasions when the reader comes into close touch with Evelyn's family is around the deathbed and the grave. The funerals of his children are devastatingly numerous, and the *Diary* is dreadfully eloquent on the subject of family bereavement. As we follow these almost annual coffins to the armigerous vault at Wotton, we recognise that we are present at a terrible commonplace of the period. Evelyn himself tries to rationalise this horror in stoic Christian language but the grief and shock show through. This capricious giving and then taking away by the Lord, his scientific mind tells him, has more to do with human ignorance than divine wisdom.

He was twenty-seven when he and Mary returned from abroad to make their home in Surrey. During the few years of his absence everything had changed. Oliver Cromwell was virtually in power and the 'rebells', as he continued to call them right up till the Restoration, were everywhere. One day Evelyn slipped into the 'Painted Chamber' (the Banqueting Hall) in Whitehall and listened unbelievingly as Bradshaw and Peters discussed the killing of the king. When the time came, Evelyn found that it was one great event which he could not witness:

The Villanie of the Rebells proceeding now so far as to Trie, Condemne, and Murder our excellent King, the 30 of this Moneth, struck me with such horror that I kept the day of his *Martyrdom* a fast, & would not be present, at that execrable wickednesse; receiving that sad (account) of it from my Bro: Geo: & also by Mr Owen, who came to Visite this afternoon, recounting to me all Circumstances.

A few days after the execution, Evelyn walked to London, 'it being a hard frost', and saw Charles's possessions being sold and scattered. Not many weeks later, having been obliged to have Holy Communion celebrated in his parlour because 'it was now wholy out of use in the Parish Churches in which the Presbyterians and Fanatics had usurped', the Evelyns prepared to return to France. An inventory was made of their treasures, 'that had been dispers'd for fear of Plundering', leases on property settled in a businesslike fashion, farewell visits paid to old friends and some keepsake drawings made of familiar Thameside scenery, 'to carry into France, where I thought to have them Engrav'd'. It was while he was winding up his affairs in the City that Evelyn saw 'his Majesties Statues throwne downe at St Paules Portico, & Exchange'. What could be more final? He swiftly obtained a 'Passe from the Rebell Bradshaw' and posted to Dover. On 1 August 1649, along with many other Royalists, he was in Paris. But a little less than a year later, back he was in London, his curiosity about the revolutionary English scene being too much for him and very much 'having a mind to see what doings was among the Rebells now in full possession at White-hall'. In February 1652 he saw Ireton's funeral and began his mordant commentary on the way saints and levellers, though swift to repress the old vanities in others, firmly retained such pomps for themselves. While reading Evelyn, it is always necessary to remember that in most matters his was a scrupulously biased vision and that he was incapable of fairness towards any views which he does not share, be they religious, political or social. So the jaundiced but fascinating description of Henry Ireton's burial at Westminster and, a few years later, the grisly glee when the body is exhumed, along with that of Cromwell, and publicly hanged at Tyburn. 'Fear God, & honor the King, but meddle not with them who are given to change,' he wrote on that occasion; this text being the central pillar of his faith. John Evelyn is the conservative mystic whose Anglican faith and English nationality are inextricably intertwined in a single rigid spiritual knot.

In 1654 he was in Oxford and visited 'that miracle of a Youth, Mr Christopher Wren'. The diary from now on reveals Evelyn's fascination with science and we get his important accounts of the first meetings of the Royal Society, of which he was a founder member, and many entries showing a fresh kind of intellectual awareness, in contrast with which his habit of sermon tasting seems prim and reactionary. For the revolutionary nature of Christ's teachings are light years away from these severe pulpit conventions listened to and noted down with such approval by Evelyn, and recognised by him as divine instructions for the correct ordering of English life. During the Commonwealth he often had to search around in order to find a pulpit containing the authentic Anglican note – so often did they echo with the rantings of enthusiasts and the like. Its tedious quantity of sermons apart, the *Diary* does give a vivid picture of the Established Church emerging from political and social confusions to become a true spiritual expression of the English. During the 1650s Evelyn witnesses a great outbreak of iconoclasm to satisfy the 'scrupulosity of the times' and is horrified by the fervour with which the Puritans 'cleansed' Christianity of its art. What Thomas Cromwell's agents had allowed to remain was now destroyed under Oliver. Through Evelyn, we see the national church in a crude kind of vacuum. On 3 September 1658 he writes triumphantly, 'Died that archrebell *Oliver Cromwell*, cal'd Protector', and has no hesitation in seeing God reaping vengeance. The funeral did not take place until November.

To *Lond*, to visit my Bro: & the next day saw the superb Funerall of the *Protectors*: He was carried from *Somerset-house* in a velvet bed of state drawn by six horses houss'd with the same: the Pall held up by his new Lords: *Oliver* lying in Effigie in royal robes, and Crown'd with a Crown, scepter, and *Mund*, like a King: the Pendants, and Guidons were carried by the Officers of the Army, The Imperial banners, Atchivements &c by the *Heraulds* in their *Coates*, a rich caparizon'd Horse all embroided over with gold: a Knight of honour arm'd *Cap a pé* & after all his Guards, Souldiers & innumerable Mourners: in this equipage they proceeded to *Westminster.* . . but it was the joyfullest funeral that ever I saw, for there was none that Cried, but dogs, which the souldiers hooted away with a barbarous noise: drinking, and taking *Tobacco* in the streetes as they went.

During the last months of the Commonwealth, Evelyn left his country house and went to live in an inn in Russell Street, Covent Garden, where he daringly published his *Apologie for the King* 'in this time of danger, when it was capital to speake or write in favour of him'. The next May, his ordeal was over, for there came 'the most happy tidings of his *Majesties* gracious *Declaration* . . . after a most bloudy & unreasonable Rebellion of neer 20 yeares. Praised be forever the Lord of Heaven, who only dost wondrous things . . .'

Evelyn's account of the Restoration years is an enthralling document and made doubly interesting because of the conflict within the diarist himself. Everything he had hoped, prayed and longed for has happened. The God-ordered kingdom is established once more, a magnificent state-ordered Prayer Book is immediately published which will put paid to both innovation and the Papists once and for all, and England itself seems to be restored to its ancient vigorous health. The arts flourish and, except for such matters as the hanging, drawing and quartering of the regicides (whose 'smoking quarters' he was to observe, with satisfaction, being carted away from the gallows), the plague and the burning down of London, a new mildness seemed to prevail. And yet, and yet . . .

As the *Diary* plunges on and on, through the reigns of Charles II, his brother James, William and Mary, Anne and into an acceptance of, if not into the actual rule of the Hanoverians, the reader senses its growing disenchantment with kings. None of them makes the least effort to live up to his or her heaven-ordained role nor, so far as Evelyn can tell (and he is in constant personal contact with them in turn) do they make any serious attempt to achieve transcendence via the Sacraments, sermons, and prayer, over lust, greed and other temporal matters, as he does. He is stiffly honest but yet ungenerous, and where he is humorous, as in the incident about Charles and Nelly having a kind of slanging match over a garden wall, he doesn't mean to be. Never for one moment during all the long years which the *Diary* embraces is there a sign of personal let up. Evelyn is the self-disciplined English gentleman from youth to dotage. He lives rigidly by Christian principles, yet never manages to convey the spirit of Christ, and the massive accounts of church services leave one intrigued only by what urged him to set them all down.

Parallel with Evelyn the lugubrious Anglican, there runs Evelyn the art-lover and Evelyn the scientist. Also Evelyn the guest whose frequent and various attendances at other people's tables belie the picture of a somewhat forbidding character. He is clearly welcome everywhere he goes, and intimacy has a habit of breaking into even the most formal occasions, as the following entry shows.

August 19th 1668

Standing by his Majestie at dinner in the Presence, There was of that rare fruite called the *King-Pine*, (growing in Barbados & W. Indies), the first of them I had ever seen; His Majestie having cut it up, was pleased to give me a piece off his own plate to tast of, but in my opinion it falls short of those ravishing varieties of deliciousnesse, describ'd in *Cap: Liggous* history & others; but possibly it might be, (& certainly was) much impaired in coming so far: It has yet a grateful accidity . . .

Evelyn's prose is a skilled mixture of the domestic, the learned and the sheer ornate, and contains periods which sometimes recall those of Sir Thomas Browne – whom he once made a special journey to Norwich to meet. Historic figures have a way of pushing through this handsome screen of words, to the constant astonishment of the reader. There is the account of Evelyn letting his house to Peter the Great, for example – who left it in such a mess that Evelyn had to send for Sir Christopher Wren to repair it. There are memorable glimpses of Lancelot Andrewes, Robert Boyle, Bishop Burnet, Marlborough, Dryden, Grinling Gibbons (whom Evelyn discovered), Sidney Godolphin, the mistresses and bastards of Charles II, Halley (whom Evelyn heard lecturing to the Royal Society), Hampden, William Harvey, Thomas Hobbes, Clarendon, Bishop Ken, Kneller, Lely, Louis XIV, Titus Oates, Pepys, Prince Rupert, Monmouth, Sheldon, Jeremy Taylor, Edmund Waller – and a vast range of public and private figures stretching from Shakespeare's to Pope's England.

But, except for such celebrated biographical essays as that written by Evelyn on Charles II, the pleasures of this great *Diary* lie in the many sentences which have a habit of bringing the reader up with an intrigued jolt by their strangeness and colour, and by its unique historical sweep as it records Britain struggling out of absolutism and many remaining medieval ideas, and into the modern age. When I read Evelyn I feel as though I have been shown to a front seat at the great parade of his time. Personally prim he may be, but what a commentator of the passing show!

There are early diaries which, with their easy jumble of pomp and homeliness, remind one of those florid seventeenth- and eighteenth-century tombs above which a fatherly peer, semi-nude, peruked and amiable, returns the adoring stares of marble cherubs with the same kind of sensible affection as at one time must have accompanied strict advice to his own little boys not to play too near the moat. The heroic paraphernalia of Greece and Rome on these monuments is supported on carved replicas of the hassock in the family pew, and their Latin inscriptions, oak-leaf mantling, stags heads, chained unicorns, pug-faced lions, swags of cannon, harness straps, rumpled drapery and extravagant gestures present a juxtaposition of formal myths too impersonal for the task they are asked to do, which is to commemorate an ordinary man.

The first Earl of Bristol's diary is a case in point. He kept it for fifty-four years, through two marriages, twenty births of sons and daughters, five reigns and countless vicissitudes on the racecourse. The entries are brief but they move so effortlessly from public to private experience, and are so ingenuously good-natured, that they leave one feeling that one has had complete access to the writer. His duties at Court never take precedent over the experiences at Ickworth, his beloved Suffolk home, and 'the sweet centre of my humble soul'. The deaths of his infant children and his dogs Fanny and Kickaninny are equally sensitively recorded. He rarely gossips but at the same time the news he has to give is always intimate and personal. Unlike Evelyn, Lord Bristol says a lot about his wife and family, and he also has an almost curiously balanced view of life in the country and life in town. In London he was the level- headed courtier, in Suffolk the ruler of local society. As his second wife wrote:

When often urged, unwilling to be great,
His country calls him from his lov'd retreat
And then to Senates charg'd with common care,
Which none less seeks and none can better bear,
Where could they find another form'd so fit
To pose with solid sense a sprightly wit?
　　. . .Well born and wealthy, wanting no support,
He steers betwixt his country and the Court
　　. . .He does with hands unbribed and heart sincere
Twixt Prince and People in a medium steer.

The diary would seem to confirm the justice of this rhyme. John Hervey's good looks added to the general opinion that he was a model of leadership and attracted such epithets as 'the lovely Suffolk swain' and 'lovely Bristol'. His son Lord Hervey was to inherit this beauty to an ambivalent degree and it was, as he soon discovered when he dared to attack Pope, made the peg upon which to hang some scathing accusations. The diary contains many references to this brilliant courtier whose acidulous *Memoirs of the Reign of George II* are a such vivid exposure of the Hanoverians. He was the first of the sixteen children which John Hervey was to have by his second wife, Elizabeth Felton, and we hear of his father taking him to Cambridge and then, at twenty, setting him off on the Grand Tour 'to perfect him ye man! wish to see'. It was Lord Hervey's son Frederick, the Bishop of Derry, who began to build the present magnificent house at Ickworth. The Bishop, a magpie who had amassed a vast collection of furniture and *objets d'art*, needed somewhere to house it and conceived an immense oval drum flanked by single storey quadrant wings. Scenes from Homer made a frieze round the drum, which is surrounded by a double ring of columns. The Bishop, who became the fourth Earl of Bristol in 1779, was a restless figure and appropriately gave his name to the Bristol Hotels which are now scattered all over the world. The modest country house which figures so frequently in his grandfather's diary as 'sweet Ikworth', and for which the diarist grew homesick the moment his carriages lurched Londonwards, is now no more than a stain on the summer grass.

John Hervey's diary displays good nature and a certain innocence. Also a personality which is in sharp contrast with those of his most famous son and grandson. He is like the principal figure in a splendid pastoral with his 'running horses' – My Hogg, Ball Manners, Grasshopper, Cobler, Mustard, Headpiece, Spider – his god-like descents on the assemblies at Bury St Edmunds, and in his unaffected magnanimity. Unlike many diarists, he kept the record of his expenses in a separate book, but this provides such an intimate inventory that it was an inspired decision by the clergyman who first edited both in 1894 to publish them together. Thus we have a truly remarkable list of the prices of eighteenth century furs, lace, railings, silver, china, pictures, wages, tips, food, glass, rates, arms, upholstery, candles, books, etc.

Among John Hervey's accomplishments was music and he had an interest in the theatre. He played the flute and violin, and helped to rebuild the Haymarket Theatre. The diary ends on 13 April 1742 with the lonely old man – his wife had died in a sedan chair in St James's Park a few months earlier – back home in Suffolk, its final words being

'Ickworth', 'which I found not sweet in her absence'.

Its bland charm apart, Lord Bristol's reasons for writing his diary are hard to define. He is present at many historic events, but he tells us no more about them than could be discovered in the most straightforward history book. He meets a whole succession of monarchs and their families, their courts and the celebrities they attract yet, unlike his son, he does not think it either appropriate or worthwhile to describe what he hears and sees. He adores Suffolk and lives there surrounded by hordes of friendly neighbours, farming people, the citizens of Bury St Edmunds, clergy, artists and the Newmarket racing fraternity, yet here again he tells us little more of all these individuals than their names. On the other hand, he is never cold and the weight of the affection shown towards his huge family and to dogs and horses makes him appear the very essence of the good Englishman. So does his modesty, for though he rose from country squire's son to earl and although during his married life he spent nearly a third of a million pounds, an immense sum at that time, he has a way of conveying these things onto the page with a lack of pride and surprise which is faintly comic. More intimately, we hear of a cholic or two, but on the whole few physical discomforts, of endless bereavements and calm acceptance, of lots of dinners but no menus, of cellars and wine but no drunkenness; of his wife's near-continuous pregnancies, but no whoring. And what we never catch is Lord Bristol looking into himself as lover, Christian, politician, human being. Had he a biographer in mind when he took up his pen? How over fifty years did he manage to write so much that was personal and nothing that was really private?

Had Dorothy Wordsworth done no more than noted the day-by-day domestic routine against which her brother worked during the years of his highest creativity she would have remained a figure of rare interest. Yet, by setting out to do little more than this, she was to succeed in revealing a brother and sister relationship of such tenderness and intensity that it haunts the imagination of everyone who reads her quietly unflinching account of it. When, added to this, one knows that by her self-effacing genius the reader is admitted to the intimate presence of a young man who was changing the direction of English poetry even as she ironed his shirt or collected sticks with him in the wood, then the inestimable value of every small detail of Dorothy's *Journals* is easy to appreciate. Particularly when we know that William himself valued his sister not merely as his housekeeper-companion, but as his muse.

Dorothy Wordsworth's *Journals* differ from the main body of diary-keeping inasmuch as they were not written to satisfy a private need but 'to please William'. Her entire existence, as a matter of fact, was to please William. He in turn saw his sister as no ordinary recorder of weather, birds, flowers, trees and the natural history surrounding their homes in Somerset and Cumberland, of the talk of friends and neighbours, and of small rural events, but as his collaborator. 'She gave me eyes, she gave me ears', he wrote in *The Sparrow's Nest*, and in *The Prelude* he acknowledged her as 'the sister of my soul'.

There are two journals, the first written between January and May 1798 at Alfoxden, and the second between May 1800 and January 1803 at Grasmere. The first entry in the Alfoxden journal declares Dorothy's quality as a writer.

Alfoxden, *January* 20th, 1798. The green paths down the hill sides are channels for streams. The young wheat is streaked by silver lines of water running between the ridges, the sheep are gathered together on the slopes. After the wet dark days, the country seems more populous. It peoples itself in the sunbeams. The garden, mimic of spring, is gay with flowers. The purple starred hepatica spreads itself in the sun, and the clustering snow drops put forth their white heads, at first upright, ribbed with green, and like a rosebud when completely opened, hanging their heads downwards, but slowly lengthening their slender stems. The slanting woods of an unvarying brown, showing the light through the thin net work of their upper boughs. Upon the highest ridge of that round hill covered with planted oaks, the shafts of the trees show in the light like the columns of a ruin.

The final entry in *The Grasmere Journal*, made almost exactly five years later on another January day, describes a visit made by Dorothy to a neighbour's cottage in the bitter cold. A man and his wife and his sister are sitting by the fire, formal in their Sunday best. The man is blind. A few weeks earlier Wordsworth had married his childhood friend Mary Hutchinson, and the evening scene in his house was of a man and his wife and his sister around the hearth. Dorothy loved Mary because William loved her. Harmony endured, but not the earlier joy.

Dorothy and her three brothers lost their parents as children, as did the Hutchinson girls. All of them were separated for years and all dreamt of the day when they could be reunited, Dorothy and William particularly. She was eighteen months his junior and was twenty-four before a legacy made it possible for William to keep his promise to live with her. This was in 1795, when he was extricating himself from his passionate involvement in the French Revolution and from guilt in another direction – his affair with Annette Vallon, which had produced a baby. In August 1802, some nine weeks before his marriage, William had taken his sister to Calais to see Annette and her child. Dorothy had walked with them on the sand while William bathed. They stayed together for a month and were happy. The journey home was portentous and leisurely, involving a stay with the Hutchinsons and William's marriage to Mary on 4 October, using the wedding ring which Dorothy had worn all the night before. Two days later they were back at Dove Cottage, William and Dorothy hurrying into the garden with candlesticks to see how their plants had grown. The purity and restraint with which these events are described is extraordinary.

But overshadowing even the interest of the delicately told personal story is the account of Wordsworth and Coleridge during the great years of their collaboration. *Lyrical Ballads* was published in 1798 and Dorothy witnessed another revolution at first hand, that philosophical interpretation of Nature which brought about the English romantic movement. It was during this time, when her every observation of the changing seasonal patterns of the countryside were of the utmost importance to him, that her brother began work on his masterpiece, *The Prelude*, although it was not to be published until after his death. So, in effect, we have in these *Journals* the day-by-day activity of a creative partnership of genius.

One other thing will strike the reader – Dorothy Wordsworth's humanity. Grasmere may have seemed like a rarefied retreat to those viewing it through hazes of cloud, peaks, streams and daffodils, but through it wandered the poor and sick and homeless. Her concern for them is total. The many sharp vignettes of beggars, lost children, wounded soldiers, stoical old men and victims of all kinds of a society in upheaval under industrial and military pressures offer a remarkable commentary on the times. Dorothy loved people, loved listening to them, and accepted each one of them as individual and unique. She approached every living soul with that special quality which her brother and his friends called 'imagination' a kind of deep luminous truth. She could catch a particular voice so that its owner, who may have only rested an hour in Dove Cottage, stays in the memory like a character drawn by a great novelist.

Finally, I must confess an addiction to the tremendous diary kept by Virginia Woolf from January 1915 to her death in 1941. The selection her husband made from it in 1956 gave only the slightest indication of its range and power. It is the by-product of a solidly hard-working, professional life and what I most feel when I read it is the pressure of a freshly running stream which is not yet diverted by analysis or polluted by wash-back. Her policy when writing it, each evening after tea, with her favourite dip pen, was one of unpremeditation and immediacy. The pen had to fly fast and at a totally different pace and rhythm to when it was writing novels and essays. It had to outrun second thoughts and to surprise the diarist herself by where it often landed up. There was to be no re-phrasing, although she quite liked an occasional re-reading and she was frequently 'much struck by the haphazard gallop at which it swings along . . . the advantage of the method is that it sweeps accidentally several stray matters which I should exclude if I hesitated, but which are the diamonds of the dustheap.' She thought it ought to be like

some deep old desk . . . in which one flings a mass of odds & ends without looking them through. I should like to come back, after a year or two, & find that the collection had sorted itself & refined itself & coalesced, as such deposits so mysteriously do, into a mould, transparent enough to reflect the light of our life .

When I read this sentence in her *Diary* covering the years 1915-19, I understood the fundamental attraction of all diaries. It was to watch

55

particles of recorded experience catching fire and providing the final illumination I was likely to have of a past day.

The poet David Gascoyne kindly gave me a copy of his published 1936-7 *Journal* a few weeks ago, and on the first page his young self states, 'The whole question of journals is absurd . . . You are reading this? But I had to pretend that no one would ever read it!' So why is he writing it?

In order to find out who I am? Yes and no. To stretch the muscles of my ego, rather; to overcome a certain timidity where my own personality is concerned and in doing so, to resolve certain intimate problems which cannot be mine alone. All this embarrasses you? That was partly my intention. Where am I now? *For Future Reference*, then . . .

Six months later he admits to liking nothing better 'than notebooks or journals which give an exact, daily record of experience – feelings, self analysis – the human being *chez lui*, naked. I think a journal should be a continual confession of an incurable passion for life.' So that could be it.

THE FABER BOOK OF DIARIES
ed. Simon Brett, 1987

'Not a day without a line', advised Pliny the Elder. 'Why?' the non-diarist has a right to ask. The compulsive creator of the book of the self tries to answer this question but rarely succeeds, at least to his own satisfaction. Boswell, that master of the book of the self, thought: 'I should live no more than I can record . . . There is a waste of good if it cannot be preserved.' Anais Nin said: 'Every evening I want my diary as one wants opium.'

Diarists began to flourish in the 17th century – although there were a few earlier journals, such as that kept by the boy king Edward VI –

and some have seen these as replacements of the confessionals which were swept away at the Reformation. 'Register those secret Faults, to which none but your own Conscience is privy . . . Often contemplate yourself in this faithful mirror', wrote the Revd James Harvey. When Richard Hurrell Froude read his old diaries he confessed: 'I can hardly identify myself with the person it describes.' What nearly every diarist reveals is not so much vanity and neurotic self-obsession as a far greater than average enthralment with the minutiae of human existence. Also an unusual energy and passion.

Diaries should not be accepted as gospel truth. To write without restraint every day about one's family, friends and neighbours must often involve cruelty and falsity. The second big question is, does the diarist, however secretive, in his heart of hearts hope to be read by another? Except for the tiniest fraction of journal-keepers, the answer is yes. Mrs Boswell loathed her husband's journalising and believed that he was leaving himself 'embowelled to posterity'. But some of the best diaries resulted from the writer's need to record what he saw on a journey or during a war. These 'log-book' diaries are often brilliant. One thinks of the dazzling journal which the 21-year-old Edmund Wheatley wrote for his girl during the Peninsular War, and the little diary which the poet George Crabbe sent to his sweetheart describing his attempt to become a writer in London.

There are many hundreds of published diaries and a vast but unknown quantity of unpublished ones, and the anthologist, after taking care to admit the titans – Pepys, Evelyn, Burney, Boswell, Kilvert, Beatrice Webb, and the rest – must reserve the right to enjoy his own prejudice. Simon Brett's selection contains some 110 diarists and they include the obvious names and a small crowd of those he particularly likes. It is pointless to grouse about why him and why not her. And, perhaps, equally pointless to whine about the flimsy approach. The book can only intend being a kind of *hors d'oeuvre* introduction to so substantial a feast, else it would not be what it is, pages and pages of appetising little odds and ends which are nice to nibble but leave one rather hungry. How to deal with diarists in anthologies has always been a problem. Should one raid them for the plums, or attempt to catch their essence? Should they be arranged chronologically, as a distinctive historic literary genre, or should they be treated like a single huge archive in which to dig for anecdotes?

Simon Brett has taken a middle course and invented his own order, choosing three or four entries from diaries of all periods for each day of the year. Thus on 13 March we have Mary Shelley, Arnold Bennett and Siegfried Sassoon and on 10 October Pepys, Queen Victoria, George Gissing and Evelyn Waugh. Except for obvious dates such as New Year's Day or 1 April, the entries cannot say anything which holds 13 March, for example, in common, but the scheme does allow Simon Brett to make a pattern from his quotations. The same diarists appear in many places, with much fracturing of their stylistic strength. Diaries are best read in fairly meaty chunks; sometimes, strangely enough in good, dull chunks, if their flavour is to be appreciated. However, the book proves that the editor does have a nice taste in diaries. If it sends some of us off to its rich and lengthy sources, it will justify its slight helpings.

One more thing. How can Barbellion be dismissed along with Mr Pooter and Adrian Mole? My old friend John Nash, Barbellion's youthful neighbour and friend, drew his portrait just before his death and was close enough to him to know that the *Journal of a Disappointed Man* was a genuine diary. It was one of those diaries written – like poor John Clare's poem – to declare *I Am*.

A MOMENT'S LIBERTY

The Shorter Diary of Virginia Woolf

ed. Anne Olivier Bell, 1990

An editor's hand, however slight, on any diary leaves its mark. The diary becomes directed. Anne Olivier Bell understands this and sets out her two courses of direction at the start. For the full text of what was so brilliantly scribbled down in a fast hand between 1915-1941 and edited into five volumes she directed us to a great diary in toto, for its abridgement she directs us to the self-portrait it contains of the diariest. *A Moment's Liberty* is a revelation of Virginia Woolf which is both candid and shadowy, tough and vulnerable. It shows her as being hard on herself as the Victorians were hard on themselves where their work was concerned. Works of the imagination, literary jobbery of a high order, running two houses, a publishing business and a social life which, for many people, would itself have constituted a full-time occupation crammed the day and were somehow expected to do so, for this to her was how writers existed. Behind her lay the immense industry of her father, Sir Stephen, in the next room could be heard the ceaseless toil of her husband Leonard, from Bloomsbury itself came the sound of a continuous making of things. There were a few holidays but little relaxation. When she wasn't working she was ill, what she called 'the dark cupboard of illness' in which she learned to put herself away. 'What a born melancholiac I am! The only way I keep afloat is by working.' So *A Moment's Liberty* is the extraction of the picture which Virginia Woolf unawarely over many years drew of herself as foremostly the dedicated writer. It shows her as being less than dedicated to anything else.

Like all the best diarists she rarely looks ahead, and likes to savour the Now. 'The future is dark, which is on the whole, the best thing a future can be, I think,' she wrote in 1915. Eventually, the Now would prove intolerable and the River Ouse would carry her from it, but it would be a fanciful error to see her being borne along on some tragic current all her days. Outside the dark cupboard lay an enviable world, and she knew it. 'How much I admire this handling of life as if it were a thing one could throw about; this handling of circumstance'. She handled it with style and never cautiously, and with great zest and energy, seeing everything through the searching, amused and occasionally ruthless eyes of the novelist. She can be sharp to the verge of cruelty or tastelessness but her honesty is often expressed in a way which illuminates everything she records, from gossip to the remarkable literary movement of the inter-war years in which she had so important a role. Her diary indeed makes her one of the latter's major historians. A week after the Armistice 'I was interrupted somewhere on this page by the arrival of Mr Eliot . . . a polished, cultivated, elaborate young American, talking so slow . . . . Will he become Tom?' And soon all the celebrated names make their bow, like the *dramatis personae* of a distinctive age, Shaw, the Webbs, the Murrys, Strachey, Forster, etc. She is never better than when she is capturing their faces and habits in a few deft sentences. Maynard Keynes is 'like quicksilver on a sloping board', Queen Mary at the theatre is 'like a lit up street with diamonds', in the aged but hopeful Ethel Smyth 'the old fires of Sapphism are blazing for the last time'.

This abridged diary brings some kind of proportion to Virginia's baroque love affair with Vita Sackville-West and, equally, a certain disproportion to her marriage with Leonard, for he seems somehow thinned down and a voice off. Her success unexpectedly eclipses him during the late 'thirties, making it difficult for them both. Her creative years are hedged in by the two wars. Although she succeeded in more or less ignoring the first, World War Two roared over her vulnerable head as Sussex awaited the Nazis. In between spread the disciplined toil and the exhausting sociability. 'To walk alone in London is the greatest rest'. Throughout 'our Bloomsbury relationships flourish, grow in lustiness. Suppose our set to survive another twenty years, I tremble to think how thickly knit and grown together it will be.' But deaths are thicker – more frequent than the longer version of the diary suggests.

Here and there a day's happenings receives masterly attention, such as the visit to Thomas Hardy. He was 86 and receiving in his simple courteous way a constant stream of visitors. Virginia recognises greatness. He gives her his *Life's Little Ironies* spelling her name 'Wolff'. She saw him 'swept off into imaging and creating without a thought of its being difficult or remarkable.' Her diary is rather like that.

PROPHESYING PEACE

James Lees-Milne, 1977

Gossip reaches out to philosophy in James Lees-Milne's diaries, the second instalment of which shows him harder at work than ever capturing houses for the National Trust, an activity in heroic contrast to that going on all around him, as architectural demolition moves towards its dreadful crescendo at Hiroshima. London's 'robot' bombs, the V1s and V2s, are to be midges in comparison; but the climate through which he battles to preserve wonderful buildings, great and small, is officially destructive.

This volume opens with a brief entry about the military decision on Monte Cassino; and it is in the light of what the British, American, German – or any – government is capable of when ·wars have established their terms, that it needs to be read. Both *Ancestral Voices* and *Prophesying Peace* contain more cogent criticisms of the last war than their author could have intended when, each flak-filled night, he described his atypical day. They are, surprising though it may seem, important war books.

The stance is patrician, the writing very good indeed, the personality revealed a vulnerable one. The ambience is that which found its way into all kinds of Forties fiction, from *Brideshead Revisited* and *Love in a Cold Climate*, to the tales of Sansom and Elizabeth Bowen in their blacked-out London moods. Here is a world as departed as snoek but infinitely more subtle and intriguing. The immediacy of the diary discipline releases its distinctive flavour with memorable effect.

Yet why is it so affecting? What can there be so disturbing in the private calendar of a young man chattering to Decca and Jamesy, and Tom and Emerald and Gerry and Grandy and Sibyl, when he isn't taking notes at Blickling, Shaw's Corner, Osterley, Charlecote and Compton Verney? Why isn't it, at the best, elegant – and at the worst, a bit awful? Because its contents are knotted to a particularly sympathetic thread of seriousness, quiet and undidactic.

'What did you do in the war, Daddy?' (Not, of course, a question to be addressed to Mr. Lees-Milne in quite this form.) 'I beavered on in the shambles, knowing that bricks and mortar, not to mention gardens, have a right to be among the most enduring of humanity's civilised statements.' While other old Etonians – and Grammarians – were busy flattening Dresden, he was shielding the work of Burton, Adam and Anon from other menaces, including the intentions of some of its owners.

Although serious, Mr Lees-Milne is never solemn, and his 1944-45 diaries supply a whole new range of anecdotes on the period. They were picked up at Sibyl Colefax's Ordinaries, Emerald Cunard's parties, clubs ranging from White's to the Gargoyle, country houses whose gilded cupolas were swathed in rugs so as not to comfort the Luftwaffe, and bomb shelters. Lord Curzon, who is keeping Sir George Clerk standing while he continues to write out invitation cards; 'I suppose you too occasionally entertain in your small way.' Colonel Wingfield Digby, MFH, on being shown Pope's Seat in the grounds of his castle: 'Pope indeed. I've no idea which pope it could have been.' Lord Leconfield, after discussing with Mr Lees-Milne the transference of Petworth to the National Trust, leads him to the street door, points to a closed cafeteria and says: 'You will get a very good tea in there. Put it down to me.'

Most of the houses to which the young negotiator makes his way by bus, freezing trains, bicycle or on foot are in the most deplorable condition, and are inhabited by troops, evacuees, Americans or worn-out servants. That charming pessimist, Marshall Sisson, sits on the grassy walls of Venta Icenorum (Caistor St Edmund near Norwich) and tells the author that he shares his disquiet about the future and that it is fruitless caring for good buildings, 'for wars will continue, and there will be underground architecture only.' Running through the fascinating pages is Mr Lees-Milne's less implicit belief that the party is over, and that – although he does not share his friend's despair, or Evelyn Waugh's dread of Hooper's arrival, or George Barker's prophecy of the ragged-arsed mechanic squatting in the gentleman's seat – the aristocratic ideals to which he is almost religiously attached are, indeed, a thing of the past. Thus a little melancholy flavours the entries, and never more so than when they are frivolous.

He is revealing when it comes to how the upper-class has to preserve its famous loyalty in the face of extremism or scandal in its individual members. While visiting America, Churchill finds time to meet Jessica

Mitford to assure her that her sister, Diana, 'was now much happier in prison because she was reunited with Tom [Oswald] Mosley', and tells her that he can get her a job with Lord Halifax. He feels 'very snubbed' when she says that she wouldn't touch Halifax with a barge pole. He is intriguing and moving on friendship, and his book is a revelation of the special relationships decreed by wars. There is the tentative, painful probing of those closenesses which must find sexual expression and those which must not. And for all his sociability, there is scarcely a page on which his aloneness is not apparent.

Finally, a word must be said about the living-through-the-blitz aspect of these diaries. Since other people's bomb stories became one of the hazards of the emergency and likely to drive one mad, it is splendid to have a version of this chaos which evokes its peculiar mixture of horror and cosiness with such freshness and fidelity. But here again privilege raises its battered head, and it has to be admitted that a good part of the reason why Mr Lees-Milne isn't a bomb-bore is because he tells us about Dame Una, Emerald, Norman Douglas, Betjeman, Sibyl, Eddy and all and all getting blasted.

The war over, 'I stayed talking to Emerald about the world's great novels, about the discontent of the rich and the still greater discontent of the poor. "It's less sad to be rich," Emerald concluded.'

THE OXFORD BOOK OF LETTERS

ed. Frank & Anita Kermode, 1995

In making their selection from a virtually limitless pile of correspondence, the Kermodes say: 'We have been compelled only to do as we please.' Which is the true art of the anthologist. To find what one would expect would be a disappointment. Letter readers will discover a few old friends but, on the whole, they will be in fresh epistolary territory. The selection is chronological and covers the years 1535 to 1985, or from Sir Antony Windsor to Philip Larkin. The latter's is one of a number of last letters which include Sir Thomas More's farewell, written 'with a coal' to his daughter Margaret.

A handful of great figures and nobodies apart – 'ordinary' writers are perhaps under-represented – the bulk of this enthralling book is made up of author's letters, as one would hope. The subject being so vast, OUP might entertain the notion of asking a scientist, a priest or a countryman to add companion volumes.

The Kermodes are well-read academics and these are the letters which give them pleasure and the sudden, brilliant access into that private world which is aided and abetted by the post office. They rightly deplore 'today's almost illiterate business letters' and find it hard to imagine an anthology of faxes.

They see the great age of the letter as 1700 to 1918. It is clear that letter-writing proper creates style and destroys inhibition. A private letter demands indiscretion, even recklessness. It is no good scribbling 'burn this' because nobody does. It goes into the drawer.

The most hilarious letter is from Groucho Marx to Warner Brothers, who were protesting that the Marx Brothers were about to shoot a film called *A Night in Casablanca*, they having shot one called *Casablanca*: 'I am sure that the average movie fan could learn, in time, to distinguish between Ingrid Bergman and Harpo . . .'

Wonderful travel, homesick letters, include gruesome days in New York and in the South with its slaves. Nothing describes so heartbreakingly being far from home in the 19th century as the long letters written to mothers by young sons. There are many letters connected with brief encounters, often awkward, such as that written by the Chavalier de Santa Rosa, an Italian refugee, to Sara Austen, a kind woman, in 1822. There are revelatory letters in which all the celebrity of the writer is discarded and a stranger with a famous name looks up from the page. There are letters which seek to justify the unspeakable such as that from Sir Joshua Reynolds after he had stood on a gallows to watch six men being hanged.

Only one letter is cut, a Fanny Burney. The rest – nearly 600 pages – are *in toto*. One is bursting to quote, but all I can say is, read the book. There is no special attempt at balance. Now and then – as with the asylum letters from the poet John Clare, who wrote many

64

magnificent letters about natural history – we are left with a distorted concept of the letter writer.

The letter is one of the gold-mines of social history and whether it be Katherine Howard's father's incontinence or Virginia Woolf being fitted with a gas mask, there is no end to each generation's facts of life. They pour along the lines. And there is what hides for all to see between the lines.

Some 'bad' people write 'a good letter', and some 'good' people a surprising one. The gossip is non-stop. We have everything from the profound and beautiful to the skittish and wicked.

THE COLLECTED LETTERS OF W.B.YEATS
Volume II, 1896-1900
ed. Warwick Gould, John Kelly & Deirdre Toomey

The Great Irish poet is now in his early thirties, and hyperactive. He has left home to live in a scruffy flat near St Pancras Church, Bloomsbury, chiefly at first to consummate his love affair with Olivia Shakespeare, a married woman, and then to create a meeting place for writers, mystics and Irish nationalists. And all this on a pittance eked out with erratic gifts from Uncle George Pollexfen in Sligo and Lady Gregory at Coole Park.

In appearance Yeats was at this time a strikingly attractive young man, with lustrous dark eyes and hair, pale skin and fine hands, tall and captivating. He had, he said, 'distanced himself from the English mind . . . meditative, rich, deliberate; it may remember the Thames valley'. This distancing went way back to pre-Christian Erin, to 'faery', and to where he believed his country's soul still existed, although buried beneath all the clutter of the Ascendancy, Christianity, etc.

The turn of the century was the heyday of the folklorist, and although not a bit interested in this as a study, Yeats recognised that some of the answers the peasantry gave to folklore-recorders contained fragments of knowledge about a kind of 'morning' Ireland which existed before foreign elements corrupted it. And thus began his famous and fey pursuit of 'other worlds than this'. It made enchanting poetry, if not much sense to patriots who were longing for Home Rule.

But gradually, as Celtic Ireland emerged via Yeat's verse and plays, the originality of his vision and the power of his language began to disturb both the Church and the British government. These years saw the founding of the Irish Literary Theatre and the 'Celtic Twilight' movement, the revival of the Irish language and a reawakening of some atavistic or dormant Irishness, unlike anything which Church or government previously had to deal with.

This five years' pile of correspondence shows Yeats the inspired poet, the complex lover of women, and the highly practical organiser of literary-political 'happenings'. A conversation with George Bernard Shaw results in *John Bull's Other Ireland*. Between managing drama in Dublin and work on some of his finest poems, Yeats is heavily involved in talismans, keeping a Visions Book, belonging to a Rosicrucianist movement known as The Golden Dawn, Blavatskian theosophy, trances, spiritualism, séances – and the occasional resorting to hashish and mescalin.

Slummy Woburn Buildings alternate with lovely Coole Park. He falls for the beautiful Maud Gonne, who says that they can be only friends, not telling him that she is the mistress of a Frenchman, with two children by him. His energies are prolix and a wonderfully detailed picture of late-Victorian London and Dublin, quite unlike that of any other of this period, is built up, letter by letter. Yeats is astute and business-like when it comes to managing publishers and committees, and yet always dream-like. It is a fascinating combination.

As for the editing of the letters, it is masterly. They're only half of a prodigious undertaking – and there are volumes more to come. Keeping open house on a pound or two a week resulted in the young writer meeting everybody. He was both remote and 'at home', and the reader sits by his stingy fire and is intimate with his simplicity and with his grandeur. The Irish Question is receiving its most exquisite answer.

Besides being a kind of autobiography, this volume, like that which preceded it, is the multiple biography of scores of now little-known authors, publishers and patriots. The editors' ability to have found out so many lives in the minutest detail is amazing, and the meticulous nature of their scholarship leaves one gasping.

What a task! What an achievement! William Butler Yeats, *aet.* 30-35, here is your early world.

LETTERS FROM JOSEPH CONRAD 1898-1902

A Writer's Day-Book, 2006

There is an acute species of melancholy attached to the early days of authorship which is often all too lightly dismissed by biographers as teething pains. The worried Conrad of *Youth, Heart of Darkness, Lord Jim*, etc. could not have imagined the Conrad of *Chance* and its revered and lucrative successors. The letters of the new man of letters are those of risk and loss, the familiar concomitants of the first freelance years. His very blessings, a wife who could type as well as create the high standard of domestic order he needed, their first son and, from the very beginning, the inestimable friendship of Edward Garnett, prince of publishers' readers, were themselves a reproach, for they had to be justified. Worst of all there was the new and still strange vacuum of the study which he had to enter each morning – or each midnight often enough in his case. This and the incredible absence of the sea. Instead there were the horrible Essex marshes, dank and crime-ridden. Eight months into the letters, Ford Madox Hueffer was to rescue him from the latter by installing him at Pent Farm near Sandgate, and within a stone's throw, comparatively speaking, of the current Olympians, including Henry James, Galsworthy and H. G. Wells. Such proximity was apt to be more crushing than anything else. There was too Conrad's natural grandeur as a Polish gentleman and incipient genius, the effect of which on others often disconcerted him. From the first he knew he was isolated and that every now and then he would need to make simple and direct statements about himself – 'I have never fostered any illusions as to my value. You may believe me implicitly when I say that I never work in a self satisfied elation . . .' He is remonstrating to Blackwood the publisher who, like his agent Pinker, goes a bit too far with his advice. At this moment both these men are hopefully thinking of Conrad as a superior yarn-spinner for boys.

He had joined the French merchant navy at sixteen, wild about the sea – some said because of reading Victor Hugo's *Toilers of the Sea* in his father's translation – but it wasn't until he was in his early thirties that he began to write what would become after some years and much shaping (and getting lost on voyages) *Almayer's Folly*, having taught himself English by reading east coast newspapers and talking to his East Anglian shipmates 'each built as though to last for ever, and coloured like a Christmas card.' He was thirty-seven when he gave up the sea as a career and retained it as a force for an entirely new kind of 'action' fiction, psychologically profound and stylistically sumptuous. It was hard to write, and hardest of all when these letters were sent.

They are chiefly to his first literary friends R. B. Cunninghame Graham, the socialist grandee who was thought by some to be the rightful King of Scotland, the wise Edward Garnett, H. G. Wells (the friendship did not last), the much tried literary agent, J. B. Pinker (Conrad's blast to him on the ubiquitous business of not delivering on time deserves a place alongside Dr Johnson's thunderclap against patrons), William Blackwood, Ford Madox Ford and Stephen Crane. There are also many letters to the generous Galsworthy, a rich and practical friend, and an exchange of mutual appreciation with Arnold Bennett. All these writers in particular are clearly aware that a novelist who is quite unlike any other novelist is emerging, and, in their different ways, are giving support to the tortured tenant of Pent Farm. Conrad's response is open and passionate. His loneliness shows. There is dawning respect and success, but a later reader would find that 'the letters abound in unhappiness'. But it is not the life-lasting gloom of some writers but the sadness of a stage of development which writers, and artists of all sorts, will recognise.

Family life itself is still odd to him. He has known nothing since he was a boy except ships' crews and their mixture of reticence and emotion, but on vast voyages he has witnessed everything, most particularly imperialism in motion. His is not an innocent's eye. In the farmhouse there is neither closeness nor space. Jessie Conrad is accorded dutiful courtesies, though once she is described as 'my wife, a person of simple feelings guided by the intelligence of the heart'. She was a bookseller's daughter, a large, capable woman on whom he depended for his spick and span home, secretarial requirements and punctual routine.

During these crucial four years, Conrad did all he could to understand what was happening to him. The hugeness of what he had seen, and maybe of what he had done, in comparison with his novelist contemporaries, plus the amazing use of a foreign language, made the usual literary placing impossible. Where was he? Who and what was he? The big first batch of letters do not wholly answer these questions but they are satisfyingly informative all the same. We do come much nearer to Conrad because of them. He made little up. Cunninghame Graham, writing to Edward Garnett about *Heart of Darkness*, said that it was written 'in the fervent contemplation of his tracks', and this masterpiece and all the rest of the work relied upon old sea-lanes re-travelled, old companions rejoined. But this kind of passage, often by pencil, was harder toil than sailing and he was constantly 'so weary, deadly weary of writing'. There was never a moment's let-up. Fresh tales pushed their way forward before he could find structures for them. 'My head is full of a story, I have not been able to write a single word except the title which shall be I think NOSTROMO; the story belonging to the "Karain" class of tales ("K" class for short – as you classify the cruisers.)' Like many stylists he was sometimes unnerved by the possibility of losing 'myself in a wilderness of endeavour' and of 'verbiage', and to this day we read him and are foxed by his artistry and his daring. He is lastingly mysterious. Seeing so many words, we think he has told all, but he never does. Explaining the deliberately bald ending of *Lord Jim* to Blackwood, he says, 'The reader ought to know enough at that time.' Will we know enough from these turn of the century letters to know how the patrician merchant seaman from Poland stepped straight into the centre of English literature? No but they help.

ARNOLD BENNETT TO HIS FAMILY

A Writer's Day-Book, 2006

Arnold Bennett's letters allow him the title of master of home truths. His celebrity had arrived early, bringing him a fortune, and it had been sustained right up to the moment of his somewhat mysterious death from typhoid in 1931. Then, almost at once, came the remorseless decline of reputation to make him, now, among the least regarded of all the famous novelists of his generation. The critic Angus Ross summed up this decline: 'His qualities of craftsmanship strengthen rather than offset the failure of his art, the failure of imagination.'

Yet the letters confirm what one has always suspected, that Arnold Bennett wanted to be an artist more than anything else in the world, and certainly more than either a popular novelist or a celebrity (although he did adore being the latter and knew how to make the most of it).

What is indisputable, and contrary to Bloomsbury's bitchy comments on him, is his kindness and decency. 'I don't care what anybody says,' he was heard to remark whilst staring at his portrait, 'I am a nice man.' And it was true.

But where women were concerned he was not a wise man, landing himself with a couple of hussies who should have been mistresses, maybe, not wife and common-law wife respectively. Their antics drew from Bennett a vast flow of domestic remonstrance which can have few equals in literary annals.

Stammering too badly to take part in verbal battles, he rowed on the page. How Marguerite, his wife, and Dorothy, his mistress, must have quailed when the postman arrived. 'You have got yourself into the clutches of an uncompromising realist with a startling faculty for detachment.' This went for both of them.

Neither could understand or accept that he was wedded to work. He was in fact a workaholic, intoxicated with output. When it was all over, weary and triumphant, he needed luxury, good food (no drink) and a bit of peace. After all, as he repeatedly told Marguerite in particular, he had paid for these things.

He also needed a little fantasy, his *Cherissime* in chic lingerie and kisses all over. Many of his letters to her are in French. Not that she is to get immortal notions, she is no Odette and he is no Swann: 'Let me suggest that you read "Swann in Love" to the end. It will give you something to think about. For it is one of the most ruthless and just attacks on woman that I have ever read.' Bennett is, of course, a Francophile. Only such a man would have set up house on the Essex coast among the yacht-clubs with a girl from a Paris dress-shop and expected the delights of both worlds. She was bored and took it out on the servants. The letters are laden with the old servant-problem chatter.

Eventually, having been given great licence where other men were concerned, Marguerite went off with Pierre Legros, a lecturer at London University – and with £2,000 a year from her much-tried husband, a tidy sum then. Many women will read Bennett's non-grumbling letters to her and wonder how and why she could have behaved as she did.

Friends like Frank Swinnerton, seeing how ill he sometimes looked, couldn't bear the way in which both Marguerite and Dorothy treated him. As the grumbling letters all too devastatingly prove, he must have frequently got his own back. Each lady was a malcontent, a whiner (something he abhorred in a woman) and each suffered, as minor artistic talents, by being outshone by what Marguerite testily referred to as her husband's 'gloire'.

Two children intervened, as it were, in the wordy, sexy warfare. The first was Richard, who was the eldest son of Arnold's brother Frank. Richard was adopted by Arnold and Marguerite to, at first, his cool disgust.

They sent him to Oundle and Cambridge. Arnold's letters to him there are so crammed with a kind of exasperated instruction that they make one laugh. They certainly didn't make Richard cry.

He emerges as a wonderfully hard-hearted lad whose truculence captured his uncle's respect, then his affection. With Auntie Marguerite it was a very different tale. When he told her to her face that he disliked her, the heavens fell, though mostly on Arnold.

The other child was Virginia, the daughter by Arnold of Dorothy Cheston, who was from then on known as Dorothy Cheston Bennett. Arnold could not marry her as Marguerite would not give him a divorce.

Bennett wrote to his mother every day, and sometimes twice a day, but only one letter from this group remains. All the rest were destroyed at her death.

The family correspondence reveals a man who appears to know that he brought difficulties upon himself by straying into marriage and into a marriage-like relationship when by temperament, and also by the requirements of his type of work, he should have stayed a bachelor.

Either this, or he should have had a wife who could run a country house, etc. But he appears to have wanted his cake and eat it too, exciting demi-monde ladies and capable companions for life all in one.

His letters are vigorous, buoyant and intimate. There is a sound of fame and royalties rushing in and lasting happiness, as they call it in fiction, draining out.

FROM MY SICKBED

Letters of Katherine Mansfield 1918-1919

A Writer's Day-Book, 2006

Between January 1918 and September 1919 Katherine Mansfield's brief life entered upon all its major events and opened towards both destruction and a modest, though certain, place among the best short-story writers of the twentieth century.

It was during these months that her tuberculosis was confirmed and she set out on the classic route of the incurable. It was then that her embarrassing husband for a night, George Bowden, at last divorced her and she was able to marry her lover, John Middleton Murry; it was then that the war which had claimed her brother ended; and then that her mother died. It was at this time, in a world so utterly transformed and sharpened, that she began to write those New Zealand via Chekhov tales contained in *Bliss, The Garden Party* and *The Dove's Nest*, which were to make her name.

As so frequently happened with consumptives, the illness weakened her and yet gave her increased creative energies: 'Darling Life is still here – waiting to be lived – not merely frowned at from a sofa. So I shall shut myself away. After all, six months' hard should be an amazing opportunity for work.' She had in fact a little over four years in which she half succumbed to the conventional treatment of the day and half resisted it, dying at last while undergoing Gurdjieff's alternative medicine.

Her fate, as with all the mortally sick, was to find herself – immediately her tuberculosis was diagnosed – on some kind of ledge outside ordinary, normal existence. While she resented this position, she recognised that it did give her a privileged view of the loveliness of the earth, and these letters contain long and grateful descriptions of what the healthy fail to see. Although she struggled hard '*not* to cut the malade off from life, neither in a sanatorium nor in a land of milk rivers, butter mountains and cream valleys', as she told Murry, the disease itself forced her to accept its own indifference to what was happening beyond its sphere.

Friends were sensible and kind, and one or two of them were devoted. Murry himself, who was only twenty-eight, took the line of supporting whatever it was that would make her content, if only for the time being. He was up to his ears in work at the War Office and editing the *Athenaeum*. There is much anxious talk about money, but between them they had over £1,000 a year, a considerable income then. Each of them dreamt of Arcadia, a cottage in the country and simple everything. As it was, they got no nearer to this retreat than Hampstead.

Almost the worst thing about her disease is the way it keeps her from him, either in cold hotels in the South of France or Cornwall, or in a separate bedroom. Instead of the closeness of his body she has to endure the 'virgin' closeness of Ida Baker, which she loathes. She is charming in her letters to Ida, who doubles as nurse and companion, but cruel about her in letters to others.

The celebrated treacherous aspect of Katherine Mansfield comes across in many other ways and, making allowances for her tragedy, does not exactly excuse it. More justifiable and understandable are her periodic spurts of anger and disgust for the boring, rather horrible hotel-lounge world her TB has levered her into, a world of guzzling old folk and hideous furniture. She writes longingly of colour schemes and pretty rooms. She is a symbolist, investing, like Chardin, good everyday objects with a spiritual power.

The illness letters open in midwinter Paris. She is on her way to Bandol and has to admit to Murry: 'It has been a bit of a bang though, hasn't it?' She means having to face up to their separation because of her symptoms. Bandol is icy. They write to each other daily. She will get better and come home in the spring to marry him just as soon as she gets her decree absolute. 'Until I get back to you and we are safe in each other's arms there is only one thing to do and that is to *work, work, work*.'

When she does manage to return to London it is only after getting caught up in the bombardment of Paris by Big Bertha and, nearly as bad, in visa red tape which delays her for weeks. Murry and she are together for less than a month, which includes their wedding, when it becomes obvious that she must travel south once more and urgently this time to Looe.

The remote, pre-tripper climate of Cornwall is wonderfully evoked. She is funny – something Murry never is – and irritable, full of plans and protestations. It is at this point that she appears to recognise without hubris or hopefulness that she is a true writer, even an important one. Now and then her letters become mannered and even a bit play acting, but her situation is a dramatic one, it has to be acknowledged, and not one of her own choice.

The flow of flowers from Garsington are those to a difficult but now dying friend. Katherine's response to Lady Ottoline Morrell appears to take stock of this factor and is so passionate that one senses it would not have been acceptable in different circumstances. The letters to Virginia Woolf, on the other hand, whose brilliance privately awes Katherine, go out of their way to avoid the perils of openly displayed feeling. Virginia never really liked or trusted her.

A serious rift with the Lady Ottoline camp had to be healed when Murry dared to give Siegfried Sassoon's war poems a bad review. Not the least fascinating content of these letters is the insight they provide on a group of young writers at the outset of their careers who are as yet without 'reverence'. There is more spite than exists now – maybe.

The mass of letters that are to follow will all have been written 'within' Katherine Mansfield's illness and during those four last years when she was at her creative height. They are the letters of a young woman under notice of death. With a 'flat-iron' where a lung should be, and smoking heavily, she accepted what after all was in her day a dreadfully ordinary fate. All she asked in return for enduring it was to complete what she had begun: 'How unbearable it would be to die – leave "scraps", "bits" . . . nothing really finished.' Her wish was granted.

THE LETTERS OF G.B.S. 1911-1925

A Writer's Day-Book, 2006

Shaw's letters are the very cornucopia of correspondence, the ultimate overflow of the epistolary urge. Recipients either received the full rich splash or the deliberate non-letter of those famous postcards. There was no drip of a note in between.

Shaw is openly intimate, if that is not a contradiction, a kind of public private man who provides enquirers with the most personal information if he thinks it will benefit society. He is the human equivalent of the standard which kings set up on a hill above the battlefield as a symbol of order amid chaos, and a sane rallying point. He is also an unrepentant busybody putting his oar in wherever he fancies, whether it is 10 Downing Street or the composition of an Elgar quintet – fearful cheek, the latter.

The intelligence is formidable. Shaw is a Dubliner Voltaire at large, and popularly licensed to speak his rational mind. He is a great public figure of the old type but with the beginnings of today's media excesses following him at every move, which he likes. He is a theatrical Irish gentleman who coats his message (and a very serious message it is) with amusement. To him the earth is a vast, noisy debating chamber in which daft views require his swift correction, and which is daily packed with fools and rogues who have to be kept in order. It is also a palace of art and language – not to mention a free space through which a paper-lover can aim his missives.

These years found the dramatist at his peak, with *Heartbreak House, Back to Methusalah* and *Saint Joan* being written and Shaw's polemics being both controlled and driven home by his now fully realised artistry. Neither he nor the world can have any doubts that he is a phenomenon, something he loves to be. He gives miscreants some of the worst drubbings ever sealed in an envelope, never posting a page on which, somewhere or other, his literary skill is not seen at full pelt. And there is Shaw the 'virtuoso trifler' and his amorous blarney, although the letters to Mrs Patrick Campbell go far beyond this ('The feet I kissed with my pen since I could not reach them with my lips'). One is struck here as never before by the sincere emotions of this celebrated affair.

When the Great War so inevitably and predictably broke out, Shaw's own opening salvo in that crazily patriotic hour was to make him one of the most unpopular men in the country. If there was a medal for literary courage, Shaw would certainly have earned it with his *Common Sense About the War*, which Robert Blatchford called 'the meanest act of treachery ever perpetrated by an alien enemy residing in generous and long-suffering England'. The idiot fury which this book generated, and the remorseless slaughter of so many of his friends' sons, had their deepening effect, and between the springs of 1915 and 1917 he wrote *Heartbreak House*, 'creeping' through it 'to prevent myself crying'. His letters to bereaved mothers who did not share his views contain a profound kindness. One of his horrors where wars were concerned was that they quintupled 'the influence of born fools and placed level-headed men at a heavy discount'.

And then there is Ireland, of course. Shaw never returned to his native land after 1923, but kept up the type of 'insider' criticism that was guaranteed to keep both the British and the Irish ratty. He is quite heretically unsentimental about events such as the Easter Rising, and regretted his country's insular heroics. 'The Irish adore a successful man or an executed man (the latter for preference) but a fiasco they never forgive.' The letters reveal all too shatteringly how little has changed in Protestant versus Catholic Irish attitudes since Shaw was a boy. The Irish have achieved world eminence because of their mastery of the English language, 'which is very imperfectly spoken and written in England'. His long letter to Horace Plunkett on the Irish dilemma is staggeringly relevant to much that is happening now.

A CRAVING FOR THE POST

The Letters of Virginia Woolf 1912-1922 and 1936-1940

A Writer's Day-Book, 2006

The 700 or so letters belonging to the war and peace decade of 1912-22 constitute the spring tide of Virginia Woolf's flooding correspondence. While it seeps into all levels, and can spread itself out in huge, flat puddles reflecting the Servant Problem, or trickle along with train times, or even suddenly run dry when madness dams the flow, for the most part it presents an hypnotically interesting ocean in which can be discerned many of the artistic and social currents of the 20th century pushing their way to the surface. Its big fish, too, also announce themselves. 'We've been having that strange young man Eliot to dinner' (November 1918). 'Never did I read such tosh [*Ulysses*] . . . merely the scratching of pimples on the body of the bootboy of Claridges . . . and this is what Eliot worships' (August 1922). 'Proust so titillates my own desire for expression that I can hardly set out the sentence. Oh if I could write like that! I cry. And at the moment such is the astonishing vibration and saturation and intensification that he procures there's something sexual in it – that I feel I can write like that, and seize my pen and then I can't write like that. Scarcely anyone so stimulates the

77

nerves of language in me: it becomes an obsession' (May 1922).

In *Jacob's Room*, published at the end of this period, Virginia Woolf wrote, 'Life would split asunder without letters,' and whatever one may think now about her prevaricating attitudes toward the collapse of the old order, it is impossible to come to the end of this huge pile of correspondence without concluding that it proliferates with those binding qualities which civilisation still demands.

She would write as many as six letters a day. The number was not all that extraordinary for the time, when etiquette prohibited the use of the telephone for most social and business arrangements, even where that still rare instrument existed. But it certainly was, given the strength and brilliance of her letters on the whole, a great achievement, by an often ill woman, who was continuously engaged upon a form of novel-writing which demanded the heights of feeling and imagination, a vast quantity of mainly unsigned literary journalism, running two houses, and running a press. Clearly, there was more than a need to just correspond in any ordinary sense, in this regulated activity. She evidently found it steadying; and when she stated 'Life would split asunder without letters,' she might have been saying: 'I know 1 shall get through this day if I get through my letters.'

They show that, although she was pathologically condemned to an ineradicable solitude and aloneness so dreadful that every now and then her mind buckled under the pressure, she was also vitally cliquish, and driven to putting in a lot of very hard work to keep her coterie intact. Both serious and riotous notions chase across the pages, as she trapped the group soul in a web of its own intrigues and affirmations. Now and then, however, instances arise in which fractions of the coterie displayed an awkward independence, or a wish for privacy which broke the rules. There are hints of this at 'the mill on the Pang', for example, where Lytton and Carrington occasionally seemed to be downright defensive about their bit of backwater.

This brings one to the business of Virginia Woolf as scandalmonger, something for which we, her readers, if not her friends, can be grateful. Nigel Nicolson has quite a lot to say about her celebrated bitchiness and her 'scatological jokes of a shocking nastiness', and yet when we close the volume at '29 December 1922', her bursts of cruelty and tastelessness seem to be little more than the familiar old period vulgarity, while her words for the most part declare a passion for literature, for her husband and for her sister, which is profoundly moving. The Bloomsbury Group itself provided her outer bulwarks, and she deliberately kept it up to the mark with wit and gossip. But what drove and preserved her was her art, Leonard and Vanessa. The Group was her periphery; beyond it lay the abyss.

The letters begin immediately after Virginia's marriage in August 1912. It was done 'in a Registry Office, in the intervals of a thunderstorm', she told Lady Ottoline Morrell from the honeymoon inn down in Somerset. A few days later, in Spain, she is pouring out its intimacies for Lytton's benefit, and kindly adding a few things which are more up his street. While he reads Pope and 'waits for when the bell rings and the sandy haired girl, whom you wish was a boy, says, "Dinner on the table",' she will be walking by the Mediterranean to a military band playing Hoffman's Barcarolle and watching 'the naked boys run like snipe along the beach, balancing their buttocks in the pellucid air'.

To Ka Cox, herself recovering from her affair with Rupert Brooke, she is less fanciful, 'Why do you think people make such a fuss about marriage and copulation? Why do some of our friends change upon losing chastity? Possibly my great age [30] makes it less of a catastrophe; but certainly I find the climax immensely exaggerated. Except for a sustained good humour, due to the fact that every twinge of anger is at once visited upon my husband, I might still be Miss S.' A confession of another sort clinches the new situation: 'My God! you can't think with what fury we fall on printed matter!' There lay their true lust till death did them part.

Yet, from the very beginning, Leonard's contribution to her physical and intellectual survival was immeasurable, and she adored him. He was her 'Mongoose' and her 'Jew'. He was 'beautiful and indispensable' and she loved his 'little ribby body'. 'When they were apart, she would write daily. A few months after the honeymoon, his devotion was put to the test when she became insane, and swallowed 100 grains of veronal. A grim letter-less gap in the correspondence sixteen months later witnesses to an even worse attack. In one of the finest letters, written to Gerald Brenan on Christmas Day 1922, Virginia challenges his beginner's envy of the established writer, and says outright that there still were times when she would rather be dead than go on:

You said you were very wretched, didn't you? You described your liver rotting, and how you read all night, about the early fathers; and then walked and saw the dawn. But were wretched, and tore up all you wrote, and felt you could never, never write – and compared this state of yours with mine, which you imagine to be secure, rooted, benevolent, industrious – you did not say dull – but somehow unattainable, and I daresay, unreal. But you must reflect that I am 40: further, every 10 years, at 20, again at 30, such agony of different sorts possessed me that not content with rambling and reading I did most emphatically attempt to end it all; and should have been often thankful, if by stepping on one flagstone rather than another I could have been annihilated where I stood . . . we live, all of us who feel and reflect, with recurring cataclysms of horror . . .

At the end of this remarkable letter, she tells Brenan: 'I was wondering to myself why it is that though I try to limit myself to the thing I do well (writing), I am always drawn on and on, by human beings, I think, out of the little circle of safety, on and on, to the whirlpools; when I go under'.

Millions were going under as she wrote, and the Great War, as they called it, can never have been more slightingly treated, more ignored, more reduced to 'noises off' in an extensive contemporary correspondence than it was in hers. The most that one gathers is that Bloomsbury, which was feminist, antiimperialist, socialist, elitist and (most important) extremely busy with books and paintings, found it the limit. Just when the despised Victorians were receiving their *congé*, and the twentieth century was showing its progressive paces, along comes the old male guard with its patriotic cant and mystique, followed closely by the mob, and both sections rowdily orchestrated by the yellow press, the Church, etc. to spoil everything. It was unspeakable – certainly not worth putting into letters to friends.

By 1916, Virginia Woolf says that any news of the war men puts her in mind of an African tribe and that she cannot understand how 'this preposterous masculine fiction keeps going a day longer'. The only time she gets in any way caught up in the engagement is when conscription threatens Bloomsbury. 'The whole of our world does nothing but talk of conscription and they're all taken up with different societies (the No Conscription Fellowship) and wire-pulling.'

Friends and relations perished, but often do not get a mention; and the letters surrounding the time when Leonard's brothers, Cecil and Philip, are respectively killed and wounded by the same shell are tremendously animated and high-spirited. When it was all over, she is disparaging as her servant hangs a flag from every window, and Lady Ottoline puts a lighted candle in each one of hers. 'Peace seems to make much more difference than one could have thought possible,' wrote Virginia to Vanessa, 'though I think the rejoicing has been very sordid and depressing.'

Her resentment of the war – 'I'm beginning to think that I'd better stop writing novels, since no one cares a damn whether one writes them or not. Do you ever feel that your entire life is useless – passed in a dream, into which now and then these brutal buffaloes come butting?' – was the familiar one for the dedicated artist. Yet, where her life's work was concerned, there had been no stagnation and no interruption, save her insanity.

In 1915, she published *The Voyage Out*, settled in Hogarth House, Richmond, and Rodmell, Sussex, and in 1917 was dividing her time between writing *Night and Day* and setting-up type. 'The work of ages, especially when you mix the h's with the n's, as I did yesterday. We get so absorbed we can't stop; I see that real printing will devour one's entire life. I am going to see Katherine Mansfield, to get a story from her . . .' The pattern is set for the next quarter century, and there would be no further madness until the attack which took her to the river in 1941.

At this point in the correspondence, the novelists and poets of the interwar decades push forward. While Lytton is writing 'like a snake insinuating himself through innumerable golden rings' in order 'to bring us down such rare fruits from the poison tree', Mr Eliot from Lloyd's Bank insists on something quite different. So does Joyce. So does 'a man who is dead called Gerard Hopkins'. Publishing some of the new promise requires certainty, and Virginia and Leonard have it. 'We are becoming rather full blown and important,' she tells her old socialist friend, Violet Dickinson. The letters to her and to Janet Case reveal Leonard's exhausting involvement in left-wing politics under the auspices of the Webbs, and Virginia's sincere, if unsuccessful, attempts to give more than lip service to the Co-operative movement.

She is far more practical about getting Eliot out of the bank and into a country cottage to write poetry full-time, and there is a mass of detail about the Tom Eliot Fellowship Fund, which failed. Eliot, whose wife was mentally ill, and whose *Waste Land* was being read aloud to Bloomsbury but not yet in print, demurred at the £300 a year which the Fund set out to raise, and said that he must have £500 before he would leave the bank.

The glimpses of him in the letters are obscured by his own personality, not by Virginia's reticence. She likes him, but cannot quite reach him, although the silhouette holds the gaze. Myriad other portraits, some full oils (Ottoline), other pastels (Forster), offer no such resistance, with the result that they loom out at us as entertainingly as she can make them.

As with all letters, the virtue is in the immediacy. With her famished eye glutting itself on interiors and her ear for an inimitable word (of Ottoline: 'She always hangs to "wonderful" like a rope dangling in her vacuum') and the poise of news against reflection, Virginia Woolf is magnificent on writing-paper. The kernel – it is a fat one – is the portrait of Vanessa, the earth sister, with all its mocking, loving homage.

In *Letters, 1936-1940* we see Virginia Woolf finding it increasingly difficult to write books. Revision of *The Years* had turned into a drudgery which brought her close to collapse, and she told Jane Bussy: 'In another life there'll be another Virginia who never writes, but always talks and talks and talks and talks.' In 1941, due – Nigel Nicolson thinks – to an overwhelming but mistaken conviction that she would never be *able* to write any more, she took the short walk from her house to the Ouse. This tension between the compulsion to work, the dread – and even the hatred – of the toil involved, and the fear of having nothing left inside is, of course, a common one to writers, probably the most common. However, during the five years separating her own extreme bouts of such a tension, write she did, with a vengeance and excellently. Played too. Readers expecting to trace a line of sad clues from page one to the river bank are going to be surprised to discover themselves being taken off, for the most part, in a completely opposite direction. To robust encounters of the publishing kind, to newsy and courageous reports from the home front, to much delight and pleasure, and to a vehemence of living which conceals, almost to the final week, that the depression which blackened it would not lift like all those which preceded it, and let her resume what has always sounded like a very wearing domestic and social regime for a writer. Her voice doesn't gradually fail, it cuts out abruptly like the hit plane above the downs which one minute is flashing along its route, and the next is spinning out of control to death and silence.

Was it the war? Most people thought so at the time. Leonard, recalling how ill finishing *The Years* had made her, blamed it all on the strain of completing *Between the Acts*. But Nicolson suggests this deeper motive for her despair – her being convinced that she had lost the art of writing. Was it an insane act? 'No, it was a combination of fantasy and fear. She would have recovered, as she had before. She was not mad when she died.' Since suicide is tentacular, reaching backwards and forwards for decades from the day on which it happens, and feeding friends with the most unhealing form of sorrow, it created fertile ground for speculation and signs. But such detection is pointless in this case. One must not read into such statements as 'I can't moon off to the river and let head drift on the stream' (letter to Ethel Smyth in 1938) anything more than that, although Virginia has been writing *Roger Fry* all day and would be the better for a stroll along the footpath, she can't because it's raining.

On the contrary, throughout this correspondence there are signs everywhere which reveal her desire for more time. She was fifty four in 1936, a successful and distinguished woman of letters with a perfect husband and a remarkable group of close companions, and her letters glow with undisguised satisfaction in all these assets. Although they slip into occasional profundity, their main note is a sustained cheerfulness. Without ever being shallow, they are surface communications to people who understand the depths of their particular mutual situation and don't need them spelt out. She wrote, too, to receive letters, often pleading for them and sometimes seeming to find in them a more supportive quality than if the friend himself had arrived in person. Or the friend herself, as it mostly was.

The chief topics covered here are the political situation from the Abdication to the Battle of Britain, literature to the birth of *Horizon* and the first of *Four Quartets*, the deaths of Julian Bell in Spain, Lady Ottoline Morrell and Ka Arnold Forster, a more cautiously continuing fascination with Vita Sackville- West, a positively all-caution-to-the-winds development of the friendship with Dame Ethel Smyth, who was one of those bulwarks of Sapphic constancy and sound sense which only England knows, and the beautiful florid epistles which she needed to rain down on her sister Vanessa.

To take the times first. The Abdication crisis gets short shrift, and she is cynical about 'the lovers', as she calls them, having been told that Edward is 'a cheap second rate little bounder'. She declines Vita's invitation to meet Mrs Simpson. Leonard fills their house in Tavistock Square, and later Monk's House, with political meetings which distract her, sympathetic though she is to their pacifist and socialist causes. She tells Victoria Ocampo, the Argentinian founder-editor of *Sur*, that they are living under the shadow of disaster – 'I've never known such a time of foreboding' – and Julian Bell, who is in China, that she has never dreamt so often about war – 'It's rather like sitting in a sick room, quite helpless.' But when Ethel Smyth protests about Virginia's husband dragging her into his activities and making it hard for her to write, she swiftly replies, 'Oh dear me! I entirely misled you – about L. and politics. He never made me go to a meeting in my life.'

In April 1937 she writes to Stephen Spender and asks him to have a talk with Julian Bell who wants to drive a lorry in Spain, and tells Spender that a disillusioned letter from his friend Jimmy Younger has arrived 'in the nick of time to set him against the CP – we of course kept your name and confidence intact: it was most interesting.' Julian was driving an ambulance when he was killed a few weeks later. The letters say little more than that it was 'terrible', the main pendant to this great tragedy being the generous literary advice she gives to Ling Su-Hua, a Chinese friend of Julian's. Contrary to what one might have expected, her spiritedness and gaiety even increase as the war approaches.

When her Tavistock Square house is destroyed in the blitz, she and Leonard base themselves permanently at Rodmell and show no panic at all at the constant raids and the threat of invasion. But at the beginning of 1941 her mood changes. The village bores her and she often craves for London. She feels that something is happening to her imagination – nothing makes it 'flash'. 'I read and read like a donkey going round a well; pray to God, some ideas will flash' and she asks Ethel, 'Do you feel, as I do . . . that this is the worst stage of the war? I do. I was saying to Leonard, we have no future. He says that's what gives him hope.' In March she tells Elizabeth Robins, the American novelist and actress who is now almost eighty:

It's amazingly peaceful here, you can almost hear the grass grow; and the rooks are building; you wouldn't think that at 7.30 the planes will be over. Two nights ago they dropped incendiaries, in a row, like street lamps, all along the downs. Two hay stacks caught fire and made a lovely illumination – but no flesh was hurt. Indeed, every bomb they drop only casts up a crater so far. It's difficult, I find, to write. No audience. No private stimulus, only this outer roar.

She had accomplished much before this hollowness overwhelmed her – enough, one would have thought, for her comfort in a barren spring. *The Years,* begun in 1932, had at last been published and had become a bestseller in the United States (25,000 copies), and had fairly quickly been followed by *Three Guineas* and *Roger Fry.* Although she had sold her half-share in the Hogarth Press to John Lehmann in 1938 in order to rid herself of much tedious work, she still continued to read and advise for it. She wrote her diary and her customary amount of exhausting literary journalism. While researching *Roger Fry* in 1938 she had a sudden 'longing to be off on fiction' and by that autumn had rushed 'headlong into a novel' called *Pointz Hall.* This was the future *Between the Acts,* which Leonard believed literally worried her to her death.

Both her *Letters* and her *Diary* show a quite burdensome amount of literary toiling and moiling around Virginia Woolf's central and finely-sprung creativity, much of it no more than a part of a way of life which belonged more to her father's day than her own. Young authors pursued her, old curmudgeons laid into her. Nobody suggested to her a considered change of the entire pattern, and she herself admired the driven-hard personality.

Finally and ultimately there are the celebrated friendships, each one fuelled regularly at her desk with what she knew would make it glow. For Vanessa, who shrank from her demonstrativeness unless it arrived in the post, there are the best letters which Virginia can devise, letters of genius, and written as though she knew that they were her only access to the core of her sister's being. For Dame Ethel there was a bluff wit and sometimes a moving kind of dependency, like a yacht signalling a Dreadnought. When Ethel's memoirs are published, their excellence staggers Virginia. Her letters to the composer are intriguing as she attempts a matching bluntness, prods Ethel into declarations – 'Do love me' – drops all her guards in plain admiration of her so unexpectedly splendid writing, or tentative break-out from feminist movement language into that of homosexual women.

Having Dame Ethel for a bosom friend presented difficulties about which Virginia was obviously aware, for she was a great figure of fun in the world. It is touching to see Virginia getting beyond this comedy, especially as it was of the kind which appealed to her cruelty, and during the last years of her life drawing from the relationship a quality which Ethel would have called fortitude.

On 1 March 1941 she told Ethel that she was trying to write a new *Common Reader* but was glued on a fly paper and couldn't move backwards or forwards. On 4 March she told Vita that her orchard is 'one of the sights I shall see on my death bed'. On 8 March Eliot sent her his *The Dry Salvages*. On 10 March she was spring cleaning Monk's House. On 14 March she consulted John Lehmann in London about the typescript of *Between the Acts*. On 18 March she may have tried to kill herself. On 27(?) March she told the recently widowed Lady Tweedsmuir that 'you have a great deal more than most of us to look forward to.' Vanessa, worried by her breakdown, was now telling Virginia, 'You *must* be sensible' and Leonard was taking her to Brighton to consult a doctor. On 27(?) March she told John Lehmann that *Between the Acts* had to be revised and must not be published as it was. On 28 March she wrote to Leonard, 'I shall never get over this,' filled her pockets with stones and threw herself into the river. Children discovered her body nearly three weeks later.

YOURS, PLUM

The Letters of P. G. Wodehouse

ed. Frances Donaldson, 1991

It is not often that one finds a writer's art and his everyday existence coming together in such a seamless merger as in these letters. Although not without its tragedies, Wodehouse's long life was all about accepting a fair amount of bliss as a norm. Life was essentially absurd, yet at the same time very beautiful and well worth having nearly a century of. He worked hard and regularly, he shared it with a managing wife – 'My precious angel Bunny, whom I love so dear' – three or four old mates with whom he certainly had genius in common, and a succession of demanding dogs.

On the whole it was plain sailing, natural brilliance and the ability to create his own new order in the shape of Bertie, Jeeves, Aunt Dahlia, Lord Emsworth and company making it impossible for Wodehouse to be anything other than the unchallengeable head of the happiness department. Quite properly, he took himself very seriously: 'You're quite right about my books being early Edwardian. I look upon myself as a historical novelist.' Here he was not strictly accurate. His comedy derives from various collisions of exquisite ignorance: that of inter-war London and Hollywood getting their comeuppance in the monumentally ignorant Shires. So, as well as being a historical novelist, Wodehouse is classically Modern.

His letters are enchanting. He left such an avalanche of them that Frances Donaldson, the schoolfriend of Plum's adopted daughter Leonore, has given us no more than a handsome sample of them, making sure that he comes through as both writer and private man. There is no attempt at analysis, and only the most essential linking comments are given. It is hard to see how a selection could have been better produced. The photographs alone make a Wodehousian treat.

The main recipients of the letters are Leonora ('Snorky' or 'old lad'), the novelist Denis Mackail, the musical comedy collaborator Guy Bolton, and William Townend, 'the second most important person in Wodehouse's life' and a study-sharer at Dulwich. With Townend he could be conspiratorial, getting him to stash away not very large sums of money in foreign banks. The beloved Ethel kept him short.

The self-revelation is unsophisticated and very moving. Wodehouse knew his worth but never his greatness, and was naïve in many ways. There are a number of letters about the disaster which befell him during the war, when some jokey broadcasts on Hitler's radio branded him pro-Nazi. George Orwell, in his magnificent 'Defence of P. G. Wodehouse', and others scraped these accusations from him. He lived on in America, long past the cocktail hour, the flow of glorious crackpot tales never ceasing, and writing the last, *Sunset at Blandings*, at 94. 'Talking of the world, what a place!'

BORDERLANDS

THE CREATURE IN THE MAP

A Journey to Eldorado

Charles Nicholl, 1995

This work is both a demystification of a famous English-American journey, and the writer's own setting out on the same route. Such things have been done before but rarely as informatively.

In the spring of 1595, Sir Walter Ralegh rowed up the Orinoco delta to find and then present to Queen Elizabeth the golden city of a New World. The New World was real enough, El Dorado a myth. The Queen had been furious with Ralegh – 'Water', as she called him – for making one of her attendant virgins pregnant and then marrying her without permission. So, first a cooling-off in the Tower, then banishment to his Dorset estate. Before this, as it turned out, suitable marriage, the great poet-explorer had been at the zenith of his career and was styling himself 'Lord of Virginia'.

Returning from his failure to find a city which did not exist, he wrote a ravishing travel book called *The Discovery of the Large, Rich, and Beautiful Empire of Guiana, with a Relation of the great and Golden City of Manoe (which the Spaniards call Eldorado . . .)* It is via this wonderful guide that Charles Nicholl goes off to search behind the myth and to brush the popular clichés from the extraordinary person who was Walter Ralegh.

The story is a mixture of navigational scholarship of a thrilling order and the kind of events in which a film crew would be plunged while on a difficult location. The author uses a kind of 'Englishness' – an unapologetic love of the English language and of adventure and a tolerance of hardship – to join the two together. He has scanned the records for the men and boys who accompanied Ralegh and found out how they behaved in this 'sullen' climate. He analyses the origins of the tobacco culture, something which was to divide Jacobean society

91

as sharply as it does ours (James I's *Counterblast to Tobacco* came out in 1604). Nicholl then moves on from gold myth to gold rush. His learned tale is supported by a mass of fascinating contemporary letters and pictures, by charts and constellations, and especially by the strange map used by Ralegh, and now in the British Museum, on which is written, plain as a pikestaff, or the latest Ordnance Survey, the alluring El Dorado.

As a writer, Nicholl has the advantage of knowing his way round the Elizabethan world as well as he does ours. He views the Queen's court as a kind of 16th-century tinsel town in comparison with the true glories of the globe. In 1617, after twelve years of false imprisonment, Ralegh set forth once more to Guiana, and to tragedy. The expedition was disastrous, for he lost both his son and his reputation for bringing back great riches. When he returned home, without gold, they executed him.

THE CAPTAIN'S WIFE

The South American Journals of Maria Graham, 1821-23

ed. Elizabeth Mavor, 1993

It has always been the fervent hope of the committed journalist to be on the spot when it happens. Due to her marriage to the young captain of HMS *Doris*, one of the finest journalists of her day found herself in Brazil and Chile when the whole of South America was freeing itself from the long rule by Spain and Portugal. Maria Graham's account of these years is candid, elegant and touching. It is also deeply personal, for she was a widow and one of a great many Englishwomen socially stranded all over the globe due to her country's expansionist trade and sea-power.

The journals contain a wonderfully open account of her's and their plight, if it can be called that. Her eye for the domestic and the political gives her writing an enchantment and intimacy which raises it above so many of the popular diaries of the period. Small but significant details catch the attention. Dreadnought, the name to be given to battleships, was originally thick cloth from which to make warm gloves for sailors. As for her female compatriots in Brazil: 'What can I say? They are very like all one sees at home, in their rank of life and . . . would require Miss Austen's pen to make them interesting.'

Mrs Graham does make them interesting – she makes everything absorbing. But she has to be careful. For an intellectual woman writer to be discovered a gossip would probably ruin her career. She is not scribbling a diary; she is an author. She has tremendous intelligence and style, strong opinions and commonsense.

She is 'Mama' to the boy-midshipmen who adore her. She is regularly informed by naval officers and English mercenaries engaged in the liberation of Chile and Brazil of their plans. She loves plants and makes gardens. She is also, as any woman like her would be, essentially lonely. And it goes without saying that she is intrepid, like St Paul, enduring earthquakes, gruelling voyages, illness, privation and all the perils of not staying at home. She is pleased that we lost our North American colonies, pleased indeed with every kind of freedom, and thus outraged and ashamed when she sees the slave ships in which Britain has so vast an investment docking in Brazil.

Her reaction to Roman Catholicism in South America shows the corruption and the truths of a religion distorted by the beliefs onto which they had been grafted. She misses nothing and succeeds in combining in these journals a gentle autobiography with a robust report of the New World at its turning point.

This diary, originally published in 1824, is nothing less than a treat. Elizabeth Mavor knows better than most how to blow away the library dust from these wandering, chronicling ladies, and the doughty Mrs Graham emerges as fresh as wet ink. She was to become Maria Callcott and the author of that Victorian bestseller *Little Arthur's History of England*.

INDIA REVEALED

The Art and Adventures of James and William Fraser, 1801-35

Mildred Archer & Toby Falk, 1989

THE LAST DAYS OF THE RAJ

Trevor Royle, 1989

These books prove, if proof were ever needed, how complex and enduring is the Indian connection for the British and the British connection for Indians – and Pakistanis. It goes far beyond empire, trade and politics: more than 300 years of shared existence have affected the psyches of the three nations.

During the 1820s, Britain was astonished by the publication by James Fraser of two volumes of aquatints of the Himalayas and Calcutta. Fraser was a young merchant in the indigo business who had been sent to India with his four brothers to raise funds to pay off the family debt. The aquatints were of such beauty that they overwhelmed the senses.

In 1979, a mass of diaries and other papers was discovered in Scotland, revealing the world of James Fraser, one of the finest traveller-artists, and of his brother William, a member of the East India Company and one of nature's nabobs. The custom of sending sons to India in the hope that they would send money home was particularly strong in Scotland. Health-wise it was a risky venture and many never returned. Sir Walter Scott called India 'the corn chest for Scotland, where we poor gentry must send our younger sons, as we send our black cattle to the south'. Mr Fraser had his sons painted by Raeburn before parting with them.

James was not suspected of being an artist himself, but in Calcutta he met George Chinnery and William Havell and took lessons. The result, as seen in *India Revealed*, was nothing less than enchanting. Men and women, costume, landscape, and Calcutta itself which was being built by the British in the best Grecian style: everyone and everything is set against fresh blue early-morning skies. Some of the paintings are by James, others are by Delhi artists commissioned by the East India Company. Mildred Archer and Toby Falk set them in a biographical context, in an essay drawn from the brothers' letters and diaries.

Pre-Raj India was magnificent – and fatal. William was assassinated and James returned to a still poverty-stricken lairdship – though with an unequalled folio of what he had seen there. William's descendants must have proliferated, for he had about ten Indian wives.

Trevor Royle was born in India two years before independence. *The Last Days of the Raj* is a sober, temperate account of Britain's exodus from the sub-continent. None of our other Empire withdrawals was so traumatic. The very notion of a self-governing India was unthinkable to Empire romantics like Churchill. Early in the discussions, no one anticipated partition, and certainly not bloody parturition.

Royle isn't romantic, but he never tries to dismiss the attachment we all feel towards a birthplace. What he seeks to do is to rid the events leading up to 1947 of colourfulness, caricature and apocalyptic din to give us the facts. Reputations are examined. Wavell and Attlee come off better than we once thought. Mountbatten worse. Novelists and film-makers have had a great hand in establishing reputations and popularising the story; Royle gives us the historical framework in good, quiet language.

CHARLES WATERTON

Traveller and Conservationist

Julia Blackburn, 1989

Eccentric means not being concentric, and the British like to boast of their tolerance of this. But the tolerance soon fades when some eccentricity begins to reveal itself as an indictment of some profitable or amusing social practice, such as slavery or blood sports, for example. Or, in Charles Waterton's case, of Coketown poisoning his squirearchal patch of Yorkshire. To be exact, the defiler was a ghastly entrepreneurial soap-boiler whose son was to buy the estate after the great naturalist's death, and after Waterton's son had sold thousands of its trees for timber and allowed sporting yobbos from Barnsley and Wakefield to shoot all his father's beloved birds.

Far from being an odd tale, this English gentleman's life story is as sane and noble an epic as can be discovered anywhere. His offence was to turn his park into an Eden-before-the-Fall. He enclosed it with three miles of wall (£9,000) and there it flourished for many years, a conservationist's challenge to everything which both the Landed and Industrial interests of his day stood for. His tender attitude towards nature apart, there were myriad other reasons for his being beyond the pale. He was an Old Catholic and a man of prayer, he lived in a mansion but dressed like a farm labourer, his two sisters-in-law who, after his wife's death, looked after him were suspiciously dark-skinned, and he had written a very curious book called *Wanderings in South America* which was full of strange admissions such as a belief in vampires and making huge journeys with bare feet. The more idiosyncratic side of Waterton might have found its right level, and his brave genius as a conservationist have come uppermost had not his doctor libelled him in a little book after his death in 1865. It made him wonderfully mad and thus a candidate for all those popular works on English eccentrics, including Edith Sitwell's. No mention of this fondly regarded type can be made without crew-cut Waterton springing up. Julia Blackburn's enchanting biography emancipates him from this circus and shows us a founding father of today's ecological Enlightenment.

Waterton was a descendant on his mother's side of Sir Thomas More, and his wife the descendant of an Arawak Indian. He was educated at Stoneyhurst, which he loved, and he read from *Don Quixote* every day. Two brothers were priests and his aunt was the Mother Superior of a Bruges convent. Some men make no secret of their lusts and are considered honest; Waterton's 'holy fool' behaviour was to make no secret of his pranks. Such as climbing St Peter's and tying his white gloves to the lightning conductor. Pius VII was not amused. Hideous events were to intrude upon his blameless existence.

A dreadful son and heir who destroyed his life's work and who himself deserves a place among the nation's boobies, and the soap-boiler, a creature straight out of Dickens. But what a tale! And how perfectly told. And what a turn-up for the crazy-squire hunters. Waterton's last days were made happy by the son he should have had, a teenage apprentice from a local cotton mill who was to become Sir Norman Moor, President of the Royal College of Physicians. There was a glorious funeral before the new squire sold the shooting rights of Paradise. A procession of boats carried Waterton's coffin and the mourners across the bird-crowded lake to his grave. There were thirteen priests, four canons and a bishop, and many thousands of wild creatures and plants whose slaughter was imminent. Meet the real Charles Waterton, the kind and clever outdoor boy who – mercifully – never quite grew up.

DEAD MAN'S CHEST

Travels After Robert Louis Stevenson

Nicholas Rankin, 1987

If you like 'in the steps of' books, this is an altogether exceptional volume to add to the shelf. Moreover, it proves that there can be no correct or complete understanding of certain writers unless every effort is made to tread in their geographical tracks. At the very least Nicholas Rankin deserves ten out of ten for going all the way, which in the case of Robert Louis Stevenson is a vast distance. The pilgrimage element which might have weakened the narrative is avoided by the successful device of running a travel biography and autobiography in parallel. Rankin is a graceful and persuasive apologist for Stevenson whom he sees as having been ousted by Leavis and others from his rightful niche, and *Dead Man's Chest* is going to make a lot of people turn to that strangely mixed achievement of *Weir of Hermiston, Dr Jekyll and Mr Hyde, Virginibus Puerisgue, An Inland Voyage*, etc., and make their own evaluation. It is likely to be a high one. It is certain to alter one's feelings about journeys.

Stevenson is among that sickly army of writers and artists who were forever being 'ordered south', he to Bournemouth, Davos and ultimately to Samoas. South spelt time, not cure. The ill man and the healthy man (Rankin sounds as fit as a fiddle) arrive with greatly contrasting views on the landscape. 'By a curious irony of fate the places to which we are sent when health deserts us are often singularly beautiful,' wrote Stevenson. In some ways his work-packed, shifting, ailing life which covered so much ground before it ceased in his early forties reminds one of D H Lawrence and his southern treks, the restlessness of which makes a healthy or post-T.B. era writer quail. Rankin doesn't just let Stevenson go off to these time-providing destinations with a ticket and some luggage, he recreates all the conditions of the 19th century train, liner, hotel and cart, putting his own plane and car, bus and foot experiences beside them, and not always to show all that much advancement. Stevenson maintained that it was not until someone like himself arrived at the latest southern corner that he began to understand 'the change that has befallen him' and realises that he has 'a cold head knowledge that he is divorced from enjoyment'. This must have been scribbled during a black day, for if there is one thing which lies undiminished in his novels and essays it is their open display of enjoyment.

Rankin makes some important statements on the travel-book as it existed in the 1880s and as it exists a century later. Stevenson himself thought that 'A voyage is a piece of autobiography at best.' Rankin makes a telling distinction between travellers who write, and writers who travel, and sees *Travels with a Donkey* as 'the first of a genre of literary travel-writing which has become a British speciality'. R L S made his own position clear: 'For my part I travel but to go; I travel for travel's sake. The great affair is to move; to feel the needs and hitches of life a little more nearly, to get down off this feather-bed of civilization, and to find the globe granite underfoot and strewn with cutting flints.' Rankin, on the road to Monterey, finds plenty of 'cutting flints' in the 1980s' U.S., Reagan's America and Victoria's Empire jog by in critical juxtaposition. Rankin struck on Stevenson's route by reading him aloud to the blind Borges in a London hotel. It was the *Fables* which led to the backpack and the roads to Edinburgh, Suffolk, California and the Pacific. Pegs on which to hang a modern traveller's tale are rarely on this scale and one is impressed by the integrity and the effort. Also the scholarship.

Fanny Stevenson has always been depicted as rather a trial but it as much via her enormous journeys, which were those of the mid-19th century semi-settled, who were legion, that Rankin is able to reveal the extent of that urge 'to move' which her husband confessed. She emerges here as a loving presence, if a formidable one. The story takes one not only to her, but to everybody in the R S L address-book. Rankin looks them up, each and every one of them, whether they be Henry James (a true admirer), or Father Damien, about whose sanctity the Vatican continues to reserve its judgement, even if R L S had no doubts about it. Throughout *Dead Man's Chest* Rankin the fellow-traveller keeps close friendly contact with his subject, and this without hubris. He is not an investigator or a sightseer; he is a writer who started out as a follower, who eventually caught up with Stevenson and who became his a-hundred-years-on-companion.

.

FLINDERS PETRIE

A Life in Archaeology

Margaret S. Drower, 1985

One day somebody must write a book about the anguish and fantasies which James Ussher's biblical chronology imposed on modern science. Both of these very different founding fathers of archaeology were intellectually confined by an Irish archbishop's discovery that God made the world in 4004 BC, although Flinders Petrie only for a youthful moment. His background had much in common with that described in Edmund Gosse's little masterpiece, *Father and Son*, where a brilliant mind had no option but to force its way out of the sacred certainties held by a fundamentalist sect.

With William Stukeley, flourishing in the early 18th century, it was a quite different matter. He seems to have given up the freedoms he had gained as a doctor and historian for the security of a nice Georgian rectory, although his behaviour and sermons after a late ordination say much for a latitudinarian Church of England. But what enthralling measurers and diggers they are! Margaret Drower says that Petrie found Egyptian archaeology a treasure hunt and left it a science. Stukeley, on the other hand, after inaugurating many of today's fieldwork practices, including the study of crop marks, went off at a Druidical tangent which, while it inspired poets and eisteddfods, not to mention those unhappy sunrise-seekers who had such a bad time at Stonehenge this last summer solstice, thrust archaeology in a very cranky direction.

But first the master, Flinders Petrie. It was the need to put a stop to crankiness which laid the foundations of his splendid career. In 1866 he read a book by a member of the British Israelite sect, which said that the Great Pyramid was not a tomb but a gigantic stone history of mankind which supported the chronology of the Bible. Great Pyramid theology became all the rage among Bible literalists, and its excitements engulfed the youthful Petrie – until he went to see the monument for himself. As Margaret Drower says, 'the great adventure had begun'. She means that long, toiling, scholarly separating of the past from the sand which was to occupy Petrie until his death in Jerusalem in 1942, when not only scientific Egyptology had been established, chiefly by him, but the archaeological awareness and skills which have altered our concept of time and artefact alike.

When Petrie arrived in Egypt in 1880 it was 'like a house on fire', with the Egyptians themselves shamefully indifferent to their historic treasures, which were being simply dug up and sold. The Great Pyramid was being used as a quarry for road-making and on a good day 300 camel-loads of stone were being taken from it. 'My duty was that of a salvage man, to get all I could quickly gathered in.' The British Fleet was showing the flag by bombarding Alexandria. The tough young man, sometimes working naked in the heat of the tombs, gradually imposed order and method – and reverence. His hordes of workers loved him and called him 'father of potsherds'. When his finds reached London they created a sensation, as did his books and lectures. All was changed. He moved on and on from site after site in a progression which would have shocked today's archaeologist – 'One year of life is enough to give to a single king and his works.' The most overwhelming royal pair were Akhnaton and Nefertiti. Petrie saw this sun-worshipping king 'as perhaps the most original thinker that ever lived in Egypt, and one of the great idealists of the world'.

For years Petrie managed on a salary of a little over £100, and was repelled on his visits to England by 'The merciless rush, and the tumult of strife for money, and the writhing and wriggling of this maggoty world.' He was, in fact, an ascetic, and the conditions in which he lived on a dig appalled visitors. He discovered the very first mention of the word 'Israel' in an Egyptian text and the grave of the pharaoh of the oppression, Rameses II, a personally gratifying find for one whose boyhood had been steeped in Bible-worship and who would be buried on Mount Zion. Margaret Drower, who knew Petrie towards the end of his rich and busy life, and is herself a celebrated Egyptologist, tells a fine tale with authority and style.

JOHN CLARE AND THE GYPSIES

A Writer's Day-Book, 2006

Sometimes I watch a film or read a book, come to and tell myself, 'But I was there! I heard it, I saw it.' It is a not uncommon experience. It occurs when I read John Clare on the gypsies. He both hobnobbed with them and was fastidious where they were concerned, was prejudiced and unprejudiced at the same time. He wrote many poems about them which envied their lot, their freedom, their women, and one poem which envied them nothing.

> *The snow falls deep; the Forest lies alone:*
> *The boy goes hasty for his load of brakes,*
> *Then thinks upon the fire and hurries back;*
> *The Gipsy knocks his hands and tucks them up,*
> *And seeks his squalid camp, half hid in snow,*
> *Beneath the oak, which breaks away the wind,*
> *And bushes close, with snow like hovel warm:*
> *There stinking mutton roasts upon the coals,*
> *And the half roasted dog squats close and ribs,*
> *Then feels the heat too strong and goes aloof;*
> *He watches well, but none a bit can spare.*
> *And vainly waits the morsel thrown away:*
> *'Tis thus they live – a picture to the place;*
> *A quiet, pilfering, unprotected race.*

It is masterly in its realism. Though one observation would not be ours – 'a picture to the place'. Today's Travellers' encampment has swapped the vardo for the mobile home, horses for horse-power and horse dealing for scrap metal, and is anathema in our twinked countryside. We, the council, intended the Traveller (is 'gypsy' P.C? – or not? – it is all rather worrying) to just winter on the official site, then push on, not to purchase them and turn them into messy caravan additions to our village. We like the gypsies best at the horse fairs, when they return to being their colourful selves, painted wagons, fortune tellers, dark-eyed beauties, lively yearlings and all. Appleby Fair is where they should be. No scrap-dealing there.

I was a churchwarden of St Peter's Charsfield, Suffolk, when I was writing *Akenfield*. It was the mid- Sixties, a moment of seismic change in East Anglia as all over the countryside, although, like everyone else, I had no notion of it. One afternoon I found Mr King, our gravedigger for miles around, throwing up clay by the churchyard hedge. He was one of those not uncommon men who would hold back on some subjects and hold forth on others, being what we called 'contrary'. You could never be certain whether he would tell you everything or nothing. Thus,

'Whose grave is it, Mr King?'
'Never you mind. You wouldn't know her.'
'Her?'
'No one you would know.'
'When is the funeral then?'
'Friday they reckon.'

Dig, dig, dig. Then, seeing my still inquisitive face from down below, he said, 'Ocean'.

'They are burying Ocean?'
'They are.'

It was then I experienced one of those close connections between John Clare's world and my own. I had never seen Ocean, just as one rarely sees a legend, but I knew what she looked like, which is someone he would have seen – this in the purely native sense. Ocean was one of East Anglia's most celebrated Romanies. She had travelled our counties for nearly a century, leaving tales in her wake, a formidable woman with a magnificent name. And here she would lie, in our churchyard. There were family connections. Her grandsons, gone Gaujo, lived just up the road in a square bungalow at the edge of an orchard which was never picked and behind windows which were never uncurtained. And there was a copse where she may have wintered.

Clare's gypsies were everywhere when I was a boy. They came regularly to the house, for mother would only have their split ash clothes-pegs with the little tin band. And they did piece-work in summer, pea picking, soft fruit gathering, hence the chalked board outside the pub, 'No Gypsies, no Travellers'. There was a green lane known as the Gull where we found stamped-out hearths and blackened cans, and evidence of ponies. In no time fireweed came to hide the mess. Grandmother, born the decade when Clare died, had actually witnessed a vardo being burnt on Lavenham common. Lavenham churchyard was full of Petulengros. George Borrow had put 'our' gypsies in *Romany Rye* and *Lavengro*. My old friend John Nash, wretched in the trenches, told me how he had been cared for by a young gypsy who had been called up and who comforted them both with promises of the Open Road. One day they would be 'out of all this' and on the Open Road. They would be friends and live again. On and on they would walk – in Buckinghamshire, which was where they truly belonged. No more Artists' Rifles, roll on sleeping in haystacks. John's only reading in Flanders was Borrow, and when Passchendaele threatened he sent *Lavengro* home to his girl for safety.

We knew a woman tramp called Nellie Eighteen and her lover Boxer who refused to sleep in the Spike (workhouse) and who resided briefly in ruined buildings of all kinds, and were accepted as part of the wandering population. Fanciful things were said about them. But they were tramps and not gypsies. We all knew the difference. You wouldn't find a gypsy pushing a pram.

Jonathan Bate wrote, 'Clare loved to spend time with the gypsies who camped on the commons and margins where they were to go once the "waste" grounds became private property. It was through such eyes as these that he saw enclosure.' The enclosure of Helpston put many of Clare's best-loved spots out of bounds, and not only sometimes out of bounds but beyond recognition, for they were in our terms bulldozed. His wrath flares up in poem after poem:

> *The silver springs, grown naked dykes,*
> *Scarce own a bunch of rushes:*
> *When grain got high the tasteless tykes*
> *Grubbed up trees, banks and bushes,*
> *And me, they turned me inside out*
> *For sand and grit and stones*
> *And turned my old green hills about*
> *Picked my very bones.*

He made Swordy Well protest. Bad enough for the villagers, now being pauperised, but quite terrible for the gypsies immemorially camped at Langley Bush. The Vagrancy Act of 1824, swiftly following the Enclosure Act, made it an offence, among other things, 'to be in the open air, or under a tent, or in a cart or wagon, not having any visible means of subsistence, and not giving a good account of himself, or herself'. Ocean had given a memorable account of herself, we believed. But for generations after the Vagrancy Act her kind were regularly sent to prison for merely existing. And then, only two years later, came the Commons Act of 1826 which allowed the local authority to set its own rules for its own common land. And soon most commons were closed to gypsies. When the Gypsy Council was at long last created in 1966, Gordon Boswell, a member of a leading gypsy family, at once proposed that permanent camps should be made by law where his people could winter without being moved on by the police. The Council was legally aided by Gratton Puxon, the son of a Colchester solicitor, who was a friend of ours. Gratton was the kind of practical romantic one would have met with among Clare's rural 'intellectuals', who thought and acted outside their own sphere, as it were.

Erotic gypsy women, with their freedom, were a frequent subject of Clare's songs during the asylum years.

A gipsey lass my love was born
Among the heaths furse bushes O,
More fair than Ladies on the lawn,
Whose song is like the thrushes O.
Like links of snakes her inky hair,
The dandy bean she kisses O.*
Her face round as an apple fair
She blisters where she kisses O.

(*There was an ancient law forbidding men to make love in a beanfield because its scent made them irresistible. Fellatio.)

And then we have 'Sweet legged' Sophie, and Maria 'who sleeps in the nightly dew'. He:

Loves the flowers that she sees,
The wild thyme bank she beds on
Mid the songs of honey bees.

105

These 'cozy blanket camp' girls exist in a sexual dimension beyond the conventions. Free as air, the poet can take them at will. Part of Clare's life might be called a vagabondage in a native place. This is still not unusual for the artist/writer. He belonged as few writers have ever belonged – yet he knew that he did not belong. Not as the rest of his community belonged. His was the fate of the insider being an outsider. In order to write and read and look and listen, he would walk to the edge of his own birthright territory, and it was there that he would sometimes find those who quite clearly had no claim to it, the gypsies. He would spread himself on the earth where they had been.

Wednesday 29th Sept, 1824

Took a walk in the fields . . . saw an old woodstile taken away from a favourite spot which it had occupied all my life. The posts were overgrown with ivy and it seemed so akin to nature and the spot where it stood, as though it had taken it on lease for an undisturbed existence. It hurt me to see it was gone, for my affections claim a friendship with such things. Last year Langley Bush was destroyed, An old white thorn that had stood for more than a century full of fame. The Gipsies and Hern men all had their tales of its history.

A few weeks later Clare attended 'Another Gipsy Wedding of the Smiths family, fiddling and drinking as usual'. He learned some gypsy medicine which was based on like for like, such as how to cure a viper's sting. Boil the viper and apply the broth to the wound it made. A sure cure, the gypsies said. Some of Clare's poems show both pride and prejudice for his Romany friends, calling them 'a sooty crew'. Though before this he assures them:

> *That thou art reverenced, even the rude clan*
> *Of lawless Gipsies, driven from stage to stage,*
> *Pilfering the hedges of the husbandman*

His frequent preferences for the parish boundary caused comment: 'My old habits did not escape notice – they fancied I kept aloof from company for some sort of study – others believed me crazed, and put some more criminal interpretation to my rambles and said I was a night walking associate with the gipsies, robbing woods of the hares and pheasants because I was often in their company.' But sometimes he was at the camp for music lessons. A gypsy named John Gray was to teach him how to play the fiddle by ear: 'Finished planting my auricolas – went a-botanising after ferns and orchises, and caught a cold in the wet grass has made me as bad as ever. Got the tune of "Highland Mary" from Wisdom Smith, a gipsy, and pricked another sweet tune without a name as he fiddled it'. Jonathan Bate reminds us that Clare had been writing down dance tunes for many years, and that one of his oblong music books is entitled *A Collection of Songs, Airs and Dances for the Violin*, 1818. His fleeting vagabond Scottish grandfather had taught the villagers of Helpstone music among other subjects before going on his way. One of Clare's lime-burner workmates at Pickworth had actually joined the gypsies – married one of them. His name was James Nobbs. And such was their fascination that a Suffolk Archdeacon, Robert Hindes Groom, a friend of Edward FitzGerald and George Borrow, had also wed a Romany woman. A certain fastidiousness in Clare seems to have marked their relationship, their 'disgusting food' for instance. But he recognised their artistry, and he was an early precurser of folksong collecting. Recalling the 'No Peapickers' sign outside our Suffolk pubs when I was a boy reminds me of Vaughan Williams taking a young gypsy into a bar in order to take down his song – and both of them being thrown out by the landlord. It wasn't a 'singing' pub.

It was George Borrow, a near contemporary of John Clare, whose Romany books would offer an alternative life style to many Victorians. *Lavengro* was published In 1831, *The Romany Rye or the Gypsy Gentleman*, in 1857. Clare might well have read them at Northampton. Borrow was famously touchy and bad tempered, and hard to handle. Stories of his picaresque wanderings and encounters are told in Spain, East Anglia and Wales to this day. During a walking holiday on Anglesey a few years ago my host said, 'George Borrow stayed in this house'. Returning from gathering material for *Wild Wales* he saw a lad mending the roof and spoke to him in Welsh – and was answered in French. Much put out Borrow demanded to know why. 'Sir, you spoke to me in a language which is not your own, and I reply in a language which is not my own.' Speaking Romany became quite a cult in the nineteenth century although nothing like the heady cult of the Open Road. The Open Road cult descended from a celebrated passage in *Lavengro* which, if it had come John Clare's way during his last years in 'Hell', his other name for the 'Madhouse', would have sent shivers through him.

'Life is sweet, brother.'
'Do you think so?'
'Think so! There's night and day, brother, both sweet things; sun, moon, and stars, brother, all sweet   things; there's likewise a wind on the heath. Life is very sweet, brother; who would wish to die?'
'I would wish to die –'
'You talk like a Gorgio – which is the same as talking like a fool. Were you a Romany Chal you would talk wiser. Wish to die, indeed! A Romany Chal would wish to live for ever.'
'In sickness, Jasper?'
'There's the sun and the stars, brother.'
'In blindness, Jasper?'
'There's the wind on the heath; if I could only feel that I would gladly live for ever.'

Two years after Lavengro was published, and still several years before death made it possible for Clare to return to Helpston, Matthew Arnold wrote *The Scholar-Gipsy*. It told of an Oxford undergraduate who walks out of the University, having seen through its claims, to join gypsy freedom. His life is furtive, shy like that of a woodland creature, and the world to which he belonged now has only glimpses of him. He is not pursued. His realm is Oxfordshire not Oxford, and the county is given a tempting pastorality which excludes such realities as the local vagabond law. Rather, the area is proud to harbour such a learned tramp. In his note on the poem Arnold said, 'After he had been pretty well exercised in the trade (of Romany lore), there chanced to ride by a couple of scholars, who had formerly been of his acquaintance. They quickly spied out their old friend among the gypsies; and he gave them an account of the necessity which drove him to that kind of life, and told them that the people he went with were not such impostors as they were taken for, but that they had a traditionol kind of learning among them, and could do wonders by the power of the imagination, their fancy binding that of others . . .' Arnold said too that he had found the story in Glanvil's *Vanity of Dogmatizing* (1661). *The Scholar Gipsy* concludes with the wonderfully hazardous lines on how such a persistent foreign element may have reached our shore:

Outside the Western Straits, and unbent sails
  There, where down cloudy cliffs, through sheets of foam,
  Shy traffickers, the dark Iberians come;
And on the beach undid his corded bales.

During the High Beach exile, each winter surrounded by gypsy camps, Helpston dragged at Clare's thoughts all day long. Homesickness frequently overwhelmed him. The plants and birds of Epping Forest, the close knit gypsy famiilies with their music and nasty food and skinny dogs seemed like an extension of Helpston and yet was a hundred miles from it. One Sunday afternoon he met some gypsies who said he could hide away with them until there was a propitious moment for his escape from the madhouse. Money was mentioned. But Clare the patient did not have the same welcome as Clare the fiddler, and the gypsies cleared off without helping him. When he went to their camp it was empty save for an old hat. He picked this up and kept it – may have worn it during the walk out of Essex. On Tuesday 20 July 1841, he took their suggested route. Epping was a very confusing place. When he at last managed to find the main road a man from the discouragingly named pub The Labour in Vain directed him towards Enfield – towards where Cowden Clarke had introduced Keats to Chaucer – and thus to the Great York Road. Now, as Clare wrote, it could only be 'plain sailing and steering ahead, meeting no enemy and fearing none'. 'Here shall he see no enemy but winter and rough weather.' Later he would give his own sanitised version of the gypsies. No pilfering, no stinking mutton, no being let down now. Just one more freedom song from a poor prisoner doing life:

109

> *The joys of the camp are not cares of the Crown,*
> *There'll be fiddling and dancing a mile out of town.*
> *Will you come to the camp ere the moon goes down*
> > *A mile from the town?*

> *The camp of the gipsies is sweet by moonlight*
> *In the furze and the hawthorn and all out of sight*
> *There'll be fiddling and dancing and singing tonight*
> > *In the pale moon light.*

DROMENGRO

Man of the Road

Sven Berlin, 1971

The longing to reawaken an intuitive response to the natural world lies behind most attempts to understand and, if possible, rejoin primitive communities. But such communities themselves are ancient organic structures which, on the whole, have a way of rejecting this sophisticated new tissue. In the Gypsy Kingdom the *rai*, the wholly acceptable non-Gypsy friend, is a phenomenon. As with that other kingdom, many are called but few are chosen. Sven Berlin includes Walter Starkie, Augustus John (although his freedom with their women was resented and remembered). George Borrow, Francis Hindes Groome, Dora Yates and John Sampson among true *rais*: but he leaves it to the reader to judge whether he himself qualifies. This is less modesty than honest doubt. After many years of as total an identification with these persecuted wanderers as any 20th-century man has attempted, Berlin hesitates to place himself among those who offered disinterested love and received in return absolute trust. John Clare called the Gypsies 'a quiet, pilfering, unprotected race', and it is the last point in his description which is most conspicuous in this vivid

110

confession of a tense and violent relationship.

While Sven Berlin correctly identifies his own central interest in the Gypsies as similar to that of artists like Jacques Callot, John and his Edwardian aunt Dickie Slade, for whom the roadside encampment was the shore of Bohemia, he had soon to face up to the fact that there existed in his nature a wild quality which needed no tutelage from the Lees and Coopers, the Smiths and the Wellses. It is this struggle between similar, rather than foreign temperaments which gives the book its flavour.

While he is with the Romanies, Berlin is mentally and physically motivated by all the stresses and emotions of a blood-brotherhood which does not exist. In another place, beyond the bent-ash tent, outside Ishtar's bed (she, too, though showing all the attributes of the Gypsy, is a foundling and can never be certain), is the St Ives of Hepworth, Peter Lanyon, Ben Nicholson and Bernard Leach. Or Augustus's and Dorelia's Fordingbridge. Or Lady Ottoline. The painting and sculpting is beyond the encampment too, for except for their music and dance the Romanies are quite uncreative. Berlin's method has been not to run all the threads of his life together to present the full pattern but to pick out this particular experience which has had a way of trapping him, on and off, ever since he accepted that classic cure for the Thirties slump, the 'open road'.

He describes the result of many an Urban Council's attempt to provide some humane final solution for what is obviously the worst challenge to their tidy-mindedness. He calls it 'a slow and persistent oppression' and says that, when the Welfare moves in, 'the blood is bred away' and that 'the gift of the council house is the death-warrant of the Gypsy people.' Police harassment is often extreme and the selective nature of intolerance is neatly illustrated when the landlady of a country pub allows a drunken bus-outing to bawl its songs in one of her bars but ejects some young Gypsies when they sing ballads in another. They happened to be singing them to Vaughan Williams, but that made no difference. There are some delightful pictures of Vaughan Williams, majestically at large in the remote villages, listening for the old music and prudently accompanied at all times by a case of Tollemache's beer. A *rai* unawares.

Sven Berlin's book is a brilliant piece of rural observation. The key to the Gypsy ethos lies not in their beautiful fragmentary language or in their family relationships, which are of a Victorian bourgeois strictness – though the children are treated with an enchanting degree of love – but in their animal sensitivity towards the fields and woods. There is something in that quick dark glance which makes its owner fair game for authority. Prejudice falls like a knife on whatever it fails to comprehend.

The Gypsies have their own cunning answers for the age-old verderers and vagrancy legislation, and have learned to live naturally in opposition to both. What is causing them their present difficulties are the new bribes and pressures with which the static men are urging them to settle down. 'Dromengro' means man of the road and, denied his nomadry, the Gypsy is denied his ancient outdoor instincts, as well as a whole range of innate expression which neither he nor the great *rais* are able to put into words. Sven Berlin himself confesses to some defeat by these enigmatic people. He has followed them since his youth when he set out on the romance road from Cornwall in a painted van. 'I searched for a dream and found only a stark reality.' In spite of their famous begging – 'by the sheer magic of persistence they take things from you' – it is the Romany who has been, century after century, rooked and robbed. Now all the secret traditional resting-places are being forbidden and in exchange there is the special compound and the designated area. Civic hygiene waits impatiently beyond the scrapyard.

THE RUNAWAY
Laurie Lee

A Writer's Day-Book, 2006

The stint of vagabondage and the romance of the open read were at their zenith in 1914, the year Laurie Lee was born. Vain were the attempts of squire, parson and the local press to stem what was called 'the flight from the land'. This wholesale rural exodus was created primarily by the great farming depression which was well set in by the early twentieth century. It would dominate village life until the second world war. Young men just walked off the farms to the towns, and out of their ancient traditions, leaving behind a kind of beautiful inertia beloved of watercolourists, a penniless scene of 'tile-spilling farms', as Lee put it.

Both he and his father fled from rural Gloucestershire, though differently, and leaving their wives behind them. Lee senior went off because he was driven by the excitements and possibilities of the new freedoms which life promised, Laurie because he had to gain some perspective on who he actually was, being a poet and all that. 'Young men don't leave a lush creamy village life solely for economic reasons', he said. But there were not many youths, faced with fieldwork and penury, who would have given a thought to its topping of lush creaminess. And to give Laurie Lee his due, he never forgot the hardships and limitations which he so famously coated with opulence. He knew what lay beneath.

His books are retrospective, that of the countryman in perpetual exile and who is always young. Lee believed that 'the only truth is what you remember', but he would worry a bit about what he called 'the censorship of self' and 'some failure between honesty and nerve'. But access to a lyrical language gave him just the right balance to record what he felt had happened to him. One of his great attractions as a writer is his admittance to making journeys without a cause. His interest in the Republican cause in Spain was minimal and yet his wonderful account of the defeat of the Republican Army in 1937 makes *A Moment of War* (1991) an unforgettable addition to the literature which came out of that conflict. He had walked into that war as he had walked out of Slad, with his fiddle under his arm and with his open, watching face, apparently never asking himself Why? A road led there.

After an office job in Stroud – it was the day of the office-boy – he simply walked to London to live 'in the flats, rooms and garrets of this city, the drawers in the human filing cabinets that stand in blank rows down the streets of Kensington and Notting Hill'. The analogy fitted him well because from then on he would exist happily in a papery mess with daily outings to the pub. After *Cider with Rosie* (1959) the bar became his court and he was always the author on show, both in London and Slad, though giving little notion of what it cost him to write and re-write his books, the long crafting of them in soft pencil, and especially the difficulties of hauling back into his consciousness events that had occurred sometimes decades ago.

In order to achieve this he had to become the young wanderer he had once been. There are few middle-aged or elderly views on a Laurie Lee page. 'One bright June morning, when I was nineteen, I packed all I had on my back' – and the reader is away. And so is the author.

Lee's first poems were published in *Horizon*. He was then working with the G.P.O. and the Crown Film Unit during the early Forties, and then as Publications editor for the Ministry of Information. Although at this time in casual pub contact with the literary world, it was not until a friend showed Cyril Connolly some of his work that he decided to be a writer. He was immediately prolific and promising. Collections with lovely titles, *The Sun my Monument* (1944), *The Bloom of Candles* (1947), *My Many Coated Man* (1955) were praised for the originality of their technique but criticised for their absence of depth. But what did they expect from a troubadour? Just as light tunes start feet tapping, so Lee's lines made his readers long to walk out of things.

And then came *Cider with Rosie*, that evocation of rites of passage in Lush-creamy-land – boys do not wait to grow up there – and its brightly coloured happiness. Few who had witnessed the realities of the time would have countenanced its existence. Yet it did exist. The wild flowers grew, the birds flocked, the cottages burst with brothers and sisters, the teachers taught rot, the churchbells tumbled, mothers worshipped the Royal Family, fathers were liars, and life was incongruously exultant. What could be done? Nothing. Slad is situated in a darkish valley, anyway.

Laurie Lee's parents, although festooned with a rich, loving, head-shaking array of words, are nonetheless archetypal products of the 1870 Education Act, domestic service and the collapse of agriculture. Unlike their son, they were mad on books. Each was a dedicated escapee from the humdrum, father spinning away to the suburbs in his new car (cranking it in one of them would kill him), mother into total romance which involved loading the house with pretty nicknacks, adoration of the gentry and novels. Laurie sees his mother as both an artist and a buffoon, and his father as deplorable. His portraits of both of them are relentless yet amused, rather like his description of rural education. All the characters in *Cider with Rosie* are involved in perpetual rites of passage, and are absorbed more in touch, scents and glimpses than sights.

Despite Leonard Woolf's apparent lack of enthusiasm when the manuscript arrived at Hogarth Press it would sell six million copies. Under its flowery bower of language countless readers have found a tough enough social history to reveal to them just how things were for their own country relations not so very long ago. The success of *Cider with Rosie* would commit Laurie Lee to autobiography and he made it the first volume of a trilogy.

As I Walked Out One Midsummer Morning followed in 1969 and *A Moment of War* in 1991. Try as he might, Lee could never quite convince people why there were such huge gaps between each volume, none of which was of great length, and the last one honed to the bone, so to speak. Whilst *As I Walked Out One Midsummer Morning* trails many of the by now famous enchantments of *Cider with Rosie* and allows the author, the vagabond boy with the violin, to enter a Spain as yet untouched by tourism and to do what can never be done again, wander around in near medieval scenes, encountering generous girls whose innocence is on a par with his own, and with still no connection with hippiness, *A Moment of War* abandons all those elements in his previous work which had been so beguiling. Instead, it is a small masterpiece of recollected helplessness and terror, the result of 'a number of idiocies I committed at this time'.

These were to walk across the Pyrenees in the December snow during the bloody winter of 1937, knock on the door of a Republican farmer and say, 'I've come to join you'. After a few old Spanish courtesies Lee was at once locked up as a spy. Between then and his rescue by Bill Rust, editor of the *Daily Worker*, Lee would, had he felt at all strongly its ideals, have been part of the martyrdom of the International Brigade. But he did not. He seems to have just walked into a civil war simply because it was somewhere for a walker to go. But he also believed that the Spain of *As I Walked Out One Midsummer Morning* would protect him. Instead, he and another lad were thrown into a kind of St John the Baptist-type hole and, a few days later, his companion in horror was dragged out and dispatched like a rabbit.

A Moment of War is written with brilliant economy and has a place in the remarkable literature which the Spanish Civil War inspired. It is cinematic in its sharp detail and its remorseless atmosphere, and it may have some kind of throwback to the Laurie Lee of the film unit. It succeeds in doing that rare thing, documenting the helplessness and fright of the individual under ruthless soldiering conditions. *As I Walked Out One Midsummer Morning* had led him to the verge of this explosiveness. He recognised the cruelty and murderousness of Spain as he got away. When he returned for what to the Republicans was no convincing purpose, it was like stepping on a landmine which had been situated at a spot where there was no reason to cross. The narrative is simple and tense and has some of the qualities of a novella. And, as so often in accounts of young men close to death, a faint eroticism floats about it. Lee was in his seventies when he wrote it. As a writer he was both the youthful hero and the mature craftsman, the disengaged onlooker and the participant. He needed to be faraway in time and in miles from what and who were closest to him, his wife, his roots and especially his first travels. His art employed a soft pencil for hard times but he was also a young old man who appreciated being alive.

LIGHT READING
Slightly Foxed, Spring 2008

When my old friend the artist John Nash died I inherited his books. I imagined him reading them by lamplight, just as I read when I was a boy, the twin wicks faintly waving inside the Swan glass chimney. There they all were, those handsome runs of pocket-size volumes which preceded the 1930s Penguins and the subsequent paperbacks. Some were small-pack books and had gone to the Western Front. Some were hiking books and had gone up mountains. Some were still a bit painty, having gone on landscape expeditions. All showed signs of having had a life far from that in the studio bookcase. All spoke of belonging to a man who, when young, had been a convert to the Open Road.

The creed of the Open Road had been written by George Borrow:

There's night and day, brother, both sweet things; sun, moon, and stars, brother, all sweet things; there's likewise a wind on the heath. Life is very sweet, brother, who would wish to die?'

(*Lavengro*, Chapter 25)

Jack Kerouac would say something similar. As Passchendaele approached John Nash returned his beloved Everyman edition of Borrow to his sweetheart, along with the letters she had sent him, believing that he would not see her or them again.

So here they were, the very same volumes he'd carried with him. I read in their curly endpapers the great promise which good books make. 'Everyman. I will go with thee, and be thy guide, in thy most need to go by thy side.' When last read, their owner thought that he would never see his native Buckinghamshire again, either. But a gypsy boy who had been called up from the same county comforted him. They would both find life sweet once more in the Chilterns.

When I knew John Nash in his middle age he walked nowhere, but the wind from the heath would whip into his little car and blow the cigarette smoke about, and the easel would rattle in the boot, and life was indeed very sweet. Green-back Penguins breathing murder slid about under the seat. Now in what had been his studio I began to put his Everymans in order.

In 1904 Joseph Dent and his son Hugh decided on nothing less than publishing a library of one thousand of the best authors at a price the ordinary reader could afford – a shilling a volume. They got the writer Ernest Rhys to advise them and it was he who christened the project the Everyman Library. The format was a sturdy cloth with gold on the spines. Compared with today's paperbacks they were quite hefty, with sharp corners. You would know that you were carrying a book in your pocket. They had marvellous introductions by scholars like Holbrook Jackson, May Sinclair and Eugene Mason, and the keen Everyman-ist would soon, without knowing it, become well acquainted with Eng. Lit.

Joseph Dent was born in Darlington in 1849, the son of a house-painter. From childhood on he adored not only the contents of a book but also its binding. Now, during the few years before the First World War, he was able to present English Literature itself from his model factory in Letchworth Garden City to the book-hungry public. The 1870 Education Act had by the early twentieth century created an insatiable readership, though mostly of people whose wages did not run to six or more shillings a volume. The public librarian and commercial libraries thrived but there arose a longing to *possess* books, especially the great authors, and to fill one's own bookcase became an urgent pleasure. Working men and women no longer wanted a small pile of miscellaneous reading but a library which looked like a library. In his youth John Nash was an insatiable reader and at first had aspirations to become a writer rather than an artist. His brother Paul, too, was well-read. Partly because of this, the two of them would be in the van of a wonderful era of book illustration as they set wood engravings to text during the 1930s.

Now and then a bus ticket or a pressed flower or a shopping list floats from John's books. How diligently they have kept his place all these years. I am pulling from the dusty shelf his Everymans, many volumes of them, their golden spines still fairly bright. And next Dent's ambitious run of Aldine classics which preceded his Everyman Library. These were nothing less than pocket luxuries which imitated the books that Aldus Manutius published in exquisite small octavo editions during the Renaissance. Dent actually named his premises in Bedford Street Aldine House, throwing out a challenge to London publishers. The army of new readers would be given beautiful-to-handle books. One of my first buys from a second-hand ledge when I was a teenager was the Aldine edition of *Le Morte D'Arthur*. Faintly worn, in soft green leather, the four volumes had the famous Aldine owl stamped on them and Aubrey Beardsley's sensational illustrations inside many of them, and each protected by a filmy tissue. The previous buyer had written inside, 'Gerald Gurney from his beloved wife, February 1899'. What a

Valentine. What a marriage that must have been. I found several more de luxe Aldine books amongst John's youthful collection, two passed on to him by Paul, Thomas Dekker's *The Guls Hornebooke* and *The Belman of London*, each containing disgraceful advice.

From the creation of the Everyman Library onwards publishers began to notice a populace which, as well as being book devouring, was using what spare time it had to leave work and home for the countryside. Hiking, cycling, climbing and eventually motoring, these passionate new freedoms were served by some brilliant writing – and some new runs of pocket volumes. Thus came Routledge's Railway Library, Dent's Open Air Library (which included a Fine edition of Turgenev's *A Sportsman's Sketches* perfectly illustrated by John Nash's friend Eric Daglish. 1932), Argosy Books' 'For the Rucksack' and county guides printed on India paper, the easier to carry around. Cape's Travellers' Library series was 'designed for the pocket, or for the small house where shelf space is limited'. Among my own treasures in this edition are four volumes of A. E. Coppard's short stories and Sarah Orne Jewett's masterpiece *The Country of the Pointed Firs* with a preface by her admirer Willa Cather. Nearly all these modestly priced and delightfully produced editions possess introductions which are an hors d'oeuvre literary treat in themselves. The Travellers' Library was a joint venture into the easily-carried volume by Jonathan Cape and William Heinemann, immediately after the First World War. It was a swift recognition of the freedoms to be found in the countryside. Even the unemployed could and did walk away from it all, if only for a day. Designed so that all the volumes are of uniform thickness, no matter how many pages, with covers made especially durable against 'hasty packing', this pocket series, I find, becomes more beautiful with age and use. Just to hold one of these 7 x 4-inch little books is an enchantment. How have we degenerated from such publishing to the brick sized fiction of today? To carry a couple of the latter on a fell walk puts one in the company of Pilgrim and his load.

Chatto & Windus's Phoenix Library of the Thirties – 'Pocket size. 3s 6d net per volume' – is also a run worth having. My first encounter with it was when, aged 18, I saw Proust's *Remembrance of Things Past* in a Rye bookshop. I had a birthday book token which ran to two volumes of this previously unheard of novel. Thus it began, the life-long loyalty to the white and blue edition with, inside the wrapper, the glorious red and gold spine, and inside the cover the memory river briefly halted here and there by a Philippe Jullian drawing.

The Phoenix Library began with Lytton Strachey's *Queen Victoria* and there soon arrived other old friends, *Lolly Willowes*, by Sylvia Townsend Warner – 'an object lesson in the proper way of bringing Satan into modern fiction', said the TLS – and eventually, volumes three and four of Marcel Proust! The final volume had to be translated by Stephen Hudson aka Sidney Schiff, because its original translator Scott Moncrieff had died. Hudson was a friend of John Nash and there is a written instruction on the fly-leaf on how he was to read Proust. Since John only possessed this last volume, I doubt if he learned how. And I doubt even more if he ever read *Dainty Poems of the XIX Century* in Harrap's Choice Books series. When we die our bookshelves can libel us.

Thin paper was the order of the pocket edition day. In 1911 John Murray produced a thin paper edition of the works of Stanley J. Weyman, twenty two volumes in all. Conan Doyle, the Brontes, the Brownings, all came whispering from the press. There was no excuse for not carrying them about. Books were light luggage. They might also be nice to touch, like a lover or a cat. Thus the now rather unpleasant feel of suede and velvet-bound copies of the *Rubáiyát of Omár Khuyyám* and *Sappho*. Their nap clings to my fingers. Their naked girls are tipped in, making fluttering pictures which one would not like the servants to see. What a fuss it all is, this bedside binding. There were a number of these naughty volumes to tremble over. Quite my favourite is *The Garden of Kama* by Laurence Hope. Heinemann's Windmill Library. Twenty editions by 1930.

> *Were I but one of my serving girls*
> *To solace his pain to rest!*
> *Shake out the sand from the soft loose curls,*
> *And hold him against my breast!*
> ('The Regret of the Ranee in the Hall of Peacocks')

Two things were imperative for these publications: the word 'Library' and a spine to be proud of. The latter after all is what one sees on the bookshelf. I confront them discerningly, giving them the due that they deserve. For the years have not dimmed their gold but have actually brought a radiance to their design. Here comes something wonderful, a rare edition of *Poems* by John Clare edited by Arthur Symons. It is bound in a rich dull green and has a lotus pattern art noveau spine. It is 'Grangerised' with a letter from the publisher Henry Frowde and a letter from Mrs Symons. This is the selection of Clare's poetry which Edmund Blunden read as a boy and which he took to the Western Front, and which, when he taught at Oxford, became the seedcorn of all future Clare studies. This little book.

Macmillan's Golden Treasury series of easily carried literature began with Palgrave's *Golden Treasury* itself in 1861 – 'a uniformly printed series in 18mo, with Vignette Titles by J. E. Millais, T. Woolner etc.' It was the sculptor Thomas Woolner who drew the piping Pan on the cover. My particular treasure in this edition is *Letters of Cowper*, 1884. John Constable died with Cowper's *Letters* in his hand. And here comes the copy of Sir Thomas Browne's *Hydriotaphis* in the Golden Treasury format, which Paul Nash gave to his brother in 1929, and which gave Paul his 'imagery' and also his philosophy. He has inscribed it elegantly.

Lolling here, I could go on for pages. I am like Jean Rhys who, when she was old, forgot time, breakfast, lunch, combing her hair, and would topple out of bed towards the nearest bookcase and – read! The chapters and the hours, and the cigarettes would pass. Poring over the little volumes I am glad to have been given them – grateful, happy for them. Dear, dear books, never shall you go to the Oxfam shop.

JOURNEY THROUGH EUROPE
John Hillaby, 1972

Walking offers a unique release for the imagination. It pulls life into proportion, and at the same time it causes little philosophical feelers to venture forth in all directions. It is the physical action most likely to set up restless currents of thought. Keats, Wordsworth and Tennyson often walked their way into poems; country parsons set up sermon-walks in long gardens. Fabians walked as a natural preparation for intellectual action. The ideas generated by walking a fair distance seem to stem from bouts of reverie entangling with hard facts. All that one has learnt is set in motion, and the senses are assailed by the intimate proximity of stones, wind, insects, flowers, smells, sounds and the ceaselessly changing flow of landscape. But the difficulty of books about walks is to catch fancy on the hoof, as it were – to get the revelation as well as the geography down on the page at the end of the day. There may also sometimes be a need to prove the moral validity of the journey in the first place: for there is all the difference in the world between doing what John Hillaby does – this is his third walk-essay – and making the formal John O'Groats-Land's End gesture. He is always travelling, never indulging in a feat.

In an age marked by vacuous travel, Hillaby's role is that of reminder and restorer. He tells us what we used to experience, in greater or lesser ways, as we got ourselves from one land to another. Walking a long distance is one of the best short cuts to what we really are, and this is what this delightful book is primarily about. Hillaby takes the classic route from the North Sea to the Mediterranean, returning from the grey edge of the world to its warm blue centre. At Nice-*Nike*, i.e. 'victory' – he steps carefully between the boys and girls fast asleep on the midnight sand and plunges ritualistically into the waves. The young too have wandered, but with a studied indifference towards the sights. No history, no nature. They are the *autostoppeurs* from all over, but, whether in a Maine or Bolton accent, their refusal of everything Hillaby walks for is total. For them the cultural framework is either missing or has been dismissed. 'Nothing I asked about where they'd been or what they'd seen seemed to interest them.' Not condemning, but genuinely bewildered, he gives up. Thumbing and flopping, they get themselves not to Nice but to India. 'Why?' he asks, 'It's logical,' they reply.

Hillaby is Spartan and squarely fascinated all day long by what he recalls and what he passes: Yorkshire Viking settlements, Karel

Capek's analysis of bicycling, the careers of ski-bums, the Meuse mosasaurs (those whale-size sea-lizards which grin in the chalk near Liège), the gasworks at Herstal which cover the site of Charlemagne's palace, the foxes of the Ardennes, cat worship, respectable provincial brothels, the Erenz (where monumental labourers in the hayfields remind him that this is the country of that tribe of supermen, the Treveri), the soft rocks of Lorraine which Michelin describes as *couches tendres*, the cities of the long-haired Merovingian kings, the movements of the Keltoi on their long time-journey to nationalist Wales, and a thousand other threads on the historic loom. When Belloc did something like this, Hillaby observes, he kept a lively eye for scenery but never saw a single flower, a bird, an animal or a butterfly. He also walked over the Alps dressed in thin cotton and without maps.

The true traveller puts comfort and convenience last, full awareness first. The latter is not easily come by. One has to apply oneself to libraries and not to brochures. Multitudes will increasingly mill about, when young with the *autostoppeurs*, when far from old, but past the use of their legs, by the *dieselomnibusse* or the Bluebird super-coach from Stockport – and what will they see? The saxifrages of the Lenta? Who will they meet? The villagers who alone can tell one what still hasn't got into the books? It is unlikely.

PIECES OF LAND
Kevin Crossley-Holland, 1972

BESIDE THE SEASIDE
Anthony Smith, 1972

When the centre cannot hold, move out to the periphery. This is what we all feel driven to do at times. The edges of a country become a new country. Although we remain high and dry, it is the sea's writ which runs there, not the city's. It makes us think and behave quite differently, and become interested in and surprised at our new selves.

For it is regeneration we are after when we reject the hive for drift and dreams. Of course, if one is born and brought up on the edge it is a very different matter. On Eigg or Inishmore, say. One then might well discover that the sea is not a way out but a wall, as two Aran islanders found when they first saw the mainland.

'Oh Maurice, isn't Ireland wide and spacious?' 'Upon my word, Tomas, she is bigger than that.'

Kevin Crossley-Holland travelled to many of the islands round Britain both to see what they offered in the visionary sense to him personally, and to look at their different ways of looking inward. Island insularity produces something very good, the dignity, quiet and fulfilment which Yeats and many other poets have commended, or something so bad that it could be tolerated only by a keen sociologist. The average village offers much the same thing. The author understands this – and understands himself. He is a poet and he naturally responds to the good insularity. But he doesn't try to share it. 'It would never begin to do – I do not really enjoy a simple life for very long before beginning to hanker after refinements; I am unpractical; though I may be gregarious I would never pull my weight in a small community.'

Few, to be honest, do seem to pull their weight on islands, or so it would seem from these delightful glimpses of Hoy, St Agnes, Lindisfarne, Tory, Alderney, Eigg, Lundy and Inishmore. Nor is life on them simple. Often it is exceedingly complex. The refinements, however, are sparse on some of them and all of them seem to demand a decent degree of handiness.

Hoy was not the empty place waiting to be filled-out with scholarship which the author had imagined, but tense and dynamic – mostly due to the lifeboat. The lifeboat keeps Hoy on its toes and won't let it slide into torpor. All the same, it is a middle-aged to elderly population which it so stimulates; all the young have fled. St Agnes vegetates, old and young alike. It is expensive, costing a good bit more to live there than it does in Cornwall. Nobody says much about the mainland – 'As far as we're concerned, the mainland can disappear, so long as the visitors come and the flowers are sold.' Nobody can recall the old Scillonian songs; the cultural climate is that imported by the holidaymakers. It is very social although 'it would be hell if you didn't fit in.'

Sacred Lindisfarne is a very different matter. The success of the evangelistic church which made it famous can only be understood, says Kevin Crossley-Holland, if one remembers that the lives of the pagan English were dominated by *Wyrd* – implacable fate. Cuthbert, Cedd and Aiden destroyed this domination. The present inhabitants of the island fleece the pilgrims with an inescapable determination and curse the local mead factory. *Wyrd* seems to have won.

But it is Tory which provided the worst island experience, and a very revealing one it is. Very soon 'claustrophobia edged our minds.' There were lots of men and few women. And a feeling of a surface which might easily erupt were it not for regular dousings of booze and bingo. The terrible keening banned by the Church is caught on the wind, Och, ochon! Ochon! Inbreeding, feuding, horse-play. It was a relief when the boat pushed out again into Camusmore Bay.

A delicious climate wafts Alderney, making it hard to imagine what happened there during the last war. The great massacre which took place on Eigg is further away in time. Eigg is 7.5 thousand acres of more or less useless moor dotted with ruined cottages belonging to the clearances. The few people who remain are a high-mannered lot who dwell in a quiet which is neither threatening nor depressing. They could do more for themselves but they don't because they prefer to do nothing very much. The occasional ceilidh whirls things up and 'you have to watch yourself.' In the bay are the celebrated singing sands which produce a creak, a shriek, a scream or a choir of drowned sailors. Lundy is Lund-ey – Puffin Island. Old Norse. A Norman 'Inquisition' listed butcher falcons among its many birds. Nobody has lived his whole life out there for several generations; the complete population gives way every now and then to another group. There is an odd lack of continuity. But it is a dramatic island, and Clemence Dane, Kingsley, Drayton, Hardy, and Tomlinson are among the many writers it has intrigued.

It is Inishmore however which still totally captivates the island-taster. True that the old culture is weak and hesitant, and has to be listened for with a cocked ear, but the seventy-two families who live there constitute an attractive society. It was to this thoughtful place that Yeats sent the young Synge. O'Flaherty and O'Direáin were born here and the atmosphere still is literate and vital. Crossley-Holland finds in noble Inishmore something very close to the island dream of the ages. His book is deepened by his knowledge of Anglo-Saxon, Norse and Celtic literature, and marked by sharp personal reactions to everything he sees and everyone he meets. It is partly a fresh, intimate examination of the island cult and partly an inward look at himself as a man intrigued by solitudes and the spare language of the past.

Anthony Smith's peripheral travels are a very different matter. In the first place he sets out to discover Britain's coast as other people set out to discover a lost South American tribe, with a search-party of ten, a plane, a boat, a landrover and a lot of branded equipment and stores by kind permission of Dunlop, Heinz, Oxo etc. The object was to look at all 6,000 miles of our shore-line and to draw some general conclusions regarding our beach-oriented leisure-patterns and also our abuses of this magnificent and varied amenity. Although in Mr Woodhouse's opinion, the sea was rarely of any use to anybody, we have long come to think differently. We use it as our main recreational facility and as our main drain. In the course of his long journey, Smith has been able to collect some devastating statistics and correct some generally held opinions. Perhaps the most crushing of the latter, considering that the seaside is where we all feel we can do as we like, is that 'the ordinary citizen has no rights of any kind on a beach.' He questions the tradition of seaside hideousness in the form of the vast caravan sites on the North Wales coast, appalling architecture in the popular resorts and the huge wash of commercial trash which accompanies the ordinary holidaymaker everywhere. The Army is a terrible coastal defiler, too, but nothing comes up to the defilement of our chilly waters by certain towns and cities which still lack sewage treatment systems. Edinburgh is one of the worst. On some days fifty million gallons of its effluent go straight from the city to the Firth of Forth via a great iron pipe.

Beside the Seaside is a tightly presented mass of information.

Underneath the packed evidence lies a submerged adventure story about the expedition and a motor-cruiser named Barracuda Two. It is comforting to know, when one is in Newquay in July, that there are immense stretches of sand, rock and shingle around Britain which are scarcely visited at all.

THE GREAT RAILWAY BAZAAR
Paul Theroux, 1975

The world's a small place, they say. It is not: it is absolutely enormous. If the globe seems to have shrunk, it is because it is increasingly traversed by shrunken minds. Paul Theroux, a novelist in his motionless hours, refutes the fashionable view that there is nowhere left to go, by simply catching the train. Or all the great trains, to be precise. For, desecrated, misunderstood and undervalued by modern governments as they are, the enchanting tracks still more or less girdle the globe; and, as *The Great Railway Bazaar* suggests, there are still some amazing travel treats on offer. 'The difference between travel writing and fiction,' says Theroux, 'is the difference between recording what the eye sees and discovering what the imagination knows.' He doesn't look out of the window very much, and he doesn't display infantile enthusiasm for old tenders and gauges. In fact, he reads most of the time – *Little Dorrit, Bishop Blougram's Apology, Dead Souls* – or watches passengers. Stations supply convenient chapter arrangements, rather than journey's end. 'If a train is large and comfortable you don't even need a destination.'

Four months on the Orient Express, the Delhi Mail, the Khyber Pass Local, the 16.25 from Galle, the Early Bird to Aomori, the Trans-Siberian Express and a score of other trains carry Theroux into an extraordinary realm of national-cultural overlap. The flotsam of empires and the flotsam of the transcendence-seeking Sixties youth-cult merge on remote platforms. Hotels have registers 'thick with pseudonyms of adulterers'. There are breaks for lectures on the tradition of the American novel which, in the light of what the author says about practically everything else, from sex to politics, one would quite like to have heard. There are descriptions of India, Burma and Russia which possess the intensity of ancient photographs, and there are snatches of dialogue so wittily selected and caught on the wing that they have the tantalising quality of pages torn from a larger context which one would give a lot to know. Nothing is recollected in tranquillity, and nothing is diarised. Nor can Theroux exactly be described as a tourist. The railway compartment having been 'hallowed by fiction', not to say enshrined in poetry – Hardy, Brooke – he enters it with naked literary intentions. Luggage-rack, sleeper, dining-car, loo 'contain the essential paraphernalia of the culture' of the country he is speeding through, and he eyes it with fascinated disgust. For most trains on this longest journey are not like the 4.30 to Norwich. Inviting confidences but beating off clingers, he acquires company for his secret purpose. 'I decided that travel was flight and pursuit in equal parts.'

Frequently, the trains and their environs inflict an unbearable melancholy. The cooped-up cultural paraphernalia, plus fantasies, of some hippy rouse the far-from-gentle writer to the attack. He lays into a fellow-American in Ceylon because of his shaved head and saffron robe, and occasionally he lifts his eyes from Dickens or Gissing to be stunned by what is flashing by: 'Osaka, a city like a steel trap someone has forgotten to bait'.

Aptly, he quotes R L Stevenson in *Ordered South*:

Herein, I think, is the chief attraction of railway travel. The speed is so easy, and the train disturbs so little the scenes through which it takes us, that our heart becomes full of the placidity of the country; and while the body is being borne forward in the flying chain of carriages, the thoughts alight, as the humour moves them, at unfrequented stations.

It is not only his respect for the great train routes, but also his candid assessments of the nations through which they still wind, that somehow link this robust American traveller with a bookish scion of the Raj. Drip-dry luggage and all, he rattles along with panache and authority.

Like Lady Glencora, when she remarks, 'We can get to the Kurds, Alice, without getting into a packet again. That, to my way of thinking, is the great comfort of the Continent,' Theroux returns style and adventure to a mode of transport which once naturally embodied both.

OLD GLORY

An American Journey

Jonathan Raban, 1981

A river trip – it need not involve anywhere more challenging than the Deben – constitutes a number of unique assets for the travelling writer. In the first place he has the choice of two philosophical approaches to his journey, for to start at its mouth will set a thoughtful drift in motion which is likely to be very different from that which would pre-occupy him if he set off from its source. Then there is the curious sensation of being free of the land by virtue of a capriciously wandering liquid line which, bar a cutting or a lock now and again, follows a flow path which owes nothing to human directions. Rivers have origins and conclusions, and officially listed depths and lengths, and their presence profoundly affects the usually ancient societies which settle on their banks, as well as the ecology for miles around. Paradoxically, when one finds a river one finds a land. A distinct area. So river explorers are searching out a territory.

But because, as Eliot pointed out, and thinking perhaps of what Shakespeare called our 'crimson river of warm blood', a river is within us, while a sea is around us, there is also a tugging, harmonious addition to even the most difficult of river travel which makes it natural and even ideal. Was the river which was in Eliot his native Mississippi or his adopted Thames? It is a fluid question. Exceeded only by the Nile, Yangtze and Yenisey in its vastness, the Mississippi pours down the Red Lakes of Minnesota to the Gulf of Mexico, three thousand miles of wide water powerfully moving from the Mid-West to the Deep South. So huge and overwhelming a river is it that even the confiscation of one little loop of it by a human being for the purpose of self-identification would seem a vain thing, as the Psalmist said, and yet here is Jonathan Raban laying claim to the whole of it because, long ago in fields by the Wensum, the Mississippi spell-bound him, first in a story, and then in the atlas which his mother consulted to follow his father's progress during the last war. Imagination and good plain geography successfully support each other in *Old Glory*, his considered reply to the many questions which the printed river versus the home river of his Norfolk were to provoke.

I had first read *Huckleberry Finn* when I was seven. The picture on its cover, crudely drawn and coloured, supplied me with the raw material for an exquisite and recurrent daydream. It showed a boy alone, his face prematurely wizened with experience. (The artist hadn't risked his hand with the difficulties of bringing off a lifelike Nigger Jim). The sheet of water on which he drifted was immense, an enamelled pool of lapis lazuli. Smoke from a half-hidden steamboat hung over an island of gothic conifers. Cut loose from the world, chewing on his corncob pipe, the boy was blissfully lost in the stillwater paradise.

However, when one grows up, there is small chance of cutting loose from the world, not even via a river, as Kenneth Grahame found. Nor, strangely as it must sound, of getting blissfully lost on the Mississippi. Had Raban been a naturalist, or a cartographer-scientist, or an innocent adventurer like Huck, he would most certainly have got away from people more than he did, though whether he could have got any nearer to his true self in his late thirties (which is what this voyaging book is really about) is doubtful. *Old Glory* isn't about escaping. The Wensum, river of childhood piety, and the Mississippi, river of the imagination turned river of debased cultures, wind their very different ways through his consciousness, demanding answers. Is he *voyeur* or voyager? Is he looking and noting, or is he in the same boat? Who and what is a traveller anyway? He quotes Sterne:

The man who either disdains or fears to walk up a dark entry, may be an excellent good man, and fit for a hundred things; but he will not make a good sentimental traveller.

To do him justice, Raban disdains nobody, not even the occasional roughneck, and amongst the populated bank-side places where the dark entries are chiefly in the form of crushingly un-enlightened talk into which, using all the tolerance he can muster, he as a fellow-respecting human being is bound to make his way. Everywhere on the long trip, from St Paul to New Orleans, and with far greater difficulties in this line than had he been in a non-English speaking country, the reader is aware of Raban always entering a relationship wherever he glimpses an 'entry', no matter how obscure, and doing his utmost to extend his meetings with people beyond the requirements of an interview. It is this genuine but brief entering into things which makes the true traveller lonely, this receiving hospitality or love or information, or abuse even, from passing strangers. Raban worries about his 'long careless drift through other people's lives' and about learning 'to trust to surfaces and appearances, as travellers must.'

The start of his journey was a long way from the after-image of the river which had so hung about in his mind for thirty years. Friends in London, who had seen the Mississippi, said that it would be amazingly depressing with nothing to see above the banks but dead trees, and that God had made the river as a ghastly warning, to prove that things really can be worse than you think. When he arrived at the 'thorough-going charmlessness of this five-mile strip of junk food, porno movies and the kind of motels where you expect to find blood running down your shower-curtain' which was the fringe of Minneapolis and St Paul, and found that he had actually crossed the Mississippi without seeing it, he had to ask where it was. '*Lookin*' for the *river*', they said, '*Mississippi*? That ain't nothin' much.' The *raison d'etre* for these rich cities had become a nuisance and had been abandoned, along with the poor and forsaken 19th century wharfs, to a half forgotten position on the wrong side of the tracks. It was the great river-geographers of those days, the solid learning from which gives *Old Glory* its firm historical and scientific base, who restore Raban's confidence and give him lasting facts – and heart.

At the same time it was no world wonder at first glimpse.

It was just a river. From where I stood, the far bank was no more than a couple of hundred yards away. Its colour was much the same as that of my domestic Thames: a pale dun, like iced tea with a lot of mosquito larvae wriggling in the glass. I squatted moodily on a bleached rock, looking across the smokestacks of a Victorian mill and listening to the rumble of a weir upstream . . . I realised that I had seen this bit of the river before, in a dozen or so bad 19th century engravings . . . It was famously picturesque. The kindest thing that one could say about the engravings was that they were a vivid illustration of the sheer bewilderment of the European imagination when it tried to confront the raw wilderness of the American West.

A degree of sheer bewilderment, most of it judiciously or kindly concealed, was to be Raban's response to the kind of gross, sub-cultural beings he was to encounter on the city waterfronts. Protected by Zadok Cramer's *The Navigator* (1814) – 'This noble and celebrated stream, this Nile of North America, commands the wonder of the old world . . .' and minus *Huckleberry Finn*, which Freudianly got mislaid the day he set sail in a little blunt-backed aluminium craft which reminded him more of non-stick saucepans than any boat he had ever seen, he provisioned and made for his first lock. At this point he had to decide whether to shape the journey into a kind of literary navigated contemplation of himself at last alone on the huge dream river, or to amalgamate his private Mississippi reverie with personal views of everything which happened to him. The book takes the latter course and is Raban reflected in the brash mirror of Mississippi cities as well as in its mottled surface. He is 'Cap' – every man steering a boat, no matter how insignificant, is a 'Cap' on the river – and critic, recorder and, in a way, poet. As someone who suspects that he has no gift to permanence, this multification of roles suits him. He can join in or stand aloof so long as he sees and hears and writes.

The variety of the experience in the different states he chugged through was what enthralled him. Sometimes berthing in two consecutive towns would be like visiting two different countries, partly still due to their German, Dutch or French origins, but mostly because of a fierce chauvinism. A particular parochial bragging was attached to the local feasting, especially in Dubuque, centre of the pork trade, where he was told 'that we've got ten times as many hogs as people. Two million people in this region; twenty million hogs . . . Right, twenty million hogs, no blacks and let's hope that it stays that way.' Dubuque was Al Capone's retreat centre after a busy week in Chicago. Now a microbus carries butcher-rabbis between the two cities to oversee the beef slaughter-houses.

Raban is as intrigued at the lengths to which bad taste can go in some Americans as he is by their often childlike simplicity and hopefulness. He is bewildered when someone pinches his old hat in Buffalo. 'The United States is internationally notorious for its thuggishness, but in ten years of visits and temporary residences I had never once had anything stolen from me or met with even the most indirect threat of violence.' All the same, enough occurs on this solitary river route to prove that he needed nerve to reach New Orleans.

It is his sharp portraits of the Mississippi towns, their architecture and general ambience, and accompanied usually by highly localised sketches of men and women who, one feels, could only come from Memphis or Muscatine, and from nowhere else, which one remembers most of all. Sadly, the cities come nowhere near offering what their beautiful names evoke, Prairie du Chein, Louisiana, Cape Girardeau, and Huck's own hometown, Hannibal, one half of which was given up to whimsy celebrations of Mark Twain's hero and the other to a grain terminal. Here Raban, pilgrim extraordinary, checked the river geography of the famous book and found it to be as exact as a map, which was more than could be said for the Mississippi facts published in the local brochure. It was a great moment coming to Gilbert's Island ('Jackson's Island') eight miles downstream and, as he says, still safely out of range of the town.

The channel would round it on the Illinois side. It would still be a good place to go into hiding, with its steep woods and outcrops of limestone like pieces of cheese tunnelled by mice. Hanging back on the drift of the current, I let it unroll as slowly as I could. Thirty years ago, I'd smelled the catfish grilling over a wood fire on the shore, and counted the stars and drift-logs and rafts. Now, watching the dark places where the boughs leaned far out over the river making dripping caves and grottoes, I was full of the nervous pleasure of being a poacher. Gilbert's Island was posted as a wildlife sanctuary. I was hunting a memory out of season . . .

Others, not so much hunting as dodging a memory out of season were the GI brides of Louisiana, one from Cardiff who had worked hard to turn herself into an American but who was referred to everywhere as 'the English lady', and one from Colchester who was a kind of post-altar Miss Havisham, a ruined *abandonné* in a ruined house, her Essex accent intact. The two women lived a mile apart but had never been introduced.

As a shaky agnostic of East Anglian rectory descent, Raban makes many a compulsive foray into the river-bank churches and chapels. He reminds one of sermon-tasting Hardy, all eyes and ears and doubts. Recollections of his early communions in Norfolk, of a church floor paved with the gravestones of the grandparents of those who sailed off to New England in the 1630s, of a perfect liturgical language, have to be suppressed when it comes to some of the wilder fundamentalist groups, squatters, as he calls them sadly, 'in the ruined house of Christian belief.'

What is admirable about *Old Glory* is the absence of detachment and egotism alike, Raban is neither on an information-giving nor an ego trip. Using his earliest experience of place-magic as a loadstar, he has completely understood that a successful travel book has to be as much an exploration of the traveller as the territory he selects. He is thorough-going, eloquent and interestingly private, and he deserves to be put alongside Thoreau's *A Week on the Concord and Merrimack Rivers*, the Reverend Timothy Flint's *Recollections of the Last Ten Years Passed in Occasional Residences and Journeyings in the Valley of the Mississippi* and, of course, Mark Twain's *Life on the Mississippi*. As Raban's grandfather could have said, he has the advantage of a wellstocked mind. This pays off when one is going places.

LITERARY LIVES

Introduction to
WILLIAM HAZLITT
Selected Writings

Penguin, 1997

A conspiracy of caution has grown up around William Hazlitt. Unquestionably a 'great author' in the system which measures writers for posterity, he has to be admitted, yet grudgingly, warningly. An impression persists of a man at odds with all and everything, someone to whom his friends had to offer an almost saintly response if they were not to get their heads bitten off. He was a bitter creature, a malcontent. Equally persistent is the hint of scandal: a rumour about making a fool of himself over young girls which, in the case of Herrick, say, carries with it amusement and forgiveness, but which in connexion with Hazlitt is loaded with Sunday newspaper innuendo. He was an irritant and a grit in the eye of his contemporaries. But he wrote as marvellously as any essayist who was not Montaigne could, so his work has always received high praise. Yet, in spite of this, most of the assessments of Hazlitt have a certain maggoty quality and are eaten through with reservation.

In the many editions of his work there are numerous attempts to present him in the best light. Because there was in his fretful nature a sublime streak of joy and serenity which allowed him to write perfectly about human happiness, the essays in which he does so have been singled out for constant reprinting, with the result that the average Hazlitt-taster has not met the real flavour of this extraordinary man. His great hedge of thorny comment, which runs parallel with the retreat from revolution politics of the early nineteenth century, has too often been chopped away in order to show a calm view of a journalist- philosopher hanging 'Great Thoughts' on the type-line and meditating on such absolutes as fame, time, death, nature, etc. Yet the very essence of Hazlitt is his dangerousness, and not only with respect to the reactionary climate of his own day but when and wherever freedom and truth are compromised by those actions which are summed up as the 'art of the possible'. These were what he called 'the lie' and it was his refusal to either take or give 'the lie' which turned him into the uncomfortable creature he was. This, the very kernel of his character, has been seen as a kind of aberrant grumpiness, a tiresome failing in an otherwise excellent prose stylist. So his work has been tilted until it squares up to what is expected of an inexhaustible aphorist and again it is wholesome Hazlitt, rather than whole Hazlitt, which is presented.

What was it, both in his own day and after, which makes him one of literature's separated brethren, which sees to it that he is critically acclaimed but which leaves him outside the full warm fellowship of what were once called trusted writers? 'I want to know why everybody has such a dislike of me?' he asked Leigh Hunt. Edmund Gosse, giving the general nineteenth century answer, put it all down to cussedness: 'Eccentricity, violence and a disregard of the conventions were at no time unsympathetic to Hazlitt.' Except for his telling inclusion of that key word 'violence', the rest of Gosse's statement takes up the central position and is a nervous cheer for a writer who made the Olympian winning post, though handicapped. 'In his own time and way he was a transmitter of the sacred fire.' Like so many critics before and since, Gosse tries to stay neutral. But Hazlitt leaves no one neutral. Disturbed himself by every ecstatic, political and tragic aspect of the human condition, he could never believe that there were those who managed to get through life without feeling and knowing these things in all their intensity. He could not understand the rules of selection which made some of the subjects on which he wrote praiseworthy and socially acceptable – art, Shakespeare (although once his analysis of Desdemona brought shouts of 'obscenity!'), the countryside – and others – class, war, money, slavery, sex – taboo. His England had been at war with France for twenty years and had, like the rest of Europe, been fed on cruelties; His London was famous for its prostitutes. The great mass of his fellow men were near starvation. Yet he was to be polite in print and draw the line. It was impossible.

'Hazlitt was not one of those non-committal writers who shuffle off in a mist and die of their own insignificance,' wrote Virginia Woolf.

His essays are emphatically himself. He has no reticence and he has no shame. He tells us exactly what he thinks, and he tells us – the confidence is less seductive – what he feels. As of all men he had the most intense consciousness of his own existence, since never a day passed without inflicting on him a pang of hate or of jealousy, some thrill of anger or pleasure, we cannot read him for long without coming in contact with a very singular character – ill-conditioned yet high minded; mean yet noble; intensely egotistical yet inspired by the most genuine passion for the rights and liberties of mankind. . . .So thin is the veil of the essay as Hazlitt wore it, his very look comes before us. . . . No man could read him and maintain a simple and uncompounded idea of him.

There is a noticeable broadening of judgement here but it is still 'less seductive' to know what Hazlitt feels than what he thinks. He is all right until he allows his private life to run so unchecked onto the page. But of course it is when Hazlitt is most privately concerned that he touches on those public affairs which involve political, sensual, happiness-seeking, disappointment-finding mankind. The reader, encountering this form of literary nakedness, must either acknowledge its reality or join the prissy mob which defines what is permissible. But whatever his reaction to that 'brow-hanging, shoe-contemplative, *strange*' creature of Coleridge's jittery description, ordinary conforming, tax-paying, shibboleth-swallowing man must inevitably encounter guilt, cowardice and regret when he encounters William Hazlitt. The oil which runs the smooth society was not for him. Nor did he ever pretend otherwise.

I am not in the ordinary acceptance of the term, *a good-natured man*, that is, many things annoy me besides what interferes with my own ease and interest. I hate a lie; a piece of injustice wounds me to the quick, though nothing but the report of it reaches me. Therefore I have made many enemies and few friends; for the public know nothing of well-wishers and keep a wary eye on those that would reform them.

William Hazlitt was born in Maidstone on 10 April 1778, the fourth child of an Irish Unitarian minister. The Reverend William Hazlitt and Grace his wife were revolutionaries and intellectual deists, thoroughly familiar with the teachings of Franklin, Priestley, Price and Godwin. Having such direct access to this radical spring was to create in their son what he described as 'that unfortunate attachment to a set of abstract phrases, such as liberty, truth, justice, humanity, honour. . . .' Weaned on absolutes, quite unable to judge anything without the use of both head and heart, Hazlitt inherited a code which lacked all social flexibility. What was not truth was a lie. And what made the world swing, far more terribly than merrily when the movement was honestly examined, was, for him, chiefly a set of myths. What was not liberty was slavery. Where and what was compromise? It was a word on which he stumbled, never seeing it, never able to convince himself of its uses. 'If we only think justly,' the good simple father told the son, 'we shall easily foil all the advocates of tyranny.' Hazlitt believed this and continued to believe it to the end of his life; and long after the great dream of replacing kingdoms (government by superstition) with republics (government by reason) was being repudiated as a kind of youthful excess by his friends. For them it was just a phase and to remind them of it became a breach of good manners. Students and young writers said wild things. The sign for them to accept the world as it was came when Napoleon crowned himself in Notre Dame. Their loyalties, they then knew, were elsewhere.

Hazlitt, dedicated to the revolution, became a lone voice speaking against the full blast of windy rhetoric needed to prosecute a national war. Allied to his revolutionary politics there were notions of personal freedom which not only disturbed and shocked, but which could endanger the kind of blanket patriotism required during a national emergency. He insisted that to deny discussion of any aspect of the human condition was cant. His contemporaries disagreed. What they could not bear in the public sense they called 'sedition' and what they shrank from in the personal sense they termed 'filth'. Hazlitt met invective with invective. His abuse was an art in itself. It coruscated with brilliant side issues. This was the Hazlitt who believed 'in the theoretical benevolence, and practical malignity of man', and who was able to turn every dirty thrust with such skill and panache that reading his rage and abuse at this length of time is as exhilarating as watching an immense gale from a safe room. Both enemy and friend hoped that these periodic great uproars, with their close engagement with life as it was, would somehow loosen Hazlitt from his untenable ideals and bring him into the ordinary arena of debate. Somewhere where his white face and black looks did not spoil the comfort of the day. But he could not be drawn into any cosy circle. He remained on the edge to remind friends who had done a deal with the establishment of the time when they would have refused to settle for little improvements on earth and pious hopes of heaven. Humanity might have had its heart's desire, as the young Wordsworth had plainly stated,

Not in Utopia . . .
But in the very world, which is the world
Of all of us – the place where in the end
We find our happiness, or not at all!

The chance to 'find happiness in the world of all of us' had occurred in a rare and wonderful way during Hazlitt's lifetime. Then had come this blank refusal on the part of the very heralds of change. How could they have gone back on all the bright promises? He was unable either to understand or to forgive.

I have never given the lie to my own soul. If I have felt any impression once, I feel it more strongly a second time; and I have no wish to revile or discard my best thoughts. There is at least a thorough keeping in what I write not a line that betrays a principle or disguises a feeling.

Hazlitt's youth had spanned an incredibly ecstatic moment in human history. Shackling traditions were being overhauled; the status quo questioned. The American colonies had freed themselves with surprising ease from Britain and the French people had rejected the hereditary principle in government. He was still a boy when Captain Tournay had ridden against the very symbol of the old power, the Bastille, and it had fallen. Hope reached out far beyond Paris at this event and involved change makers everywhere in the actual possibility of creating a society which up until this moment had seemed to belong to the geography of romance, or the hereafter. It was the first of Hazlitt's personality-shaking, soul-forming experiences. Others were to come and each would exalt and afflict him for the rest of his days. His anger was only equalled by his astonishment when, later on, others were to describe similar experiences and the commonsense they had grown out of them. Enthusiasm – a word then used to sum up a well meaning but weakheaded eagerness – should not be applied to the new and the non-traditional. Yet some had never presented enthusiasm more magnificently:

> *For mighty were the auxiliars which then stood*
> *Upon our side, we who were strong in love!*
> *Bliss was it in that dawn to be alive*
> *But to be young was very heaven!*

This was the clear trumpet note which Hazlitt heard in his head and felt in his heart until he died. He had stayed, the rest had retreated. (He had actually advanced, that was his trouble. Although so exactly late-Georgian Man, there was that in his nature which anticipated radical concepts and behaviour which are only now being accepted as possible alternatives to the existing structure.) He was often so far ahead that he was fighting evils which his contemporaries simply could not see. He called their conduct cant – a favourite epithet – but it was true that they often did not know what he was so angry about. When his strictures became too much, too outside anything they could comprehend, it became charitable to call him mad.

But for him there were worse things than being called mad. Nicknames. 'A nickname is the hardest stone that the devil can throw at a man. It will knock down any man's resolution. It will stagger his reason. It will tame his pride. . . . The unfavourable opinion of others gives you a bad opinion of yourself.' As so often happens, the least apt, the most moronically inspired nickname cut deepest. In March 1818 he was described as 'Pimpled Hazlitt' in *Blackwood's Magazine*. The fact of his notoriously sharp, set face with its pale clear skin became irrelevant. He believed that his entire image in the eyes of the world

142

had become pustulate and obscene because of this false description. It heralded the grand attack on him and he met it with the most dazzling set pieces of invective which, with the exception of Swift's, can be found in the language. But the damage was done all the same and, as he confessed to Bryan Procter ('Barry Cornwall'), 'it nearly put me underground'. Procter tragically summed it up when he said that Hazlitt 'was crowned by defamation'. There was another young friend who had reason to take sides with the figure in the pillory. Why should not Hazlitt speak out on anything and everything? What was the fear – it could be nothing less – which made the *Quarterly*, for instance, attempt to reduce his influence by declaring that his essays were dished up in 'broken English' and left behind them a trail of 'slime and filth'? Since when was the world unable to endure the truth? 'Hazlitt,' cried John Keats '. . . is your only good damner, and if ever I am damn'd – damn me if I shouldn't like him to damn me.'

But however deep the wounding, Hazlitt was never changed by it. Society was never to teach him a lesson. Sweet reason and threats alike could not sway his commitment, whether to an individual or a cause. 'These bargains are for life,' he said of his decisions, once made. Had not his father been equally uncompromising? Old Mr Hazlitt's outspokenness had forced him out of his comfortable living at Maidstone, and his protests about the barbarous treatment given by the English garrison to American prisoners of war in Ireland had made it necessary for him to leave that country. Greatly daring, he had in 1783 emigrated to the new and hopeful republic of the United States of America, only to find as much bigotry in Boston as in Kent or County Cork. William, aged eight, thought so little of his new land that, writing to his father, he said, 'that it would have been a great deal better if the white people had not found it out'. His only memory of America, from which he returned a year later, was the taste of barberries. In 1788 the family settled in Wem, Shropshire. Mr Hazlitt's gradual withdrawal from 'the world of all of us' to a dreamier habitation is described by William with absolute tenderness, and without accusation. A note of wistfulness too intrudes. Hazlitt, though never an agnostic, has parted from the comfort of his father's God. There will be no such retreat for him when the world becomes unendurable.

After being tossed about from congregation to congregation . . . he had been relegated to an obscure village, where he was to spend the last thirty years of his life, far from the only converse that he loved, the talk about disputed texts of Scripture, and the cause of civil and religious liberty. Here he passed his days, repining but resigned, in the study of the Bible, and the perusal of the Commentators – huge folios, not easily got through, one of which would outlast a winter! . . . Here were 'no figures nor no fantasies' – neither poetry nor philosophy – nothing to dazzle, nothing to excite modern curiosity; but to his lack lustre eyes there appeared . . . the sacred name JEHOVAH in capitals: pressed down by the weight of style, worn to the last fading thinness of the understanding, there were glimpses, glimmering notions of the patriarchal wanderings, with palm trees hovering in the horizon, and processions of camels at the distance of three thousand years . . . questions as to the date of the creation, predictions of the end of all things; the great lapses of time, the strange mutations of the globe were unfolded with the voluminous leaf, as it turned over; and though the soul might slumber with an hieroglyphic veil of inscrutable mysteries drawn over it, yet it was in a slumber ill-exchanged for all the sharpened realities of sense, wit, fancy or reason. My father's life was comparatively a dream; but it was a dream of infinity and eternity, of death, the resurrection, and a judgment to come!

Although Hazlitt had, at fifteen, rejected his father's wish that he should become a Unitarian minister, his awakening to faith had about it much of the detail of the classic Christian conversion, word, angel and all. The latter had luminous eyes, a mighty brow and large, soft childish lips only partly concealing bad teeth. At twenty-six, Samuel Taylor Coleridge had not had the same difficulties as Hazlitt in combining religion with intellectual freedom, and in 1797 was considering the offer of a Unitarian living in Shrewsbury. In January 1798 Hazlitt, who was now nineteen and had done little since leaving college four years before except to hide away in his room or in a field and read *Tom Jones* (another bargain for life), Rousseau and Burke, having read Coleridge's *Ode on the Departing Year*, and having heard that he was a revolutionary, walked the ten miles from Wem to Shrewsbury to hear him preach. Neither he nor the world as yet knew that this magical young man had completed *The Ancient Mariner* or that he had begun the regular use of drugs. The sermon was spectacular. Coleridge's text was 'And he went up into the mountain to pray, HIMSELF, ALONE.' It was about the real Christ path, about pacifism (Britain was expecting to be invaded by Napoleon), poetry and isolation. Hazlitt listened and was both crushed and elated by the personal implications the sermon had for him. The following Tuesday Coleridge came to Wem for a dinner of Welsh mutton and boiled turnips, and stayed the night. Hazlitt walked with the poet as far as the sixth milestone when he returned to Shrewsbury in the morning. Hazlitt's walk was straight and Coleridge's meandering and constantly crossing the younger man's path. Hazlitt saw that they did not collide and listened to the quite unimaginable flood of talk. All was changed, all was new. His confusion and dullness had gone. His joy in Coleridge was almost like that of a lover at times, making him sick and exhilarated by turn. When, on parting, the poet invited him to visit him in Somerset, where he and Wordsworth were collaborating on a book of poems (*Lyrical Ballads*), Hazlitt's happiness was overwhelming.

Years later, in one of the most wonderful descriptions of a turning-point in life – 'My First Acquaintance With Poets' – Hazlitt recalled the moment exactly.

On my way back, I had a sound in my ears, it was the voice of Fancy: I had a light before me, it was the face of Poetry. . . . I had an uneasy, pleasurable sensation all the time, till I was to visit him. During these months the chill breath of winter gave me a welcoming; the vernal air was balm and inspiration to me. The golden sunsets, the silver star of evening, lighten me on my way to new hopes and prospects. *I was to visit Coleridge in the spring.* This circumstance was never absent from my thoughts, and mingled with all my feelings. I wrote to him at the time proposed, and received an answer postponing my intended visit for a week or two, but very cordially urging me to complete my promise then. This delay did not damp, but rather increased my ardour. In the meantime I went to Llangollen Vale, by way of initiating myself in the mysteries of natural scenery; and I must say I was enchanted with it. . . . That valley was to me (in a manner) the cradle of a new existence. . .!

Thus the first meeting with Coleridge and Wordsworth possessed all the dramatic power of a curtain rising on a tragedy whose first scene is the deceptive and lulling idyll. Yet, in spite of what was to follow, when Wordsworth, sunk deep in reaction and apprehensive of what the world would think of his youthful friendship with a man who was now a notorious radical, was not above spreading gossip about Hazlitt's sex life in an effort to discredit him, and Coleridge, as marvellous during this period as his own drinker of the milk of Paradise, had sunk into a comfort-seeking hulk, the essayist allowed nothing to dim or qualify the glory of his twentieth year. 'What I have once set my hand to, I take the consequences of . . .' We see Coleridge at this moment as one who commits others to great doctrines which he is unable to follow himself, and we see Hazlitt's frightening vulnerability for the first time. 'My First Acquaintance With Poets' reveals, as well as happiness, that ultimate defencelessness which marks all his writing.

It was art, however, and not literature which received its fillip from this meeting, although in Hazlitt's mind at this time the two activities had begun their inseparable fascination for him – 'Till I began to paint, or till I became acquainted with the author of *The Ancient Mariner*, I could neither write nor speak.' But painting for Hazlitt was to be neither a career nor mere interest. Mania might best describe it. It is doubtful if any words – his beloved Shakespeare's excepted – were ever to involve him heart and soul as did Rembrandt, Titian and Raphael. Throughout his life he thrust these masters forward like a salvation-bringing icon, insisting, 'Believe! believe!' It was not enough that he should become rapturous in picture galleries, he had to bring others to this state, for he knew nothing to equal it. A few weeks after meeting the poets he left home to become an art student in London. His hero now – for Hazlitt was a man who insisted on heroes – was James Northcote.

Hazlitt's conception of painting was strictly retrospective. The nearer it turned back to its sublime source – Titian, Rembrandt, Raphael – the greater it became. Northcote's special attraction was that he had known Sir Joshua Reynolds and his circle, and, as one who had had direct contact with an artist who had reaffirmed the inviolable laws of art, he possessed a special mystique for Hazlitt. Eventually he Boswellised the gossipy old man in *Conversations with Northcote*, a book which contains many amusing anecdotes including one about

Romney and a painter friend first seeing the Sistine Chapel, and the friend gasping, 'Egad, George, we're bit!' Hazlitt, the entirely open and inquiring, the radical and the sceptic in most matters connected with human activity, became fiercely orthodox and academic the moment he entered a gallery. Nor could he ever see a picture without needing to place a written description beside it. He quite baffled old Northcote – 'Very odd – very odd! I can make nothing of him. He is the strangest being I ever met with.' But when, in 1821, he published his essay *On the Pleasure of Painting*, the need for such an enthusiasm is explained. Reading it in the light of his multiple tragedy, his inability to relate to everything from the accepted pattern of politics to the average notions of love, we see his faith in painting as a great stabilising factor in his sad, triumphant life. Old Mr Hazlitt, after half a lifetime's engagement with callousness, had sought Jehovah's arm. His son, fighting the same evils but never to know a moment's rest, found in landscapes and portraits harmonious statements from which he could draw strength. Art was for Hazlitt a mixture of religion and medicine, and he envied those engaged in it.

No one thinks of disturbing a landscape painter at his task: he seems a kind of magician, the privileged genius of the place. Whenever a Claude, a Wilson, has introduced his own portrait in the foreground of a picture, we look at it with interest (however ill it may be done) feeling that it is the portrait of one who was quite happy at the time, and how glad we should be to change places with him.

Where his own painting was concerned, Hazlitt was a fundamentalist, restating the dictums of the old masters as faithfully as he could. He painted his father in the manner of Rembrandt and Charles Lamb in the style of Titian. On two occasions, in 1802 and 1824, he visited the Louvre. No one in search of Europe's great pictures need have gone further, for Napoleon had looted the Continental galleries and palaces of their treasures and had heaped them up in Paris. There had never been so great a concentration of the major European schools before and certainly not one so easily available to the ordinary people. Hazlitt, a shabby student of twenty four when he first sat copying one of his beloved Titians in rooms so recently closed to all but the privileged few, felt that he was present at some kind of breakthrough in the frustrating rules governing humanity. 'You have enriched the museum of Paris with 300 masterpieces . . . which it required thirty centuries to produce,' Napoleon had told his troops. For Hazlitt, this was not the customary spoils of war but a taking of art out of the exclusive hereditary sector and making it available to all. In France, he heard tales of the Emperor's taste, charm, courage and general superiority at every hand, and there began that process – and one involving the hero of all heroes – by which he could accept Napoleon as the enemy of absolutism and all the stale systems devolving from it.

Wordsworth, who was also in France in 1802 – the Peace of Amiens had brought the British across the Channel in their thousands, all eager to see this sensationally transformed nation – watched Napoleon's imperialism and lost all belief in revolution. He wrote sneeringly of the eagerness of the recent destroyers of the Bourbons to

> *bend the knee*
> *In France, before the new born Majesty!*

For Hazlitt, Napoleon remained the hope of the world and when, at Waterloo, the final crushing came, his despair was terrifying. 'It is not to be believed how the destruction of Napoleon affected him,' wrote Benjamin Robert Haydon. 'He seemed prostrated in mind and body, he walked about unwashed, unshaved, hardly sober by day and always intoxicated by night, literally, without exaggeration, for weeks; until at length, wakening as it were from a stupor, he at once left off all stimulating liquors, and never touched them after.' (This latter teetotalism was not the good thing it might appear, for Hazlitt took to drinking green tea of such strength and in such quantities that it probably contributed to the stomach cancer which was to kill him.) Another witness of Hazlitt at this time was Thomas Talfourd, the first biographer of Lamb. 'When I first met Hazlitt in the year 1815,' he wrote, 'he was staggering under the blow of Waterloo. The reappearance of his imperial idol on the coast of France, and his triumphant march to Paris, like a fairy vision, had excited his admiration and sympathy to the utmost pitch; and though in many respects sturdily English in feeling, he could scarcely forgive the valour of the conquerors . . .' He added, 'On this subject only was he "eaten up with passion", on all others, he was the fairest, the most candid of reasoners.'

Hazlitt's last great task was a monumental *Life of the Emperor*. It was mostly written in Paris and he intended it as both a vindication of Bonaparte and the pinnacle of his own career. He also relied on it to bring him some real money and to put a stop, at least for some time, to the hand-to-mouth existence of essay writing. But whereas these had seemed to simply fly into print with no difficulty beyond that created by Rightist claques, the great *Life of Napoleon* seemed hardly able to totter from the press. Nor was this all. Like some hideously uncalled for blow from a person for whose sake one has endured much, the publishers went bankrupt, involving Hazlitt in a loss of £200 when, with his last illness approaching, he was in desperate need of money. The Emperor who had alighted like the bird of promise had turned into an albatross. Hazlitt could have found reasons for getting Napoleon off his neck. It would have made life easier. It would certainly have widened his influence as a radical journalist, for there were those who saw his defence of Napoleon as something which at the best was irrational and at the worst, mad. But as he wrote to William Gifford:

The reason why I have not changed my principle with some of the persons alluded to [Wordsworth, Coleridge and Southey] is, that I had a natural inveteracy of understanding which did not bend to fortune or circumstances. I was not a poet, but a metaphysician; and I suppose that the conviction of an abstract principle is alone a match for the prejudices of absolute power. The love of truth is the best foundation for the love of liberty. In this sense, I might have repeated –

Love is not love that alteration finds:
O, no! it is an ever-fixed mark
That looks on tempests and is never shaken.

Besides, I had another reason. I owed something to truth, for she had done something for me. Early in life I had made (what I thought) a metaphysical discovery; and after that it was too late to think of retracting. My pride forbad it: my understanding revolted at it. I could not do better than go on as I had begun. I too, worshipped at no unhallowed shrine, and served in no mean presence. I had laid my hand on the ark, and could not turn back!

To trace the second disastrous strand in Hazlitt's life, we have to return to his second meeting with the poets. This occurred in the summer of 1803. They were kind and welcoming but they were different. They sat to the almost penniless artist for their portraits, but when they introduced him to their benefactor, Sir George Beaumont, a famous patron, he disgraced them by airing his radical views and contradicting Coleridge, Sir George's latest protégée, in his – Sir George's – actual presence. Other complications followed. Hazlitt drifted along with the poets, now including Southey, all that autumn, becoming more and more bewildered by the great change which had come over his friends, and feeling upset. On 14 December 1803 he left. Southey, writing at the time, makes it sound a perfectly ordinary departure and even goes so far as to describe Hazlitt as a painter 'of real genius'. Wordsworth, writing twelve years later, had a very different tale to tell. Hazlitt, the moralist on all things, had when staying with the poets in the Lake District attempted to violate a village girl against her will and it was only through the generosity of his friends that he had escaped from the indignant country youths, and possibly from transportation! Charles Lamb, who received this news from Wordsworth in December 1814, laughingly reduced it to a pastoral frolic but Henry Crabb Robinson, who actually heard the details from Wordsworth's own lips, was so fascinated by them that, in the selfish manner of educated prudes, he resorted to Latin when setting them down in his diary. An obscene gossip proliferated at once from this story and from now until the close of his life Hazlitt's name carried with it the overtones of depravity.

Wordsworth's motive for making the serious charge stemmed from his volte-face politics of 1802-3. Both he and Coleridge had sided with France during the first half of the Napoleonic war because they regarded their own country's action as a war against the birth of democracy. But they were able to change sides when the second war was decided upon because they saw that Napoleon was no more democratic than the Bourbons and was in fact planning a great imperial military adventure. Eagerness to begin this second war, which had actually been declared by the time Hazlitt reached Keswick, was rowdily apparent and he saw, to his disgust, that Coleridge of all people was in the van of 'the war whoop', as he called it. Coleridge had, in fact, invented Napoleon's most damaging nickname – 'the Corsican'. Such fervent patriotism was reassuring to Coleridge's new patron, the High Tory Sir George Beaumont, and came as a natural relief to Wordsworth in his new mood of Olympian withdrawal to the Cumberland mountains. Hazlitt's disgust at their revised positions when he arrived in 1803 was one thing, but his morbid pursuit of them in print as turncoats – something they could not have imagined the confused young artist would ever be able to do – was another. Hazlitt, fighting his own private war for liberty, was a menace. The note of accusation never ceased. The accuser needed to be accused – but of what?

Because his enemies so often reached through his private life in order to discredit his politics and, in Wordsworth's case, even his literary opinions – for one reason why the Lakes escapade was made public in 1814 was fear of what Hazlitt might write about *The Excursion*, which was published that year – it is necessary to take a brief look at Hazlitt and women. They were very important to him but his neglect of 'manner' in his approach to them and what seemed like a tacit assumption on his part that they would reciprocate his feelings without going through the usual charade of high-flown talk and artificial gestures, got him nowhere. His lack of success, and subsequent fear and hostility towards 'young ladies', was well known among his friends, who found it very amusing. Crabb Robinson had seen his nervous confusion and shock when, still a boy, some well-bred girls had teased him during a holiday at Bury St Edmunds. It enabled the diarist to state, when the outcry against him as an immoralist was at its height, that 'Like other gross sensualists, he had a horror of the society of ladies, especially of smart and handsome and modest young women.'

Hazlitt was married twice, each time to a 'lady'. But an early Rousseau-like idealisation of simple, unsophisticated girls, a conception of companionship which at first had for him a dreamy innocence, grew naturally into a sexual desire for such women. Although they let him down every bit as much as the ladies, his forgiveness of their inability to accept him as a lover showed that in these encounters he was not self-blind. P. P. Howe, his best biographer, sees the Keswick incident as the sketch, as it were, of the marvellous and remorselessly worked out *Liber amoris* story in which both the bathos and the splendour of obsessional sexual love have been set down on the page in their entirety. It is the type of love which those who have not experienced it call infatuation because to them it is undignified and pathetic. Hazlitt in love was, to his friends, a comic sight, to his enemies, a disgusting one. Hazlitt did not pretend to find love, as he recognized it, in either of his wives. The first union, to Sarah Stoddart, was almost as much an arranged marriage (by Charles and Mary Lamb) as if the bride and groom had been Chinese. Lamb, for whom Hazlitt's sex life was the only thing about his friend he could never take seriously, laughed so much during the wedding that he was nearly turned out of church. Sarah was to bring Hazlitt little happiness in herself but she gave him a son, whom he both mothered and fathered, his wife being cold in such matters and, anyway, frequently away from home on great walking tours. Neither lover nor home maker, she was yet what he vaguely wanted a woman to be – a free agent, an untrammelled soul. Sarah Hazlitt was, in fact, a New Woman born a century before her time. How she would have enjoyed 'rational' clothes for all that hiking! By the time of their – inevitable – divorce, in Edinburgh, her craving for the open road forced her to walk nearly 150 miles through the Scottish countryside during the proceedings. As well as his adored son, she gave her husband one other thing that pleased him, a small cottage in Winterslow, Wiltshire.

It was from this address, immediately after his marriage in 1808, that he began to bombard the London editors with outlines for literary projects, and that he wrote his Life of Holcroft. The choice of subject was interesting. Thomas Holcroft, who had died the year before, had been a friend of Tom Paine and a believer in Godwin's revolutionary ideas. He had also been a stable boy who had become a successful novelist and playwright.

But neither painting, his wife's fortune of £80 a year, nor the solid books he was managing to turn out, met the expenses of married life, and in the autumn of 1812 Hazlitt, with Lamb's help, became

Parliamentary reporter for the *Morning Chronicle*, a Whig newspaper edited by James Perry, whose snobbery and scant scholarship did not prevent him from becoming one of the most progressive figures in nineteenth century journalism. Within a year of accepting this job, Hazlitt was filling the columns of the *Morning Chronicle* with far more exciting things than could be heard in the House of Commons, essays such as *On the Love of Life* and brilliant accounts of what was taking place on the London stage. Both these discursive essays, in which profound and extraordinary matters were dealt with wittily and with a personal conviction which made an immediate contact with the reader, and the dramatic criticism, were of a kind previously unknown to journalism. The excellence and unusualness of his work provided Hazlitt, now in his early thirties, with the influence which he could never have hoped to have derived from any other literary activity. Whatever the world thought of his politics, both his style and the strangely intimate tone of his arguments were things which no one cared to miss. 'Once he had started,' says P. P. Howe, 'we find his dramatic criticisms, art criticisms, political letters and leading articles, "Common-places", and contributions from "An English Metaphysician", all going up together in Mr Perry's columns.'

As this hardly-to-be-expected burst of literary power and excellence coincided with such national self examinings as the meaning of patriotism, inquests on the value of the French Revolution and what to do with Napoleon, a reactionary Britain – including the Lake District – saw with horror that a Daniel had come to judgement. Worse, Hazlitt's very catholicity, his perverse refusal – or inability – to specialise in a subject, as other men did, made him hard to handle. A piece that, when produced by the eighteenth century essayists and their followers, would have contained a few ounces of elegantly wrapped morality, often contained an ethical explosion when it left Hazlitt's hand. He lacked all restraint. Anything which threatened the total liberty of the individual, the little deceits by which society managed to get by, the areas of human behaviour which it was 'civilised' to ignore, speciousness of all kinds and *cant* – his four-letter word for describing the talk which covered the naked truth – these were his natural targets. He attacked them with a mixture of gaiety and rage. Those who had

153

reason to fear waited nervously for his blow. His concept of truth as a once revealed thing to which a man remained loyal no matter what happened later on placed everybody in the somewhat religious position of either the 'faithful' or the 'apostates'. Southey, who at nineteen had written a revolutionary play called *Wat Tyler*, was aghast to find something he hoped the world had forgotten being reissued by a pirate publisher at the very moment he had accepted the Laureateship. Hazlitt gave no quarter in this affair, and others with radical pasts which, up to now, they thought well buried, shivered. He was no believer in the woolliness which society permitted to shelter public and private lives, but however much people might deplore his stark honesty, they could not forbear to look.

Yet he was never simply out for a scoop, and journalism in the ordinary sense of news-plus-comment meant little to him. A magnificent writer who would have preferred to work quietly on metaphysical treatises in the tradition of Locke and Hobbes, he was driven to the newspapers and the magazines by the need to make money. He wrote spasmodically and with a certain resentment. He was daydreaming and indolent. His real pleasure never stemmed from work but from drifting, idling, unplanned days made up of lying on the chalky turf of the Wiltshire downs, playing racquets on the St Martin's Street court and chatting to strangers or chance acquaintances. Like so many artists, he was never reconciled to one or other of the country-versus-the-town choice. His compassion for the village people of England during their extreme misery of the 1820s also showed indications of his personal fear of them. As a village-intellectual, on and off for the best part of his life, he could not forget the countryman's narrowness and meanness of spirit, and as a townsman he could never be sufficiently man of the world to exist without shock amidst scenes of accepted greed, indifference and hypocrisy. In both village and town he recovered his shaken belief in life by reading the poets and by looking at pictures.

Yet, although shy of contact with the masses and often scathing about them, he saw them as few people did at the time – as the real England, crushed by the land evictions, reduced and starved by the famine caused by the war, and tragically inarticulate. His emergence as a trenchant and controversial writer, in 1807, came with *A Reply to the*

Essay on Population, when his attack on Malthus revealed his brilliant radical pen. The Reverend T.R.Malthus was exactly what the establishment needed after the drums of revolution had petered out, a clergyman prophet able to supply fact and figure for the inevitability of inequality in human society. For the ruling class Malthus had provided a mandate for going on as before. To back his theory he had put forward a plan for dealing with 'the poor', that inconvenient nine tenths of the nation. This included, among many other things, notions for restraining fatherhood among the rural males and the blue print for the extensions of the Poor Law which was to harass countless simple families right up to the First World War. Hazlitt's attack on Malthus was violent and emotional but it displayed his freedom, and less apprehensive friends than Wordsworth and Coleridge came forward to acknowledge him. Among these was Charles Lamb, Hazlitt's senior by only three and a half years, but in whose (much tried) relationship there was a stable, protective element suggesting a much older man. The great difference, in fact, between Lamb and Hazlitt was that the former seemed to have received the gift of perpetual early middle-age and the latter, with his moodiness, his iconoclasm, his physical energy, his hero-worship, his passionate love and his general recklessness, appeared to have been cursed with everlasting youth. To outgrow innocence – i.e., one's initial reflexes to important matters – was for Hazlitt a sin. James Knowles, one of his disciple-like young friends, said, 'There was ore in him, and rich, but his maturer friends were blind to it. I saw it. He was a man to whom I would have submitted my life.'

From 1816 onwards Hazlitt's work has to be seen against the churning unrest which provoked the government to suspend Habeas Corpus in 1817 and which was violently epitomised in the massacre at Peterloo on 16 August 1819. His collected essays from the *Examiner* were published under the title of *The Round Table*, and dedicated to Lamb. The essays so excelled the usual literature of radical protest that one critic described it as being 'like a whale's back in a sea of prose'. We have a number of glimpses of him at this period, including the one Haydon painted in his enormous *Entry into Jerusalem*, where Hazlitt is shown 'looking at Christ as an investigator'. The same year as this portrait appeared, Wordsworth was writing to the artist, 'The miscreant

Hazlitt continues, I have heard, to abuse Southey, Coleridge and myself in the *Examiner*. I hope you do not associate with the Fellow, he is not a proper person to be admitted into respectable society . . .' A less hostile witness gives this vivid description.

His face was indeed indifferent, and his movements shy and awkward; but there was something in his earnest irritable face, his restless eyes, his black hair, combed backwards and curling (not too resolutely) about a well shaped head, that was very striking. . . . At home, his style of dress (or undress) was perhaps slovenly, because there was no one to please; but he always presented a very clean and neat appearance when he went abroad. His mode of walking was loose, weak and unsteady; although his arms displayed strength, which he used to put forth when he played at raquets with Martin Burney and others. . . . His violence (if violence he had), was of very rare occurrence. He was extremely patient. . . . Had he been as temperate in his political views as in his cups, he would have escaped the slander that pursued him through life.

Temperance, however, was not something which Hazlitt understood. 'When I see a spirit of intolerance I see a great Devil,' he said.

This, then, was how he looked at the moment when he was at the height of his power as a writer. The man who in life so disliked being touched and human contact generally, and accepted friendship on chilling terms – and then complained of lack of warmth: 'I want to know why everybody has such a dislike of me' – was, on the page, to generate a glow which admitted the reader at once to his intimate presence.

In 1820 Hazlitt and Lamb were contributing to the *London Magazine* the wonderful essays which were to become, respectively, the first volume of *Table Talk* and the *Essays of Elia*. It was also the year of disaster. Hazlitt lost all hope 'I believe in the theoretical benevolence and practical malignity of man' and eventually almost lost his reason. Why? Because at forty-three he had fallen in love at first sight with the nineteen year old girl who waited on him in the two back rooms of a lodging-house in Southampton Buildings. 'Love at first sight is only realising an imagination that has always haunted us . . . our dream is out at last . . .' At twenty six, the Lakes girl had led him on, laughing, and (according to Wordsworth) he had struck her. Now he was middle aged, Sarah Walker was to do the same, with 'mock embraces' and lips 'as common as the stairs'. Yet sometimes she smiled, and in analysing the effect this had on him, he had immortalised her. His refusal not to treat the situation rationally – with a straightforward sexuality – bewildered Sarah and puzzled his friends, to whom he was compelled to pour out his troubles. Strangers, too, had to listen to every humiliating detail of the affair, for he was an obsessed creature – 'the fool of love'. It was the kind of behaviour which appeared to justify De Quincey's later verdict that Hazlitt 'wilfully placed himself in collision with all the interests that were in the sunshine of this world . . .' The love affair, grotesquely compounded with divorce proceedings concerning the other Sarah, and followed by a nervous breakdown during which he considered suicide, produced the extraordinary *Liber amoris*. Once he had been merely bitter when a simple girl let him down – 'Choose a mistress from among your equals. . . . Those in an inferior station to yourself will doubt your good intentions. . . . They will be ignorant of the meaning of half you say, and laugh at the rest' – now he gave himself up to a total declaration of the nature of the only sexual love he understood. The *Liber amoris* endorsed posterity's claim to distrust him long after his politics had ceased to offend. Robert Louis Stevenson thought of writing Hazlitt's biography, then discovered this book and withdrew in horror. Augustus Birrell was simply astonished that a grown man could let himself in for anything so idiotic – 'The loves of the middle aged are never agreeable subject matter . . . a fool at forty is a fool indeed . . .' He added, '*Liber amoris* now sinks below the stage, and joins the realm of things unspeakable . . .' Charles Morgan, in an excellent introduction to the book (1948), reminds us that Hazlitt's unguarded account of love and sexual madness was published at the same time as Stendhal's *De l'amour*, and he says that 'the whole story of the *Liber amoris* is a flawless example of Stendahl's theory of crystalisation'. To write it, Hazlitt had to abandon the only thing which could have made it even remotely socially acceptable – dignity. It was not 'manly' declared *Blackwood's*. This it all too shatteringly was. Love is frequently a pitiable state.

Recovered from the débâcle, he settled down to his familiar unsettled life, working when he must but now with a greater sense of his own coherence. In 1825 came *The Spirit of the Age* and a year abroad with his second wife, the all but unknown Isabella Bridgwater. Also a meeting with Stendhal – 'my friend Mr Beyle'. He returned looking ill. His writing grew in its intensity, breaking in on the privacy of those who read it with irresistible and sometimes unbearable news. There was no escape from his meaning; the language which conveyed it shone with precision – 'I hate to see a load of bandboxes go along the street, and I hate to see a parcel of big words without anything in them.' The exposition of an idea would start out on the page in light, happy phrases which threatened no man's complacency, and then the skilful strengthening would begin, and intellectual involvement would bind the reader. Each essay shows the build up of numerous small climaxes, such as are sometimes employed in the novel. Excitement and expectation mount. Hazlitt is the word juggler who never misses; his almost casual use of ornament, epigram and fancy is hypnotic. Some, like De Quincey, resented that they should be morally got at by this 'abrupt, insulated, capricious . . . and non sequacious style'. Hazlitt's method of writing essays had something in common with his action on the St Martin's Street fives-court. He would begin by pleasantly spinning his subject around, work along various entertaining possibilities until he found a possible break through, then score for all he was worth. He never regarded journalism as an inferior literary activity. His only regret was the voracious way it had of swallowing up work, and thus the time he would have preferred to spend in a kind of unambitious reverie. 'All that is worth remembering of life is the poetry of it.' Yet it was, as Virginia Woolf saw, the chafing and goading of many of life's unpoetic asides which kept Hazlitt on the stretch. One of his most amazing accomplishments is his abolition of the time barrier, not for himself – he is primarily the spokesman for the inarticulate, the exploited, the self-deceived and the less brave inhabitants of George IV's England; the conscience of an era – but for future readers. He has an uncanny ability to involve us across the generations in his hopes, hates, enthusiasms, fury and sensuality. It is also possible to see in him the warring extremes of the Puritan nature. He is a writer who must always remain more than 'works' and it is both thrilling and sobering when one investigates the latter to find so much flesh and blood, so much anger and so very much love. His was a uniquely unsublimated life. For him, writing never took the place of living.

He died of cancer on 18 September 1830 in a poor little room at 6 Frith Street, Soho. Bryan Procter heard him speaking his last words in a voice 'resembling the faint scream I have heard from birds'. He was fifty-two.

LIZZIE PYE
An Autobiography
Edward Blishen, 1982

Reading the new Edward Blishen (who is an expert on the matter) made me think what a curious book might be written on the way in which literary children have managed to deal with their parentage. It would encapsulate plain duty, pure hatred, vengeance, satire, unbounded criticism, guilt and passionate love. But whatever it was that got put down on the page, a common obstacle would have been surmounted: that intimacy of the relationship itself which keeps most of us a tolerable distance from the real truths.

Yet dealing with mother or father is clearly a creative preoccupation for quite a lot of writers, and has been for centuries. Fair copy, if you can bring yourself to look; amazing copy, if you dare to penetrate; the tenderest of all loves, should such a love exist and you are able to confess it. Given the compulsion to get one of them down, father is usually the easiest to tackle and, if one is a writing son, there is now social approval for giving him one in the eye.

But mother: she has to be a very different tale. To tell it, one has to cut into oneself as well as into her. Blishen has done both, although with little evidence of having had to steel himself for the task. It is all due to the unflinching nature of what they saw in each other, and of what they were when he was a boy, and of what they had become when they were, respectively, very old and no longer young. A long process for which his book had to wait.

Although its title is his mother's maiden name, it is subtitled 'an autobiography', and this is its key. Not her life with his own and his children's dangling like a pendant from it, but a series of generational waves in which the family strength transfers itself across almost a century. The movement was precarious in socio-economic terms, as most family movement was over this period, but the delight in being alive was strong enough, and Blishen's latest book is, as well as much else, a vindication of his mother's claim (not that she made it in so many words) to have had a full and unique existence in this world.

If there is a filial element it is this, the uncovering of Lizzie's modest life to exhibit its inner brightness, drama and vitality. On the face of it, she possessed very little, this little between-maid from Dickens's London with her minuscule education and malapropisms, her more than seventy years' dominance by an egotist-husband who, exasperatingly, managed to remain irresistible, and her other 'disadvantages' (as they would be described). Yet, as her son has the language to prove, she had a great deal. His constant pleasure in her for a start. As 'next of king', as she called him, he writes to preserve utterly the sense and flavour of someone who, born in the late nineteenth century, wandered on and on through most of the twentieth without quite taking it in, so to speak. It is a study in isolation, for although her son in no way grew apart from her, culturally and emotionally, her origins kept her alone.

Blishen tells of her need to touch and embrace which became frantic and unconsciously erotic towards the end, as she beguiled almost anyone, from other old people in the home to her grandchildren, to accept her as a flesh-and-blood creature of the present. Blishen's problem was how to prevent Lizzie slipping into Barrie-like sentiment or into a memorable character-sketch. But he need not have worried; he has got what most parental recorders have not, a lack of obliqueness and a decided nerve.

He faces Lizzie dying, missing nothing, though never clinically. She is a Victorian and he allows her a fine deathbed scene. But everything which precedes this receives his challenging full glance, and as well as being an often very funny and uncomfortable piece of mother-observation, Blishen gives a profound account of ageing in the modern

160

world, and in the circumstances which have now become commonplace. It is not really admirable and he never pretends that it is. It is what happened to Lizzie and what will no doubt happen to the rest of us, those last days with strangers in cheerful yellow rooms until we or our savings run out. Cataracts, senescence, spinning chatter.

Set skilfully between the grouped opening, and closing chapters which deal with Lizzie past and Lizzie passing is the balancing factor or corrective of Blishen's setting up house in a London suburb after the war. He and his family live in a flat underneath that of friends. There is a ramshackle garden and literary ambitions, hardly any money and the gradual arrival of better things, including a distracting au pair. It is a tranquil period beyond war noise, and with no notion of the racket to come. He uses it to write *Roaring Boys*, discover marriage and to take stock of his universe. Lizzie, still firmly controlled by the handsome Selfridges van-boy-turned civil servant, dreams of a riotous widowhood which is not to be. At the least sign that their child looks like becoming a writer, mothers and fathers should pull their socks up.

DOUBLE ENTRY
Richard Middleton

He remains one of those individuals, like Connie Gilchrist, Hannah Glasse or Mackworth Dolben, about whom one knows practically nothing or practically everything. We, who are, of course, in the latter category, will find it impossible to join the shrill audiences at the Palladium, Olympia, the Scala and the Queen's Theatre during the next few weeks without expecting to see any minute the arrival of a stocky, sullen young man edging his way down the clamorous aisles to his seat in the pit. Those to whom he is not even a name will once more take a look at the hammy old transvestist chestnut called panto and marvel again at the power it has to draw its huge innocent audiences in this knowing and over-entertained age. The secret of its success is also the secret of the Pantomime Man's failure.

Richard Barham Middleton was born at Staines in 1882 into that prim clerking class whose arbiter was Mr Pooter. It was an appalling day for Richard Middleton when the full meaning of his situation in life dawned upon him. For a poor young clerk in 1903 there was small joy in an endless prospect of lower middle-class rectitude, in the certainty of a life-time of cheap top-hats, paper cuffs and chops at Slater's. Particularly if one knew one's self to be a poet. Poets did not hope to look like clerks in 1903.

From our plastic eminence we look down somewhat fondly at the Edwardians. We see with affection miles and miles of bobbly chenille, endless marble mantelpieces *garnée*, oceans of Nottingham lace frothing at the bows of countless squat stucco terraces; the despised (and despising) skivvy lodged on high in her oilclothed attic and a horse-bus pulled right up against the area railing so that afternoon tea, with doilies and three kinds of bread and butter, is lacerated by the crossing sweeper's screaming shovel as it whisks up the droppings. 'Gissing . . .' we say. Even the million or so City clerks balancing their thin shanks on a million pitch-pine stools, their slender wrists aching on cold ledgers, have now the warmest literary charm. For a moment we are back into what the interior decorators persist in recognising as Spacious Days, but which, for Pooterdom, were the very narrowest days human nature has ever been called upon to squeeze itself into. Fine manners, percolating downwards, had reached Pooterdom as a finger-crooking sediment which stiffened it against art, deafened it to reason and set it, like a Ptolemaic frieze, in the most respectful attitudes. It was Leonard Bast's world, not Helen Schlegel's and poor Richard Middleton, being a far cleverer person than Forster's hero, regarded it with horror.

So, being trapped, what for it but to escape. People were less concerned with the moral implications of escapism in 1903 than we are now. If you could, you did. For Middleton there was no going forward – that would only mean sinking yet deeper into the slough of the Royal Exchange Assurance Company. So he went back, or did his best to, retreating to a vision of childhood.

'Feb. 5th,' he notes in his journal, 'Went to *Alice in Wonderland* . . . exactly twenty times during the run . . .' And then, towards the end of

December, 'I went to the theatre ninety-seven times this year . . .'

Of those ninety-seven visits we can be sure that most of them were to the pantomime. Middleton adored it, its gaudy warmth and its optimistic everything-possible transmogrification, its guileless harlequinade and its sensuous music-hall bombast. Above all, its unreality. He worshipped the great gold and red shell of the traditional theatre, its tiers banked with flouncing little girls, purple uncles, grave boys, florid aunts, creaking nannies and mysteriously isolated adults like himself. He said it was like 'being marooned in a turbulent sea of children'.

Middleton's short stories and the curiously virtuous *Journal of a Clerk* hold one man's key to the meaning of this annual gallimaufry of puns and patter, stupendous manipulations of scenery, interchanges of sex and the bravura morality of the finale, itself a happy secular Magnificat in which the mighty give up their seats to the humble and weak. Nobody who has read Middleton can go to the pantomime and not cast a glance round the boisterous auditorium before the heavy curtains tremble and go up just to make sure that the morose phantom from the Royal Exchange Assurance Company is present. He is unmistakeable. From a distance, it is true, he might be the young William Morris. His thick dark beard – he had never touched his face with a razor in his life – quite fails to hide a puzzled resentment in his expression. Nor does it hide, as he hoped it might, a large wet-cherry lower lip. But his eyes are serene and beautiful and his shoulders are very broad – as indeed they would need to be to carry their outsize chip – and his hands are plump and sad and white. He is not entirely admirable, but then how few of us are.

We are watching a man who has exchanged the too solid streets of Tooting for the primrose paths of the Surrey, the Old Britannia, Drury Lane and the Lyceum. We see him being artificially revived with the delicious stale air he loves. The smell of camphor and oranges, dirty plush and best clothes, the acrid stench of massed children; he rejoices in them all. The boxes are stacked like Sickerts and the fiddles grind away. In a minute Dan Leno will strut and leer, and corrugate his raddled cheeks and be suggestive, and it will all be received with a roar which shakes the chandeliers. But one tongue will not have added its acclaim. Belle Bilton (later, Countess of Clancarty) might smile right

163

at him in the way women once did, showing just a hint of her pebble-white teeth, but even she will not destroy the sturdy Middleton's inherent sadness. Only the children can do that. It is their laughter, and not what causes it, that carried him away. He follows the children and not the stare. Little Tich, Johnny Danvers, Ellaline Terriss, Fred Emney, Queenie Leighton, Marie George, Fred Eastman and Ada Reeve shout and bawl from their spangly Hymettus. All is sweetness, all is electric lights. But he has payed for ooohs! and aaahs! and shining eyes.

There comes a time when the most applauded curtain must fall for the last time. One cannot emigrate to a pantomime. Unfortunately for Richard Middleton there was no life worth living outside it. He had striven, by casting himself adrift in the resounding happiness of multitudinous children, to trace his way home to the glory and the dream. He failed. On 1st December 1911, at some lodgings he had taken at 10, rue de Joncker in Brussels, and by the aid of chloroform, he drifted into a less transient oblivion than that offered by the theatre. He was twenty-nine. The same week, in London, Renee Mayer in *Hop O' My Thumb* was singing tritely to a huge audience of nannies and children.

Mid . . . mingled hopes and fears
We still would seek to charm your eyes and ears . . .

A few days before his death, a little girl lodging in the same street as Middleton called after him, *Monsieur le tricheur!*. The dispute had been about marbles, but perhaps the child was right in other respects. It is worse to cheat at life than to cheat at games. The world he fled from hurried on. London Bridge carried its sable tide of clerks. In Wandsworth, Pimlico and Fulham doorsteps were whitened and scrapers blackened. Correctness of dress, of demeanour and address was worshipped and glorified. Pooterdom was at its zenith and showed not the least hint of ever being otherwise. Yet just three years later it is marched and saluted its way down to the trenches.

J. M. BARRIE AND THE LOST BOYS
Andrew Birkin, 1979

It is hard to know quite how to begin with Andrew Birkin. Having created one of television's biographical masterpieces, he follows it up, not with the now customary book of the programme, but with his documentation set out in another form but with an equally compelling artistry. 'May God blast anyone who writes a biography of me' said Barrie towards the end of his dark and brilliant life – to which Andrew Birkin replies, this is not a biography, but a love story. What shakes one is not the nature of the love but the dumbfoundingly dreadful tragedy which clambered all over it, not during one fateful season but perennially, until all those involved had suffered to the utmost.

There is no conclusion, and the question of Barrie's guilt is left shivering in the air. Birkin neither absolves nor indicts. His purpose is to narrate, not to enlarge upon the strange tale, and finally he leaves the strong draught of Edwardian sentimentality and agony to swirl around in our Freudian responses and burn the kind of holes in them which absinthe was said to have done to those marble-topped café tables. But he admits to not being totally objective, and that the very act of choosing photographs and letters, and the placing of them in a certain order, carries with it opinion and judgment. At the same time, we learn that he approached this love story from the truest angle – from Barrie's works, which he unfashionably reads and admires. It is the ability genuinely to feel the worth and power of Barrie as a writer which acts as the steadying factor in Birkin's book – which, whatever we think about its astonishing contents, is a tribute, not an exposé.

'Oh, miserable Jimmie. Famous, rich, loved by a vast public, but at what a frightful private cost', wrote Peter Davies in his account of Barrie's multiple passion for the beautiful Llewellyn Davies family which he had picked up in Kensington Gardens while walking his wife's St Bernard, Porthos, and made his own. And then not just as an entity, which is how some of us become attached to families, but possessing the group and successive members of the group with two different kinds of obsession and admiration.

What this arrangement of the letters and journals reveals is the family's inability to escape from their captor, and how rapidly each one of them found himself trapped forever in Barrie's web of wealth and devotion. But Mary Hodgson, the family's stalwart nurse, was not deceived, neither was society, which viewed the whole thing as an interesting public event via its allegory, *Peter Pan*. And one is filled with grief for poor, noble Arthur Llewellyn Davies who, after providing this ugly, rich little Scottish playwright with five enchanting companions and their dream-mother, is hideously mangled in surgical operations paid for by the strange intruder. One of the sons wrote later that his dying father 'put up a smoke screen' about liking or tolerating Barrie in order to leave 'Mother a little less sad and try to show her he didn't grudge the Bart (the boys' name for Barrie after he had been awarded his baronetcy) being hale and hearty and rich enough to take over the business . . . it must have been extraordinarily bitter for him.'

But shatteringly bitter for Barrie, too. When he was a child in Kirriemuir, he used to change clothes with a boy who wore mourning so the latter could play for an hour or so. As the boy played, Barrie, in his friend's black, would weep 'though I knew not for whom'. He would have done the same for the surviving members of the Llewellyn Davies family, as all-too-mature horrors broke upon it, if he could. As well as a stealer of filial affections, he would, had it been possible, have taken on himself any kind of torment which threatened the idyll which he had set up around 'my boys'. Scottish fishing, Eton, daily letters and, most magical of all, knowing how to re-enter boyhood from the wilderness of being middle-aged, divorced and a literary solitary. At Kirriemuir, he had done his best to become his dead brother, standing like him, whistling like him, so that when the bereaved Margaret Ogilvy would repeat yet again, 'Is that you?', he could answer yes and be the handsome David who had died in a skating accident when he was fourteen. Later, Barrie lowered the age limit for happiness – 'nothing that happens after we are twelve matters very much.'

But it did. What one wonders, reading this fascinating family album, is: was Barrie at first grimly reconciled to the fact that 'my boys' would naturally outgrow his love, and was not the fact that they could not his real tragedy? It would seem that Barrie was somehow prepared for a limited or contained relationship with the small Llewellyn Davies brothers, but that they, and Michael in particular, as they grew up, drew him on into their adulthood, with desolating results. Had Michael drowned at twelve, it would have been appalling yet at the same time fitting, but to drown at twenty-one and in a friend's arms was a disaster which dragged Barrie into an emotional territory which was too terrible for any words of his. There is a photograph of him just after the funeral which tells all, as they say.

What emerges from this careful documentation, and as much from the illustrations as the text, is that Barrie was a poet of death. Not a great poet, by any means, but an intriguing death-poet of his day who played around with dangerous fads like popular morbidity and alternative eternities. He has been dismissed by critics for his whimsy and sentimentality (and enormously underrated for his dramatic skill) but it seems never to have dawned on anyone before Andrew Birkin that Barrie made his name and fortune by a delicate and fanciful articulation of yearnings and emotions that were widespread in middle-class society itself just before the First World War.

The error, both in respect of his huge readership and of Barrie himself, was to equate this sentimentality with weakness when, in fact, it was often as hard as nails. Birkin, describing the success of the Thrums stories which put Barrie on the map, says that the reverse side of his sentimental streak and humour was a kind of genial sadism. After 1915, he cut from *Peter Pan* the famous curtain line: 'To die will be an awfully big adventure.' When he took the five-year-old Peter Scott, his godson and a prospective ward, to see the play and asked him what he had liked best, the child had replied: 'What I think I liked best was tearing up the programme and dropping the bits on people's heads.' It was an answer which gave the author much pleasure.

Birkin has made a specially effective use of Peter Davies's unpublished journal of Barrie's involvement with his family, a book called *Morgue*. Some forty years after Michael's drowning, Peter, a successful publisher, a du Maurier on his mother's side and named after *Peter Ibbertson*, and with *Peter Pan* named after *him* ('What's in a name? My God, what isn't!' he exclaimed after years of Eton persecution), left his office, crossed to Sloane Square station and threw himself under a train.

It is indicative of Andrew Birkin's creative use of restraint that this astonishing history justifies his claim of 'love story' from beginning to end. It is a lesson in revelations.

VANESSA BELL
Frances Spalding, 1983

LYDIA LOPOKOVA
ed. Milo Keynes, 1983

Copious though they have been these past 20 years, the histories of Bloomsbury have been missing an essential study, that of Vanessa Bell alone. Scarcely without company for an hour, it would seem, during all her long life, on her own she paradoxically remained. Her 'inviolable reticence' is how her sister, Virginia Woolf, described it, although this suggests choice and preference, whereas we now know through Frances Spalding's full-length portrait that she had no choice. It must have been a hard book to write due to all the print already, but Frances Spalding's admirable decision to deal with them briefly, and to save all her best writing for those reaches of Vanessa's experience which have until now remained confused and shadowy, has brought every kind of fresh light on what might otherwise have turned out to be a very familiar matter. She speeds over the well-documented dramas such as Lytton and Carrington, and Virginia's death, and slowly and meticulously presents Vanessa as a total artist-cum-a monumental kind of house-mother against whom every type of distraction beat, from mere tiresomeness to deep tragedy, from egotism in those who surrounded her to the demands of running houses full of children and guests.

This study also reveals, in a way which others have failed to do, something of the emotional, rather than moral, dilemma of those happily plunging through the new sexual freedoms which the children of Leslie Stephen and their friends – and many other young people –

claimed. Although, as Frances Spalding says, 'few women in any age have managed their loyalties so diplomatically, keeping husband (Clive Bell), ex-lover (Roger Fry) and lover (Duncan Grant) all within her orbit and all reconciled to each other', this management of her men by a deeply sensuous Vanessa was not achieved without great suffering. Nor was it achieved without resort to some of the old taboos, for Angelica was grown-up before she learned that the homosexual Duncan Grant was her father and that also, in that home where her mother's talk was often bawdy, there was no one prepared to tell her the facts of life. She had to seek advice from a doctor. It was David Garnett, Duncan's erstwhile lover and the cause of so much heartache for Vanessa long ago, who married her, although twenty-six years her senior.

Francis Spalding deals with all this now wearisome bisexualism with exceptional skill, knocking whatever sensation there remains out of it, successfully returning it to convincing areas of true feeling and love. The key to Vanessa's emotional development was not her husband, who left her, or Fry, who indeed meant much to her, but Duncan Grant, who stayed with her to the end, and with whom she *worked*.

Their decades of painting, all the pictures and decorations set out against a background of English art ranging from Sargent, who taught Vanessa, to the last vestiges of Post-Impressionism during the 1950s, have received a serious and comprehensive attention which puts everything else into perspective. Frances Spalding allows Vanessa's and Grant's paintings somehow to colour her narrative. Their combined spirituality and hedonism spill from her account of their creativity and its fiercely protected disciplines, rather like Bonnard's spill from his.

Between them they turned Charleston itself into a picture in which they could live. It was very beautiful, often very cold, frequently over-populated and always exclusive. Vanessa discovers it, after finding Suffolk unsympathetic during the First World War. From 1919 to 1939 it was just a holiday house, but thereafter it became her home until she died in 1961. The other Vanessa house-discovery was, of course, 46 Gordon Square. It marked her emancipation from her father's tyranny. A mid-Victorian workaholic who required a formidably conventional upper middle-class domestic life, Leslie Stephen fastened on Vanessa to preside over it. No sooner was he in his grave than she sold off most of his furniture, disposed of the huge Hyde Park Gate house and distanced herself from all that it represented. When Virginia saw Gordon Square some time later, she too found it 'the most beautiful, the most exciting, the most romantic place in the world.'

Vanessa possessed a combination of enchanting looks, vice and poise which made her very formidable and even frightening. She made no allowances and could be ruthless. Her radicalism, like that of so many of her circle, was entirely opposed to all notions of equality, and thus it was used entirely for personal ends. She was mean to her servants and severe towards outsiders. She was also wonderfully enduring, emotionally generous, and incapable of burdening others with the kind of disasters with which they freely burdened her. Her sufferings were profound – the loss first of her daughter, and then of her son Julian in Spain, her sister's suicide and Grant's affairs with Keynes, Garnett and other men. She became fascinated with Mediterranean culture and was able to channel it through herself so that eventually she became a mixture of aristocrat and Madonna rigged out in clothes of no definable fashion. Keynes, who had written *The Economic Consequences of the Peace* in a couple of months in a Charleston bedroom managed her money. Frances Spalding's book is not so much one more addition to the packed Bloomsbury shelf as a study in depth of a late 19th-century woman who paid dearly for her freedom.

In the Spalding biography Keynes's surprising marriage to a ballet dancer makes an intriguing repeat of a celebrated Charleston crisis. 'To an intellectual like Maynard she was as rare as a hoopoe in a hop garden,' and he swooped uncharacteristically upon the pretty creature with the inconsequential wit and wed her, in spite of Vanessa's wrath. Milo Keynes, Lydia's nephew, in *Lydia Lopokova*, has drawn together twenty past and present assessments of her by those who knew her, and they scarcely need to make a case.

To quote her is to know her. Any woman who could say the things she did would be a treat to live with. The daughter of a theatre attendant in Petersburg, she came to be Lady Keynes and have a role in such disparate dramas as the international monetary conference of the Forties and the founding of the Arts Council via Diaghilev and the

Sitwells. She knew a lot about bliss. She had artistry as a dancer and artlessness as a person. Maynard adored her, but Vanessa more or less barred her from Charleston although their house was only a few hundred yards distant. Maynard: 'What are you thinking about?' Lydia: 'Nothing' Maynard: 'I wish I could.'

Vanessa's son Quentin, asked to contribute to this book, writes an apologia for his mother's conduct which is honest and downright. What Maynard loved was what Lydia's brother called her 'jubilation'. She got on with E. M. Forster best. 'When I am on the Downs in the morning I feel that I am having a cocktail with God,' she said. She deserves all this new attention. She found *The Economic Consequences of the Peace* 'just like Bach'.

HILAIRE BELLOC
A N Wilson, 1984

Belloc wrote too much, talked too much, drank too much and indeed did nothing by halves. What survives from all this turning out of books and strenuous engagement is minimal in comparison with what began to sink from sight long before Belloc himself did in 1953. Some of the best light verse of his day, two enduringly good little travel books, *The Path to Rome* and *The Cruise of the Nona*, and the fading rumble of hobby-horses being ridden hard: these popularly comprise his legacy. To overturn this assessment required a singular perception of certain previously half-glimpsed or neglected threads in the 'Georgian' weave, and a lot of hard labour.

Some men take to loud-mouthing to hide their complex souls, and in Belloc's case nobody has ever doubted that behind his lifelong hunger for a row and his robust polemics, some of them so grisly that it would be charitable to call them mad, there existed a more important and more intriguing figure than the author of *The Bad Child's Book of Beasts*. Here he stands, incomparably more interesting in himself than any reference to him in a history of 20th-century English literature would allow, and casting a deal of light on it into the bargain. Treading not so much delicately as knowingly into the always ramshackle, often deplorable but also frequently brilliant Bellocian edifice, Wilson has been able to reveal how both its virtues and its cracks have to be understood if we are to understand many of the more subtle elements in British society. He seeks neither to reinstate Belloc nor to dissect him, but to show him. It is not a pretty sight, but always a fascinating one – the quarter-French Sussex countryman for whom dogma was holy writ and who yet remained a wild one.

Belloc, writes Wilson on page one, 'was born during a thunderstorm on 27 July 1870, nine days after Pius IX had declared the doctrine of Papal infallibility, and two days before the outbreak of the Franco-Prussian War. Both these events shaped the pattern and texture of his life. But neither would have done so – indeed, he might never have existed at all – had not the Archdeacon of Chichester, Henry Edward Manning, become a Roman Catholic in 1851. 'The conversion of Manning is the most crucial event in Belloc's pre-history . . .'

It's a great start. Belloc's mother, Bessie Parkes, being the kind of person who 'knew everybody', as they used to say, knew Father Manning, part of whose cross was having to wear a Roman stock in the streets of London, 'a bizarre, foreign and outlandish' garment. She also soon came to know Newman and placed her small son in his Oratory school, where he had an appalling time and where he ran into the snobbery of what he was always to call the 'Old Catholic clique', a sect which was soon to enthral English novelists. Belloc's Catholic position proper, as it were, was adopted after these encounters, and soundly reinforced by youthful talks with Manning, who told the pugnacious boy that he never could admit 'the possibility of compromise between Catholic and non-Catholic society' and that he saw 'the necessary conflict and gloried in it.'

Belloc, who was able to believe anything which the Church told him, believed this. It also suited his temperament to believe it. Although he saw himself as the defender of the Faith, he was really the battler for an antique rock-solid system of human management which the Roman Empire had handed over to the Papacy. He hated with all his heart, and reviled with all his might, everything and everyone who questioned this system, and was led to putting its record straight after centuries of Protestant history. He was also led to obey the Roman Catholic Church's medieval edicts against the Jews which forbade the faithful to have anything to do with Jews because they had condemned Christ to death. Wilson, balanced throughout on as biased a man as ever existed, is balanced on this. The Church's law was 'piously harsh; as are the similar prohibitions placed by Holy Scripture on the Jews themselves, against mixing with the Gentiles'.

His ferocious Catholicism apart, received as it was by Belloc from Church of England clergymen become cardinals, the other factor which was to have a lasting effect on his life was the having to choose when he was seventeen whether to be French or English. He decided on the latter because, as a would-be writer, he recognised even then that he would only achieve literary success through this language. But France and the scrap of him that was Irish added an edge to his best prose, giving it on occasion a style which is quite unlike that of any of his contemporaries.

After leaving the Oratory, and while he was thinking about becoming a journalist in London, he met through his sister, the future novelist Marie Belloc-Lowndes, an Irish-American girl named Elodie Hogan, and eventually tramped to California to marry her. Wilson is never better than when he is dealing with what on the face of it seems this tepid liaison held together by the Post Office, for after he had settled her at King's Land Belloc was always off somewhere and a chronic wife-neglecter. Yet they adored each other, and when Elodie died at 42 he was to spend the next 40 years hungering for her, kissing the locked doors to her rooms as he passed them and in as elaborate mourning generally as Victoria's for Albert. Wilson admits that he cannot fathom what made Belloc's apparent misfit of a marriage work, but proves that it did, adding: 'The happiness of other people is much harder to penetrate than their sorrow.'

After experiences at Oxford which brought dons on to his anathema list, Belloc had to force himself to accept that there really wasn't a fortune behind him (his maternal grandfather had owned three houses and had left seventeen pictures to the National Gallery) and that he would have to make his way in the world as best he could. He wrote and lectured prodigiously. His social connections were as varied as the subjects of his books and journalism. El Vino cronies, the Souls, politicians (he was for some years the Member for South Salford) – the range of his gregariousness was vast. Special friendships included George Wyndham and, of course, G.K.Chesterton, although the famous 'Chesterbelloc' was more a popular notion than a fact. Wilson's remorselessly complete account of Belloc's drudgery leaves one stunned. It was unlike the breadwinning toil of most successful writers in that, the money apart, he actually needed a punishing regime of drink, hackery, train journeys, public events and arguments to soak up his giant energies. Once he had his secretary type and deliver a dictated book to his publisher without looking at a word of it.

Yet although he was often careless or just uncaring, there were frequent occasions when a superior vision and imagination swept away mere tradesmanship and produced something strange or excellent, or both. As he worked, so he drove his stocky person into the grubby mould which challenged the averagely clean-and-tidy, and whose smell (like a fox, said Waugh) he overlaid with Floris scent. What with his incessant work and filthy clothes, and the neglect of his body, there was something in Belloc's progress which reminds one of a flesh-mortifying medieval ascetic, praying at all hours and alive with 'God's pearls'.

Early in his biography Wilson has to decide what to do about Belloc and 'the Jew question', which confronts him with what he calls a serious technical difficulty. Yet he must chronicle it. He surmises that Belloc's frightful, obsessional interest in Jews began when he was doing his French military service and was confirmed by the Dreyfus case. However it began, it seems to have lasted him for life. In 1922 he published *The Jews*, 'my admirable Yid book', a work which Wilson found too upsetting to be read today, but which is also prophetic about Israel. Even allowing for the pre-Holocaust permissive anti-Jew language of his youth, Belloc goes far beyond such commonly held opinions and into his own squalid fantasies. Wilson is too good and true a writer to let this side of Belloc off as 'aberration' and uses it to throw a beam of murky light on Britain's attitude towards its Jews this century. He includes a savage rerun of the Marconi scandal.

This remarkable portrait concludes with Belloc's ponderous, slow-motion demise. Senility is a fragment of life and when a man like Belloc has a decade of it, it has to be taken into account. Wilson uses it as Belloc used the death-bed scenes he was so impressive at rendering, as a grand passing of a subject from his attentions and of a spirit from the earth. There he goes, Manning's disciple, whose religion was 'triumphalist, baroque, certain, glorious and hard', and who was 'a pioneer in exposing the fundamental absurdity of the Whig view of History'.

HERSELF DEFINED
Hilda Doolittle

Barbara Guest

PRETTY GOOD FOR A WOMAN
Elsie Dunn

D.A.Callard

Other than their being beautiful American women of roughly the same generation who early on broke from their differently exclusive backgrounds to become part of the movement which was to transform literature at the beginning of the century, Hilda Doolittle and Elsie Dunn, the subjects of these biographies, had little in common. Publishing coincidence has drawn their fading (H.D.) and all but vanished (Evelyn Scott) faces before us. They knew each other, of course. No two such writers in the propinquitous New York-London-Paris modernist literary field of the experimentalist and direction-changers could have avoided contact. It was Ezra Pound who told Hilda Doolittle to call herself 'H.D.' and Elsie Dunn became Evelyn Scott because the middle-aged man who persuaded her to elope with him from her Southern belle mansion had borrowed Scott of the Antarctic's name in order to vanish from his wife and family. Evelyn was a guest at the wedding of H.D's great friend Bryher in New York.

Bryher (Annie Winifred Ellerman) had named herself after a Scilly island. There is a certain pathos, considering her fate, that although there is this one reference to Evelyn Scott in the H.D. book, she has been missed out of the index. Both biographies will make the feminists sit up and shake their polls. Barbara Guest's book is likely to be the definitive one on the Imagist poet and D. A. Callard's life of Evelyn Scott is certain to have a place among 'quest' biography of the finest category. She is prolix, he is terse. Between them they unroll a very strange scene.

Herself Defined is, among a thousand other things, a study of sublime self-indulgence. To prevent gusts of exasperation at their conduct it is necessary to have some of H.D.'s poems and a novel or two by Bryher at hand, for there are very few quotes from these and unless one knows them, at least a bit, the writers themselves do tend to become on occasions a pair of trying, rich women. Bryher and H.D. were partners for almost half a century but did not think of themselves as lesbians. Barbara Guest sees them as being a little like Colette and Missy. H.D. was almost six feet tall, fair and very attractive. She met Pound at a Halloween party when she was fifteen and later, when studying at Bryn Mawr, fell in love with him. They became engaged and he initiated her into literature, about which she knew nothing. Two other teenage friends were William Carlos Williams and Marianne Moore. Her background was that of the gravely beautiful Moravian sect, and this for many generations. In 1911 she accompanied somebody she loved more than Pound, a girl named Frances Gregg, to London and almost immediately met the twenty year-old Richard Aldington. Frances disliked him, resented the way he brushed H.D.'s shoulder and found him 'beautiful . . . but unclean.' Meanwhile, H.D. was writing poetry and one day Pound, also newly arrived in England, took up her *Hermes of the Ways* and signed it 'H.D. Imagists' 'There were to be no muddy abstractions no superfluous words . . . What the symbolists had put in, the Imagiste took out.' Imagism wasn't Pound's invention at all and having involved H.D., Aldington and others in it, he lost interest. But it was to play a significant role in the development of modern poetry. H.D. herself was to later resent the appellation. In October 1913, at the Kensington registry office where D.H. Lawrence married Frieda, Middleton Murry; Katherine Mansfield and James Joyce; Nora, H.D. wed Richard Aldington. Soon she would see him off to the Western front, soon have a child by another man, and soon meet a small, plain Jewish girl, the daughter of Britain's reputedly richest man, Sir John Ellerman, a shipping magnate.

Bryher – 'semitic little face, clear skin, wide brows, hair twisted in two enormous coils and that odd commanding look and that certainty and that lack of understanding and that utter understanding that goes with people . . . who were simple and domineering never having known of anything of scraping, or terror at the wrong thing, of the wrong people.' (H.D.) – was twenty-four. She saw herself as a boy and not as a homosexual. H.D. lived with her, off her (although she had a lot of money herself) and near her for the rest of her life. Their relationship admitted extras, 'young squires' for H.D. and girls with plenty of boys in them (Elizabeth Bergner) for Bryher. When Bryher married and divorced the penniless Robert McAlmon he became known as Robert McAlimony. Still in need of a male protector, she married Kenneth Macpherson so that H.D., who loved him, could be with him.

Eventually and predictably, huge wealth made a huge difference to whatever and whoever they encountered. Bryher's father left some £800 million in today's money and she herself liked finance. Yet they lived not very stylishly or comfortably in Kensington flats, foreign hotels and a Bauhaus tax-haven structure in Switzerland. H.D. was analysed by Freud and, in old age, she and Bryher succumbed to the usual wealthy old ladies' fooling about with the occult, spiritualism (with Lord Dowding), tarot, etc. Barbara Guest swells this tale of dedicated writing, humourless ambivalence, suffering and first-half 20th century freewill with wonderful unstale period descriptions, anecdote and some sense of proportion. Self-centredness of an alarming kind seeps through everywhere.

Pretty Good for a Woman is a far more honed and firmly turned affair. D. A. Callard is a biographer who is ceaselessly astonishing himself as much as his readers. His material, unwearyingly tracked down, is the stuff of a great novel, a Flaubertian tragedy. He sees in Evelyn Scott parallels with Jean Rhys, whom she knew. It is a riches (though not on the Ellerman line) to rags tale, via bohemia. A Southern

177

aristocrat tumbles down and down, dragging her mother with her, from their Grecian mansion to the welfare hostel and, in Brazil, from landowners to near-peons. Mysteriously, considering their isolation, the revolutionary concepts which were to produce Joyce, Eliot, Pound, etc. penetrated the distant and dreadful world to which her lover had taken the twenty year-old Evelyn, and they both began to write. Eventually, she was able to make her somewhat vociferous way to Greenwich Village, there to queen it with the wildest of them. The casualties would have been her small son and his friend, the son of her later lover, had not these boys beaten back her moral squalor for art's sake with extraordinary eloquence. The lover's son was Thomas Merton. Evelyn trailed through Bermuda, Algeria, Cornwall, hurt and impeded by men, yet writing her fat fictions and preaching the new radicalism. That is, until the pressures broke her and she reverted to Southern reaction, a toothless old woman writing letters to the C.I.A. about communists. Callard has grasped all the real facts of a much written-about world, showing them to be harder for the women caught up in it than we imagined.

MAN AND MIRAGE
T. E. Lawrence, 1988

There can rarely have been a more obliging subject for the biographer than T. E. Lawrence. Every barrier he set up to keep the curious out of his life has proved to be an invitation to explore it. The paths leading to his motives and his soul may be labyrinthine, but they are carefully docketed.

It is a century since his birth and more than 50 years since his death, and it is disconcerting to find him, a little male sphinx crouching just beyond the reach of detractor and admirer alike.

'Simplify me when I am dead,' demanded the poet Keith Douglas in the Western Desert during the last war. This would have been the last thing which Lawrence would have wanted and when, in 1955, Richard

Aldington had the nerve to take him apart and reduce him, once and for all, to a heap of fears, claims, poses and aberrant drives, it was only to leave us with an even more complex and intriguing figure than ever.

The only way to keep on the right track is to see him as some kind of artist, a master of heroics and anti-heroics. He was certainly a most interesting writer. Fresh editions of *Seven Pillars of Wisdom* and *The Mint: the Complete Unexpurgated Text*, plus a new influx of volumes of interpretation and homage, prove him to be a strange winged creature who refuses to be put down.

Most Lawrence lives begin at Tremadoc with Mr Chapman (Sir Thomas in 1914) and Miss Maden welcoming their second son. But they should mention that the child and the text of his destiny arrived together – not that Lawrence knew of it until his teens. The book which was to route the way he had to take was C.M.Doughty's *Travels in Arabia Deserta*, a massive tale about a young man from Suffolk who, after appointing himself 'God's Wanderer', had so convincingly turned himself into an Arab that he had been able to join the two-year pilgrimage from Damascus to Mecca.

Lawrence was 20 when he was introduced to Doughty's *Travels* by one of Doughty's keenest admirers, the archaeologist David Hogarth. Also while still a child, Lawrence had been introduced by his father – via long bike rides to castles and church brasses – to the first Englishmen to become obsessed by the East: the Crusaders.

So grounded was he in the path he had to take, that Doughty's advice 'Don't go' had to be ignored. The advice was in any case bewildering. 'The populations only know their own wretched life and look upon any European wandering in their country with at best a veiled ill-will,' Doughty had written to the undergraduate.

How was he to know that what most people termed 'wretched life' was for Lawrence as appealing as hardships were for saints? Or that when this small man with the big head arrived among the Anglo-Arabists that he would be recognised as some kind of brilliant, if dangerous, incarnation of their Saxon-Bedouin philosophy?

Almost the first thing Lawrence did was to wear Arab clothes, some said to hide his figure, which seemed unrelated to his face. Faisal eventually robed him in princely white and gold. In none of his costumes, whether Arabian or R.A.F. A/C's best, was it sufficient for him to act the part – he had to *be* it.

Reading Lawrence himself in 1988 sometimes makes writing about him superfluous. He is all there, all the versions of his self, in his books and letters and photographs. As deaths reach a million in the Iran-Iraq battlefield (his beloved Mesopotamia) read him on corpses. He is the poet of defilement and degradation. Such torrents of blood have passed under the bridge since he elevated his desert war into scenes from Malory that this painstaking part of his writing is boring beyond belief. But the landscape on which the action takes place, and the characters, and the confessions which fill *Seven Pillars*, guarantee that we will be reading it for a long time yet.

It should not be forgotten that Lawrence and his contemporaries were Victorians raised on Great Men. And one reason for Lawrence's impact was that his adventures were so Victorian, so 'clean' (a word often used to defend T.E.L. from accusations of homosexuality), in comparison with the incomparable filth of the trenches, that it was a treat to watch them sparkling and jerking across the newsreel screen.

Stephen Tabachnick and Christopher Matheson, in *Images of Lawrence* have done a good job by including the post-Aldington Lawrence of Terence Rattigan and Robert Bolt. All in all, a spirit of generous give and sensible take prevails. One thing which strikes the eye is the casualness of the young man in the photographs. The last years in the choking R.A.F serge show him coarsening and stocky. They also show him as a kind of secular monk, someone with a vocation for severity. All the new writing harps on the self-immolation of the Prince and the creation of the Ranker. *The Mint's* explanation seems more than adequate: that loners are often most blissfully alone in hugger-mugger groups, like the army of Arabs digging up Carchemish, like the close tents of the Negev, like the foetid, secretless sleeping huts at Cranwell or Karachi. Lawrence always wanted the best of both worlds, nor thought it disreputable to pursue it. That total lack of privacy in the hut could be balanced by silent Clouds Hill, the effing this and effing that (as they used to say before he spelled out normal soldiers' conversation) balanced, if that is the word, by talk with Forster, the Shaws, Hardy, and the airmen friends who borrowed his books and listened to Beethoven on his gramophone. *Images of Lawrence* sees him, correctly, as a man who respected ambiguity.

A Touch of Genius: the Life of T. E. Lawrence by Malcolm Brown and Julia Cave takes its title from Lawrence's friend, Aubrey Herbert's summing up in 1914, long before his achievement and notoriety: 'an odd gnome, half cad – with a touch of genius'.

Brown and Cave re-tell the entire familiar tale so lucidly that all manner of old confusions and attitudes are demystified. They deal particularly well with his education and with his unhappiness – something ignored or avoided by most writers.

They rescue him from adventurism and set out in an admirably clear way the background to the Arab Revolt. They recognise Lawrence's talent 'for energizing and enthusing people', his efficiency and high intelligence. They show how to his colleagues he could be both nerve-rackingly unconventional and a successful bringer-off of 'wonderful stunts'.

But a sense of proportion is their watchword. The Deraa flogging took place the same month as the Russian Revolution, with its incalculable effect on the Middle East. Lawrence, in fact, is put in his place in the right sense. The authors are apologists for a puritan romantic whose mixture of expertise and unorthodoxy made him useful and yet an awkward little number to deal with – whether by bureaucrats and politicians, and in the forces.

What would have happened had he not crashed his motorbike? It has often been suggested that he would have joined the British Fascists to energise and enthuse recruits. Almost certainly he would have not. But what on earth would they have done with him in World War Two?

THE HAUNTED MIND
An Autobiography
Hallam Tennyson, 1984

This naked autobiographer doesn't mention Hazlitt, yet it is the unguarded essayist and self-confessed 'fool of love' who swore to remain faithful to his youthful ideals that he frequently resembles. Tennyson is actually more the fool of sex, but the restlessness and energy with which he goes on living according to the progressive convictions of his early years are often reminiscent of Hazlitt's fidelity to the politics which claimed his twenty-year-old self. The compulsion not to conceal, not to change (not to grow up, some would say), is essentially a moral one. In a worldly sense, like so many good men, Tennyson is unwise. And if there is a central tragedy or dilemma in his life, it surely must be his inability to discover and then accept some kind of religious discipline for it. Not a structure of dos and don'ts which mocks the intelligence, but some house of the spirit in which to take shelter from the ego.

The first paragraphs of a well-written but uncomfortable book are a kind of ethical *curriculum vitae* to tell us what we are in for:

> The comforts of inertia and compromise have been denied me for reasons which I sometimes regret . . . the contradictions in my life seem deep-rooted and innumerable . . . I am an economic Marxist . . . yet the chief preoccupation of my inner life has been to experience something of the mystery that lies beyond all materialist explanations of the universe. I am a bisexual . . . I enjoyed married life for 25 years and helped to bring up two children . . . but I do not believe I succeeded psychologically until, at the age of 50, I openly declared my homosexuality.

This no-holds-barred confession then moves off in the usual chronological order to expand on these contradictions, or rather, this dualism, and to show on the one hand a man in his sixties who, because of his father's longevity, is still within conversational distance of the Great Victorians and, on the other, someone who is the personification of the late twentieth-century's radical, wholly committed, full-frontal

182

individual conscience. In between lie the formative 1930s.

Having been so strangely close to Farringford, the Tennyson family house in the Isle of Wight, and his mother's friendships with Reginald McKenna, Bertrand Russell, Lord Napier's son (to whom she became engaged) and Lloyd George, Tennyson never quite appreciates how intriguing for the rest of us all these family connections are. While his father, Sir Charles, was to remain overwhelmed to the end by the fact that he was the poet's grandson, Hallam managed to escape this vast literary shade and sees himself more the inheritor of his mother's characteristics. His portrait of Ivy Tennyson, née Pretious, a petite, emotional, businesslike, litigious woman of probable Mediterranean origins, and the begetter, he thinks, of his 'earliest ambiguities' deserves a place in literature's gallery of powerful parents.

Although to some degree free of the monumental laureate, Tennyson says that he was never to find his own reality, and that his personality seems illusory. His story is that of the hopelessly divided man candidly told. So persistent has been his sense of loss that he wonders if he could actually have inherited a tendency to experience life 'as a system of deprivation'? He was the third of the Tennyson brothers and he writes vividly on Penrose and Julian, both killed during the last war, when he stuck to his pacifist guns, joined the Friends' Ambulance Unit, married a German Jewish refugee and set out on a dedicated and complex career of deep involvement in bringing relief to the world's disaster areas, and especially to Italy and India.

It was in Italy, just before his marriage, that he began the long and, as he admits, often ugly process of cutting out emotion in his affairs with men, preserving all this side of his nature for women, particularly his wife. Although honest to the point of display on the basic, early adolescent-like character of his sexual activity, Tennyson is no Boswell and no Joe Ackerley, and it is proof of the broad drama of his life, and of the vividness of his writing, that his book survives some of its confessions. Yet, negative-seeming though many of them at first appear to be, they do eventually lead up to brief experiences of love, which is one of the reasons why they are present. Another, of course, is that for Tennyson no life is truthfully told which leaves out its compulsions. The price exacted is also included, and often it is as much as any individual can pay in the way of domestic comfort, and from the losses accrued when conscience overturns the conventions.

The Partition years in India, when Tennyson and his wife were involved in the restructuring of the economy of some villages near Calcutta after the terrible 1942 Bengal famine are described with a mixture of social detail and self-analysis which makes these pages belong to that huge and ultimate pile of footnotes which so many enthralled British witnesses added to the official history of the Raj. Tennyson met – and still defends – Gandhi, and in rural India recognised for the first time 'that I had come home'. Illness, alas, soon brought him back to these native, alien islands, where as a result of his ever-searching need for a teacher, Gandhi was succeeded by Canon Fitzgerald, an East End priest whose stark post-bombing church in the Commercial Road was to remain for Tennyson a potent haven when things got really rough. During the early Fifties occasional broadcasts led to producing at the BBC. Like so many before and after him, he muses on the ephemerality of what he toiled to create, adding his experiences of the famous stresses and strains of the Corporation. 'Looking back it seems surprising that I should ever have been as happy as I undoubtedly was in that mammoth, hierarchical, "masculine" structure'. Working with Martin Esslin, plus his own gifts as a producer, were the source of this undoubted happiness.

The final chapters are not so much a conclusion as a staring around at what could or should come next. A brief return to India, a very necessary man-woman emotional friendship in Italy, but chiefly a description of someone who, although constantly in close touch with family and friends, is isolated, and knows it. A certain strandedness prevails, leaving him where he can see most things, and most of all himself, painfully clear.

NANCY MITFORD
A Memoir

Harold Acton, 1975

Towards the end of a memoir which is not much less amusing than any
written by its subject – which is high praise – Harold Acton quotes
Logan Pearsall Smith's remark about malice and loyalty as an
assessment of Nancy Mitford: 'Hearts that are delicate and kind and
tongues that are neither, these make the finest company in the world.'
She died agonisingly and courageously two years ago of Hodgkin's
disease, after providing a stream of some of the most irresistible
literary entertainments since the war. Her books rested upon a vision
of the world as it appeared to comically self-obsessed British and
European autocrats. She pillaged her family and her friends ruthlessly
for cranky and hilarious material for her tales, and where history was
concerned, she revealed a remorseless understanding of its monstrous
burlesque. She was, says Harold Acton, 'more a novelist in life than in
literature, superimposing her own image on what she was seeing'; and
if his funny-affectionate account of her frequently reads like notes she
might have made for further novels, then this, too, is praise.

Some comic writers are driven to inventing a comic situation
because their own is tragic. Not so Nancy Mitford. She wholly
believed that she was born special and privileged, she stayed young
and pretty, and without illness, until the end of her days, and she had,
as well as literary ability, all the energy and discipline to exploit it.

More or less self-educated, and with little money, her progress from
bookshop assistant to the most elegant and dizzy pinnacle of best-
sellerdom was made via massive reading and a serious passion for the
desk. Or for the armchair and the pad on the knee, as it was in her case.
Nothing else mattered to her all that much. Just friends when she
needed them, and not when they wanted to come, a few absolutely
first-class creature comforts by way of food, clothes and furniture, a
doting slave – 'Maids are so much more important than men' – and a
tightly interlocked circle of sisters and gossips at which to aim a
regular volley of letters: these were her basic necessities.

It is from her sisters in particular, that Harold Acton has extracted the correspondence which forms the basis of his book. It chiefly covers the twenty years of Nancy Mitford's francophilia when, after the terrific success of *The Pursuit of Love* in 1945, she set up house, first in Paris and then in Versailles – which was her notion of the ideal village, big house and all.

At this period, her marriage to Peter Rodd was defunct, although not yet annulled, and she had found exactly the kind of affection she required in 'the Colonel', an aide to de Gaulle whom she had met as a Free Frenchman in London during the war. The colonel turned out to be the perfect companion for a fashionable woman who also happened to be an artist and a natural bachelor.

One of the complexities of Nancy Mitford's milieu was that it tended to polarise its males into opposing non-communicating camps of brave boneheads and what it called 'pansies'. It was a division which served her well for comedy, but less well for relationships. Adoring the military as she did – 'It is the sorrow of my life never to have been in (a battle). I suppose a cavalry charge must be the nearest thing to heaven on this earth' – it was bliss to adore a sensitive colonel on conditions which did not interfere with her writing. Four hours a day were enough, Evelyn Waugh told her, but instead she worked all hours, given the chance, reading her eyes out, and working with intense concentration against an essential background of hard frivolity. When she lay dying, she said that, in another world, she 'would like to be a pretty young general and gallop over Europe with Frederick the Great and never have another ache or pain'.

Her hates were doctors, Americans ('Govs') during the war, Heywood Hill's bookshop in Curzon Street was known as the Ministry of Fear by US soldiers, due to the treatment they received from assistants like Nancy and her friends), actors and bores. Her group practised a cruel, perpetual laceration of each other by pen and tongue. The most riotous examples of it here concern her wrenching of the crown from Violet Trefusis ('Lady Montdore'), who, until Nancy Mitford arrived, had reigned as queen of the English literati in the Faubourg St Germain.

Mrs Trefusis made a fine butt because she was too outsize in awfulness either to miss or to feel sorry for, although thoughts about giving hurt were unlikely to stay Nancy Mitford's hand if she thought she could score a hit. Many less-deserving victims, in the words of James Lees-Milne, found themselves gulping her 'sharp little barb, barely concealed like the hook of an angler's fly beneath a riot of gay feathers'. The quality of her malice, however, was of a less intolerable order than that of her old friend and mentor, Waugh, whose posthumously-published diary left her stunned. He was her master at first, and had begun to influence her even when she was doing her best to write like Wodehouse (in *Highland Fling*, for example), and the favourable climate for her fiction owed much to him.

Once financially independent in France, Nancy Mitford settled down in the type of domestic security and good order which attracts those whose universe has shown signs of unreliability. Skeletons rattled in the Hons' cupboard. Her Hitlerite sister, Unity – second name Valkyrie – had attempted suicide at the beginning of the war, but had not died of her head wound until 1948; her sister, Diana (Lady Mosley), had been interned, and her brother had been killed in Burma. Her parents, like Redesdales, spent their last years living apart. And she herself, out of some kind of quintessential indifference in her attitude towards marriage, had wasted years with Peter Rodd (Waugh's 'Basil Seal'). The strict disciplines of authorship were rewarded with celebrity, and this she thoroughly enjoyed. She believed that the ultimate aim in life was to have fun, and with a stylish mixture of stoicism, pride and industry, she pursued her aim at all costs.

Harold Acton's portrait of her is intimate, waspish and loving. What we glimpse remains witty but seems infinitely longer ago than it was.

SYLVIA BEACH AND THE LOST GENERATION
A History of Literary Paris in the Twenties and Thirties

Noel Riley Fitch, 1984

The lost generation of this book's title is not that of the First World War but of those liner-loads of Americans who, during the Twenties, became lost in Paris. One of their most important addresses was 12 rue de l'Odéon where Sylvia Beach, a girl from Princeton, ran a circulating library, a bookshop and a kind of non-stop practical party for the new Parisian-American-Irish writers. Shakespeare and Company, the famous bookshop, is familiar old ground, and at first one doubts if there is enough that is fresh about its owner and its customers to warrant this latest, extensive stocktaking. Then, before many pages have passed, one sees why it is justified. In all previous accounts, Sylvia herself is not much more than a smudge on the decadal group photograph in which Joyce, Stein, Hemingway, Carlos Williams, Sherwood Anderson, McAlmon, Gide, Romains, Valéry, Fitzgerald, etc. are hogging the camera for all that they are worth. As Noel Fitch proves, Sylvia's trim personality is every bit as interesting as that of any lion which, often as not, she fed from her never very rich table, and it is something of a treat to make such a full acquaintance at last. Even so, she has to put up quite a fight in the middle chapters to stand free from the monstrous shadow of Joyce.

St John Perse gave the best description of her. She looked, he said, like the daughter of a Wild West sheriff. She was actually the daughter of a New Jersey parsonage, and had arrived in Paris when she was fifteen as the result of her father being appointed to look after its American Presbyterians. She never went home again. Neither, for long, did her mother, a chronic Europhile who, once her children were off her hands, spent the rest of her life wandering about the continent until a classically horrible shoplifting charge resulted in suicide. Sylvia remained very loving towards her parents and sisters but never allowed them to threaten her independence. As a family, reverend father and all, they possessed a little of the diceyness of certain Edith Wharton characters. Sylvia's more potent influence derived from those selfless, flat-heeled English parsonage girls whom she met while on war work.

After the Armistice she was dissuaded from opening a bookshop in the States by her father and from opening a French bookshop in London by Harold Monro. Only a few months later, the whole of the rest of her life was inaugurated, as it were, during a chance visit to a bookshop in the rue de l'Odéon owned by a girl named Adrienne Monnier. Adrienne believed that a 'private fixing of the soul' occurred whenever a customer entered because the latter was in 'a place of transition between street and house!' She was as keen on all things American as Sylvia was on all things French, and soon they were together and running non-competitivenesses opposite each other.

Sylvia's shop opened just eight months before James Joyce arrived in Paris. She ran it with a casualness which concealed her genius. Although a declared handmaid to literature, aspiring to no more and no less, she was no doormat, as some who gave Parnassus as their address soon discovered. On 16 March 1920 Gertrude Stein crossed her threshold, with 'the face of a Roman emperor on the body of an Irish washerwoman', as somebody said. Unlike Sylvia, she spoke poor French and said 'You betcha', but each recognised the other's role in the swiftly expanding community of independent women which Paris was attracting at this time. They crossed swords over *Ulysses* and Sylvia was able to demonstrate her fearlessness by writing to Gertrude, 'A thorn is a thorn is a thorn.'

Joyce and Pound also entered Shakespeare and Company in 1920. It was the heyday of the little magazine (it was considered shameful by many of the new wave 'moderns' to see their stories and poems in any other kind of periodical) and fractions of *Ulysses* were already appearing in the *Little Review*. Pound was busy being John the Baptist to 'Crooked Jesus', as Sylvia and Adrienne dubbed Joyce, and by the end of the year the decision which was to internationalise Sylvia's name and stretch her goodness to breaking point had been taken; she was to publish *Ulysses*. The author is obliged to spell out yet again the familiar episode, but by carefully filtering every sentence of it through Sylvia's part in it, much is gained. Miss Fitch has it in for James Joyce, and a good thing too, one is bound to say. But she brilliantly evokes the contemporary effect of this novel on Paris, New York and London, plus Joyce's complex dependency on women.

How could Sylvia and Harriet Weaver (another parsonage girl) have endured it? one is yet again forced to ask – they so austere, he so like a Scottish solicitor whooping it up on a windfall. Hotels, dinners, cabs, clothes, tips and booze, and every bill remorselessly passed on, as well as a little army of youthful worshippers, including the twenty-two-year-old Beckett, devilling for him in the libraries. Sylvia stood it for ten years. *Ulysses* did indeed bring her celebrity, but at every kind of cost. Not the least of her troubles was with the printers, a third of *Ulysses* having been added by Joyce on his page-proofs.

Other figures join her library, chat to her under the framed photographs, are introduced to Whitman, Melville, Henry James on the shelves at a time when America itself ignored its great writers. Stein was cross with her because she refused to stock Gene Stratton Porter. There are glimpses of macho Hemingway and young Cyril Connolly. Rebecca West, purchasing Joyce's *Pomes Penyeach*, has the booklet handed to her 'as if it had been a saint's medal on the porch of Westminster Cathedral'. Catty though this is, Sylvia's attitude to literature was reverent – but never precious. She possessed antennae which led her to the very centre of the literary imagination of her day, which is why she deserves such a fat book on herself alone. And Noel Fitch was the right person to tell her, on the whole, self-effacing tale, for without perhaps knowing it she reflects Sylvia's voice.

HELEN WADDELL
A Biography

Dame Felicitas Corrigan, 1986

Between the wars, published some half a dozen years apart, two eccentric studies of medieval Christendom astonished and, more importantly, delighted the world. They were *The Wandering Scholars* (1927) and *Peter Abelard* (1933), and their equally surprised author, for she could not have dreamt that she would appeal to the general reader, was Helen Waddell. How one envies those about to open these beautiful romances – from the Latin – for the first time. They are eccentric in that they sparkle well outside the circles of conventional learning and theology, and still remain in a starry orbit that is all their own.

To change the metaphor, a young woman from an Ulster Presbyterian background did what whole academies of historians had until then failed to do: she unblocked the channels of Europe's ancient spirituality and let it flood into the 20th century. Most of what she released had been well within the reach of the experts and specialists, but only she was sufficiently inspired to restore its tumultuous liveliness.

Of course there was much criticism. Latin history and Latin literature were far too sacred subjects for people to queue up for at the lending libraries. Something had to be wrong with these studies, which were at the same time novels and poems. But there wasn't. They were correctly learned, yet also distractingly imaginative. As Helen Waddell possessed the style of a wittily forgiving recording angel, it was no wonder that she was able to introduce the 'age of faith', in all its tangible, talking, singing, loving strength to the age of Hitler. Not that her work is confined to that grim period. *The Wandering Scholars* and *Peter Abelard* hold their freshness, and if you haven't previously encountered them, you should pick them up at once.

It was a rule of the old healing to confront like with like, and so at a time when the biographer's art is under attack, how fortuitous it is to have Dame Felicitas Corrigan confront – if that isn't too aggressive a stance – Helen Waddell. Only a religious with literary power of a high order could have revealed such a woman without shattering her in the process. However, the subject remains unforgettable in its wholeness. The writer from Stanbrook Abbey and the writer from the manse meet on common sacred ground, intellectual and simple ladies both. Discipline acknowledges discipline.

Scene one is old Tokyo, where Helen's father was a missionary and where the great Daibutsu of Kamakura – the Buddha – and the Christ doubly influenced Helen and her big family. They had arrived in Japan the very year – 1873 – Christianity had been officially legalised. Life was barefooted, austere, but brilliant. Helen looked back on it always but rarely mentioned it after the return to Ulster, with both parents dead and her splendidly problematical career ahead of her. For what was to be done for someone whose haven was so obviously the senior common room of an Oxford college and yet who needed to pursue the kind of free-range reading that ran wide of the academic pattern?

Ditto where marriage was concerned. Her pretty-pug looks brought her a long line of young hopefuls, but very early on she settled for father-daughter relationships, first with Professor George Saintsbury and finally with Otto Kyllmann, her publisher. Her women friends were her sister Meg, Cathleen Nesbitt the actress, and the historian Maude Clark. What Helen required, and got in full measure, was a kind of passionate companionship without sex. Behind the baulking at a university career and marriage were her ordinary artist's self-protectedness and a succession of rooms of her own.

Dame Felicitas's treatment of Helen's schooldays and studentship is itself a work of art – as it had to be if we are to be excited by what happened, which wasn't the mere getting of results but the early and rapid unfolding of her extraordinary power to reach the Christ of the medieval Church via its Latin poets and teachers. The power began to show itself in still-medieval Tokyo, but positively shone during the years at Queen's University, Belfast. It made life in her horrible stepmother's horrible terrace-house very difficult. All the backgrounds, Japan, First World War, Ulster, '20s Paris, blitzed London, the Armagh countryside, are fascinatingly evoked. But the biography's real achievement is its successful account of the way in which Helen deflected from everything which threatened her true destination – the single-language universe of her scholar-lover-saint Abelard. And all this without 'deviating a hair's breadth from her Presbyterianism'. This was her strength.

She became very famous and, as they say, heaped with honours, and she enjoyed it. She made her home in 'London, so old and tolerant', and read and read her way into a past where none before her had been able to catch such music and recognise such ordinary human pleasure. But her ivory tower was shaken by more than flying bombs and the usual ups and downs of existence.

Dame Felicitas has to fit them in so that the pain and drama of them doesn't overwhelm the narrative, the many deaths and most of all the long death in life which was to be Helen's strange fate when her intelligence failed, leaving her mindless and helpless, understanding nothing at all. Her art was the piecing together of joyful, confident but near-forgotten holy declarations about Christ and humanity, the blowing away of library dust, and the amplifying of necessary but time-faded voices.

DENTON WELCH
The Making of a Writer
and
The Journals of Denton Welch
Michael De-la-Noy

I LEFT MY GRANDFATHER'S HOUSE
Denton Welch

These three books are an interleaving of each other, and to read them in sequence, Life, Journals and Journey, brings substance to a literary reputation thought by some to have been a bit on the gossamer side. It is now nearly forty years since Denton Welch died, locked, it has always seemed in the neo-romanticism of the period, the archetypal sick genius perishing, in his case, from multiple injuries. Now the mere decorativeness vanishes as the depths of his experience are reiterated in a kind of antiphon between himself and his biographer. The accident on the Beckenham road when he was twenty divided his life between great and small journeys – the latter often minute, though picaresque to the last step. Once they had included Korea, Canada and China, and teenage trampings across England; then everything he was hungry for had to be discovered in a corner of Kent.

He never lived long enough to become philosophical about being 'spoilt', as he called it, by the woman's car running over him and his bike, and he got through the thirteen remaining years by cramming them with sensations which he could record. The slightest happening, like the odd porcelain saucer, had to be treasured, set out to its best advantage. The mixture of homoeroticism and missish (his own word) aestheticism intrigued his contemporaries, while his terrible suffering, although described as truthfully as Barbellion described his, tended to be glossed over.

Because he lacked a future, Welch hugged the past to him. The important past was that of the 18th and 19th centuries and of his own lifetime, and he reached out to both via ornaments, furniture and architectural detail. He was crushed by the brevity of his lot and preoccupied by transience. To posses beautiful objects which had managed to survive generations of rough handling made him their honoured protector. He learnt, almost from the minute he came to in the awful hospital, 'that to be ill is to be another person' and that whatever happened from now on he would be unreachable. His intensely self-presenting writing brought him immediate fame and could have turned him into a rococo guru had he allowed it to; but the idea of being an exponent of anything other than his own brief days appalled him.

The ceaseless accumulating of the facts and feelings relating to his existence, the careful listing of them in stories and diaries, has, quite incidentally made Welch a World War Two social historian – something he would not at all have liked to be. No sooner had an essay in *Horizon* and his brilliant autobiography, *Maiden Voyage*, launched him than he made astutely youthful advances to the Sitwells, Lady Oxford (not to be charmed), Lord Berners and others. For their pains, almost everybody who became his friend or simply his host was unforgettably docketed. His books and his life spoke to very young men and to sophisticated middle-aged women. The sexual candour which once so bothered the publishers and editors now proves to be nothing more than a compulsive ringing the changes of first encounters, plus a voyeurism resulting from a mixture of his knowing himself to be too 'spoilt' to go further and a writer who needed to see bodies both lyrically and clinically. Slow dying through one's twenties is a fleshly business.

Michael De-la-Noy's role is not that of the apologist who has to justify such a lavish re-entry of a writer who is now chiefly of historical significance. What such a full assessment has done – the careful and necessary filling-out of the cool family background which produced the classic rebel, and the doubling of the *Journals* after the narrow glimpse of Welch allowed by Jocelyn Brooke in 1952, but especially the publication for the first time of the short novel *I Left My Grandfather's House* – has been to demonstrate Welch's tenacity, not to mention a prose style which keeps one feeding as greedily on his pages as he did on the treats that supplemented his ration-book.

De-la-Noy understands the nuances of the period. He is expert, too, in managing Welch's difficult combination of tragedy and fashionableness, objectivity and fantasy, class awareness and anti-authoritarianism. The central fact which these intriguing variations on his life confirms is Welch's determination to have one, in spite of the fractured spine and the successive bladder and kidney infections which drove him to death at thirty-three. The life included an impressive literary and artistic output, a long love affair – and even more bike rides. But all of it remained hopelessly circumscribed by Welch's black recognition of its meagre helping where he was concerned. He stretched out all it held for all he was worth, dwelling on its tiniest detail.

How it comes over to me that my life is really too limited to bear . . . Is reverie really what people live for, and do they just do things to feed their reverie? . . . I do not think that people want love most, they need the settled reverie, the calm testing and tasting of their past and the world's past.

There had to be an obverse to these deathly reflections if stories were to be written and pictures painted, and it shows a vital, life-worshipping, occasionally ruthless figure working hard against time.

SURVIVAL TACTICS
A Literary Life
Peter Vansittart, 1999

Many writers keep notebooks or day-books. One thinks of André Gide, Somerset Maugham or Virginia Woolf and their self-illuminating jottings from their constant reading and from their various encounters with the world when away from their desks. As is often said, a writer's life is essentially a solitary one. Bouts of talk with other writers tend to give it a club-like gregariousness which it does not actually possess. As time passes, the conditions of the trade create preferences and lay down conditions. 'They tell me that life is the thing but I prefer books', said Logan Pearsall Smith. But for writers like Peter Vansittart literature *is* life and it is this kind of vitality which keeps him going. He is prolific and the amount and variety of his work has long since allowed the reader to penetrate the many aspects of his existence, as well as to enjoy the beauty of his prose style. *Survival Tactics* presents the framework of a life on which has been hung a wonderful collection of the sayings and anecdotes with which he has been filling his writer's notebook since he was fifteen.

For a great many of us, the pleasure of *Survival Tactics* will lie in the Vansittart version of our own reading experiences since the last war, for he is a master of evocation, quietly resurrecting in just a page or two the often short-lived climate of a particular literary period which engrossed us then but which has half-slipped from memory. He reminds us that, like him, we have gorged on novels and poetry and reputations, and have been made what we are – by books more than by anything else. Schoolmastering kept food on the table but could not stop the flow of stories.

He – uncomplainingly – confesses to small sales which are, in his case, evidence of his distinction as the kind of novelist whose work is rooted in the rich culture of twentieth-century writing. His attitude to everything is patrician and faintly melancholy. He gives the main distresses of his own life and the unparalleled evils of this century but does not dwell on them. He has escaped very little; but language, the inner world, the obsessive craft of writing; and a good eye and ear for what is happening at the moment allows the emergence of a philosophical if gently sad view of what has been happening since the 1940s.

He is delightful on his loves, who range from Baroness Orczy to V.S. Pritchett. It is difficult now to describe the atmosphere when the latter reigned as literary editor of the *New Statesman*. Pritchett taught young and coming writers not to be pompous or awed – or even ambitious. Just write well and read everything. Vansittart is a defender of the writer's faith, which is highly individual and complex and cannot be generalised. Like all the best writers, he never forgets gossip and how often there is nothing better as a summary of either a period or a person. He is excellent at giving a revised version of reputations and his account of what happened to Angus Wilson is just and kind.

Wilson was about the kindest man that ever lived, the most hard-working, the funniest, and Vansittart's reassessment of that enormous talent makes one want to start reading him all over again.

Survival Tactics is a cascade of authors. Some continue to sparkle, some are early lights, none is wholly out. Vansittart shows us a fire which had to be fed. He concludes with a saying by Isaiah Berlin. 'There is something singularly attractive about men who retained, throughout life, the manners, the texture of being, the habits and styles of a civilised and refined milieu. Such men exercise a peculiar kind of personal freedom.' Such a man is Peter Vansittart.

TIME AND THE PRIESTLEYS
The Story of a Friendship
Diana Collins, 1994

To write in depth about our friends is one way of writing about ourselves. Boswell's *Life of Johnson* remains one of the great autobiographies. *Time and the Priestleys* is about the meeting and the staying together of like minds, Jack's and Jacquetta's, Diana's and John's. Minds, it should be added, which were never independent of hearts. The intimacy of their relationships was actually increased by the public role each of them had to accept during the 1960s onwards when all four friends, in their different ways, took action against certain political policies both here and abroad, and voiced a familiar British sanity when it came to a nuclear arms race, apartheid, etc. In this intelligent and frequently moving book Diana Collins tells what it was like for essentially private people like themselves to go public, as it were, and how their brave campaigning and shared principles were to bring them close in every other respect.

They met in the autumn of 1957 after an article in the *New Statesman* – 'Britain and the Nuclear Bombs' – by Priestley brought the whole debate on this moral question to life. Priestley was sixty-three and had been married to the strangely beautiful and learned Jacquetta Hawkes, as she was to continue to call herself as an author, for four years. His celebrity as a novelist and playwright continued to be enhanced by his 1940s BBC postscripts in which, as Diana Collins says, he provided the perfect complement to Churchill's broadcasts. Between them they provided the country with exactly the right kind of patriotism for the hour. She gives a vivid picture of him at work. His output was not so much phenomenal as Victorian, a brilliant play completed in a week, an encyclopaedic survey of English literature covered in eighteen months. And all the time those ably-finished essays in which a writer of his period could exercise his style and thoughts. Whilst offering no critique of J.B. Priestley, Diana Collins has a way of making the reader take fresh stock of him. She reminds us of his *warmth* as a writer and that, to comprehend him, this warmth has to be met by warmth. He was at times testy and given to venting his native bluntness in all directions, yet everything he wrote is given balance and hope by a kind of gratefulness for being in the world and by a sanity which conquers all the madnesses he lived through, the two world wars, the depression and the old social hypocrisies which he satirised. His 'cheerfulness' and rumbustiousness used to be mocked but the centenary of his birth has seen a recognition of his real position as a writer which many of his contemporaries failed to understand. This memoir adds to the understanding. It takes an affectionate and yet an intellectual view of two very different writers, of a marriage, and of a circle which did more than most of us, even now, are willing to concede to change for the better the direction so many things were taking after the last war.

Literature and politics apart, *Time and the Priestleys* can also be read as an exceptionally clear-eyed view of marriage. Although it is the custom for us to avoid if we can, or to carefully not see 'marriage' when it involves our closest friends and families, to look away politely when it comes too close, Diana Collins does no such thing. Marriage itself and the companionship which often grows up between married couples interests her greatly. She witnesses two ultimately unknowable private planets in conjunction, each allowing glimpses of stress or bliss, and it fascinates her. Jacquetta Hawkes, nee Hopkins, was Jack

Priestley's third wife. She was one of those Cambridge ice-maiden girls – her father was Sir Frederick Gowland Hopkins OM, the discoverer of vitamins and Nobel Prize-winner – who have cool heads and cool feelings until poetry in the first instance and the late middle-aged Jack Priestley in the second, turn them into fire. This marriage, a mismatch on every account, blazed. She was the scrupulously brought-up agnostic, he the Yorkshire Baptist inspiringly stuffed with the Authorized Version; she upper-middle, he working-class moving to middle; he Promethean in output, she slight in hers, his appearance like the human equivalent of beef and two veg, her's lovely – exquisite. His feelings towards women open and passionate, her's towards either sex ambivalent. Yet what a union it proved. Nor is the Collins marriage left as a cipher. Although Diana has given this the full treatment in her biography of Canon Collins, she adds what is necessary here to convince us that it was the strength of their marriage which must have played a part in the late love-story of the Priestleys, proving to them perhaps what can be achieved.

Future biographers and historians of the Cold War years will turn to this modest, well-written book for information which cannot be found anywhere else.

DEAR DODIE
The Life of Dodie Smith
Valerie Grove, 1996

It was baffling to have been for a decade or two so in step with the times, and then for ever after so out of step with the world. Dodie could not understand what had happened to her, nor did she try to. She just went on writing to the end. Somewhere in her path strode the uncouth Mr Osborne and the puzzling Mr Pinter, master of the pause. But although popularity may have deserted her, celebrity never did. Her long life was one of many misses and two or three terrific hits – *Dear Octopus, I Capture the Castle, A Hundred and One Dalmatians.*

Money poured in and out like tides, but whether flush or next to Queer Street, she dressed well and hung on to essentials, such as the white Rolls Royce.

Dodie lived as famous playwrights and novelists of the 1930s were expected to live, with a Syrie Maugham flat in London and a Tudor cottage in remote Essex; with a table at the Ivy and the best seats at first nights. She also lived to write and read, and sociability apart, her pen or a book was rarely out of her hand. To give her her due – and Valerie Grove does just this – as an author, Dodie was the genuine article. But like Rattigan and others she became stranded by the revolution which swept through the theatre during the 1950s, and then lived to be so ancient that she had to be respected for what she still was, and not as a has-been.

'Dodie belonged essentially to the theatre of comfort and reassurance,' Valerie Grove says in this marvellous biography. Dodie's journey to the theatre of comfort was hard: RADA, bit parts which even when serious provoked mirth (it was her diminutive height and oddly fitted together limbs), and cheap lodgings. She felt wounded by all this and got herself a job at Heal's in Tottenham Court Road. Heal's prided itself on being a shop where one could find everything, and nothing could be truer where Dodie was concerned. She found herself Mr Heal's mistress (deliciously described here), she found herself as a writer and not an actress, and in the next department she found beautiful Alec, some years her junior and her devoted partner for the following half century. As told here, the story of their marriage offers the best justification for what Dodie put on at the theatre of comfort and reassurance.

When the Second World War came, she fled to America, accompanied by the first dalmatian. Stricken by guilt and nostalgia, with the money from West End and Broadway plays alternately flooding or trickling in, renting Hollywood houses, wrecking scripts for semi-literate moguls, Dodie worked like a Trojan. Compensations included the friendship of the dubious John Van Druten, author of *Young Woodley*, and the devotion of Christopher Isherwood and Don Bachardy. Although tolerant of their many gay friends, Dodie and Alec found their love inexplicable.

Before coming home Dodie wrote a novel about Wingfield Castle, Suffolk, in which one of the girls, Cassandra, is herself. *I Capture the Castle* has a strange, magical quality not unlike *Rebecca*. It was followed by *A Hundred and One Dalmatians*, which sold a million copies and for which Walt Disney himself came to remote Essex to arrange the filming.

Dear Dodie could have got by on anecdotage. Instead, it is an example of what life of the 'total' writer should be, for this is what Dodie Smith was. Her husband knew this but frequently her publishers and producers did not. Nor, really, did the middle class, whose ethos was to her a kind of ideal. Valerie Grove knows how to respect such a life while seeing its funny side. Her book is a delight and an education.

ROBERT FROST
A Literary Life Reconsidered
William H. Pritchard, 1985

When Robert Frost died in 1963, it was as the most nationally venerated figure in American literature. Two generations had sat at his feet and accepted his poetry as the true distillation of their country's soul. Armoured in honours (he actually sewed the hoods of his honorary doctorates together to make a bedspread), popularly worshipped, summoned to ornament Kennedy's court, his final years were such that any post-mortem assessment of his work must seem more like an act of desecration than of legitimate criticism.

Years before his death at 88 he had blocked the rush on his papers by choosing his own biographer – one of his most ill-judged acts, as it turned out. For, as the huge three-volume life proceeded, a not entirely unknown thing began to occur; the writer began to despise his subject. Entrusted with a craggy national monument, Lawrance Thompson ran into so much smoothness that he had no option but to expose it. Or so he believed. A dreadful man emerged. The tumble from seer to monster was at first too bewildering to be either instructive or diverting; then began the extraction of the poetry from the revelations.

Writing when Thompson's book was still coming out, Ian Hamilton said: 'It is too early to say what the effects of it will be on Frost's popular standing in America but one thing is immediately clear; it will never again be possible for him to be viewed in quite the old way. And this, it seems to me, is all to the good – if Frost's popular following does fall away . . . this will remove a major obstacle from the path of his genuine, and informed, admirers. It will also make it possible for the poetry to be got at in a new, uncluttered way, much more directly and sympathetically.' Hamilton also reminded Frost readers, no doubt to their initial astonishment, that 'there *never was*, at bottom, anything very lovable about the appearance he makes in his own poems.' This is surely the key to a double deception which millions of Americans (the majority of whom believed Poetry equalled Frost) fell for. They loved him because he sang simple American virtues, as they thought. And he allowed them to imagine lovableness where he knew very well it could not exist – deep inside himself. The rhythms he sought were those of colloquial talk, which made him easily accessible and flattering. Thompson's biography hustled him from his plinth into the dock, this Yankee 'Georgian' who was almost grown-up when Whitman died, who had been the close friend of Edward Thomas but whose regularly spaced output was contemporary with those of Eliot and Auden. Overloaded with honours, then stripped of honour, how now was he to be approached? Entirely as an artist, says William Pritchard – how else?

Frost: A Literary Life Reconsidered is not a picking up of the pieces but a finding of the parts. Quotation is minimal and a good collection of the poems needs to be at hand. And then, what surprises, what excellences, what routing of irritants concerning the notorious careerism, and, above all, what fresh understanding of the work itself, cleansed now of all its deplorable homage! Pritchard challenges those biographers who know everything about collecting material, documentation and good narration, but who also know that they possess little real ability to reach an artist's inner life. 'Since we care about the life because of the poems which came out of it, a literary life of Frost could only be written by someone who had an informed inwardness with that poetry. (By "poetry" I mean not just the poems, but also the prose reflections: essays, interviews, notebooks – above all, the letters.) One of Frost's favourite words for poetry was "play", and everything he wrote or did could be thought about in the light of that notion.' Gradually, economically, with no omission of either the self-promoting ghastliness or the tragedy which included his sister's madness and his son's suicide, the maker of the poems emerges. Pritchard leads us into the strangeness and originality of the work.

Was Frost a victim of his own ability to be ceaselessly lionised? He was almost the proto-'writer in residence' and maybe the day has come when the corruptions of academe where certain poets are concerned need to be examined. Frost 'the cracker-barrel sage' possessed natural immodesties which were inflamed by decades of attitudinising on platforms, in common rooms, university libraries and classes. Life down on the farm had been brief in comparison. When he was actually teaching he was masterly. His method was to just read aloud, provide pleasure from literature, and to tempt the young 'to fall under the influence of great books'. He ignored the marking system. Pritchard is at his Frost-discovering best when he investigates the poet's 'guardedness' and his development of a style which 'kept back as much as it gave away'. He says that 'whether in his poems or in his life he needed to make it difficult for those who thought they had the right names for him or for his work.'

STEVIE

A Biography of Stevie Smith

Jack Barbera & William McBrien, 1986

When Stevie died of a brain tumour in March 1971 it was as a popular, much-loved poet who, it was beginning to be recognised, had done the minimum of loving in return. A considerable actress herself, she would have been astonished to know her potential as a future dramatic subject. The wispy businesswoman (as they were called) from Palmer's Green, who chose an aunt in preference to men, and who used up office hours to say and draw querulous things about human and other creatures, was to go on having her uncomfortable appeal.

Her transmutation of the ordinary, not to say the dreary, and her views on the desperate continue to be seen as a kind of cranky magic. Moreover, there is the unforgettable cadence of the voice itself, plaintive as some lamb's when trapped on a ledge, and used with devastating effect. Part of Stevie's good luck (she had a good deal more than she was capable of assessing) was to have reached her peak at the moment when the poetry-reading gig swept the lecture-halls. Glenda Jackson describes her stunning performance. To Stevie it was all part of the proper role of poets to speak their work. She rightly deplored the reading of poetry by actors.

Stevie, her sister Molly, their mother, a grass-widow, and mother's sister, the later immortal Lion of Hull, fled that town in 1906 for 1 Avondale Road, Palmer's Green, a semi-detached house whose effect on the literati who surrounded the poet from the 1930s on was one of puzzlement more than anything. Shabby, unaltered since the furniture van arrived from Yorkshire, full of poor things, as somebody said, they could not see it as *dolce domus*. Yet for Stevie it grew in bliss. Aunt – possibly named Lion after Aunt Leonie in *Swann's Way* – and her niece-partner were soon to have the exclusive run of its grimly cosy rooms, and settled to their roles of cosseted and cossetter.

A seaside snapshot reveals Aunt as one of those ample, majestically frocked and hatted ladies who glare at the young in old *Punches*. We hardly need to be told that she is High Anglican, likes stocks and shares, is above all else respectable, or even that her favourite reading is Francis Younghusband's *The Relief of Chitral*. She lived to a considerate 96, thus sheltering Stevie for almost the whole of her life. Stevie then said: 'People think because I never married, I knew nothing about the emotions. When I am dead you must put them right. I loved my aunt.'

After school and secretarial college, Stevie went to work for, in succession, Sir Neville Pearson and Sir George Newnes, and to return each evening to find 'her ordinary suburb as somewhere wondrous'. As her biographers have at times quite a struggle to retain our sympathy for someone whose closest friends provide fearful evidence of her selfishness, much praise must go to the way in which they show us the higher Stevie, as it were, the artist-writer-child transmogrifying her nipped and grey territory into zany gold.

She began to write her first poems in 1924 but didn't begin getting published until a decade later. *Novel on Yellow Paper*, published when she was thirty-four, created a small sensation and admitted her to London literary society. From then on it had to face up to the fact that it had an extra task, which was 'looking after Stevie'. It is here that the legends begin. The ruthless hitching of lifts home – or anywhere she needed to go – from those unfortunate enough to possess a car; the finding of oneself, all too recognisable, in a story; the witty disloyalty.

Rosamond Lehmann, one of the battered, sums it all up when she tells Stevie about 'your talent for pointing the deathly joke and causing the wry smile'. But whatever she said or did, the friends, Elisabeth Lutyens, Kay Dick, Norah Smallwood and a little regiment of males from publishers' offices, literary festivals, and so on, stuck to her. She told John Hayward, during the war, that she wrote less for fame than to find company. Company was certainly what her books brought her, that of anyone she wishes to meet. She was a celebrity and behaved like one, demanding and usually getting whatever she wanted.

She became agnostic yet increasingly theological, and grumbled away at God and the Church. Always comforted by the notion of suicide, in 1953 she cut her wrists. There was not so much despair as ennui behind the gesture. She thought that 'women are more affected by boredom than men . . . The capacity women have for just hanging on is depressing to contemplate.' She was just hanging on in Sir George's office, and its small drudgery, like that of the 'governess trade' for Jane Austen, became all at once insupportable. Three months earlier, she had written her best-known poem, 'Not Waving but Drowning'. She said it was for those who were not at home in the world. Was she among 'the too far out'?

This full but not 'official' life points to the contrary. It shows an old nestling who chants strange songs and expects Aunt and the world to take good care of her. The pleasures of being alone, after Aunt's departure, took her by storm. She wrote many poems about isolation, but no sooner had she finished one than 'the happiness of being alone comes flooding back'. The authors have spoken to everybody she knew and sought to balance their caustic, occasionally touching but always intriguing reminiscences. It was clearly no small task. Not nice was the verdict of Francis King, Olivia Manning and most of her circle. Perhaps a student at Sussex University, Colin Amery, got her contradictions in some kind of order: 'a middle-aged woman behaving like a child; not being able to sing, but singing.'

VAMP TILL READY
Further Memoirs
Roy Fuller, 1982

THE INDIVIDUAL AND HIS TIMES
A Selection of the Poetry of Roy Fuller
ed. V. J. Lee, 1982

Introducing a selection of his poems, *The Individual and his Times*, Roy Fuller says that 'every poet cuts into English literature at a certain point in the game, when all sorts of what may be called purely literary preoccupation exist.' It would be a fitting statement with which to preface the second volume of his memoirs, although one must add that he understands the knack of cutting back into the first volume and cutting ahead into volumes still to come, thus avoiding that decadal neatness which is so unlike life.

Vamp Till Ready, which is the tale of a newly grown-up Fuller acquiring his Marxism, his legal career, his wife, his war and proof that he was indeed a poet, grows most naturally out of *Souvenirs*, which is the tale of his childhood. The tone continues to be one of laconic eloquence. The flavour of the Thirties, now so familiar to us because of its endless evocations, is given a stranger, more compelling taste because of the economical way in which he handles it. The signposts pointing from slump to call-up indicate the usual old road, but the sights and comments on the way provoke a fresh attention. Again, it has something to do with their descriptive frugality, their never going on and on. 'Poetry is on the whole, a succinct art,' remarks Fuller, and so in his view is autobiography. The title refers to that extemporary rhythmic strumming, so popular at the time with pianists, which preceded the song.

The style is one of affectionate irony, reticence and bursts of wayward colour having to contend with an amused formality. Although Fuller reminds us that the 'I' of a poem is not necessarily the poet himself, here on every page it is made absolutely plain that the 'I' speaks for his 1930-42 self as exclusively as art and memory can persuade it to. Although the 'I' of 'Obituary of R. Fuller' is decidedly that of the poet at his most self-candid –

> *We note the death, with small regret,*
> *Of one who'd scarcely lived, as yet.*
> *Born just before the First World War,*
> *Died when there'd only been one more:*
> *Between, his life had all been spent*
> *In the small-bourgeois element,*
> *Sheltered from poverty and hurt,*
> *From passion, tragedy and dirt*

– the 'I' of the autobiographer has been able to speak with more justice. In poetry, says Fuller, a writer can be free with the details of his personal life, can 'give himself away as a lesson, not a confession'. In prose, as we see here, it is quite another telling of the same story. True confessions, nothing less. He rakes them out of his past with wit and civility.

Certainly, it appears to have been a life minus the traditional conflicts. That fundamental one of whether he should become a full-time writer or a lawyer, or a poet and a lawyer, or a lawyer who writes poetry, for example. To be able to recognise 'almost from the start that I should never abandon a "job" in favour of "writing"' is a type of self-knowledge which puts paid to a whole mass of struggles, confusions and hurts from the word go. He treats it simply as a basic fact and then, of course, has to describe how two such apparently opposing strands, that involving the orthodoxies of a successful legal career, and that involving an equally committed role as a poet, began, right from the start, to work in tandem.

There is no apology; that is the essence of it. He has also had to deal with the characteristics which made him conventionally attractive and acceptable, these being obvious and unavoidable. In this volume we see their emergence. Modesty, mercifully, doesn't really come into it; something more obliquely unpretentious allows Fuller to take close stock of what was clearly in most respects a fortunate being with the minimum of self-regard.

The secret seems to be to reveal himself without dwelling on himself. Hence the concise and brief form of each revelation. 'Perhaps my whole life could be depicted in terms of the destruction or modification of public and private illusions . . . In the areas dealt with by the pages that follow, I see, looking back, that what my generation proposed to put in place of illusions had been formed by the illusions themselves.'

The book begins with Fuller playing cricket at Blackpool, cramming for the Law Society's Intermediate Examination, continuing his friendship with Gilbert Waller, the born 'foot in the door, picture-snatching' journalist, living in London and hanging around Soho, going to music halls, encountering Harold Nicolson on a train (a faint pass), joining the CPGB and selling the *Daily Worker* on the Saturday streets, reading prolifically, as all young writers-to-be must, and, by Chapter Five, becoming a salaried solicitor at £3 a week and writing his first poem. One of them was published in Grigson's *NewVerse* in December 1934. It was about excessive rainfall, not the fate of the West. And then, disconcertingly, in 1935 came unemployment, his mother's illness from Graves' disease and his 'immense trek' to Ashford, Kent, to work for a firm that was to make him an experienced solicitor of a quite exceptional kind.

All this is a brilliant glimpse of interwar provincial life. 'Writing these last few pages, I have been struck by the contrast between them and what has come down the years as the atmosphere and aspirations of the Thirties (I say nothing of the almost unrecapturable density of life – people, objects, sensations, in their actuality, not simply as traditions . . . This period inculcated a pessimism that lasted far beyond the period itself),' He goes on to speak of 'the decade's amazing historical tergiversations, of the closeness of great change'. As well as conveying an unforgettable whiff of the politics of the time, he remembers things like the psychology of cigarettes, the impact made on him by Auden and Rex Warner, and a pervasive fatalism.

In April 1941 he gets his call-up papers. Why the Navy? Because of the horrific trench-warfare anecdotes he had heard as a boy. Thus, 'a non-games-playing solicitor in his 30th year' reports to HMS *Ganges* – the Equitable Building Society, which was his last employer, making up his pay. Archaic, gruesome disciplines at Holbrook, Chatham and Lee-on-Solent, relentless profanity, 'Ath' for atheist on his identity disc, poems for *The Middle of a War* getting themselves written in 'a bizarre mixture of the bellicose and the domestic', it comes together in as vivid an account of Forties' forces experience as any written under the searchlights.

V J Lee's selection of Fuller' poetry, is non-chronological, a device that works well:

> *Incredibly I lasted out a war,*
> *Survived the unnatural, enormous danger*
> *Of each enormous day. And so befell*
> *A peril more enormous and still stranger:*
> *The death by nature, chanceless, credible.*

209

JOHN STEWART COLLIS
A Memoir
Richard Ingrams, 1986

The fields speak with two voices, that which comes directly from them, Clare, Cobbett, Hardy; and that which comes, somewhat indirectly, to them of those who have produced a huge rural-based literature. There is no question of authenticity. A poet, novelist, historian or ecologist coming to a village will often see more than any local has ever done, and certainly be able to say more than any local would ever dare. However, two books published just after the last war blurred these two forms of articulation and should have had an immediate effect on both – except, as they say, the time wasn't right. The books were *While Following the Plough*, a masterpiece of its kind, and *Down to Earth*, and they were the work of an Irishman with an English education (Rugby and Balliol) who had toiled alongside the last of the old farm labourers as one of them, and not as a man fallen on bad days but as a man who had achieved what he had long desired, to work in a field. A philosopher, of course. In the early 1970s these by then forgotten essays were re-issued in a single volume under the at-first forbidding title of *The Worm Forgives the Plough* and to great acclaim due to perfect timing. The Green movement was springing up and in the poetic-philosophic-sociological pages of this most beautifully written book were many of the roots of its gospel. It's until then obscure author became a celebrity, and justly so. He was in his seventies, a wiry, brown, youthful old man recently married to the widow of the art connoisseur Sir Edward Beddington Behrens, and living at Abinger Common, E. M. Forster's old territory.

Who was John Stewart Collis, the writer who had so mysteriously bridged the space between the fields' own indigenous voices and the voices of those who, through the centuries, have been drawn to them? Richard Ingrams provides the first complete outline of a figure who has for a decade or more greatly intrigued the literary world. Collis had no wish to be outside, very much the reverse. He had taken to writing as a vocation soon after leaving Oxford. His brother Maurice was a well-known author and he himself had written some dozen books as well as *While Following the Plough* and *Down to Earth*, and was perplexed and hurt by the neglect which he couldn't understand, but which was plainly his lot. It caused him to retain many of the naïve responses to publishers, literary editors, reviewers, etc. of a beginner, so that as a distinguished elderly writer he could be touchy or easily impressed by matters and people which someone in his position would not normally have bothered himself with. Ingrams, who became Collis's friend and whose acknowledged privilege it was to bring him out a bit via his colleagues at the *Spectator* and elsewhere, is both intrigued and touched by the complexity of the neglect and eremitism which surrounded the writer. In one sense Collis was in traditional flight from the rat race, a man who would trade-in any of the jobs and ways of life commensurate with his background and education just to lie in the sun; in the other sense he was forced to experience the agonising indifference of London's publishers to his existence. His marvellous *While Following the Plough* was turned down by twelve of them, he told Ingrams. How could it have been? Just read the first six pages.

Getting past Collis's pride and pain wasn't easy. Being ignored for forty or more years had not wrecked the high opinion he held of his own work and when I, and others, after his 'discovery', began to recommend it, and received letters from him, it was clear that what he needed most of all wasn't fame, but connection. This was how Ingrams first came to know him, and with this welcome result. His complex mixture of the austere and the worldly was just right for drawing out Collis's equally complex amalgam of sensuousness and severity. By nature he was no confessor and his past got into not quite accurately piled-up episodes due to his not caring to look back. He was the twin who wasn't loved – there is much evidence of twin preferment, of one child getting all the love and the other the cold shoulder. His father was a Dublin solicitor and the whole family was thrusting and competitive. Because he was cast in the Cinderella role, Collis felt early on that he must at all cost outdo his brothers. 'Ambition is rarer than is often supposed. The family idol loves to shine much more steadily than the English sun, but he is not filled with a burning ambition to do so since his light is already so luminous. It is the non-spoilt children who build empires and found dynasties . . .'

Lack of success, including the breakdown of his marriage, plus an enchantment with the open air, led gradually to rural isolation and then to farmwork, and to forestry. He was slight, very strong, socially somewhat unplaceable in the English countryside and so peculiar in his approach to it that his friend Ruth Pitter called him 'the village idiot'. He was in fact shatteringly realistic and sane, and if there is any dottiness to be found it is on the farm. Farmers, labourers and their wives, here they were in his books, as they frequently still are, little insular pockets of humanity fretting against each other in their hard rituals and determined limitations. Collis was an artist, not a chronicler, so his interest lay in himself, not in the now much described passing of the old rural economy. 'My chief aim has been to present my physical and mental reactions regardless of their consistency, and to give a truthful picture of what I found in the agricultural world'.

It is ironic that it was Charles Morgan, a writer who is thought little of now but who in his day enjoyed vast respect, who first recognised Collis's brilliance. The two close friends who alternately helped and influenced him most were Stephen Potter and G. B. Edwards, an author even more neglected than himself. Collis's epitaph for Edwards might just as well have been his own, says Ingrams: 'He suffered throughout his life from three terrible things: poverty, publishers and women.' No doubt a fuller revelation of this strange and excellent man will appear in the not so distant future, but this penetrating though affectionate glimpse of him by Richard Ingrams will do very well until then.

FROM THE HEADLANDS

FAMILY CIRCLES
At the Yeoman's House, 2010

Jasper continues to cast a long shadow across the flint fields. He was an eclectic collector of Stone Age artefacts to bronze penny-in-the-slot machines from the old seaside, and anything in-between. Immensely tall and fragile, always growing until his fine tousled head was far beyond us in more ways than one, his voice would descend in a run of rough barks. Myself being the only walker on the flint fields other than Jasper would watch him stalking the winter wheat, usually just after Christmas, a scavenger of Wormingford's Neolithic litter, every now and then giving his stork-like swoop when he suspected a find. For the worked and unworked stones could each be deceitfully alike until held in one's hand. On we would go, a long way apart, eyes down, Jasper filling his pockets with treasures, me picking up stuff which usually proved to be more plough-chipped than hand-chipped, and throwing it away. It was always dreadfully cold. And the rooks would kaaa-kaaa their way over us in black shoals.

At the farmhouse, and at any time of the year, Jasper would suddenly descend on me in search of company and priceless Huntley and Palmer's biscuit tins or 'that old wireless or those old bottles with marble stoppers'. His hoarder's gaze would alight on the yellow peony in full bloom. 'You can have a bit in the autumn, Jasper.' But as we would soon discover he could not wait. Where did I keep my old fork? He would bend his way through the low rooms, never banging his head, leaving a belated adolescent musk in his wake. Did I want that old clock? He could make it go. There would be a tender meeting with the ginger cat. Wound back into his dilapidated van, he would crash up the track.

It was in our Stone Age village by the Stour that Jasper's aloneness was most evident. Also his happiness. My only real find was a beautifully weighty palm-fitting gold and white stone which we both took to be a polishing tool or smoother. Jasper's loot was a very different matter. He arranged it in one of those handsome Victorian cabinets especially devised for a birds-egg collection. Axes, arrows, flint saws, knives, beads, flint, everything nestled in yellowing cotton wool. Never quite trustingly, he would place a particular treasure in my hand and then snatch it back like a child. And these brief exchanges would always make me imagine the original warm human hands of the ancient craftsmen. The archaeologists call the loop of the river which flows past the flint fields a meander. It was the River Meander which, changing course at Ephesus, left the harbour low and dry. The Stour meanders all the way from Cambridgeshire to the North Sea but at Wormingford a community turned its C into a D by sealing a meander with a linear cemetery of six ring-ditch graves. Jasper did not know this.

One lovely summer's day Jasper died. He was thirty-three. Never again the tall finders-keepers walker through our first settlement in the valley. Never again an eye like his for a find. I took his funeral at the Crem. 'Nothing religious,' his family said. And, 'No one will be there. Just us.' It was a burning noon and everyone thirty-three or thereabouts in our world was present. A multitude of upset young men and crying girls all dressed in shirts and jeans, all carrying skimpy flowers. I led them in. Jasper's absurdly long coffin swayed in my wake. Outside lay stone-filled acres, countless tombstones, miles of gravel, thousands of carved names and declarations of love, mossy hands, wings, chippings. The undertaker's cars were fiery chariots in the sunshine. It was all too hot for what had to be done. The elegant Crem man saw to it 'that I had everything'. During the Middle Ages it was presumed that we would all be aged thirty-three in heaven, the same age as Christ.

As we passed up the aisle the Icelandic sculptor who lived in Penny's barn leant forward and placed a carved seagull on Jasper's feet. A woman strummed *Ave Maria* on a guitar and then, after the last notes had faded away, I told the sad crowd what most of them knew, but adding things like the walks in the winter fields to look for 'finds' and Jasper's jackdaw habits in, I supposed, all our houses. I then read one of those threnodies from the *Oxford Book of Greek*

Verse which commemorate young men on whose stele, or thin stone monument, their laurels would hang until leaf by leaf they vanished. Euripides had written it ages after our flint princes whose circular tombs had sealed-off the river's meander had existed. Having no knowledge of the wooden seagull, it seemed a small miracle of suitability.

> *Bird of the sea rock, of the bursting spray,*
> > *O halcyon bird,*
> *That wheelest crying, crying on thy way:*
> *Who knoweth grief can read the tale of thee:*
> *One love long lost, one song for ever heard . . .*

There is a little button beneath the Crem desk which brings the curtain down on life. Jasper slid slowly from sight. Would this last movement disturb the seagull? It trembled but stayed with him. As most of the mourners were too young to know what a funeral was, the grief was terrible. They stood outside in the heat amidst the cellophaned flowers, as much shocked as grief-stricken. Back in the village Jasper's parents and I walked by the lake to get over the jolt of it all, saying little. A mile or so down the lane the Stone-agers' bones were as usual ossifying with flint. It was calcium to chalk under the corn. 'That seagull!' said Jasper's mother, 'what a good touch'. I still have no idea what happened to him. At the time we called it 'outgrowing his strength'. This cannot have been right.

A long time after this, returning from the Bluebell Party at Tiger Hill in Tony's Range-Rover, splashing across the stream as we used to do with our bikes and entering the village via the ford bridge, we heard a pistol shot and then the flap-flap-flap of a burst tyre. Doug and his lady happened to be passing. Joy lit up his face. 'A puncture!' For there is an indescribable pleasure in helping to change someone else's wheel – to being on the spot. 'And no wonder!' cried Doug, holding up a flint axhead. 'Come in handy at last!' When Tony ran his fingers along its edge one of them bled. Doug repeated what luck it was for us that he happened to be passing and the axe trembled on the dashboard.

217

Aircraft fly over all the time. Those carrying a crowd fly high. The aerial photographers fly as low as they dare and hitting the long beams of the winter sun, their cameras combing the crops. The Suffolk and Essex gliding Club saunters overhead. Also a farmer from his private airstrip. All this once on a Boxing Day or the Feast of Stephen. I thought of the young saint standing in the stoning pit and the tentmaker guarding the clothes of the executioners, and behind them the city getting on with its normal business. Boulders, not flints, would have been thrown. We call our boulders 'sarsens', from Saracens, stranger stones, for they do not belong to our ecology. Too hard to cut into shape, they go into a church tower just as they are, or are humped to a garden as a kind of wonder. I have dragged one or two of them from where a ploughman has left them on a headland. Sarsens are hard blocks of tertiary sand, some a youthful pink having endured less than seventy million years of pressure. Unlike most oddities, they have no history of being unlucky. Just foreign. Once possessing a Lower and a Higher Stoney Field, my farmland must have often pulled out, like Little Jack Horner, this plum of building material. Undetected like some ground iceberg, a plough could sail into one of them and get wrecked. The ploughmen called them 'they bloody grit things'.

Paul Gilman, who looks after our Historic Environment Records at Chelmsford, has given me one called *A Cropmark Landscape in Three Dimensions*. I am enthralled. It stops all other reading for days. Holding it before me, I am able to stand exactly where the Neolithic and Bronze Age dead encircle one another in a kind of remote and caring intimacy. The earth rings are linked in a line across the space left by the river's meander, enclosing a ritual ground. It is where Jasper picked up his best finds. So maybe also a barter market. Or even a thanksgiving place for the gift of flint. Holding *A Cropmark Landscape in Three Dimensions* in front of me like a kind of literary divining-rod, I note the shimmering river, the rising reeds, the mirrored clouds, the devoted swans and the deep silence. The wheat looks scanty but is well up and there could be a kingfisher. Brown dace swim against the current. In January the crop seems to grow on a beach, in March on a water-meadow. Sprayers will make tramlines through it

218

and these will become highways for historians.

It was the flint itself that the village harvested right up until the Great War. Bent low in family groups, women and children gathered it to mend roads. They filled a pail and then a tumbril up to the chalk mark. The first school registers are furious with stone-picking absentees. The farmers were bewildered. When hadn't a child of eight been put out to work? None of these toilers was aware of the circles of the dead. They themselves were called the poor.

Ages would pass before further circles would be added to our landscape. Robert Morden was thirty-two when he published his map of Suffolk. It was covered with a rash of green spots, i.e. the parks of the nobility and gentry. Except for a few churches there was no other geographic information. No windmills, no herring-boats being blown along by Zephyrus and certainly no farms. Morden was an ambitious geographer who was aiming his map at the country-house where such industries had to be beyond the pale. Or out of sight. Not long after abbeys and priories became palaces a process of 'imparadising' began which walled or fenced-off farming and the peasantry in general. There was no rough husbandry in the Garden of Eden, just fruit trees and seed-bearing herbs, and a lovely river (the Euphrates). God walked in it in the evening to chat with his highest creation Adam.

To 'impark' or enclose a country-house was a word first used in 1535. To call this house a 'seat' first appeared in 1607. Such dwellings became rural hubs of taste and learning, and local power-bases. Park-fences and brick walls ran for miles round them. A Suffolk feature is the serpentine or 'crinkle-crankle' wall. Fanciful lodges and gates flaring with heraldry permitted entrance to wonderful horticulture, architecture, music, 'society', local government and, often, the parish church. This having occupied the holy place since a Saxon cleared the wood to make the first field would still be adjacent to the mansion which now occupied the site of his wooden hall.

Most of Robert Morden's ringed worlds remain in situ although searching for a few of them will lead one to the ghostly grandeur of forsaken gardens and owl-visited ruins like the incomparably sad Houghton House in Bedfordshire, which was John Bunyan's House

Beautiful. One finds them by the straight lines of World War Two airfields, these tell-tale fragments of pride driven into the concrete runways. At Stoke-by-Nayland, which I glimpse through a framework of oaks as I walk down the farmtrack, and all of five miles distant, the medieval park remains but its hall has vanished. The youthful John Constable passed its miles of fencing many times. The gamekeepers were instructed to 'Pray, permit Mr Constable to draw the trees' – a pass to a place where he did not belong. The hall-owners commissioned him to paint portraits of their houses and were angry when he included farm animals. His landscapes with their agricultural contents were too 'low' for a gentleman's drawing-room and were not purchased. Having spent a fortune keeping the village out of sight one was hardly likely to hang views of it on one's walls. However, the student of agriculture might equally find a Constable questionable, for it was often an imparadising of what was happening to the workaday countryside, at that moment in starvation and ferment. Yet the great artist was not deceitful: as a boy he had witnessed farming harmony and prosperity in the Stour Valley, and his work was a declaration of how things should be. He watched the park-owners flee to their town-houses for safety, the stacks being fired and the labourers starving.

The map-maker's green rings are confident. They declare park-rule, park civilisation. They cluster for the most part in West Suffolk and in the Blythings, a hundred to the north of the county. Great stretches of the county are parkless. The oddest thing about Morden's map is that many of the place-names are printed as they used to be pronounced and not as they are spelt. Laneham (Lavenham), Carsey (Kersey) etc. And all the time, not even the highest church tower being able to let one see a ring of graves in a field which grew flint, there existed below the surface of things communities which preceded the angels.

Park walls are an architecture in itself, and a vast undertaking. There are still lots of them to walk round both inside and out. Industrial revolution magnates continued to build them almost to the time of the First World War and the pinnacle of country-house culture. They support an entire brick or wooden fence natural history of life on their own. Plants, insects, birds, creatures of every kind occupy them like an elongated abandoned city. Alec Clifton-Taylor says that all bricks were called 'waltyles' before the fifteenth century and he describes the ascendancy of the brick we know today. There are still two main bondings. The brick park wall, often running for miles around house and grounds, was for the most part a Georgian extravagance. Jane Austen comically exaggerated the bliss contained within them and the terrors which lay beyond them. Also their moral purpose and economy. In *Emma* feeble Mr Woodhouse and his daughter do not so much reside as reign. Their park wall would no doubt have been built in English garden wall bond (three or five courses of stretchers to one of headers) or in Flemish garden wall bond (three stretchers to each header in each course). Such a bonded circle would contain within it virtues, pleasures and feelings unknown to those without. It was said in Suffolk that a Victorian park wall would cost as much as a pound a yard. They spared no expense.

It is quite a thought that in these days we might have a greater understanding of the society who made the ring-ditches by the river than of what walled-out most of their village neighbours. Sir George Sitwell, staring across the whole of Sheffield from Renishaw, observed to his son, 'Do you realise, Osbert, that there is no one between us and the Locker-Lampsons?'

My stackyard was walled-in to stop the animals from getting out. A few yards remain. And here and there is a stout buttress supporting hanks of ivy. Tall nettles green the powdered mortar. I quarry it for rubble or nice hand-made edging bricks. Let tottering boundaries be. Our squire's hall is on high ground and sheltered by trees. John Constable's Uncle Abram rented it for years. Our churchyard wall leans out, due, it is said, 'to the dead having a stretch'.

MAN AND THE NATURAL WORLD
Changing Attitudes in England, 1500-1800

Keith Thomas, 1983

Anyone, and that must mean most of us, who has been caught in the drift of the vast ecological literature of recent years must have noticed how repetitively it cites the same relatively few authorities: John Ray, Linnaeus, Constable, Gilbert White, Cobbett, plus the pundits of the present.

Keith Thomas did not set out to challenge these producers of the great advances in how we interpret and understand nature, but he has succeeded in doing so nevertheless. And very eye-openingly even if, after reading his surprising book, common sense tells us, men and women being what they are, whether their sovereign is Mary Tudor or Elizabeth Windsor, that there must always have been those who simply shared England with its flora and fauna, as well as those who knew they were a cut above the non-human natural order.

Thomas invites the sharers to speak or rather he masses a collective voice which few would have believed existed until he released it from the stacks of sermons, pamphlets, poetry, village records, diaries, etc. to which no modern naturalist and conservationist would think of turning. He makes his case by the unsuspected eloquence of fugitive witness, and by all the big names too, of course, when necessary.

But it is the freshness and power of all these little known or unknown people when they give their views on bloodsports, flowers, pets, trees, farms, cities, vivisection, pollution and especially their notions on where they stand in the natural scene which takes one's breath away! All these attitudes being held at the same time as ladies dismounted to personally cut the throats of the hunted deer, and lords, with a mandate from Genesis, being certain that they were lords of creation.

Gradually, by building up a whole new edifice of supportive quotations, Thomas sets back the commonly held idea that our enlightened thinking towards the land is a late phenomenon by some centuries. As he says, 'nowadays one can hardly open a newspaper without encountering some impassioned debate about culling grey seals or cutting down trees in Hampton Court or saving an endangered species of wild animal. But to understand these present-day sensibilities we must go back to the early modern (Tudor) period. For it was between 1500 and 1800 that there occurred a whole cluster of changes in the way in which men and women, at all social levels, perceived and classified the natural world around them.'

And go back he does, but not via the celebrated signposts. Instead, the return to the grassroots of our own environmental convictions is made by the most enchantingly minor paths. In a way, *Man and the Natural World* is an anthology of forgotten or ignored viewpoints on ever-threatened subjects, and they should make everybody, from the nuclearists to the producers of the latest field studies documentary, very humble. Far too many to quote, they simply tumble over each other in their brilliantly selected forcefulness.

Developed from the author's George Macaulay Trevelyan Lectures for 1979, this book shows the English moving from a position which held that everything which grew, swam, flew or grazed existed soley for their food or amusement to one in which, gradually, and pleasurably in a different way, they recognised that they simply had a place in nature.

It was this revolution in seeing where they stood, anthropologically speaking, 'which generated both an intense interest in the natural world and those doubts and anxieties about their relation to it which we have inherited in magnified form'.

Being part of nature instead of being master of it brought a close examination of it, of flowers, fruit and beasts living for themselves even as the human use of them as nourishment, medicine and work-power increased. Curious things happened. The horror of 'bestiality,' for example, all that unspeakable dissent by a few from the divine image state to the animal state, vanished. ('It was no accident that the symbol of anti-Christ was the Beast.') Men even began to have a conscience about eating beasts.

But it wasn't all sweetness and light, because 'To say that there was no firm line between man and beast was to strike a blow at human pride,' which eighteenth-century Europeans in general soothed by what is now called racialism. There being no superiority where there is no inferiority, the notion of 'lesser' states of humanity, most particularly negroes, bolstered up an otherwise collapsing sense of lordship.

On the credit side, there was the delight of all classes in England in nature study, both as a science and a recreation, and the incredible development of cultivated plants from some 200 species in 1500 to more than 18,000 in 1839. This is the period when nearly all our garden flowers arrived, from the New World, from the East, from, it seems, every seaman's locker.

Thomas goes so far as to say that our craze for gardening, pets and hobbies has vitiated our political impulse. Maybe now that the builders are pushing mortgages into mean little boxes with yards just big enough for a pram and a clothes-line, the conditions will soon generate an uprising.

It is a dense and rich work, crammed with anecdote and telling little facts, and all held in place by a strong yet calm and unindignant commentary.

The humanitarian impulse remains as inconsistent and illogical now as when, in the eighteenth century, Dr Johnson fed live oysters to Hodge and passionate squibs against fox-hunting were bound up in calfskin. Horace Walpole said that he knew that a friend was turning Methodist because in the middle of their talk he rose, opened the window, and let out a moth. Christopher Smart reminded his readers of the beetle, 'whose life is precious in the sight of God, tho' his appearance is against him.' Shelley inveighed against castration, and Thomas himself is excellent on the long and conventional and even now more widely practised evil of animal mutilation.

He allows the Church to come out with flying colours in all this transitional sensibility and many of his best quotes are from the country clergy. And he is at his wittiest when it comes to trees – a magnificent essay, this – and their sublime role in human affairs. 'It was not on Tower Hill that the axe made its most important contribution to human history.'

THE ILLUSTRATED NATURAL HISTORY OF SELBORNE
Gilbert White

ed. Richard Mabey, 1988

THE JOURNALS OF GILBERT WHITE, 1774-1783, Volume II

ed. Francesca Greenoak, gen. ed Richard Mabey, 1988

It is now just two centuries since an elderly Hampshire curate took the liberty of 'laying before the public his idea of parochial history'. The idea was novel and the public that small erudite group which habitually subscribed to the works of scholarly clergymen. In no circumstances could the author or his first readers have imagined that, within a generation, a village annal in which the local antiquities came a very long way after the local fauna and flora would take a place beside the King James Bible, the *Book of Common Prayer* and *Pilgrim's Progress* in the nation's literary priorities.

There have been as many explanations of Gilbert White's success as there have been editors of his *Natural History of Selborne*. Most put it down to his prose-style which amalgamates in an entirely original and marvellous manner the learned and common languages of his day. But Richard Mabey, his latest and best interpreter, puts his finger on the perennial enchantment of *Selborne* when he stresses its parochiality. By allowing generations of readers to take great gulps of real parish air, and not vestry-chest dust, by letting us into a village which is a helter-skelter of dips and hangers, beeches, house martins, yews, bees, masses of boys and girls, etc. and not just the site of a family-tree, White engendered a sense of parochial thanksgiving and release.

Mabey mentions the 'vivid, sensuous, attentiveness' of White's approach and his quick village lad's eye for anything which arrives on the little scene or vanishes from it. One as yet not suggested reason for his popularity must surely be his quite unselfconscious ability to reconcile us to death. His descriptions of natural senescence envelop humanity and our deaths lose their fears and importance. Being a priest, he might have moralised, but he never does. Insects have their hours, Timothy the tortoise an age which is wasted on him, as he sleeps most of it away, the neighbours tumble from their beds into the churchyard, and become part of Selborne's compost as well as immortal souls.

It was an earthiness which appealed to White's readers and which applied to any parish, as did the 'heavenliness' of birdsong, summer meadows, gardens, toads even. His book struck at the grimness of country life. It taught a form of observation which caused the boundaries of the smallest hamlets to become illimitable. It also created longings in city-dwellers and colonialists for the classic English rural scene, now made intellectually challenging.

The Whites had been indigenous to the Selborne area for generations. Gilbert, born in the vicarage in 1720, might have succeeded to the living had he not gone to the wrong Oxford College, Oriel instead of Magdalen, which held the patronage. This rankled a bit, as did career failures in other directions. Known as Busser-White when young because of the way he kissed girls, there was little initially which pointed to the future bachelor genius which was to revolutionise the study of natural history by noting what exactly lay outside his own back-door.

This in the first instance was the neglected garden of the Wakes, a house occasionally packed to the rafters with Whites. Gilbert, always crazy about gardening, transformed its grounds and recorded the process in one of the 'garden kalendars' which were so popular at the time. He was thirty and the habits of a long life to come had been rooted. A few years later his friend Daines Barrington, who invented them, would send him another kind of calendar, a printed form called a Naturalist's Journal which had to be filled in daily.

White's first entry in the *Garden Kalendar* was about planting Spanish beans (Jan. 7th 1751), and that in the *Journal* about the ghastly winter of 1768. The discipline which eventually was to produce the famous book (the author and Timothy the tortoise had some things in common) was thus established by a sublime version of form-filling. The actual format of *The Natural History of Selborne* was created by the letters which White wrote to Daines Barrington and to another friend, Thomas Pennant, most of which are an inspired expansion of the brief entries on the forms. If ever a great book grew like a tree which would dominate and delight its particular world for many human lifetimes, *Selborne* certainly has.

It is quite a shock to discover in such an old work almost everything we currently believe in. White's philosophy is 'go outside and look' and 'know your sharers of the earth'. One reason for his loyal following is that he is the undisputed master of the British preoccupation with weather. 'The weather of a district is undoubtedly part of its natural history' – thus those unrivalled accounts of wild and bitter days or blissful suns. We recognise, too, a man who, for one reason or another, has become more detached than he realises from the central conventions of his day. As with all scientists, these go out of the window when one needs the help and eyes of the whole community. Critics have repined that White did not include a full study of the human inhabitants of Selborne in his book, but although the references are brief, did local faces ever shine out more memorably than those mentioned here?

Selborne was odd in White's time and far from being the typical Georgian village. It had never had a squire, it was both deeply sunken and dizzily raised up, and extremely difficult to get in and out of when it came to travelling by coach. Everybody lived in good stone or brick houses and in a decided seclusion where the rest of Hampshire was concerned. White offers no idyll but he does, quite unaware, depict a rare kind of rural freedom. Crabbe's Suffolk parishioners rush off from their toil to botanise or collect butterflies, and there are escapes from 'condition', but there is none of that commonly-breathed air which blows through Selborne. The poet John Clare once thought of Selborne-ing his beloved Helpston. What a natural history that would have been to place beside White's.

In his study and editing of Gilbert White, the most comprehending we possess of Britain's favourite naturalist, Richard Mabey sees us as the inheritors of something enormously valuable, something untouched even by later scientific discovery, or modern methods of social history. His work, and that of Francesca Greenoak, gives us such

227

close access that it is like trailing within earshot of the little clergyman and his nephew Gibraltar Jack, and all those girls, through that humpy parish with its skimming hirundines and highly respected crickets. The beauty of it is, as everybody has known since 1788, that *Selborne* remains a useful guide to any village to this day, not to mention being a path to its poetry.

THE BANVILLE DIARIES
Journals of a Norfolk Gamekeeper 1822-44

ed. Norma Virgoe & Susan Yaxley, 1986

Rather than a diary, this is a book created around one, though it has nothing to do with the now familiar style of book-making whereby some, usually nineteenth-century, journal or album is provided with a glossy package. The Banville Diaries is, in fact, an important work made readable by means of a sensitive interpretation, a linking narrative and an inspired selection of pictures. A sample of the original, opaque text is offered as justification for the heavy editing. All the same, one hopes that the diaries as they were written may eventually find a publisher, as Banville's wonderfully inexact words, the Irish-English confection of literacy, illiteracy, eloquence and ignorance, hard-hitting comment and pure story-telling, would be treasure trove for the etymologist, 'He got me a Pear of Barls from manstearter when I was there we had some astrs to Eat we also had som Bear with Mr Wust Mr masts keeper from Barningham Hall' (He got me a pair of (gun) barrels from Manchester. When I was there we had some oysters to eat. We also had some beer with Mr West, Mr Mott's keeper from Barningham Hall).

Banville's reason for keeping a diary was to show the world what it was to be a servant who experienced particularly the actual relationship between master and man. He left all 2,000 pages of it to his master's son, requiring that it should be printed. As gamekeeper to

Thomas Buxton he was in the customary awkward position of sporting and travelling companion, as well as a simple cottager on the estate. The Buxtons themselves had a somewhat complicated position in Norfolk, using the country, as the editors say, rather like a Scottish moor for their shooting, while their real centre was near London. Norfolk grandees such as the Windhams were sniffy about the celebrated philanthropic circle made up of Gurneys, Hoares, Frys, Buxtons and others. Banville the gamekeeper, meticulous when it came to rank, noted it all. Thomas Buxton treated him pretty well and captured his affection. Llewellyn Lloyd, his first employer, did not, and as a result receives in these pages a spate of insubordinate home truths very like those which Boswell deservedly suffered – and accepted – from his servant.

As with most diaries, Banville's fascinates because of the way in which private matters play against the history of the times. In his case there is added interest in that he was a poor Irish Catholic in the midst of very rich Quakers turned Anglicans. During his visits to Ireland he could see the changing conditions which were soon to lead to famine and the abandonment of the country by half of its population. In East Anglia starving labourers have become Luddite rioters and the Evangelical gentry are raising funds to save the heathen. Banville attends a service in the local workhouse, where the new Poor Law has separated wife and husband, and wonders why the parsons, whom he detests, have the nerve to export such 'Christianity' to the natives. But laurels are fixed to the church walls in 1833 to celebrate the passing of the Abolition of Slavery Act, inspired by his master and others. The diary is uncomfortably astute in its judgements. 'What a bottle of smoke with the cork out!' is his verdict on a humbugging sermon. His great adventure is a journey to Sweden to fetch home to Scotland the capercaillies, a giant wood-grouse (*Tetrao urugallus*) once native to the Highlands but shot out of existence there.

Banville's life was, on the whole, secure, but its necessities often came to him somewhat capriciously, and there can be few diaries which so exactly relate what it felt like to be both an independent spirit and a man who comprehended and accepted his condition. He existed in a radical whirl of Emancipation and also in the brutal

England of the enclosures, game-laws and a torpid religion, surveying both with his sharp outsider's eye. He could never have imagined that his diary would make such a handsome début, Lord Buxton's introduction and all.

THE LONG AFFRAY
The Poaching Wars In Britain 1760-1914

Harry Hopkins, 1985

Trenchancy is much avoided these days. It requires nerve and certainty, also something formidable in the way of legalised injustice to be cuttingly incisive about. We try for a balanced view of the past, re-assessing its passionate issues without giving way to indignation. The strong feelings displayed by the Hammonds, for example, in their descriptions of farm labouring poverty create an awkward emphasis for many of today's historians.

Harry Hopkins is incapable of the detached view; moreover, he has the tough hitting partisan style which would have made Hazlitt cross the road to shake his hand. It is hard thumps or profound pity all round, according to which of the two sides is being investigated in this often quite overpowering account of the long and often horrible village skirmish between the Big House and the cottage. Here is a classic radical outburst which is going to make much current rural writing sound very mealy mouthed.

The gist of the ancient quarrel which was to bring such disasters on to the heads of the 19th century British peasanty in particular was the law which said that a gentleman could take the wild creatures of the fields and forests for his amusement, and for his table, but that a non-gentleman could not. As this law ran contrary to the natural taking instincts of countrymen of all degrees, not to mention the near-starvation which was the common lot of countless field-working families, *The Long Affray* of this study became inevitable.

Hopkins deals with the period when the aristocracy and squirarchy, plus their invaluable aid the tory parson, set up the pheasant as their god, consolidating its sacred status with a series of Acts which kept the gallows busy, populated Botany Bay, and filled every village with spies – the gamekeepers and their watchers. Here is the grim, and often mad, chapter and verse which fed a wry balladry and inspired the best village voices, Clare and Hardy.

Such pretensions! Such victims! If Hopkins doesn't now and then make your blood boil you need to be checked for anaemia. We are, the majority of us, after all, descended from farm-workers.

Hopkin's starting point is the Hampshire village of North Baddesley where, in the churchyard, a young man hanged for wounding a gamekeeper's watcher lies under two tombstones, neither of which correctly states his tragedy. One of these stones was erected by William Cobbett soon after the execution and the other by the Hon. Evelyn Ashley over eighty years later.

Cobbett concludes his inscription with a text from Ecclesiastes about 'the oppression of the poor and the violent perverting of Judgement', Ashley his with a suggestion that the reader might care to consult the original records of the trial which he has placed in the church chest. He is protecting his kinsman Lord Palmerston, owner of nearby Broadlands and the Home Secretary who dismissed his Romsey neighbours' heartfelt petition against the death sentence on this particular victim of the poaching war. Cobbett, who farmed nearby, is of course protecting the countrymen of Britain against the dreadful Ellenborough Law of 1803 which created no less than ten new capital felonies, including one for resisting a gamekeeper.

'Property, once exposed', the Ellenborough's family friend Archdeacon Paley had written in his influential *Principles*, 'requires the terror of capital punishment to protect it.' What more exposed property could there be than game? And what could be done with the strange and threatening forces of the rural masses beyond the park who had never been entirely able to believe in game as property?

Thus Hopkin's melodramatic tale begins in what he calls Palladian oppression and pride, and peasant bewilderment. Commons are enclosed to swell the landholdings which alone can make a gentleman and give him the 19th century's most desired entitlement – the right to shoot pheasants on one's own acres.

The sport reached its apogee when the Prince of Wales bought the Sandringham Estate in 1861, where the second largest game larder in the world was built (the Hungarian Baron Hirsch owned the vastest) and the *battues* brought mountainous piles of slaughtered creatures. All over Britain the crops of tenant farmers were despoiled by birds which they dare not touch, and the protection of the game exceeded the caring for humanity up and down the land.

Dissent – what Sir Philip Sidney had unforgettably described as 'the affects, the whisperings, the motions of the people' – began to unify the agriculturalists. Clare's 'parish hind, oppression's humble slave whose only hope of freedom is the grave,' took to chapel instead of church, got himself unionised and enfranchised and gradually, almost heretically – for the game laws had been made to so indoctrinate his ethos as to lend it a religious dimension – began to lead a fuller life beyond the reach of a sporting tyranny.

Hopkins will have no truck with the latter's romanticised culture, as we view it today via art, literature, and the National Trust. Behind the façade we now so greatly admire lay a legislature which allowed a gentleman to have some very strange sport at the assizes. The Restoration Game Act of 1671 provided the basis of what was to occur later on and Cobbett thought that the Act of 1770 the first to 'Lay on the lash'. But the huge tangle of laws enacted by a group legislating entirely for its own benefit during the Regency and after were what were to brutalise the countryside.

For when a man's happiest activity is killing and he will employ other men – gamekeepers – to destroy on a relentless scale anything living which might threaten what he loves to kill, and when he can virtually do what he likes with a neighbour who is found with a hare, the idyll slips in blood. By 1844, committals under the game laws had risen to 4,500 a year and the gamekeeper's trade was more dangerous than a soldier's. A great telling of a shocking story.

W H HUDSON
A Biography

Ruth Tomalin, 1983

There is a perverse satisfaction in discovering that some writers, in spite of today's penetrating biographical arts, still manage to hide their tracks. What Ruth Tomalin has to reveal about the private life of W. H. Hudson, the great naturalist and author of *Green Mansions* who helped to transform the world's attitude toward wildlife, is not much more than he himself intended us to see after he had made a bonfire of his papers. Thomas Hardy did much the same thing at the same time but with a famous lack of success, the flames of his bonfire actually throwing light on what fed them.

But the motives behind the attempts of this pair of rural literary masters, born a year and 8,000 miles apart, to obliterate their pasts were very different. Hardy utilised every scrap of his personal experience, especially its most painful aspects. Hudson could not. His horrors, which included a fear of ageing, crushed the spirit he needed to face each new day, and so he ignored them as best he could. Although an able explainer of natural history, Hudson was spiritually and physically taken over by forces that no longer governed the societies in which he found himself. Both in Argentina, where he was born in 1841 and spent much of his life, and in England, to which he migrated in 1870, he constantly sought out people who seemed to him to be in harmony with the universe. No previous life of Hudson has demonstrated so well the resulting sense of isolation.

Ruth Tomalin's major addition to what we already know about Hudson is a vivid description of the attitudes toward the environment of his post-Darwinian epoch when, gradually, the lens took over from the bullet. Her account of a world in which every creature that swam, flew or ran was killed either for fun or to provide scientific specimens is simply amazing. How could it not have been thought mad for railway companies to run weekend excursions to the coast so that Londoners could spend a happy day potting at sea birds? How could women of every class insist on the deaths of millions of the loveliest birds so that they could wear feathers? Great collectors, sportsmen, artists such as Audubon and John Gould and their admirers, scientists, taxidermists catering to the glass-case parlour trade – all were united in pitiless slaughter. Villagers, Hudson said, 'thought birds were only made to be destroyed,' and he knew of a gentleman who, in about 1850, had all the nightingales on his grounds put down because 'their late singing disturbed his rest.' Wild birds were caught, caged and blinded with red-hot needles to make them sing. Boys were expected to practice atrocities on wild creatures as a sign of their normalcy.

Hudson's part in the bitterly slow reversal of these practices was to prove that to watch and revere the life all around one was a far tougher and more dramatic activity than eliminating it. His popularity as a writer was attributable to the way he himself represented both the human and the natural, for it was the age-old belief in the inferiority of the natural that gave men the authority to do what they fancied with it. As a child on the pampas he had been asked by a gaucho, 'Why do you come here, English boy, frightening and chasing away God's little birds?' As a young man he was shooting and skinning hundreds of rare Argentinian and Patagonian birds for the Smithsonian institution. By the age of 33 he was a gaunt migrant bird himself in the vast confusion of Victorian London. 'One might figure him as some bird pressing forward against a gale,' a woman friend said, 'The eyes were bright and dark, the regard narrowed continually in a sort of wild, astute vigilance.'

The absence of a formal education – he described himself as being 'unschooled and unclassed' – benefited Hudson by making it impossible for him to become a professional ornithologist and thus forcing him to become a loner. For years poverty blocked his path to London; then, after the publication of his superb *The Naturalist in La Plata* and his inspirational role in what is now the Royal Society for the Protection of Birds, the path ran where he had always wanted it to, deep into a still remote rural England full of little farms and wildernesses, introverted cathedral cities and stray encounters with fieldworkers.

Before this change of circumstance he had married a London boarding-house keeper a good deal older than himself, the still enigmatic Emily, whom Ruth Tomalin has not gone out of her way to explain. Similarly, her account of Morley Roberts, Hudson's life-long friend and first biographer, should have been fuller. But there is some sense in avoiding more than a passing mention of that baffling taste, common to so many high-minded Victorian males, for the companionship of little girls.

As well as deserving high praise for its first-rate chapters on the revolution in the world's thinking about wildlife and Hudson's noble role in it, this latest assessment of him unravels what might be called the bi-hemispheric factor. It is the effect of the time spent in South America on his English responses that makes Hudson so enduringly interesting. As an amalgam of naturalist, novelist, memoirist, poet and oral historian, he is as much an outsider now as when he lived. Ruth Tomalin makes one long to rediscover him in such classic and still-mysterious works as *The Purple Land, Idle Days in Patagonia, El Ombu, Green Mansions* and *A Shepherd's Life*. There he is the rara avis on the wing.

JOURNALS OF A METHODIST FARMER 1871-1875

ed. Jean Stovin, 1982

The publication by Jean Stovin of her grandfather's journals, documents which have been consulted by agricultural historians for some time now, is a most welcome event. So often such nineteenth-century records are little more than a kind of briefly personalised set of farm accounts. Not so with Cornelius Stovin, whose intention was always to bring the profit and loss account of his fields, a huge tenancy of some 600 acres, to the point where it would receive the approval, not of cold Sir Edmund Beckett, his landlord, but of Christ. Thus we have one of the most intimate and self-revealing of farmers' diaries, a book which throws an astonishing light across the mid-Victorian rural scene. The sight of one of those stiff little village chapels recalls not such matters as the Non-Conformist conscience or vernacular architecture, but its God-enchanted priests, complex figures like Stovin who longed 'to throw my farm into the treasury of Christ'.

He did not succeed, of course. Confronted by an ill and down-to-earth wife, an implacable class system, which left him isolated in the neighbourhood, an outlook formed by an addiction to reading, and the first rumblings of the great disaster which was to ruin British farming for decades to come, Stovin was obliged to take the usual worldly measures. But during the four years covered by the *Journals*, the complexity resulting from the contrast between what he knew he should do, and what he was able to do, gave his life a dramatic edge which goes far beyond that which one associates with such an existence.

Stovin had farmed Binbrook Hall, Lincolnshire, for twenty years before he began writing about it. The whole of his youth had been spent in dragging it out of its stagnation and in perfecting his preaching. These two activities, his acres and his Methodism, were for him an undivided path, which, by 1870, when he was forty, appeared at last to have become united. Thus, when he begins his first Journal during the harvest of 1871 (prompted perhaps by a pamphlet about Bunyan), he is all praise and confidence. Newly invented machinery speeds the field work. The weather is glorious. His wife and his foreman are – and here follow panegyrics fit for memorial stones. A lighted window at night gives a glimpse of a labourer and his wife at prayer. He has leisure for reading (his greatest passion) and is uncharacteristically absorbed in a novel, *Lothair*. His wife is poorly but 'Never fail' is 'written on her banner'. As for his men, were there ever such workers? The sheaves seemed almost to fly from the ground to the wagon and from the wagon to the stack. Mr Gladstone has made a just and powerful criticism of the landed interest.

But then all kinds of worms begin to emerge from the bud of holy toil. To the historian they are inevitable, and it is proof of Stovin's truthfulness and lack of self-deception that he notes down all the first small indications of a collapsing agricultural economy, combined with a subtle alteration in the thinking and attitude of its workers. To the writer, many of them must have seemed like peculiar, unrelated incidents; to the reader today they are vivid evidence of his sensitivity. During the winter of 1872, for example, two of his labourers come to the door to ask him to raise their wages just when he has been boasting that his kindliness as an employer saved him from such an expense. One of the labourers gives notice and Stovin 'came in the house confused with grief and consternation. I felt injured by his ingratitude. I considered and followed him into the yard. He softened in his manner but held firmly to his own terms.' All over the country 'they are forming themselves into organic companies for the purpose of dictating their own terms'. This unnerving independence shown by his men highlights the 'grossly servile prostration' of tenant farmers like himself before absentee sporting landlords who are putting up the rent. He feels deserted by both sides, which indeed he is.

The *Journals* continue with Stovin struggling hard to correct the social and economic forces which are creating the imbalance at Binbrook. Parallel with his transparently honest description of these, are accounts of equally acknowledged fulfilment. Although his men 'seem to have set their forces like flint against work' and 'are advancing in intelligence and folding their arms simultaneously', although the farmhouse is damp and badly run due to Mrs Stovin's sickness ('the world had proved a very sharp grindstone to her'), although weeds and Sir Edmund's coverts diminish his crops and his waggoners are singing, not the glories of Zion but obscene songs in the yard and, most frightening of all, although despite all his efforts, by 1876 he is in debt to the tune of £1,675, he is as capable in his way of responding to the countryside as thankfully as Kilvert.

COUNTRY LIFE
A Social History of Rural England

Howard Newby, 1987

Howard Newby has achieved what has long been needed, a single and authoritative telling of village England's economic tale over the past two centuries, an uneasy story of triumphant and desolating fluctuations in which the ordinary farm worker and his family were thrown about with little care of what would become of them. When we now see, with enjoyment and conservationist concern, the pattern of arable, pasture, ditch, woodland and river-management which to us spells landscape in its most perfect form, let us remember that it is the 'handiwork', as the psalmist puts it, not of the landowner or often of the farmer, but their poor labourers. The latter's ever dwindling descendants are well out of that poverty, although a long way from being well into today's wage earnings for the highly skilled employed. The persistingly curious situation of this group has been analysed by Newby in his previous study, *The Deferential Worker*. In *Country Life*, a title no doubt intended as a corrective to what ever-expanding hordes imagine living in a village is all about, Newby follows the very mixed fortunes of the plough from the first Agricultural Revolution in the mid-18th century to the eve of the current C.A.P. decision to reduce production, and thus yet once more profoundly change our never really peaceful rural scene.

It is a great drama and it makes a lot of what now passes for country life horribly trivial. For generations three classes ground against each other, landowner (both aristocrat and gentry), tenant farmer and landless labourer. Wars brought prosperity via government protection and subsidy. Peace, more often than not, brought bankruptcy and even starvation. But in 1959, uniquely, a war-inspired modernisation of farming brought such a flood of plenty that, forty years on, it had now to be turned off at the mains, first the dairy-acres and now the grain. Newby travels along at an admirable pace, his quiet style with its underlying edginess producing fresh insights and making hitherto unsuspected connections.

The chief outline is now most familiar. Tull, Townsend and the first 'Golden Age'; then the Industrial Revolution and its rationalising spin-off the Enclosures, to be followed by riots and Captain Swing. Then another brief 'Golden Age', soon to be dismissed by rain and a depression which ruined country people for generations. The coming of the farming slump coincided with the arrival of the National Agricultural Labourers' Union and Joseph Arch, a thrilling event to hear about even now, and this hopefulness to be succeeded by what Newby calls 'the Diaspora' and what was then described as the Flight from the Field. Surveying England in 1900 Henry Rider Haggard found empty cottages and wholesale abandonment of their native places by, usually, young labourers. Age-old custom and the ancient understanding of the fields were fled from, as was the grim subservience demanded of its toilers by the farmhouse and Big House. Newby is good on the social shifts and their often catastrophic effect on the ordinary villager. Late-Victorian Britain saw much buying of land to support new peerages – ennoblement required at a least a thousand acres of estate and a country seat. A survey published in 1873 revealed that 7,000 men owned four fifths of England. And as for Ireland – ! But after the First World War, due to these new and old landowners losing their heirs as well as to the farming doldrums, a quarter of the land surface of Britain changed hands. There had, says, Newby, been nothing like it since the Dissolution. Those who have been brought up on a farm or in a village can still sense these upheavals behind much of the flamboyance of today's agricultural 'industry'.

This monstrously successful best, born of the War Ag and raised by the EEC, is now in process of being reined-in. Newby traces the wild gallop from a gloriously revived farming in the late forties to the shocking agribusiness of the late eighties, and shows how very little the farmworkers themselves have benefited from the boom. They and the farmer himself stand yet again at a crossroad as many fields are about to come out of their intensive cultivation. Newby's well-rooted history should be read by the new-villager, that huge populace which is now able to live in the countryside, chiefly due to the car, and which sees itself as its protector. It will ground them in the realities.

BACK TO THE LAND

The Pastoral Impulse in Victorian England from 1880 to 1914

Jan Marsh, 1987

THE COUNTRY HABIT

A Year in the Working Life of the Land

Josphine Haworth, 1987

Here are two earthly factual accounts of the polarised situations which have made up rural life for many years, the agrarian and the philosophical. It is still as much a common longing among the English to be a villager as it was generations ago, hence the incredible distances now commuted to the city work-place, and the flight to even deeper country once work is finished and retirement sets in. Josephine Haworth describes by means of fragments of talk and her own commentary what one has to be quite fly to see these days, the actual toil taking place in the fields and stock-yards. Her polarity is that of the indigenous farmer and his men – and women. Jan Marsh's far opposite is comprised of that far more numerous population which has been crowding into the countryside over the last century in order to have a healthier and happier existence than that provided for by what we now call, rather nervously, the inner city. Both of these still wide apart village groups, the one tiny, the other ever swelling, have a huge literature and neither writer tells us much that we don't already know. But their calm, somewhat bemused factuality and the realisation that village England is approaching yet one more of its cyclic crises, not to mention their attractive writing, does add a fresh significance to what they are saying.

Jan Marsh has chosen late Victorian idealisation of country life to make her point on today's obsession with village values. *Back to the*

Land was the command of Ruskin, Morris, Edward Carpenter, the founders of the folksong and dance movement, the fresh air fiends, food faddists, simple lifers, Fabians (though not all of them), the arts and crafts brigade and a host of very good poets and essayists. What this account of them does is to dust-off the familiar social history in which they have been so long covered and bring them all out, individuals and movements alike, as fresh as daisies. Were they cranks or pioneers? asks Jan Marsh, leaving the reader to decide. They certainly posed a lot of very awkward questions which had to be answered, either in their own day or in ours.

What is so attractive about this book is its old classic liberal tone. One has become so battered by today's hard-nosed attitudes towards the old ethics that it comes as a very nice shock to see them so unapologetically on display once more. It is easy to sneer or laugh at these men and women who opted out of the acquisitiveness and conventions of their time either to rescue what was left of England's ancient village culture, or simply to do their own thing, whether it was making a garden or living, as Hazlitt put it, 'for one's self'. Given an economic chance, what multitudes of us would not live like Gertrude Jekyll, C R Ashbee or any of the totally absorbed plantsmen, craftsmen or just idlers who set in train all the notions which have developed to create what we now accept as the best kind of life ever? Before the First World War it required a lot of nerve and very little money to opt out of both society and industrialism. Landowners, made jumpy by Henry George's crusade and his bestselling *Progress and Poverty*, hated to see the countryside being turned into a hotbed of ideas but things like the rapid spread of suburbia and the uncontrolled developer soon hurried them into the first conservationist lobbies. In *Back to the Land* we have the birth of myriad England-saving, English-thinking transforming institutions from the National Trust, the Garden City, the National Footpaths Society and the Society for the Preservation of Ancient Buildings, to Bedales. But most of all we have a new respect for what a whole host of intellectuals and ordinary villagers achieved, which was the laying of the foundations of all that we know we must believe in and act on now, if our countryside is not to be ruined. Lampooned though they once were, they don't strike us as the least

241

odd now, rather the reverse.

Tragically and ironically, the moment chosen by the Simple Lifers to discover the virtues and arts of the countryside was that when the farming community left in their droves in an agricultural collapse known as the Flight from the Land. Now, in an economy which employs only 3% of a village's workforce in the fields, today's seekers after rural values have to look hard to see actual farming taking place, and it is this apparently empty scene which Josephine Haworth fills with accuracy in *The Country Habit*, a round the year commentary on the basic tasks of sowing, reaping, bee-keeping, shepherding, etc. With the villages filling-up fast with people who intend to be villagers, this calendar of the inescapable seasons, as they are currently toiled through, will be an eloquent reminder of why such places exist.

THE SHEPHERD OBSERVED
Going to Meet George, 1999

The vicarage children have descended from exploring the roof-space with armloads of old newspapers. 'There are hundreds-thousands – of them'. Don't exaggerate. They turn out to be a Victorian insulation against the draughts. The boys dump them on the carpet in clouds of dust. There is a smell of another day. They are almost exactly one hundred years old, *The Times, The Church Times* and *The Ecclesiastical Gazette*. Ancient Anglican news crumbles from them and into our nostrils. We sit on the floor and read out the juicy bits. Fearful assizes, angry deans; Mr. Stanley is 'gradually emerging from the black depths of the dark continent' after his efforts 'to rescue one who, it seems, was not quite sure whether he wanted to be rescued or not'. 'General' Booth is being tiresome about money, needing lots of it. He needs to be watched. Magic lanterns are £7.17s and fares to Sydney on the Orient line £17.17s. The 'largest and loveliest cemetery in the world' is near Woking. The letters page is fretful. 'Sir, can any of your readers tell me if any legal means exist of stopping irregular marriages?' Villagers are getting wed in town churches, rather than in their own parish church, in order to find some privacy in their lives. There is advice on how to recruit farm-labourers for the army. Nearly three thousand acres of first class farmland near Beccles are to be let for shooting. Polite journalism is no more than a veneer for the rough news, the rough voices, the rough prospects.

Grandmother, it occurred to me, would herself have been getting married when Mr. Hargraves' back'us boy heaved all this newsprint into the loft and spread it between the joists, and on her way to Cuckoo Tye. Not that she would have seen this vicarage because it was all of thirty miles from home, although the same winds howled through it. Her 'Tye' would be on the high ground equidistant from Long Melford and Lavenham, both of whose church towers would stand as markers in the landscape for the rest of her life. These tyes were a feature of our part of Suffolk. They were little communities which had grown up around either a remote farm or a common pasture far from the main village, although hers had been gathered in by Earl Howe, whose coronet marked one of the main buildings. But generally, like Thomas Hardy's woodlanders and heathlanders, the folk spent centuries out of sight. It did not make them especially independent, simply isolated. Cuckoo Tye itself was – is – a small moated farm at the end of a wide green land. The once common pasture close by was a hamlet named Newman's Green, a place full of relations once or twice removed, so that we never did quite know the connection. It was the heyday of honorary aunts and uncles, rather as all cooks were called Mrs. Concealing bastardy became an art-form, the truth only coming out when some liaison threatened to come uncomfortably near the list of whom one may not marry which hung in the church porch. The list was so long that most rural populations would have died out had it been obeyed to the letter. However, obedience has never been East Anglia's strong point.

Paths from the Tye were grassy and fugitive, and much ploughed over now. They tended to skirt the main village but make bee-lines for the neighbouring town, as though those travelling them longed occasionally to be swallowed up. Grandfather, taking Suffolks to Norfolk, would have by-passed Acton, his native village, but most likely have driven his sheep through Lavenham, Bury St. Edmunds and all metropolises to Dereham, simply to see the sights, though staying hidden on the way. He died when I was six and remains a quizzical authoritarian whose sky-blue eyes and brown face under a weathered hat created uncertainty. He petted and mussed children much as he did sheep-dogs or, similarly, bade them to be quiet and sit. 'Do what he says,' advised Grandmother. Their house, although never free of people coming and going, was at heart impressively still, a place where clocks were encouraged to have their own voice. After Grandfather's death she married an aged widower, once a schoolfriend who had missed her the first time round, and the quietness of the house continued to defeat the noise of talk and feet. She lived long enough to glimpse our first television set, a sturdy affair with the lines of a fruit machine. 'I have to ask a question: can *they* see *us*?' In the quiet house she and her second husband used their wireless for the Service. Born in 1860 – years before Thomas Hardy had written a word – they were thankful for such modern convenience as being able to have the Service without having to go to church.

Whilst she was alive I found myself less fascinated by Grandmother's ancient farming roots than by her longevity. Dwelling on it eventually produced a non-gerontological defence of old age. My researches, some of them at least, were to be as fugitive as the boy shepherd David Blythe's travels with his flock. And thus I entered the centre of Lavenham to meet Major Bush né Michael Home, who was ninety and lived at the Great House. Major Bush, as Michael Home, had written a dozen books about his childhood in the Breckland in what could be construed as an attempt to reconcile his early self with the person he became after success as a writer of Thirties' whodunnits, and what he called 'novels of military intelligence'. He was born in 1885 and had been a prolific author, his village tales full of fierce loyalty to Hockham, the place where mallows grew. The Breckland was East Anglia's heath, not an Egdon with furzy arms upraised to dash human hopes, but an airy desert where rabbits and foxes excavated the flint axes and chisels left behind by neolithic walkers. It was all farmed and afforested out of existence after the First World War. Major Bush as Michael Home gave scrupulous chapter and verse on the life led there, the rabbits grown to a great plague, the bracken closing-in the paths, the gamekeepers rubbing their hands, the farmers perishing. But sitting by an old man's cindery grate in the kitchen of the Great House, we did not talk of such things, or of shepherd David brazenly running his sheep across the market square outside, or of anything literary. I saw the little Breckland cottage and the Great House, the shuffle through the fine rooms to the warm, sweet-smelling kitchen and the wooden armchair. And I saw, as in many an ancient man, a recidivist. Outside, Lavenham's late-medieval glories were in the restorative hands of a new race, the retired, with its understanding and appreciation of such things. Taking stock of these beam-worshippers, the postman observed, 'They say Lavenham is God's waiting- room'. It is quite something to have lived long enough to have known a man who drove sheep through a Suffolk wool town now filled with Japanese photographers, and no lament is intended. It is just the phenomenon, the outlandishness, which cannot be avoided. As boys, my brothers and I would climb the church tower, the mightiest in the county, and look down on the ploughing and the entire world of what in the fifteenth century was a millionaire's manufactuary. The scene was concise, the church excepting, a town of wood in High Suffolk, with orange tiles and its fairytale roofs abundant with stonecrop and house-leeks, the latter to keep the witches away. And to the south, far off, the magenta rise of the Essex hills. Below lay Shilling Street, Water Street, Lady Street and Prentice Street. The masterly church itself appeared to us to have tree-like origins, for it was the creation of men named Spring and Branch, and of Lord Oxford, whose badge was a boar. The churchyard was full of gypsies, whose vardoes wintered on the heath. Grandmother remembered seeing one burnt after a death. There would have been gypsies on the Breckland when Major Bush was Michael Home. One of the legendary travelling women was Ocean, whose territory stretched to south Norfolk. Moving about so much herself, would Ocean have noticed 'the flight from the land'?

This is what they called it, anxiously, in the late Victorian newspapers. The labourers, the servants, they were taking wing. Henry Rider Haggard, the farmer who wrote novels, prefaced his

Rural England – 'being an account of agricultural and social researches carried out in the years 1901 & 1902' – with a quotation from the Book of Judges. 'The highways were unoccupied . . . the inhabitants of the villages ceased.' Lavenham was half empty between the wars and the poor who lived in the huge timbered loom rooms shivered in winter, and papered the beams to make some cosiness. Some biked seven miles to Sudbury to make silk for, among other things, Queen Mary's parasols and frontals for cathedrals. Also old school ties and corsets. They cycled in groups singing songs. There was a lot of movement as if to balance so much stillness. It was penury time and if you weren't on the go you could hear a pin drop. Keeping on the go was the thing.

Collecting information for his book on 'the flight from the land', Rider Haggard arrived in Grandfather's home ground. The novelist was in his mid-forties when he took stock of this countryside, much the same age as David the shepherd of Cuckoo Tye, whose only flight was the swift return from the depressed markets. Haggard himself farmed 365 acres of beautiful land where the Bath Hills and the Waveney Valley opened towards Bungay. Two years before he had made a brave effort to put the heart back into East Anglian agriculture by writing a candid diary called *A Farmer's Year*, in which nothing was held back and the profit and loss, chiefly the latter, was set out to the last penny. This bitter-sweet journal of what was happening on his own farms – then two of them, one in Ditchingham, the other in Bedingham – was suggested by Tusser's *Hundreth Good Points of Husbandrie*, a rhymed farm book written by a professional musician in 1557. The scene was Tusser's riverside farm, at Cattawade, the scene which John Constable would paint when, yet again, British agriculture had collapsed. Tusser was wry.

> *Who minds to quote*
> *Upon this note*
>   *May easily find enough:*
> *What charge and pain,*
>   *To little gain*
>   *Doth follow toiling plough.*

246

Haggard was hopeful. The prosperity would come back if only the labourers would cease to fly away. Why flee to the towns? 'What kind of places are these cities to live in, for the poor?' What kind of places were Ditchingham and Bedingham – and Acton – for that matter, for fieldworkers on ten bob a week? Or indeed for near bankrupt farmers? A few months before writing his honest, pleading journal, (come back, Hodge, all is forgiven for it acknowledged the men's wonderful skills), Haggard had visited Egypt and seen the paintings and reliefs on the royal tombs at Sakkara, and had thought how very like he himself was to the 'gentlemen-farmers of the Fifth and Sixth Dynasties who, whilst yet alive, caused their future sepulchres to be adorned with representations of such scenes of daily life and husbandry as to them were most pleaseant and familiar'. Egypt had had its plagues, but they passed, and the joy of the cornfields remained. So stand firm, was his advice to East Anglia, 'although how the crisis will end it is not possible for the wisest among us to guess today'. He could not have guessed that the crisis would not end until 1940, when Hitler's war inaugurated the second agricultural revolution and today's corn and dairy surpluses.

Haggard was a celebrity when he came to Grandfather's patch. Not only had he written *A Farmer's Year*, 'my commonplace book for 1898', but *King Solomon's Mines, She*, and *Allan Quatermain*. These colourful African bestsellers stemmed from his other life. At nineteen he too had fled the family acres in Norfolk for opportunities in South Africa, where he joined the staff of Sir Theophilus Shepstone and had with his own hands raised the Union flag in Pretoria's main square. Revered by the Africans, detested by the Boers, Shepstone had annexed the Transvaal for Queen Victoria almost single-handed, and without consulting her government. The resulting turmoil finished his career. Shepstone's unorthodoxy and dash enthralled the youthful Haggard and fed his imagination. When he returned to Norfolk, still only twenty-four, he became a very unusual member of the county's farming, sporting gentry. These too, as much as the labourers, he saw, were stuck in some kind of inertia and fatalism. Why could not both be like those glorious tillers of the soil on the tombs at Sakkara? What had happened to make English farmwork so despised, so appalling? He visited Heckingham Workhouse.

247

What do these old fellows think about, I wonder, as they hobble to and fro round those measureless precincts of bald brick? The sweet-eyed children that they begot and bred-up fifty years ago, perhaps? Whose pet names they still remember, now dead or lost to them for the most part; or the bright waving cornfields whence they scared birds when they were lads from whom death and trouble were yet a long way off. I dare say, too, that deeper problems worry them at times in some dim half-apprehended fashion; at least I thought so when the other day I sat behind two of them in a church near the workhouse. They could not read, and I doubt if they understood much of what was passing, but I observed consideration in their eyes. Of what? Of the terror and the marvel of existence, perhaps, and of that good God whereof the person is talking in those long unmeaning words. God! They know more of the devil and all his works; ill-paid labour, poverty, pain, and the infinite unrecorded tragedies of humble lives. God? They never found Him. He must live beyond the workhouse wall – out there in the graveyard – in the waterlogged holes which very shortly . . .

In all Haggard employs some fifteen men on his farms. Their dogged strength amazes him, isolates him from them. In January he had watched a pair of them bush-draining a huge expanse of clay land. It had taken them ten weeks and at the end 'such toilers betray not the least delight in the termination of their long labour'. It was just the same with dyke-drawing, the toughest of all winter jobs. They dug a twelve-hour day in summer and when ever it was light in winter, and without holidays. And yet, something 'teaches them that there are places in the world besides their own village' and makes them aspiring and restless. More and more of them disappear, making for the army, the colonies, the Lowestoft fishing smacks, anywhere preferable to a Norfolk farm. It grieves him. Their lives are dreadful, but they should not be. He should be like them, a Boaz gathering-in the harvest beside them, but he cannot be. Sir Theophilus was nearer to his Africans than Squire Haggard to his ploughmen. Unwittingly, *A Farmer's Year* captures the sullenness of the flying away and the coming down time.

Rider Haggard's report from Grandfather's world was severe. Ruined cottages at 1s. 6d. a week. Labour at thirty shillings the acre.

248

The farmer saying, 'the better you farmed the less you made'.

Within two miles of Lavenham the country was bleak, lonesome, and undulating. Here we saw some empty cottages, also winter barley, which is grown to a certain extent in this district. The cottages were very bad and had leaky roofs. My companions informed me that, taking the average of these parishes, they were badly farmed and full of misery. Indeed they all declared that 'the industry is in a parlous state – on the verge of ruin, in fact.

Wages were 10s. for old men but up to 20s. for engine drivers and stockmen. Horses were cheaper than steam ploughs. Farms were being sold for £7.10s. the acre. There were masses of poultry and few sheep. The pastures were going back, the arable land becoming wilds. A Clare farmer told Haggard that 'for the eight years that he had lived there he had been trying to get on better terms with his men, but was as far as ever from this consummation. The feeling between employers and employed was bad, and to get a job done he must stand over his labourers, and nothing but actual poverty would drive a man to hard toil. He was sick of Suffolk men and, if he could house them, he would bring down men from the Shires, even if he had to pay them £1 a week.' The Rector of Earl Soham deplored the badness of the Suffolk roads. 'The primary cause of this, I believe, is the doing away with the system of picking stones in the fields, due to the advance of education'. Rider Haggard said he had been thrown off his bicycle when riding along equally atrocious roads nearer home. At Acton and its Tye the farmers were 'rubbing along'. The men there 'took no interest in their tasks', he was told. All the young fellows had gone fifteen years later when Rider Haggard passed by, longing to ennoble the disenchanted scene, aching to make it like the fields of Sakkara, where the husbandry was touched by divinity. Instead, Lord Howe's agent told him that things were as bad as they well could be, and that there was no hope for the future of Suffolk agriculture. But when, as a boy, I sat with the ancient relations and honorary relations in their apple-scented houses, I cannot remember them being marked by despair. Physically, even when thin, they had a monolithic quality, a presence not unlike the reapers and herdsmen at Sakkara. They were cagey about their lot, or perhaps unable to put it into words. Due to the camera, they were the first generation of farming folk to possess a portrait gallery. There they hung, two or more generations of the family, the photographs blown up until they were a mass of pointillistic dots, and heavily framed, among them the departed. Not only the dead but the fled.

Whilst Rider Haggard was writing *King Solomon's Mines* at Ditchingham a young American doctor arrived in East Anglia to photograph the 'peasants'. The name P. H. Emerson drifts around in the local consciousness in a still quite powerful way, and there might still be cottages with an Emerson on the walls, for he was kind to his sitters, or usually toilers. His masterpieces had titles like 'Coming Home from the Marshes', 'Women Raking', the marvellous 'Gathering Waterlilies', which is a Monet done with a lens, and 'Yarmouth from Breydon Water'. He has been seen as the first photographer-poet to arrive on a frenetic scene in which men with cameras were striving to make much the same reputations as men with palettes and engraving tools. Dr. Pedro Enrique Emerson (he became Peter Henry) was twenty-seven when he first saw East Anglia and instantly recognised it as the ideal region for providing him with the material for his big statement, which was that photography was better than painting and sculpture. Superior. A great step forward. Fair, tall, freshly wed, a cousin of Ralph Waldo Emerson, possessing dual English and New England nationality, he might have come straight out of a Henry James novel. Before coming to Southwold, he had been to Rome, where the pictures and statues shocked the Puritan, agnostic and anatomist in him. Somebody gave him a camera and with it he intended to give the lie to Art. The intensification of the natural view, via the lens, was to remain for him the camera's ultimate glory. He agreed with his Suffolk and Norfolk 'peasants' when he permitted them to put their heads beneath his focusing cloth, and when they caught their breath with delight at a brilliance which they had never before seen, and said, 'Ah, if we could only get it like that!' Life, they meant. For Emerson and for his subjects revelation came through ground glass.

Emerson had a few lessons, not from a photographer, but from his old tutor in physics and chemistry at Cambridge. He was one of those artists who require just a feather-like instruction, as had Julia Margaret Cameron, his heroine. Presented by her daughter and son-in-law with a lens and dark box – 'It may amuse you, Mother, to try to photograph' – she turned her coal cellar into a dark-room, her hen-house into a glass-room, and began to take pictures immediately. When Emerson came to Southwold he at once gave up medicine, engaged the local artist and naturalist, T. F. Goodall, to guide him around the district, and set-to on a series of albums, *Life and Landscape on the Norfolk Broads, Pictures of Life in Field and Fen, Idylls of the Norfolk Broads, Pictures of East Anglian Life* and *Wild Life on a Tidal Water.*

When published these wonderful picture books were received with every kind of hostility and criticism. Also with some kind of awe. The new photographic establishment, with its journals and medals, and its crusade to place itself as an equal among painters and engravers, saw all that it believed in threatened by what Emerson called his Naturalistic Photography. It was all too natural for photographers like Henry Peach Robinson, who said, 'It is the photographer's duty to avoid the mean, the bare, the ugly, and to correct the unpicturesque.' Emerson, who quite liked a row, attacked this school for years and years. In a way, it assisted him to draw ever closer to his controversial vision, that of the half-marine, half-agricultural society semi-starving on its watery acres.

There was another enemy, the local press, which had no doubt what this grand American doctor was getting at, which was something called 'making trouble'. Its columns were filled with Tory rage by this exposure, in captions, and essays, as well as photographs, of the miserable conditions in which the rural poor lived. Emerson, unlike Peach Robinson and his tribe, who combed the alleys and seafronts for beautiful or striking faces, and bodies which could be dressed up to create genre-pictures, published his portraits of a coastal people in order that his work 'would help in the understanding of this peculiar region and to the outcry against abuses'. He recorded the local dialect and learned all the local crafts and customs. And, as a doctor, he noted the local health and welfare. He became, in Nancy Newhall's words, 'a prophet crying in a strange, dry mechanised and mercantile wilderness'. Dry in the Eliot sense. In 1891 Emerson gave it all up. He sent a letter to every photographic magazine saying that 'the medium must rank the lowest of all arts . . . In short, I throw my lot in with those that think photography is a very limited art. I regret deeply that I have come to this conclusion'. He lived on until 1935, ten years after Grandfather, who never came into his view-finder but who would have made a good subject. Especially in the 1880s when he was in his twenties, and journeying on and on with his flock. Emerson immortalised, if photography can do such a thing, his peasants on a grey day 'when possible'. Staring into his view-finder, they saw one another vivid as dragonflies and existing in a jewel. Critics began to talk of Courbet and Millet when they looked at his work. Visiting the Broads cottages and hovels, Emerson gasped at the closeness and the stench.

If Rider Haggard describes the abandonment of the villages, his Norfolk neighbour, Mary Mann, provides us with the most relentlessly truthful account of village existence at its nadir. Her husband farmed 800 acres and from their home, Shropham Manor, she observed without camera and economics exactly what was going on. It was the age of dialect, folksong and folkdance collecting, and her popular country novels were at first vehicles for rustic speech and customs. Then something happened. The caste tragedy of 'condition' suffuses the text and dialect becomes the cry of the trapped. Here are men and women planted as immutably in the Norfolk clay as were their ancestors, and as are the crops. When they talk it is the speech of plight, and Mary Mann puts it all correctly down, offering no assistance, and it is only by stoically enduring their misfortune of birth, their ignorance and their incessant labour that her characters are able to achieve something which her readers can admire. Her terrible understanding of what is happening in the local cottages and in her own land is at its best when it comes to describing the actual nervelessness, apathy and inertia which comes, not so much from being stuck in a rut, as from being tethered from birth on a few sour acres. She states that these villagers inhabit 'an insignificant landscape, black fen-land, gorse-choked heath, familiar ponds and pits and puddles, rank turnip fields, flat distances . . .' They inhabit, in fact, all that we now find conservationally desirable.

However, the common dilemma of the Emerson-Haggard-Mann fieldworker is to find 'the Book of Life practically closed'. Against the stark facts of their education, religion, diet, marriage, toil, sickness and death, Mary Mann now and then pulls out some not quite done for creature from these 'poor units of the brutish, measureless human undergrowth.' Also, and unlike Henry Haggard, she fails to acknowledge the skills of the farms, the wonderful ploughing and reaping and care of the animals. What she does see is an understandable running away from rural depression for those with the strength to do so, and an equally understandable collapse into drink and squalor by those left behind. Shropham, her own parish, which she calls 'Dulditch', is depopulated by a third during her lifetime. The flight feeds her radicalism and she often appears self-surprised by the relentlessness of her own pursuit of the sad stay-at-homes in their muddle of fortitude, eccentricity, vice and penury. She must have worried the Edwardian lady. There is no 'politeness'. The politeness is in the local press which cannot bear to think that if everything in the cottage garden isn't lovely, it will soon be so. Mary Mann, the farmer's wife, thought that the average field-worker's fate was so ghastly that he must be under some special curse from on high. Henry Rider Haggard wanted to stand in the field, a man with his men, but found them more unlike himself than a Zulu. Pedro Enrique Emerson from New England captured them body and soul on a grey day. Mary Mann, infinitely better than any dialect-lorist, has caught their actual voice, thus undermining her sense of their hopelessness, for it comes through witty and strong. There is little wrong with these East Anglians but everything wrong with the social and economic system of the day which sees them simply as 'hands'. Henry Rider Haggard, of course, believed in passing through fire to become immortal. I had no idea when I was twelve that he had composed a fat two-volume inventory of the collapse of agriculture at the turn of the century, and of the flight from it. But I read all about Ayesha and Allan Quatermain, as I lay hidden from 'jobs' in the tall summer grass in the lanes and meadows leading to Cuckoo Tye, and thrilled to the fiery transformation process. Something of this solution runs through his bitter *Rural England*. What other agricultural advisor to the government – he was to be knighted for his farming expertise, and not for his fiction – would preface a study about people like Grandfather with the text, 'I will make a man more precious than fine gold; even a man than the golden wedge of Ophir.' And, with set aside and golf courses proliferating all around me, it is salutary to read at the close of Haggard's view of Grandfather's world, 'I am sure that one of the worst fates which can befall England is that her land should become either a playground or a waste . . .'

ORAL HISTORY AND THE LOCAL HISTORIAN
Stephen Caunce, 1994

It was the invention of the tape-recorder rather than the questionnaires of Mass Observation which was to establish oral history as an invaluable addition to History with a capital H. That there has always been such a spoken past was never in doubt. The old and the young have ever added a personal rider to the main facts. But tape has provided for an orderly sequence, the capture of an actual voice, the creation of an archive and – most tellingly – a trained ear and a guided reminiscence. George Ewart Evans, a Welshman come to Suffolk after the last war, might justly claim to being the founder of oral history with a masterpiece called *Ask the Fellows Who Cut the Hay* (1956). It was his work which inspired Stephen Caunce to listen to the lives of farm horsemen in East Yorkshire and in his honest way finding them less mysterious than Evans's ploughmen.

Academically, oral history can be said to have come of age via the University of Essex and in need of an authoritative textbook. It would be hard to find a better one than this, with its examples and methodology. The tape-recorder in the hands of many an interviewer can be one of the horrors of the time and far too many people in search of a witness do not realise that listening itself often has to be taught. Dr Caunce teaches the student of oral history how to go about this new discipline. His own sensitivity dominates his chapters and his work is essential reading for anyone attempting to come close to the recent past via the talk of someone who was there. He divides his book into 'people and places', 'alternative history', 'lifestyles and language' and 'oral history and the mainstream' before coming to the techniques and practicalities of actually taping a contributor – I almost said victim – but feeling, consideration, etc. for the sources of this aspect of history are shown to be a necessary part of the access to it.

Tape-recording was once so novel that it evinced in many interviewees (a) a fanciful tale and (b) a true confession of surprising power. But now such a way of talking has become commonplace and only the skills and taste – and often the personality of the oral historian himself – is able to make it otherwise. Dr Caunce certainly can. One is constantly made aware all through his book that he is serious. A tape to him is an antenna picking up what might soon be irrecoverable. It could be a saying, a pronunciation, a working process or something which revises History itself. He teaches their value in the context of all other studies. Ostensibly for first-year students, *Oral History and the Local Historian* has a lot to offer to anyone who needs to listen to another person talking.

Like other academics Dr Caunce decries the lack of method in my *Akenfield*. I had never heard the term 'oral history' when I wrote it in the mid-sixties, nor have I ever called myself an oral historian. This book is about the Suffolk into which I was born in 1922 and was an attempt by a poet and storyteller to describe the agricultural depression and its consequences. Some of it was remembered, not taped. Most of the characters were friends and neighbours.

PITMEN PAINTERS
The Ashington Group 1934-1984

William Feaver, 1993

As Edmund Blunden said, 'This is not what we were formerly told.' What we have been told about the miners this century by novelists, poets, film-makers, historians and politicians, Left and Right, is more than about any other industrial culture. Their lives, their toil, their communities are like none other and set them apart. Over the years they have been much visited, but, it seems, with such an existing notion of who and what they are as to make it near impossible to get beyond a stereotypical image.

The wholesale destruction of all that we believed they stood for by Mrs Thatcher and her successors, albeit for the sake of the economy, that sacred excuse, leaves an unpleasant taste. And yet – and not forgiving the ruthless government onslaught – were the miners ever what we were told they were? Even by Humphrey Jennings, J.B.Priestley, Emlyn Williams, George Orwell and Clancy Sigal? Even by, if it comes to that, Arthur Scargill?

In January 1971 William Feaver, then art critic for the *Newcastle Journal*, went 'to see the Helen Sutherland Collection of Modern Art at the Laing Art Gallery and was introduced to a group of four or five elderly men, well wrapped up, standing apart . . . They were the Ashington Group.' They took him to their hut and there he saw something which seemingly everyone who made pilgrimages to the collieries during the Thirties, their heyday for the compassionate, the intrigued and the investigative, had missed: a normal artistry. Although critics and sociologists might stick labels on them (Feaver is careful not to), the miner-artists themselves go about their painting as naturally, as it were, as they had cut coal. Their pictures, the finest of which are well-reproduced here, are of their friends, their families, their landscape, their hobbies, their homes, and all of them refute the literary and photographic views taken of them during this period.

It all began when the Workers Educational Association class of 1936 stopped listening and began doing – 'a breach', Feaver calls it. Those were the days when the working-class was supposed to listen to the middle-class, or read what it wrote. The miners started with lino-cuts and moved on to Walpamur on plywood. Up the road lived rich Helen Sutherland who collected paintings and who sometimes had David Jones and other artists to stay. She took the miners to the Tate and to the National Gallery, she sent them models so that they could paint from life (the blinds had to be drawn), and very soon their work broke through the condescension barrier and existed simply and properly as art of a particular school.

Feaver places this work in its cultural context. We have Marion Richardson's exciting new art education, Pelican Books ('the WEA in paperback'), *Picture Post* and the revolutionary photo-journalism of 1938 onwards, BBC documentaries during the war and the social triumphs of the Attlee government. But most of all we have some 20 miners painting in their studio-hut, neatly dressed men in ties with pale absorbed faces. Oliver Kilbourn, one of the best artists in the group, protests, 'I'm sick and tired of miners being portrayed like lumps of wood – all downtrodden with work!' This remarkable artist wrote to Feaver:

Contsable said the River Stour and Dedham Vale made him a painter of natural landscape. Alas my River Stours and Dedham Vales were in the underworld of Ashington, and I hope by staying at home like Constable that Ashington has made me as good a painter of underground pit work.

After all the Egyptians didn't do so badly with the depiction of their underworld.

Ashington and its neighbouring colliery have vanished under a £3 million Silver Jubilee Park. The miners' pictures are evidence of a beauty and goodness which they saw all around them, from the little terraced house to the coal seam, but it was an aesthetic which escaped those who were on *The Road to Wigan Pier*.

IN SEARCH OF A PAST
The Manor House, Amnersfield, 1933-1945

Ronald Fraser, 1984

Exactly halfway through this autobiography Ronald Fraser's analyst asks, 'What purpose are you trying to achieve with the book?' and is told that its aim is to combine two different modes of inquiry, oral history and psycho-analysis. The voyage of inner discovery has to run parallel with a voyage into the social past. To this the analyst gives the somewhat priestly reply, 'Well, it's not the past but what we make of the past that shapes our future and present.' Fraser might have added a third dimension to his aim, which was to draw an analyst into an act of literary creation. The couch-talk and the tape-talk wind into and around each other, and around Fraser himself, until often his mysterious and less articulate self is seen struggling like Laocoön.

What does emerge plainly is that Fraser's boyhood at the Thirties Manor, although such a spiritual desolation in so many respects, was exceptionally rich in those elements required for a growing writer. A victim of the class-truce between his parents and their servants, he fled as soon as he could to Spain, though not to freedom. The key to this remained at home at the Manor, hence this middle-aged home-coming. He questions the servants, now to themselves incredibly distant from the time they spent in the employ of Captain and Mrs Fraser, and he counts the cost which their combined attitudes and pretensions have forced him to pay. Is he free now? Probably not, but in the better kind of captivity supplied by an imagination which has been daringly fed with broken taboos. Such as not honouring thy father and thy mother.

Of course, they asked for it. Between the wars English villages were full of people like the Frasers who took the local 'big house', filled it with servants at a pittance, and then spent nearly all their energy maintaining their social position. Amnersfield Manor and its inmates manufactured the kind of philistinism and semi-submerged violence which lies beneath the weekends and dinners in the fiction of the period. Ronald Fraser's evocation of it is brilliant and, of course, lacking detachment, shocking rather than amusing. His parents' sole purpose for many years (the war was to suggest other goals) was to be country gentry. Father was a Scottish lawyer, mother was the daughter of a rich American married to a German baron. The old servants, when questioned about them, are cagey and devastating by turn. Fraser leads them – he doesn't say quite how – into saying to his face things about his parents which he has to know if he is ever to know himself. The impossible barrier to get out of the way is the class one. Forty or so years on, it should have been possible for 'Master Ronnie' and for the astute villagers who, in their youth, had been butler, grooms and maids at the Manor to find this less formidable; but not so. One of Fraser's insistent complaints is that his parents have contaminated him with their class-consciousness. It is horrible to have such large, stale whiffs of it coming at him from Carvell, Lizzie, Ilse the German nanny, and especially Bert. Conventionally, the servants were for him the real human beings in his childhood. Outwardly, he exercised the prerogatives of the 'little master', inwardly he felt himself inferior to them. Why, after all this time, can't he let himself go?

I can't. There's something – a blackness I'm frightened of, it's like that cesspit at the Manor which Bert had to pump out, where my father's condoms used to block the pump. I feared falling into that stinking blackness. We're never going to get to the bottom of all this. I need a structure in which to operate.

The structure is this book. It holds up very well. The texture is too close to isolate Fraser's skill as an oral historian from his skill as the conveyor of his own case-history. What matters is the artistry of the mix, and this is considerable. What injured him as a boy at Amnersfield, at the grim snob prep-school, during the war when father was fighting and mother (and the servants) were dropping their masks a fraction, was the vulgarity and cruelty of it all.

He returns to Amnersfield during the time of the great linked-hands Greenham Common demo, to find it inhabited by an anti-nuclearist like himself, and with all its gloomy rooms made bright. But it is no discovery of paradise where a desert had previously sprawled. The bruisings acquired in the getting there had seen to that. During the journey analysis and social history explore others almost as deeply as he allows them to explore him. Mother with her nail polish, *Daily Express* and planchette, playing her 'lovely lady' – quite the most effective way of getting servants to drudge for you – father hard-riding and disappointed. Ilse and Nellie the foreigners, and Bert 'the most important male influence of my life'. One of the strangest things to hear is a description of oneself at ten, say, or fourteen. Those who witnessed our early selves rarely volunteer such descriptions, at least at any length. Fraser has courted them. Courted, too, faithful portraits of his parents from those whose role it was not to stare. Long ago he made up his mind to 'write about an "I" who wasn't the "I" everyone else knew'. Ironically, he has had to go to all these early observers to find him.

COUNTRY HOUSE MATTERS
1987

The country-house itself may now be immemorially settled after what has turned out to be a few post-war years of baseless alarms, but its current investigators and apologists reveal no such fixed and stable views. For them the subject provides an exceptionally rich bit of cultivation to be dug over time and again, and never mind if it throws up what have become, due to such industry, a great many now familiar facts and wonders. It is ironic, even poetic, that buildings created for the display of an exclusive inheritance are now claimed as 'our heritage' by the rest of us. When in 1976 a wealth tax proposal appeared to threaten their survival and the Historic Houses Association was formed, it was able to get a million signatures on a petition to 'save our heritage.' The cultural hand-over has been superbly managed. The old country-house owners have had their cake and eat it too, and the nation, which now also regards itself in possession, has never grudged them a crumb of it. What with the National Trust art and architecture experts, and their right-hand men the photographers, the tourist industry, the screening of novels by Waugh, Hartley, James, Austen, etc. especially on television, and last but not least aristocratic showmanship of a ruthlessly dazzling order, we can swarm through 'our heritage' and often be considerably more au fait with what is contained in its gardens and rooms than the old house-party guests – or even their hosts – ever were. The surprising thing is to find how very surprised we are by what a great house is saying when we are within earshot. The Weasels may have made Toad Hall but what it says via its proportions and contents is still able to take their breath away. Were such statements made by a church, a town hall or an art gallery, or Buckingham Palace, they could be taken in one's stride, but by an often not very large private house! How amazing!

Country-house literature ranges from the learned to the doting but for all its approaches there has been little penetration of what it was actually like for generations of villagers to exist within the climate which a local Big House generated, to worship God in a church over-flowing with icons of its inhabitants, or, most of all, of the thinking which allowed a family to set itself up so gloriously over the neighbours. Maybe we come closest to this climate in the old word 'seat', dropped now by the country-house writers, but a noun whose cathedra-plus-magisterial overtones partially explains why the earlier residents had the nerve to exist in such state. That these rural first families never had the faintest intention of being put down from their seat is the immediate impression we receive as we rattle over the cattle-grid to be nonplussed by the façade. All is most beautiful; domestic and dynastic arrangements correctly harmonised by Time. If anything browbeats us, it is so much naked stone and brick social acceptance of a bursting pride in rank. The latter was not always easily reached and could take ages. Are not a family's arms its achievement? This properly understood makes the never-ending acquisition of land (imperative) and taste (usually first class) distantly logical. Man, we are told, may not see God at any time, but when we are suddenly brought face-to-face with Blenheim, Castle Howard, Blickling,

Chatsworth, Ham, Hardwick, Longleat, or ever little Ebberston, we reel back a bit from their absolutism. More nerve. Had Nelson survived Trafalgar, Lady Hamilton might have pushed through a later Blenheim. Or so she thought. As it happened, he died Duke of some Sicilian huts and master of a nice Surrey villa covered all over with his portraits like Elvis Presley's mansion.

Great houses do not always go with great deeds, or in fact with a great deal of money. And frequently their greatness completely overrides that of their owners. They are an architectural expression of a marriage between a hard-nosed management of the surrounding countryside and principles discovered in the Classics. It was purpose-built for fanfares and posterity. Closed they may have been to the likes of the masses now pouring through them, but what were then called the better sort could wander up to stare. No less than 2,324 trippers visited Wilton in 1776. A country-house existed to be stared at, though not by the local peasants and artisans at the tasks which sustained its wealth. Parks, walls, lodges and plantations kept them out of sight, and its huge staff ran it from as much seclusion as could be contrived. The house was a paradox. It was there to be seen and to dazzle, and there to provide the utmost privacy for its residents forever. It has always been all things to all men and Henry James was as right to lyricise it in *English Hours* as Mark Girouard, in a sparkling anthology, *A Country House Companion*, is to record some of its ghastliness. At Blenheim in the 1890s it was the custom to have big tins in the dining-room for scraps to feed the poorer tenants. Consuel Marlborough risked being thought impertinent by insisting that fish, meat, vegetable and sweet scraps should not be tipped into the same tin, which they always had been. Girouard also deals in reverse realities, those of sheer happiness and a kind of monumental ease. The whole point of any country-house was that it should reflect 'the image of abundance'.

Property and Landscape is the most intriguing and original of this latest batch on the Big House, not only because it touches on scores of things which have been somewhat skirted round before, but because it is so lucid. This is a book for those requiring some ground-work on the ecological as well as economic effects of possession. It stresses the role of the park in the development of country-house attitudes. A lord's house in the Middle Ages might stand hugger-mugger in the village street and his park miles away. The latter was a hunting ground to provide sport and meat in abundance but by the 18th century it could only tell the world that its owner was an important man by being of no use at all. Tom Williamson and Liz Bellamy, besides writing well, present their information on certain notorious aspects of the house, the clearances which provided its amenities, for instance, more fully and fascinatingly than in most of its histories. They are good on what they call 'tomb churches', or the turning into mausoleums a community's common place of worship by country-house families. On the credit side they prove how often the heads of many of these landed families saw that it was nothing less than their duty to be well-read, good musicians and excellent gardeners, so as not to let their clever houses down. Botany and silviculture, ornament and symbol, Virgil and Claude, the Anglican liturgy and science, heraldry (marvellously suspect in the new Victorian country-houses) and literature, these interests were strong enough to still hang in the air when we leave the car-park and pay for our Entrance.

Lawrence Rich has something of today's landowning pragmatism and tenacity about him. *Inherit the Land* takes stock of eight representative country-houses ranging in size and showmanship from Longleat and Beaulieu to the 'slightly mad-looking granite pile' which is the home of the Seigneur of Sark. Lord Bath and Lord Montagu, the first of the great cashers-in on the heritage market, are assessed and come out smiling. Peter de Savary of Littlecote and now of Land's End is placed by Rich among the successful money-spinners of the ages who buy their way into country-housedom – 'In England a ladder has always been at hand'. In de Savary's hands the house is the fulfilment of popular dreams about the past. Waxwork cavaliers plan a battle, small boys grin in the stocks, local lads joust in the tilt yard. De Savary's 1988 intention is to have 300,000 visitors a year to 'my country home', the annual costs of which are £900,000. Rich's candid tale of what happened between 1945 – 'when all across the land great houses were being shuttered and deserted' – and the present, when our longing to see them in all their splendour has turned them into habitable goldmines, is a lesson in patrician adaptability. No country-house family seems to really speak its mind on the burden of inheritance. Somebody speaking on a Northumbrian wild-fowl preserve said, without accusation, that 90% of its visitors weren't interested in bird-watching and were there just to have a day's outing. The country-house openers aren't remotely fussed about this and their brochures say, if that's what they want, let's let them have it. 'Beaulieu is unashamedly profitable,' says Rich, and 'owes much to the techniques of Disneyland'.

The Country House Garden, the photographer James Pipkin's stunning tour through the National Trust's parterres, lawns, shrubberies and vistas, with a good-mannered commentary by Gervase Jackson-Stops, halts criticism. Here is some of the loveliest and oldest gardening in Britain whose scale and perfection would never have come into being had the landed classes not insisted on looking out of their windows onto paradise. Limitless labour produced and maintained them, and they must be among the world's most desirable inventions. We their visitors on the best of all day's outing return to our own patches with ideas above their station. If you want to get away from the official guide and into the secret, read Andrew Marvell's *Upon Appleton House*.

IN THE PINK
Caroline Blackwood, 1987

This gallop over the controversial ground begs two questions. How on earth is it all still going on, and how on earth could it ever be stopped? What this gallant attempt to balance the for and against arguments reveals is how deep-eyed and ingrained, addictive and quasi-sacred these rituals are. Also, if one can manage to put the sufferings of the fox out of one's head for a moment, how alternately ridiculous and splendid. As nobody brought up in hunting country can deny, there is what Caroline Blackwood calls 'the thundering beauty of the chase' and unless it is allowed to mask 'the high-pitched child-like screams' of the chased as the hounds get him, its colourful aesthetic has to be acknowledged. However, it is not her intention to let distance bring enchantment to the scene. This is a book of close-ups, some very nasty, some pretty hilarious. But many simply loutish and thick. Her own stance is that of abolitionist/detached, and she is as scathing on some of the anti's as she is on most of the pro's. What emerges is a lot of strange behaviour which it would be flattering to describe as eccentric, and little of which could bear rational analysis. Killing a fox requires a special language, a special soul.

In the Pink opens with a fierce hue and cry in the direction of the late Duke of Beaufort, the man the hunt saboteurs would have exhumed had not their spade broke. The Duke's life was one long fox-hunt and when, very old, he could no longer ride, he shot foxes from his Land Rover, thus becoming a 'vulpicide', which, in hunting thinking, is nearly as bad as being a matricide. But from nine onwards Henry Beaufort could not allow a fox to live. There is a very funny account of the care taken of his unreadable memoirs in the office of the League Against Cruel Sports. Caroline Blackwood is irreverent with what she calls the Opposition. Though sympathetic with their aims, she finds many of them little less repulsive than the MFH's and their crews. There are, incidentally, 77 female Masters of Fox Hounds, and the sport has always had an enormous appeal for women.

Many of the best anecdotes have been related by much-damaged ladies, one of whom pointed out that most of the wheelchairs in the House of Lords are there because of hunting accidents. Injury and death are not the prerogatives of the fox; hounds, horses and people regularly get hurt, and the sport remains one of the most dangerous, and one needing a lot of courage. Caroline Blackwood mentions Prince Charles, who has hunted with 42 different packs. If the immorality of the sport cannot deter him, perhaps its dangers should.

There is plenty of Mitfordian gruesomeness; 'Horsewhipping a hunt saboteur is rather like beating a wife. They are both private matters' (an MFH), and to represent the other side of the coin, some highly candid forays into the redoubts of the enlightened. Extreme alternative lifers, punks, etc., are dismissed as scum and are never given a hearing by the pro-hunters, and so, as John Bryant, one of the League Against Cruel Sports senior voices, told the author, 'If you want to achieve anything worthwhile it's a mistake to let yourself get a disgusting image . . . . if you want to beat the tweeds and green wellington brigade you have to have more tweeds and green wellingtons than they do.' Her encounter with the vegan Tim Morgan, the Animal Rights leader, was less amiable. Here was a 'sanctuary' which to her reciprocated the aggression and extremeness of what it wanted to destroy. She is honest enough to admit that her feelings about fox-hunting are those of the liberal rejectionist, rather than those of the passionate crusader. She speaks in some ways as an insider, and she is also, as a novelist, seduced by strong characters, of which any hunt produces a rich field. Like everything else, the hunt has its modern accretions, one of which is the car-hunter, a truly ghastly nuisance in the countryside, and loathed as much as the saboteur by the riders. Many car-hunters following the hunt which is following the fox dress to kill in caps, tweeds and boots, block the lanes and inevitably lose the horses when they take to the fields. It would be true to say that the average fox-hunter is caught up in the attractions of dressing the part, rushing across the English landscape with the air on his face and the music of hound and horn in his ears, and with a nice spot of resurrected rural brutality in his breast, and nothing much worse. But there is the wild creature in all its terror and pain ahead. Maybe the chief value of *In the Pink* is that, unlike most anti-bloodsports literature, it possesses a certain social fascination and style which in spite of its hard underlying criticism will appeal to the fox-hunters themselves. It could be one way of getting a tract through the door. Also it is full of cold-eyed glimpses of the fringe, the horrible terrier men, the old folk who hunt by telephone, the apostates and their fate. Perhaps one of the weirdest of all hunt investigations was Hans Eysenck's 1971 poll of MFHs and its conclusions. The book rarely waxes indignant and it isn't really very learned, but its anecdotal asides are often lethal, and most especially when they break into the sincere lyricism of some huntsman who is genuinely baffled not to be admired. Nor can Caroline Blackwood bring herself to like the anti as a type, he/her all too often being too

266

full of a different kind of unawareness of the violence within. The fox gets a good press and he does seem to be a pleasant enough creature in comparison with those who make up the Quorn and the Galway Blazers.

GEOFFREY GRIGSON

To docket Geoffrey Grigson as a twentieth century country writer of genius is correct enough in its way, but because of our present notion of the term it could be a limiting classification. All that I have consistently felt during a lifetime's reading him has been his distinction in this sphere, a kind of natural eminence which he shares with just a handful of writers among the ever-increasing host who go to the country for the experience needed for their books. Many who do so are genuine countrymen, of course, so here again one can only see Grigson's nearly sixty years' rural commentary in poetry and prose on a countryside whose changes and permanence I have witnessed as the superior account that it is. Wonderful, firm narration, clear, fresh imagery – and this in spite of his immersion in such rural masters as Hopkins and Clare. How has it been achieved, this bright texture covering so many decades which is so all of a piece, so classic and so unmarked by dating fashions? By Grigson's knowing rural England (and later rural France) in historic, aesthetic and botanical depth. He is erudite, learned, but the facts spring from the page in the most imaginative way, and one relishes their mixture of philosophy, tartness and lyricism. The tone, the voice is unmistakable. Private, often severe, yet at the same time sensuous, it is the highly literate voice of a great tradition of village based poets-cum-men of letters-cum naturalists.

Grigson's work is remarkable in that it shows very little decadal wear and tear. References point to when particular books were written but the output itself retains the interest and urgency of a 'latest volume'. It is very intriguing. Here I must admit to the enormous pleasure which I derive from their style. It is a vigorous, occasionally hard-hitting style which makes no concessions to the popular idea of rural writing as something minor, gentle and withdrawn. For Grigson the fields are a very intellectual place and he knows as any writer does who comes out of the country, and not to it, that those who are still in any way connected with their ancient cyclic pattern have a far more powerful mystery than any but the village-reared artist or writer can reach. In his scholarly way he touches their simple, and yet at the same time complex, nerves, those of a workaday rural landscape and its inhabitants. Even where aspects of the village have been so buried in previous descriptions and explanations, the church, plants, folklore and human types, Grigson lifts them out of past words into his own excellent language. Nothing is taken for granted, and his vision all these years has remained strong and original because he depends entirely on his own eye for what is going on all around him. Or went on, for he is a witty and individualistic interpreter of the past. Never for him the limitations of the current sociological and ecological debates where the countryside is concerned; he is into the scene at a far deeper level. I am myself such a product of this kind of multi-stratification, with Anglicanism running into literature and reading running into everyday tasks round an old agricultural setting, and everywhere seeing the old symbolism, that I have to admit to being a 'natural' when it comes to the Grigsonian view of country life. But I am full of honest gratitude for it – for such an entertaining and moving statement of it.

The poetry and the anthologies aside, my favourite Geoffrey Grigson books are *The Englishman's Flora* and *Notes from an Odd Country*. The *Flora* is a big, sumptuous gathering-up of our national plant-life whose etymology leads one into the crannies of our culture as well as our natural history. Like so much of his work, it gives the impression of having been gathered together from infinite inner resources rather than researched. It is a celebration of flower-names from the lewd to the holy, and, I have always believed, one of the few works guaranteed to change for the rich better anyone's feeling for rural Britain. It might also be seen as a mine for gardeners, poets, novelists, cooks, travellers, Christians, historians – indeed, delvers of every persuasion. I remember my old friend the artist and 'plantsman'

John Nash's love of this book, with its skilful twining together of so much knowledge and its being able to take one right to the centre of Britain's historic flower-consciousness. The 'odd country' of the *Notes* is that of the Bas-Vendomois, just below Troo, the poet Ronsard's native place on the borders of Touraine, and where an alternative farmhouse to that which forms Grigson's Wiltshire base has been his home for a long time. These *Notes* provide a perfect extension for Grigson's art. They could claim to be the most dazzling 'second house' reflections ever written! But they contain a deeper meaning than this implies. It has always made me wish that anyone who has written well about his own countryside should be lured to foreign parts and, hopefully, as they now say, be tempted to write as well about somebody else's. *Notes from an Odd Country* is a delectable English intrusion into rural France.

Finally, I must add a word about Grigson and John Clare. As president of the John Clare Society I wander annually around Helpston, often in the fields where the poet worked, and I never do so without thankfulness for Geoffrey Grigson's part in bringing Clare to where he can be seen in all his strength, truthfulness and beauty as a village writer of genius. Clare the farmworker and Grigson the country clergyman's son are involved in a tradition – and in a revolution, as all authentic rural voices are.

DOWN THE DEEP LANES

Peter Beacham & James Ravilious, 2000

The nature of Devon's terrain and climate still allows us to see farming life much as it was before recent agricultural development and much tidying-up of the village wrought their great changes in other parts of the country. In less than a generation we have tended to forget what the rural world was like for those who were part of it until 'just the other day'. The chief jogger of our memory was the late James Ravilious, son of the artist Eric Ravilious, whose marvellous photographs fill this book. Armed with Pevsner, fully informed by every kind of conservationist, aware that at this very moment Devon's farmers are in crisis, we still lack the reality of this beautiful rainy county. Between them, Peter Beacham and James Ravilious show it to us. They also reveal how often the anti-idyll becomes a poem all its own.

Compared with East Anglia, the west country is a poor place. Devon itself, due to its deep lanes and inhospitable moors, stays hidden, and this in spite of its being on a popular tourist route. Beacham and Ravilious penetrate it without attempting to expose it. They say, 'This is what is really here, only you would not find it without our sort of guide.' They are partners in truth about certain local matters. The kind of Devon they lead us to is not likely to make us want to stay there. But it is a Devon restored to its old dignity and power. Candida Lycett-Green uses the old Hardyesque word 'sequestered' to describe it. Beacham and Ravilious take the reader into a farming world which makes no attempt to be agreeable. It halts him in his tracks, makes him think hard about what happens in these tucked away settlements, and challenges his comfortable notions. At the same time he feels himself strengthened by this uncompromising corner of England which has been so intimately conveyed.

Ravilious spent many years making pictures of Devon for the Beaford Archive and here we have some of the finest. Peter Beacham's words fit them perfectly. Amongst much else he praises and explains things which get left out of the picture in ordinary topography, farm buildings, corrugated iron, a tin tabernacle, abandoned quarries and other workings. Those caught at their tasks are unenviable, yet at the same time offering a criticism of today's ideals. Devon and Cornwall are still marked by Methodism and its simple chapels and glorious hymns. Remote chapels often become holiday homes or were built so flimsily that they stand in ruins at the crossroads. In this instance Beacham accepts transience, recognising them as 'no more than tabernacles in the wilderness.' Similarly, like John Nash, who loved to paint them, he finds the smallest quarry 'a world of strange awesome beauty' and the lunar mountains of the china-clay pits near St Austell a fascinating addition to the landscape. He reminds us that there was a period when much of the necessary equipment of the countryside, power lines, farm machinery, metal Dutch barns, etc. was picked out for abuse by writers but that now they have to be taken into the actual aesthetics of the scene. They too, like the often ugly yet profoundly moving little chapels, are transient. Corrugated iron itself is now heritage material in Australia, where silver roofs glitter in the outback. Cob, of course, is Devon's old shelter for man and beast – and that archaeo-botanist's boon, for in its mixture of soil, shillet and straw can be discovered the ecological Devon of the Middle Ages. The one 'untidyness' which Beacham and Ravilious are likely to preach in vain is that of the uncut churchyard. They see 'Headstones at home in grass and wild flowers' but most see what they call 'a disgrace'. Yet churchyards, untouched as they are by chemicals and richly fertilized for a thousand years, contain many more plants and there is no happier sight than old memorials rocking about in a sea of cow-parsley.

This is an unusually interesting country book. The pictures and words come together reflectively and make us look twice at things we may not have looked at all.

A CORNER OF ENGLAND
North Devon Landscapes and People
James Ravilious, 2006

This second collection of James Ravilious's work has to be studied for three distinct reasons. Because it is in the great tradition of Henri Cartier-Bresson, because it corrects our distorted vision of the English countryside, and because it reveals the poetry of the commonplace. In 1973 Ravilious was invited to restore and add to the Beaford Archive, a remarkable library of photographs of village life in North Devon. This wonderful book shows him way ahead of his commission. His Leica records his own intimacy with the region, its landscape, its people, its creatures. No ordinary journalist or social historian could have gained Ravilious's entrée to these extraordinarily private rooms and fields, or be taught to see what he so naturally sees. The pictures have been drawn from his own contribution to the Beaford Archive and he describes them as 'rather like scenes from a tapestry I have been stitching over the years.' His wife Robin, a local girl, contributes a few hard facts. 'The small mixed farm is the commonest unit still. Short of labour, short of capital, bothered by paperwork and recession, farmers struggle stoically in a cold soil, high rainfall and awkward upland terrain . . .'

Ravilious's camera scrupulously avoids wringing the usual bitter-sweet agricultural drama out of this situation and his work is masterly in its absence of comment. He has a way of capturing a private moment without making it public, so to speak. So the reader/looker has to share his intimate views if they are to see anything at all. As one stares into these twisting lanes, stackyards, churchyards, bedrooms, kitchens, animals' faces, sheds, shops, schools, one often feels apologetic at invading something so personal, then grateful for having been shown what is actual, true and good. This is a rural world without 'characters', only people. Not even the old tramp sunning himself amidst the rubbish-tip of his belongings is a character – just a naked man on the earth. Nor do the farm animals set out to beguile but are where one would expect them to be. A snowdrift of geese on a darkening hilltop and a dog in blackening road are waiting for the first thunderclap. A sick ram rides home in a tin bath. Here is the ordinariness of the harsh and lovely pastoral. The Ravilious 'interior', whether of houses or hills, can shock or inspire. A rare country-book.

HOME COUNTRY

Richard Mabey, 1990

The conservationist-ecological-save-the-earth movements have their highly articulate apologists, and thank God for them. Their films and facts shatter our comfortable lives. They are the Solomon Eagles of our day, and well do we deserve them. Richard Mabey was in the van of this informed concern for the countryside and now, twenty or so years later, he takes stock of his position.

Whether he recognises it or not, it is plain to those of us who have learned from him, or who know classic natural history writing when we see it, that he stands not so much alone as among the best landscape philosophers. He is quirky, often despairing and full of facts, but also he is inspiring, and filled with the right kind of dreams – those which could, and should, be put into practice. This book is, among other things, a statement of his current position and how he reached it. It is an April day of a confession, gloomy and sunny by turns, erudite, tender. He is one of the few commentators on what is happening to rural Britain today in whom one can still hear the voices of White, Jefferies, Hudson and Massingham. It is this old literacy in conjunction with the latest science and protest which isolates Mabey from most of his contemporaries in the ecology lobby.

Home Country begins with Mabey's recognition of his local territory, the Chilterns, as being his most formative influence during boyhood, and ends with his triumphant purchasing of Hardings Wood. In between there are his passion for East Anglia and a critical summary of some of the major issues involving the land since the early 1970s. In one sense his limits were the Blitz and the Great Gale, in another, those two states of landscape awareness which we all have, but which few of us develop; that of infancy and first-seeing, and that of what might be called 'the informed view'. The trick is not to allow a child's wonder at the world all around him to become obliterated by grown-up statistics and hard facts.

There is in Mabey a continuing fight between the emotion which certain places create and his scientific knowledge of them, and it makes for good writing. His account of the intensity of his feelings for certain areas, north Norfolk, for example, are like those of affairs which are so thrilling in retrospect that they can never be quite over. Wherever he is, wherever he has been, he makes one long to go and see for oneself, though with a sense of trespass. His travels are markers for his years, walking and cycling distances from Berkhamsted for when he was twelve, the Norfolk coast for his teens and now, the twice-weekly drive to the ancient, re-awakened wood just outside Tring.

273

He correctly refutes the popular notion of a free and unravaged countryside until our day. One part of the history of Britain has been the constant whittling away of common land, destruction of forests and the spoiling of rivers for short-term gain. 'Improvement' impoverished countless villagers. Mabey quotes a Victorian clergyman's astonishment that some Hertfordshire folk should let a local landowner filch their immemorial wilds without a struggle. He also notes the pain caused by today's ecologists when they specify somebody's home country as 'the last wilderness'. Or a prairie or a wetlands, one might add.

This highly personal tale of a naturalist reaching out towards all kinds of discovery and experience from his understanding of his home base has to come to terms with the divide which exists between the emotion most of us feel for our native place and how it is perceived in the new Green language. Mabey is among other things an excellent teacher. Wherever he travels, among abandoned workings and dumps to find the flowers of the unofficial countryside, to Selborne itself, to the Flow Country, as he calls the peat wilds of Caithness and Sutherland, to ever-mysterious Dorset, he has a gift for handing back these scenes to those who live within sight of them in a condition which forces everybody to look again. But a touch of melancholy hangs around his vision; it is as if he cannot convince them – or himself – that it could not be a last look.

Hardings Wood acts as a tonic. Here we have the first full account of its purchase and management, and these practicalities, undertaken by friends and locals of all ages, is the kind of Green education in which at this moment we should all have a hand.

SELECTED WRITINGS
1974-1999

Richard Mabey, 1999

Mabey's understanding of the countryside is passionate, radical, informed and infectious. These essays are not journalism in the ordinary sense but what used to be called 'fugitive' pieces, good work which gets lost in various publications, so what a good idea to collect it up like this and reveal its position in the writer's opus. It is a high one. Here we have some quarter of a century of Mabey the rural educator, with his tough line and gentle spirit, and his easy way of conveying both scientific and folk intelligence without didacticism or a crusading pen. He *is* a crusader, of course, but never the usually recognisable polemicist. Instead of urging us to join causes, like John Clare, like Colette's mother the immortal Sido, he simply says, 'Look'. And what sights, what sounds, what overlookings brought to our attention! He is the master of casual instruction. 'Herts has more species of lea than any other county in England', and takes its name from the hart which once so plentifully ran its woodlands.

He is autobiographical throughout and these fifty or so chapters drawn from a life dedicated to natural history reveal Mabey's Berkhamsted, his Oxford, his seduction by north Norfolk, his spasmodic journeys to Galway, the Camargue and to Spain, his travels in Cornwall and, uniquely of course, his exploration of urban wastes and mainline crevices where so much diffident flora is rooted. And all the way through this gathering together of scattered writings there are the mentors, great and, well, call them companiable sharers of the field, Gilbert White, Kenneth Allsop, Dorothy Hartley, his late and loved friend the photographer Tony Evans, the wonderful Annie Dillard and a whole host of fellow trampers and lookers. It is eager out-of-doors, frequently boyish yet always movingly mature stuff, the kind of book which encapsulates Mabey's teachings, for teacher he has been all these many years, and none more eloquent or commonsensical.

Whether it was intended that Mabey's *Selected Writings* should appear the very moment that the government's 'right to roam' bill is announced, or not, there could be no better accompaniment to this long fought-for triumph. Every page breathes access and freedom, plus a moody kind of happiness to go with our weather. Added to which is the joy of maps. The advice is, if you want to read the landscape, read its maps – not just the Ordinance Survey but the Tithe Map, the Enclosure Map, the beautiful farm maps all done by hand. Most of all, read the map which is created by your own footsteps. Mabey writes colloquially but intellectually, avoiding the crude buzzwords of the ecology lobby, in fact he writes nobly. He has taught a whole generation what to see both on and off the beaten track. He insists upon a whole countryside, not the special site or the museumisation of rarities and gradually, because he has educated us in its delights, we are beginning to see – his vision. He is forgiving and illuminating when it comes to commuterville but he shakes his fist at any kind of fossilisation with its theme-parks and tat. As were our forebears, though less so ourselves, he remains emotionally caught up in the changing year and the powerful repetition of its nuances. In 'Art and Ecology' and 'The Painter as Naturalist', and in his description of the 'birth' of his *Flora Britannica* he shows the full compass of his intention as a writer, which is to bring us back to where we belong.

FRONT LINES

THE GREAT WAR – AND THE LITTLE MAGAZINES

The Ivor Gurney Society Journal, 2003

It is not uncommon for writers in their work to avoid areas of their own historical involvement for reasons which they find hard to explain – particularly to themselves. I have now and then written about the First World War but at arm's length, which is strange when I remember that our toy box at home contained father's Gallipoli medals and mother's V.A.D. insignia. And that some of our farming neighbours still called themselves 'captain', and that men laboured in the sugar beet fields wearing army boots and greatcoats. More pertinently where its literature is concerned I should not forget that I actually met Edmund Blunden, Wilfred Gibson, R. H. Mottram and still do meet the family of Robert Nichols.

But the real closeness comes from my lifelong friendship with John Nash and his wife Christine. John and Paul Nash were official war artists in both world wars. In the spring of 1918 they hired a seed shed in Chalfont St Peter in which to paint their celebrated pictures of the Western Front. The government paid them thirty shillings a day, a fortune, they said. When John died in 1977 I inherited his books. They included runs of English, French and American literary magazines. Also periodicals specialising in the 'new music' and the new movements in art. I have read them hungrily since then for nothing – except old film, of course, – so powerfully evokes the cultural climate of those exciting years.

These magazines are as follows: (Some belonged to Paul, who died in 1946, and some to John):

Art and Letters, an Illustrated Quarterly, 1917-20
The Little Review, A Magazine of the Arts making no compromise with the public taste, 1918. London Editor, Ezra Pound

The London Mercury, 1919-29. Edited by J. C. Squire
The Monthly Chapbook, 1919-23. Edited by Harold Monro, Poetry Bookshop
Fanfare, 1921-22. Edited by Leigh Henry.
Drawing and Design, 1926.

And various other periodicals about poetry, music and art of the period. Between them they create a world which Ivor Gurney knew and was part of. They are both international and provincial in their outlook, and their contributors, both famous or at this stage unknown, await time to sort them out. Gurney appears now and then, most hopefully and movingly for me, in *Fanfare*, when his *Five Preludes* are advertised. Granville Bantock, Manuel de Falla, Eric Satie and Eugene Goosens all wrote trumpet pieces for it. There are Paris notes and drawings by Picasso and Kokoschka, and not a little of the wild optimism of the Twenties. But Richard Aldington, staring across an English harvest, asks:

O friend, why is it that the fields have peace
And we have none? I press my hands
Softly against my aching eyes and feel
How hot they are with scanning many books;
My brain is dry with thoughts of many men,
My heart is faint with deaths of many gods.
I know I live only because I suffer.

His poem is moody with the generally experienced sense of appalling loss and possible gain. The war – its name is not quite settled and it is sometimes called the Big War or the Great European War – has both deprived the artist and poet of their natural joy and in some way in which they cannot at this moment understand, energised them.

Searching for attitudes towards the war and editorial statements on the huge calamity I found them all rather played down. It was not escapism because there could never be any escape, even in rural England where everything went on as usual: as in Auden's 'Musée des Beaux Arts' a boy falling into the sea is 'not an important Failure' for either the ploughman or a passing ship 'which had somewhere to get to'. Here before me is the first number of the *London Mercury* which Jack Squire sent to John Nash and which is dated November 1919. Exactly a year since the Armistice. Its lengthy editorial briefly mentions the paper shortage during the war and says 'We have had a glimpse into the abyss of disorganisation', then passes on to its aim, which is the continuation of English Literature. The first poem is by Thomas Hardy and is called 'Going and Staying'. He sees:

Seasons of blankness as of snow,
The silent bleed of a world decaying,
The moan of multitudes in woe,
These were the things we wished would go;
  But they are staying.

John Nash, who fought with the Artists' Rifles in the trenches, and who with his brother has completed his official war paintings in the Buckinghamshire seed shed, writes on The Fine Arts. He is twenty six. He is sad because Harold Gilman, who taught him how to use oils, has died from influenza. Paul Nash too is going to be very ill, as so many soldiers were after the war. Not wounded men but injured men. John, who has contributed some delightful illustrations to them, plugs the magazines *Art and Letters* and the *Chapbooks*. He and the Australian poet W. J. Turner have become theatre and music critics, Turner writing, John drawing. Siegfried Sassoon lodges in Turner's London house. (Sassoon will buy a house for Edmund Blunden after the Second World War at Long Melford, near my home, where I will meet him and eventually give his centenary lecture.) They all read the *London Mercury*. In the first number there is a long short story by Robert Nichols which goes as far as it possibly can from the war. An advertisement says that Rupert Brooke's *Poems* 'has gone into an enormous number of editions'. One of the sailors who helped to dig his grave on Skyros 'having heard that I was interested in such things' told me what hard work it was, what with the rock and everything. They were ordered to make a cairn over it. The sailor was now a brewer's traveller, a rotund, wistful little man who *had* got to Gallipoli. Paul

281

Nash had encountered Rupert Brooke after he had got back from the Antwerp raid in October 1914, his eyes shining with happiness and excitement. They had stood on the pavement outside Eddie Marsh's house, not believing their luck. To be young and at war!

The *London Mercury* was not at war in any sense. It was at peace with books, with that literary intelligence which had to carry on without break from the nineteenth to the twentieth century, never mind 1914-1918. It had to show an unfractured civilization in the form of Letters. To its critics it was no more than the continuation of Georgian Poetry, which died in 1922. But its retrospection can be a goldmine for those searching for World War One treasures, often small things which reveal the climate in which a poet-composer like Ivor Gurney worked. These include Edgell Rickword's *The Soldier Addresses his Body*, Max Beerbohm's essay *Servants* which presaged Kazuo Ishiguro's butler with uncanny exactitude as well as reminding the reader of that great army of footmen, gardeners and valets from all over Europe which vanished in the mud of Flanders. A staple of *Punch* humour between the wars was the servant shortage. Another army, that of agricultural labourers, hoped that the brotherhood of the trenches would continue on the farms when it returned home, but it did not. The farmer and his men, far fewer needed then because of the return of the agricultural depression, remained socially apart. Edmund Blunden, discovering John Clare, remains one of the best poets of village England after 1918. Although mocked by the Modernists the *London Mercury* was, among other things, a truthful forum for those writers who recognised the irony of desecrating one countryside in order to save another, of wrecking Ypres to save Gloucester. Although poets like Ivor Gurney were provincial city boys, the fields and meadows came right up to their cathedrals and market squares – as they still do at Ely and to countless French, Italian and German towns, if held back by ring roads to some extent. And of course having 'Gloucester' or 'Suffolk' written on one's shoulder tabs intensified the feeling that one's entire world was an English county. As did hearing the home dialect spoken in a foreign land, for its broadness had not been narrowed by outside influences then.

In 'First Time In' Gurney describes the hospitality of the trenches when Gloucestershire calls on Wales, and tenderness overcomes the foreign-ness:

After the dread tales and red yarns of the Line
Anything might have come to us; but the divine
Afterglow brought us up to a Welsh colony
Hiding in sandbag ditches, whispering consolatory
Soft foreign things. Then we were taken in
To low huts candle-lit, shaded close by slitten
Oilsheets, and there the boys gave us kind welcome,
So that we looked out as from the edge of home.
Sang us Welsh things, and changed all former notions
To human hopeful things. And the next day's guns
Nor any line-pangs ever quite could blot out
That strangely beautiful entry to war's rout;
Candles they gave us, precious and shared over-rations –
Ulysses found little more in his wanderings without doubt.
"David of the White Rock", the "Slumber Song" so soft, and that
Beautiful tune to which roguish words by Welsh pit boys
Are sung – but never more beautiful than there under the guns' noise.

Among the fascinating aspects of old literary journalism is the comment on writers whose future standing is not yet recognised. Thus, turning the pages of the poetry magazine *Wheels 1919*, the reviewer finds poems by Wilfred Owen which 'have all the earnestness, and much of the force, of Mr Sassoon's illustrations of the beastly cruelty of War' but passes on swiftly to the 'hard, clear and original language' of Mr Aldous Huxley. He quotes from 'Strange Meeting' – 'There is one poem by the late Wilfred Owen which has a powerful, sombre beginning'. Families and friends were beginning to publish the letters of the dead. Charles Sorley's parents published his, revealing that he carried Richard Jefferies' books with him in France. John Nash carried Borrow everywhere he went, he told me, longing not to die because he longed to take to the (English) open road. Charles Tennyson, who lived to be a hundred, used to say that post-World War One generations could not imagine the loveliness of pre-car Britain, its strangeness and enchantment. Ivor Gurney, of course, ached for it:

If I walked straight slap
Headlong down the road
Toward the two-wood gap
Should I hit that cloud?

He did, alas. An open-air man like John Clare, like Wordsworth, like the majority of the still non-industrialised men at the front, four walls would hold him in. By 1926 the *London Mercury* and the *Modernist* magazines in particular were sick of war writing. It was unending, not only poetry and novels but memoirs and politics as the generals and economists got going. 'The war is too much with us, late and soon . . .', despaired Edward Shanks, '. . . the predicted cessation of books about the War has not yet occurred. The public is not, as they say, tired of the subject: it only wants to be tired of it . . . It remains alive in our minds, and there is much yet to say of it before we have got it out of our system'. He is reviewing R. H. Mottram's *Spanish Farm* trilogy and F. Scott Fitzgerald's *The Great Gatsby* and finds that 'the shadow of the War hangs a little over him as well'. Early war poems catch up with post war 'freedom' poems. Patrick Shaw-Stewart's 'Lines Written in Gallipoli' face Belloc's 'Do you remember an inn, Miranda?' – who isn't a girl but a Spanish duke. Now and then Marion Scott sent Gurney's poems to the *London Mercury* where they joined the flood, then the trickle of writing about an essentially war- seen English countryside and a war-hurt Englishman. J. C. Squire anthologised some of them.

In the summer of 1917, when John Nash was a sergeant in the Artists' Rifles on the Somme and his brother Paul was being chauffeur driven along the Front as a Lieutenant War Artist, they began to subscribe to a new review entitled *Art and Letters*. The war was going badly, the casualties were enormous, and the early patriotism was waning. *Art and Letters'* apology for coming out at such a time said 'Objections on the score of scarcity of paper and shortage of labour may surely be overruled when we remember the reams of paper wasted

284

weekly and the hundreds of compositors daily misemployed on periodicals which give vulgar and illiterate expression to the most vile and debasing sentiments. Friends serving at the Front – some of them contributed to this first issue – remind us that there are educated men in the Army . . .' Slight but adventurous, *Art and Letters* took the new movement to the Front as well as bringing home some of its finest creations. Ronald Firbank, the Sitwells, Proust, Dorothy Richardson, T. S. Eliot and Wyndham Lewis were read in the dug-out and the work of soldier poets was given early prominence. War artists such as the Nashes, Edward Wadsworth and William Roberts were illustrated alongside Modigliani, Gaudier Brzeska and Picasso. It was one of those little magazines which attempted to foresee a future civilisation as the old one collapsed. It lacked the space to quarrel with the conventions, it simply gave a taste of the Twenties in order to give the young people something to look forward to. It mourned loss – the death of Isaac Rosenberg received a wonderful reaction – and Ivor Gurney would have fitted into it in so many ways. Its object was to point beyond the narrowness of war and of nations. Cyril Connolly would attempt this with his *Horizon* during World War Two, and John Lehmann with his *Penguin New Writing*. In *War Books* Gurney asked:

> *What did they expect of our toil and extreme*
> *Hunger – the perfect drawing of a heart's dream?*
> *Did they look for a book of wrought art's perfection,*
> *Who promised no reading, nor praise, nor publication?*
> *Out of the heart's sickness the spirit wrote*
> *For delight, or to escape hunger, or of war's worst anger,*
> *When the guns died to silence and men would gather sense*
> *Somehow together, and find this was life indeed . . .*

W. B. Yeats's way of dealing with war poetry was to ignore it. In his Introduction to *The Oxford Book of Modern Verse* (1936) he makes the confession that he had:

> . . . a distaste for certain poems written in the midst of the great war; they are in all anthologies, but I have substituted Herbert Read's *End of a War*

285

written long after. The writers of these poems were invariably officers of exceptional courage and capacity who . . . felt bound, in the words of the best known, to plead the suffering of their men. In poems that had for a time considerable fame, written in the first person, they made that suffering their own. I have rejected these poems for the same reason that made Arnold withdraw his *Empedocles on Etna* from circulation; passive suffering is not a theme for poetry. In all the great tragedies, tragedy is a joy to the man who dies; in Greece the tragic chorus danced . . . If war is necessary, or necessary in our time and place, it is best to forget its suffering as we do the discomfort of fever . . .

Amazing though it is that some of the finest poetry of the twentieth century should be excluded thus from what was intended to be its most representative collection, it was true that those who fought did become famously reticent about what they had seen and done. 'He never talked about it' was said of many a returned soldier. As for passive suffering, whatever that meant to Yeats, means everything to those who lived through both the trenches and the holocaust. Their particular tragedy was no joy to either John Clare or Ivor Gurney but it was part of their greatness.

Paul Nash's lifelong poet friend was Gordon Bottomley but his ultimate mentor was Sir Thomas Browne. Flanders under the shelling provided for him one landscape of death, *Urne Buriall* another. *The Annual of New Poetry 1917* contains Bottomley's 'All Souls, 1914' in which the universe is already crowded with 'the young uneasy dead' whose energies 'Are still unspent', and it was this sense of terrible waste which haunted the post-war world. They are the absent figures in Paul and John Nash's fields. In his grim asylum Ivor Gurney 'calls' to them again and again. There was 'The Silent One' who:

Died on the wires, and hung there, one of two –
Who for his hours of life had chattered through
Infinite lovely chatter of Bucks accent:
Yet faced unbroken wires; stepped over, and went
A noble fool, faithful to his stripes – and ended.

286

In 1918, painting the official war pictures in the Buckinghamshire seed-hut with his brother, John Nash, who had more than a passing interest in being a writer as well as an artist, was subscribing to *The Little Review*, with its generous serialisation of *Ulysses*, and works by Dorothy Richardson, Proust and Eliot. Modernism, now almost a century old, still reads youthfully. The contents do not reflect the last casualty lists of London, Paris and New York but a new kind of vitality and a determination to cut loose from the boredom of war, among other things. Unlike all the other magazines, the *London Mercury* in particular, *The Little Review* is flimsily and cheaply published in both French and English, and remains curiously avant-garde whilst being at the same time a museum piece. I think of the Nash brothers reading it, shocked, excited, John putting it down to continue working on *Over the Top* in which a handful of soldiers scramble out of a snowy trench to be mown down, one of them, he told me, given the face of a singer he had heard at the Queen's Hall 'to show the death of art'.

All these old World War One and post-Armistice journals are full of music. There is the Diaghileff Ballet at the Alhambra music hall in London in the summer of 1919 with Karsavina and Massine, there is Poulenc, Vaughan Williams, Prokofiev, Holst, Bax, Bliss, Bridge, Ireland and there should have been a more substantial Gurney. All the young composers and ex-music students would have heard of him, would have wondered about him, and what happened to him. What happened to him was what happened to Clare. In some ways Gurney was the soldier who could not die. For whom there would be another death.

In 1932 a stranger named Marion Scott wrote to Edward Thomas's widow Helen, to tell her that she was the friend of 'a young musical genius named Ivor Gurney who had lost his reason in the war and was in a lunatic asylum'. And could she face the ordeal of visiting him, as Edward Thomas 'had evoked in him what one can only call love'. And so they went. Helen Thomas carried flowers:

We arrived at Dartford Asylum which looked like – indeed it was – a prison. A warder let us in after unlocking a door, and doors were opened and locked behind us . . . We were walking along a bare corridor when we were met by a tall dishevelled man clad in pyjamas and a dressing gown, to whom Miss Scott introduced me. He gazed with an intense stare into my face and took me silently by the hand. Then I gave him the flowers which he took with the same deeply moving intensity and silence. He then said, 'You are Helen, Edward's wife, and Edward is dead'.

Later, Gurney played the piano to them 'and to the tragic circle of men who sat on hard benches built into the walls of the room. Hopeless and aimless faces gazed vacantly and restless hands fumbled or hung down lifelessly. They gave no sign or sound that they had heard the music.'

The next time Helen went to see Ivor she took with her Edward's walking maps of Gloucestershire and spread them across the bed. Their fingers traced 'the lanes and byways and villages of which Ivor knew every step . . . He had Edward as companion in this strange perambulation and he was utterly happy.' It is interesting that Helen did not take Ivor Gurney books and magazines. Were they forbidden? John Clare possessed an entire library at Northampton. Helen said that Gurney's room contained only a bed and a chair, and window bars high up. Nothing else. Mental health between the wars, when it was most needed, was most neglected. Poor mad soldiers.

A PILGRIM'S SONG
Selected Poems to mark the Poet's 100th Birthday
Geoffrey Dearmer, 1993

THE IMPERIAL WAR MUSEUM BOOK OF WORLD WAR ONE
Malcolm Brown, 1991

The Great War, as all these private voices would have said, still has a lot to tell the world. The voice of a still-living poet of the Dardanelles and the Somme comes as something of a shock. Geoffrey Dearmer is Wilfred Owen's exact contemporary and here he is, publishing his work, half a century after World War Two. There is a poetry in itself in knowing that the man who wrote of his experiences at Gallipoli and in Flanders will also experience this April's weather. Those who wrote alongside him, as it were, have vanished to become a period of English literature, but he breathes. It is strange, moving. And even more so when one knows that the Dearmer voice, father's and son's, must have influenced us more than we realise, for Percy edited *The English Hymnal* and Geoffrey was one of the creators of the BBC's *Children's Hour*.

A Pilgrim's Song is marked by the old Hellenic-Christian-Keatsian vision of things before horror and disillusionment swept it aside. After 1916 the gross idiocy of the war, with all its pain and loss and destruction, caused Owen, Sassoon, Rosenberg, Blunden and all the other trench writers, to abandon this culture. Geoffrey Dearmer did not. It is his clinging to it which makes his book so interesting. Lacking rage, invective, all the anger which we have come to expect from poet-critics of the later carnage, he hangs on to what Wilfred Owen in particular rejected, managing to convince us all these years hence of its strengths and virtue. This was civilisation as he knew it, before, during and after 1914-1918. Hazlitt would have admired him for sticking to his first certainties. These are elegies declaimed in springtime, a mourning for those who went down just when everything else was rising, larks, flowers, the reasonable expectations of the young. Soldiers fall in a landscape which is gardened by shells, the split earth allowing long-dormant seeds to shoot. In 'Somme Flower Talk' they discuss their luck. But Dearmer can speak of 'murdered Picardy'. The individual faces which stare through poem after poem are those of his younger brother, killed at the Dardanelles, and of a friend. Later work maps the Georgian countryside, botanical, Keatsian. And the final pages are a bestiary of 'Other Creatures Seen Lightheartedly'. Pilgrim Geoffrey has come a long way – as far as any of us can.

Voices from 1914-18 in the archives of the Imperial War Museum are legion. Those selected by Malcolm Brown from this vast cache of personal comment have never been heard outside their private reference before and most of them by no means complement what the poets said. They are accompanied by eloquent photographs and paintings, gauche posters – 'Is your "Best Boy" wearing Khaki?' – and an excellent linking commentary. So much has been written about those days that the latter can only follow a well-worn track. But not so the letters and diaries. Their contents swing from adventure to introspection, from the blessed humdrum of life to the peaks of fear, from lumpen statements to sustained passages of great beauty. More than anything one is continually surprised by a truthfulness of observation which doesn't have to look around for striking imagery, but which just forges ahead in plain, clean narrative. These unknown (except to families and friends) writers remind one of St Paul's 'cloud of witness', a swarming mass of individual intelligences, each and every one seeing for his and herself what was going on, and getting it down on paper.

These voices are not confined to the Allies or to the battlefield. There are letters from the enemy and from the home fronts. The famous 'innocence' of the day is constantly on view. This was not so much the 20th century being born as the 19th century dying. There is a wonderful description by the future Baroness de T'Serclaes of the troop trains at Victoria Station, which she calls the 'Palace of Tears'. Although late afternoon of the great age of letter-writing, it was also still the age when certain things were never mentioned, so that 'politeness' inhibited the pen on most occasions. Now and then some dreadful happening bursts through convention. But for the most part this correspondence and these memoirs seem to be light years away from the accounts given by fighting men of Vietnam, and all wars *et seq*. There is an especially fascinating section of religion at the Front. Church parades did much to destroy faith. Priests were placed in a terrible dilemma as they tried to steer a course between what Christ and some military duty required. Canon Crosse wrote, 'Before a padre could be of much use he had to throw overboard his natural temptation to be a spiritual profiteer'. He noted that 'Scarcely any soldier thought of Christianity as offering any sort of philosophy of life.' All the same, if there is one quality which reveals itself again and again in this writing, it is that of the human spirit. Around it fly all the missiles and grisly propaganda flak of the war, never in this case coming anywhere near its destruction.

SOME CORNER OF A FOREIGN FIELD
Poetry of the Great War

ed. James Bentley, 1993

This is a curious anthology – the celebrated words and images of the immense tragedy are juxtaposed, trimmed with British Legion poppies, sketches of toy soldiers, medals, and produced like one of those keepsake volumes of the period. While appearing to ask, 'How decorative is this war now to you?', this very decorative little collection does eventually make a painful wound. The complementary poems and paintings, though the majority of them are familiar to most of us, remain accusing and moving. James Bentley's addition of verses and pictures which have stayed outside, as it were, the contents page and gallery, where we look for the literary and artistic responses to the Great War, serve as sharpeners to our glance at the well-known.

Yes, here are Brooke, Sassoon, the Nash brothers, Nevinson, Owen, Gurney, Kennington and all those other critics and recorders of the carnage whose work has to be shown and read whenever Britain's role in it is mentioned. It is significant that their view of it still outweighs that of photography and official history. Recent historians have gone as far as cursing these artists and writers for making such a lasting moral song and dance about the Great War, and continuing to obscure its interesting military facts. James Bentley, by including some less instantly recognisable names, is telling us not only that there were many painters and poets saying what they thought about the war, but that it was impossible for any artist during those four mad years to be silent.

And so we have everyone and everything which an illustrated Great War poetry-book must have: Paul Nash's splintered trees – the common sight of a fallen tree stark on the ground was to seem something monstrous to him to the end of his days; his brother John's incomparable *Over the Top*; Wilfred Owen's 'pity'; and Sassoon's rage. Then comes a painting by Harold Gilman entitled *Tea in the Bedsitter*, in which two girls, if they are not actually waiting for the boys to come home, do say everything about waiting women.

While not attempting to broaden all the old comment and denunciation, or to try to stop it from seething once again over the politics which caused the war, and the blind officialdom which allowed it to go on after 1916, Bentley in this oddly pretty volume does succeed in extending that vision of the calamity which its artists and poets alone have made real to us. In their eyes, whether we are in the English countryside on a summer's day, in Croydon, or looking down on to a Welsh farm, we are at the front. Bentley respects the sentiment, even the sentimentality, of this hour, letting it hit us.

We become conscious of the stylisations of the English School when the subject is battle. The soldiers and the women doing their bit for the war are trapped in grave attitudes from the life-class, although some harden into Expressionism. But on the whole these figures possess a kind of bewildered gentleness. Khaki runs from their uniforms into the landscape which suggested it. For men having to live in a ditch, they are grotesquely encumbered, stiff with mud, hanging with mugs, weighed down with boots. Yet they are delicate.

Henry Lamb's beautiful painting 'Advanced Dressing Station on the Struma' pays homage to this delicacy, when a dozen or so massively overcoated men avoid the privacy of a dying soldier and his friend, where the stretcher is already a bier, and the trench a tomb. This picture was not painted to illustrate Owen's 'Greater Love', yet it does so exactly. Whether the images which are thrown against the screen of our minds by great poetry should be supplemented, even by good pictures, is another matter. Bentley's idiosyncratic 'marrying' of the words and art of 1914-1918, while showing a certain loss of understanding of their need to exist separately, does have its fascination.

The format of this book may be an indictment of the uses to which we have put the agonies of the Great War, even the Remembrance Day service with its perfect Georgian sadness, but there is no getting away from the fury of many of its pages. D. H. Lawrence, G. K. Chesterton, Rudyard Kipling are among the non-combatants who have been chosen for pulling no punches. Kipling's verses on a drowned woman, and on a raped woman, are not for the squeamish.

On the whole, what might be called the Christian element in retrospect grows ever more cringing. The Church's now notorious entanglement with crude nationalism, where each and all the fighting countries were concerned, was a shameful sight. From Rupert Brooke's 'Now, God be thanked who has matched us with His hour' to Kipling's Picardy Gethsemane and Studdert Kennedy's matey Golgotha comparisons, there are attempts to make connections which we can only find embarrassing. Indeed, much of the 'Christianity' of the world wars belongs to sociology.

The cult which the poets and painters followed was that of the beautiful dead, and of the poignant element in being young. The writers adored nature, the artists were intrigued by the patterns created by its destruction. Both were weather-obsessed and, as these famous and obscure words and images state, what happened, happened seasonally, in rain, in snow, when Flanders flowered and when it froze.

THE OLD LIE
The Great War and the Public School Ethos

Peter Parker, 1987

One of the most daunting of tasks for a writer is to have to travel through exceedingly familiar territory in order to arrive at some scarcely known area. A large part of Peter Parker's reading for *The Old Lie* has been in literature that has been familiar to most of us for a very long time: and it was by acknowledging this that he was able to set himself the kind of test necessary for carrying through the (again often popular) accusations contained in it to such a powerful conclusion.

There is, after all, still a vast amount of 'byways' material about the Great War, and a less redoubtable investigator would have been tempted to try his luck there and to steer clear of the now famous ground taken up by Brooke, Owen, Housman, Barrie, Sassoon, and so on. Similarly, it was brave and energetic to go once again to the heart of the matter (Dr Arnold *et seq.*) where the public schools are concerned, and not to seek to entertain us by revealing some never-before-mentioned aspect of their history. The disillusionment which Parker traces back to its roots is, after all, a most celebrated one. His telling of the old tale fascinates because of its radical and fresh re-examination of everything which went into the making of it: art and literature, patriotism, the class system, militarism, religion, Fleet Street, the *Greek Anthology*, cricket, imperialism and the pre-1914 quasi-innocent Cult of the Boy. It all adds up to something strong, original and 'not what we were formerly told'. Indeed, hurtful still after all these years.

Here we have the school photo of those who were taught elegiacs as naturally, as it were, as they might have been taught botany or French. Thousands of patrician and would-be patrician Englishmen learning how to die young as a way of not growing old – or of not quite growing up, which was just as undesirable. Who set these lessons? Beguiling Hellenist-Anglicans at Eton, Winchester, Harrow, Westminster, Dulwich. Who filched them so that the lads in the grammar school and board schools could have at least a taste of this dark and heady instruction? Well, every youth movement leader, author of a school story (vastly influential), song and hymn writer, journalist, and a great many politicians and clergymen for a start, and by the time of the Edwardian arms race the fatal inculcation from the top could hardly be avoided, even by a fourteen-year-old down a coalmine. When the war memorials arrived, his name was entered on a stone rich with symbols from the classics, Malory, the Crucifixion and the games field.

What was the basis of this public school education which drained down to the elementary classroom? It was a line from Horace, *Dulce et decorum est pro patria mori* – it is a sweet and seemly thing to die for one's country. This is what Wilfred Owen, a grammar school boy, nailed as 'the old lie' just before he was shot. Parker's book is a broad attack on the post-Arnold public schools and their dangerous obsession with often bowdlerised Greek texts, their low level of real education, their corruption and violence, inevitable homo-eroticism, and their powerful freemasonry. It traces 'the sweet and seemly thing' through the decades before the war, through the war itself and then through its aftermath, exposing not for the first time, but with a new vividness, what was really the social training of an élite leadership for the hour when the balloon must go up.

Unfortunately for those who taught the old lie, its victims were able to turn on them with a terrible eloquence in poetry, novel and memoir, and in painting. The old school and what it had preached took a dreadful hammering by its own heroes. The 'fallen' showed their ruined flesh and expectations. Dying fingers pointed at Northcliffe, the incompetent generals, the profiteers, women who promised to make a man of you if you took the shilling (they had been educated into quite a bit of misogyny), and at an establishment which had tricked them. Unlike Brooke – unlike everybody – Charles Sorley repudiated both the schools propaganda and the war itself from the beginning. About Marlborough he wrote:

O come and see, it's such a sight,
So many boys all doing right:
To see them underneath the yoke,
Blindfolded by the older folk,
Move at a most impressive rate
Along the way that is called straight.

He was killed at 20.

The Old Lie is about the overwhelmingly successful creation of a high-class tribalism, a forging of the well-off heirs of the Industrial Revolution into an instantly recognisable command force. It questions all the rituals of the machine which turned out the unmistakable English gentleman in sufficient numbers to run the Church, the Empire and the regiments. Parker gets at the emotion and sentiment which were the real activators of the public school code, and with a mixture of condemnation and delicate understanding. There is plenty about the love which, not daring to speak its name, called itself jollier things. Like so much else, this love came of age in the trenches. And what of the Other Ranks, those equally bamboozled young men who were barely educated at all (and on the whole were five inches shorter and a good deal thinner than the public school subalterns) – how did they mature under fire? Not all that unlike their betters, for an amazing amount of public school idealism had reached them. It had become a religion within the national religion. The Great War shattered this artifice and used up its language – Ardent, Golden, Youth, Life, Spirit, Sacrifice, Victory – on rolls of honour.

Parker is a brilliant analyst of British mawkishness and intellectual sloppiness, getting in some body-blows at Newbolt, Tennyson, Henley and, perhaps most interestingly, at J.W. Mackail, whose translations of the *Greek Anthology*, he maintains, falsified Greek thought and ideals. Cyril Connolly called it 'one of the sacred books of the inner culture' at Eton, and said how it 'exhaled pessimism and despair' and how he learned all the sceptical epigrams 'about love and death and the fate of youth and beauty' by heart. Parker has often to remind himself that although he is dealing with stuff which could end only at Passchendaele, it can be exquisite stuff. Whiffs of it creep into the air during any Remembrance Day service, pungent and affecting, like the scent of dusty geraniums. His last sentence is, 'That men died for an ethos does not mean that the ethos was worth dying for'. It is a verdict and a book which will make some of today's O.B.'s snort and twitch.

THE LOST VOICES OF WORLD WAR I
An International Anthology of Writers, Poets and Playwrights

ed. Tim Cross, 1988

Among the myriad questions which this unusual anthology raises, like startled birds, are those connected with achievement and 'promise'. Can Wilfred Owen be 'lost' in the sense of our being deprived of what he might have achieved had he lived – or 'Saki' Munro, if it comes to that? Need Marlowe, Mozart, Keats and Shelley to have lived longer in order to fulfil their genius? Need Alain-Fournier to have done more than write *Le Grand Meaulnes*? It is certain that Owen would have been lost to the first rank of poetry had there been no war. It was the Western Front which discovered him, both to himself and to the world. As a writer he would have been lost indeed without it.

These who had been lost, and who found, queries are not intended as criticisms to undermine the general concept of this remarkable and ambitious book, but rather as an acknowledgment of its power to shake up much of the accepted notion of what the Great War did to – and for – literature. Tim Cross's anthology does this shaking up by admitting a small army of soldier-poets, novelists and dramatists who those of us long-familiar with such names as Rosenberg, Trakl, Apollinaire, Péguy and Brooke are unlikely to have encountered. Not only do we have translations from the Polish, Serbian, Hungarian, etc., but among the faces which have become as intimate to us as those in the family album, newcomers stare out and return our absorbed gaze. The photographs can, if we like, have death read into them, although what they have most in common is a lively seriousness. Many are not all that young. The 'Lost Generation' itself was born c.1892 but the war destroyed a host of middle-aged writers and robbed their countries of mature voices.

The anthology contains generous examples of the work of 65 writers, nearly all of whom were killed in battle, although Apollinaire, for example, died from influenza just two days before the Armistice. The terrible 'flu plague of 1919 was to claim more victims than the guns. Apollinaire was 38 and quite the most wittily scathing of the war poets and a writer whose attitudes seem to reach our own as though there were no seventy years in between. Peter Read's essay on him is one of the treasures of the book. It was Apollinaire who, in his 'The Cavalier's Farewell', wrote 'the most notorious lines of all French war poetry':

Oh God! what a lovely war
With its songs its long leisure hours . . .
Now everything is enormous
And it seems to me that peacetime
Will be as monstrous as the war.

297

There was universal loathing of the patriotism-mongering journalists by the fighting poets and novelists, and the war-crazy popular press generally was regarded with revulsion by the man in the trenches. Marc de Larreguy, killed at 21, reminded the lying journalists 'of our own national and international Lamartine, who said, "I am a *human being* before I am British, French or Russian".'

Some of the greatest World War One literature is an inspired riposte to the muddy thinking which was immolating vast numbers of young men in the mud of the Western Front. Wilfred Owen's 'Anthem for Doomed Youth', Jon Stallworthy reminds us, owes its charge to a maundering Preface to *Poems for Today* (1916), an anthology for children, who are told of a poet who 'has gone singing to lay down his life' and of 'the bugle-call of Endeavour, and the passing bell of Death'. 'What passing-bells for these who die as cattle?' asks Lieutenant Owen.

Contrasting the inanities of those who wrote about the Front without experiencing it, and those who wrote out of the experience, one can see the dilemma. Writers at home could not imagine what it was like to live for weeks – months – literally with the dead, with corpses of all nationalities, whilst even the best soldier-writer believed that he had no adequate language to describe it. They were like the medieval mystics who knew that their words would run out long before they could say what they had seen. What this first of the twentieth century's huge disasters proved to writers was their inadequacy, even their impotence. Francis Ledwidge, the Irish farmworker-poet, killed at Ypres, who has a touch of Clare, says:

And now I'm drinking wine in France
The helpless child of circumstance.
Tomorrow will be loud with war.
How will I be accounted for?

The fatal scene is set by Robert Wohl in a first chapter which analyses some of the thinking and technical discoveries which brought about the war, the triple cultures of the avant-garde, of modernism and of the newly emergent culture of the masses. All the writers in the anthology were as much a part of their particular national version of these cultures as they were of the Armageddon they precipitated. So there was guilt and repudiation. And an enormous sense of tragedy, tragedy such as the Classically educated only knew about in Sophocles, and most people in the Book of Job. Another Irish writer, Tom Kettle, (the model for Hughes in Joyce's *Stephen Hero*) was one of the many soldiers who took an ironic line – 'War has long been accepted as our best aid to the teaching of geography! Blood is an expensive marking fluid for maps, but it is vivid and indelible.' T. E. Hulme, a decided loss to both poetry and philosophy, not to mention cussed argument, opted for blind endurance:

My mind is a corridor.
The minds about me are corridors.
Nothing suggests itself.
There is nothing to do but keep on.

There is a marvellously ferocious poem by the Hungarian writer Géza Gyóni who, as did all his contemporaries, regarded the home front patriots as the real enemy, in which each verse begins with 'Send them along for just one bloody night'. And there is also a good translation of Milos Marten's 'Cortigiana', a tale about a courtesan's revenge on men which not only presents a symbolic account of the destruction to come (it was written in 1911) but even more prophetically the late twentieth-century plague we call Aids.

The choices are terrible and funny, gentle and wild. Although there is not a single inclusion which fails to make one contemplate the waste of a talent, there are some items which do not suggest considerable giftedness being cut off before it could flower. In many instances the most telling and impressive aspect of the anthology is the manner in which a dead writer is presented via a brief life, a critique, a photograph and a translation which is truly eye-opening. The point is made that, like Rupert Brooke, many of the writers who perished, were not 'war' poets at all, but young men at the beginning of literary careers which the war terminated. It is for the reader to speculate on what twentieth-century literature would have been like had not, to paraphrase the famous epitaph, a bullet stopped their song.

MICHAEL COLLINS
A Biography

Tim Pat Coogan, 1990

Is this a portrait of a hero, warts, halo and all? A portrait of the proto-twentieth-century terrorist/guerrilla, or of his country's lost leader? It is all these things and more. For most Britons seventy years later, this book will offer a finely focused picture of what has become very hazy: the creation of modern Eire as seen in and around the tumultuous presence of Michael Collins.

All kinds of questions relevant to today are aired in this violent and romantic book, the biggest of which is 'what would have happened if Michael Collins had not been gunned down at the age of thirty-two?' He was large and handsome. Men obeyed him, women adored him. He came from a little Cork farm and simply took charge. Immensely able and energetic, surely he would have had a hand in shaping the new state. And how would de Valera, the half-Spanish 'Long Fellow', have fared with Collins by his side? What of the North?

In another age and another place he would have been a doughty young deliverer, routing the usurper and winning the diadem. Powerful creatures such as he had mostly abandoned Irish squalor for the rich chances of Boston and New York, but Collins stayed to take on the British Government so challengingly that Dublin Castle and Downing Street were forced to negotiate. At this distance, his staying at home in order to change things so that the best of his countrymen would no longer think in terms of flight makes a gallant tale.

Tim Coogan's biography makes one realise how stifled the debate on Irish nationalism has become in Britain. Matters which would be openly discussed in most countries are avoided here. Instead, we are fed with drearily ritualised violence and official protest, with the heirs of Michael Collins waging a war he would have found impotent. The intractability, the repetitive sadness, the unexpressed doubts, the politicised religions, the feeling that it will continue until kingdom come – how he would have hurled himself towards some solution.

Coogan follows his brief revolutionary career and in so doing tells the British reader a thousand necessary home truths which have become greyly merged in what we vaguely call 'the Troubles'. He writes, naturally, from the Irish point of view – with a vivid journalistic accuracy – but with none of the usual partnership. 'If we wish to understand today's tragedies and perhaps avert others like them, it is essential to know and learn from the story of Michael Collins.' He says that it is a book for both south and north of the Border, and if it does nothing else, it sweeps away the muteness into which the future of Ireland has fallen.

Coogan's other gift is his mastery of period detail. He describes rough times, full of hard drinking, riding around on bikes, sleeping in frowsty bedrooms with a gun to hand. Collins, de Valera and the rest, are in and out of English gaols and just one step ahead of execution.

During one of de Valera's incarcerations, Michael Collins unofficially assumed the presidency. In October 1921, aged twenty-nine, he began the meeting with Lloyd George, Churchill, Birkenhead and Austen Chamberlain, which was to free southern Ireland from England after many centuries of loathed colonisation. Collins was at work on the problems of the North when a fellow Corkian shot him.

He lived in a powerful ambience of inspired political reconstruction and blood. Coogan believes his ruthless, raffish side was not unlike that of Lord Birkenhead, but, for the most part, as this account proves, Collins was the kind of man whose maturity and earthy intelligence would never have deserted him, however long he lived.

JOURNAL, 1937-1939
David Gascoyne, 1978

A PACIFIST'S WAR
Frances Partridge, 1978

TIME AND AGAIN
Memoirs and Letters
Helen Thomas, ed Myfanwy Thomas, 1978

A recurring theme of Second World War writing is that of the resentment caused by state intrusion into the personal life at all levels. Ironically, those who felt this resentment most were the culturally and politically committed anti-fascists, those who had stuck their necks out for civilisation when the majority were far less concerned. In First World War writing, the recurring theme is of a political and social naivety which had to be thrust up against barbed wire before it could be exploded. These three books, each exceptionally well-written, are about approaching war, war-rejection and war as muse.

When David Gascoyne completed his *Journal* on his twenty-third birthday, and in the sixth week of the last war, it was with the instruction that it was to be published should he be killed. He had put a match to nearly all his other papers, and the *Journal* was to be his last word and apologia. Emerging nearly forty years later, its excitements are all to do with first words, with beginnings and promises. Many young writers draw up private manifestos and make statements of intention; but few at twenty, which was Gascoyne's age when he began his, could have known themselves so fully or have had the literary maturity for such a self-portrait. It shows him as a penniless young man in Paris and amid scenes which are like the pages from some rare novel which it tantalises one not to possess the whole of.

Like most poets of the period, Gascoyne is immersed in individualism and symbolism, in Hölderlin, Rilke, Jaurès and Rimbaud. He sides with Europe against England, and at such events as the International Association of Writers for the Defence of Culture against Fascism, he dissociates himself from the British delegation of

Day-Lewis, Rex Warner and Spender. Spender, it might be added, is busy dodging him, having just damned him in a review as a 'charming talent'.

The *Journal* certainly charms, but with something more than talent – perhaps by its ability to describe, with neither conceit nor tedium, all the initial *longueur* of a writer's existence. Lawrence Durrell tells him 'You are an expert on English Death,' but Gascoyne attributes 'our obscure perpetual frustration' to a longing to live our lives 'like a story' when the demands of mere existence 'continually thwart our desire for clarity and significance'. He interprets his own life as one which is dominated by a voracious imagination, for which he must suffer the consequences. Just as 'a kind of invisible darkness hangs in the sunlight' of the Munich summer, so it must within himself.

Although so young, he has published five books and is proposing a sixth to Allen Lane, a Penguin Special on the need for France to reassert its classic revolutionary fervour, as if there is already a whiff of Vichy in the air. He marks out where he stands in Existentialism, Marxism, Christianity and homosexual love. In poetry he wants 'emotion, a raised voice, but a clear and coherent speech'. Beautiful writing but never just fine writing.

Frances Partridge's diary seeks, among other matters, to rehabilitate her husband, Ralph, from the obfuscation of his personality begun, she feels, by Gerald Brenan. Not that Ralph shines even now, though we do see him as his positive self and not just as Lytton and Carrington's not quite explicable appendage. A major and an MC in the First World War, his subsequent pacifism made him refuse to join the Home Guard during the second, and thus brought down on him that nastiness peculiar to an affronted rural gentry. One of the most interesting aspects of this book is its atmosphere of that special social isolation which dissidence creates.

The Partridges, plus intermittent servants, evacuees and visitors from Bloomsbury, sat the war out in a Ham Spray House still redolent of all that had happened there a decade earlier. Because of what had led up to it, as much as because of the war itself, they feel as if they have been condemned to endure one of those recurring outbreaks of man's unutterable stupidity, like old Madame du Deffand when she wrote, *'L'horrible chose que la guerre! . . . la guerre est de toute les folies la plus atroce'*.

The first entries are of a cold disdain at what is happening. When Frances goes up to London for the day, she is struck by 'the fierce animal faces of the passersby, and felt like a tame rabbit among so many dogs, birds, wolves and monkeys' whose every chance remark she overhears is about food. Confessing that her – almost only – object in life was to be as intensely conscious as possible, and that what she most dreaded was the possibility of its slipping by unnoticed 'like a scene half-glimpsed from a railway-carriage', her dilemma is caused by the war insinuating itself into her experience at every level so that, try as she might to preserve it for nobler things, it mops up the whole of her attention. The diary protests and struggles between a consciousness bred by the war and that bred by Bloomsbury's liberal values. In April 1945, when 'R sits by the wireless all day, with an anxious face, tuning in to stations like a doctor taking the pulse of a dying man' it is to hear the BBC's German newsreader 'saying slowly and weightily *"Es ist das ENDE".'* Frances likens their shifting response to the great calamity to that of Flaubert's in his *Letters* during the Franco-Prussian war, which indeed it is.

'Do you remember, Janet, when I saw you last I told you of a plan I had made regarding the boy who Father is taking up, and who writes Nature sketches? I think it will succeed, although it will take ages, for he is fearfully shy. He wants a girl friend and I want a boy friend.' It did succeed, as we all know, in spite of his not turning up for the first appointment and her having to give the first kiss. *Time and Again* is what used to be called fugitive pieces, and what a mercy that Helen Thomas's daughter rustled them out of their corners and linked words of her own. With those marital masterpieces, *As it Was* and *World Without End*, they demonstrate the workings of the posthumous principle in all that Edward Thomas ever did, or was. When, as Wilfred Owen said, 'a bullet stopped his song' on Easter Monday, 1917, none had heard the singing. He could not have dreamed of his celebrity as poet and husband. It was Helen who was the beneficiary. She used the legacy of his life and work as few writers' widows could. She made it so that she was never without him.

This final grouping of what pertained to them both rounds the whole thing off. Helen's life began when black flags warned of typhoid in the street and ended when she was taking an interest in Nureyev and Albee. She is adept at the portrait vignette and gives some sharp little pictures of Lawrence (dressmaking for Frieda). Robert Frost, W. H. Davies and, unforgettably, poor Ivor Gurney. There are, too, memorable glimpses of working-class life viewed without a hint of class-consciousness, particularly one of Edward's tinplate factory relations in South Wales. She knew her place, which was at the literary periphery, and she had a perfect understanding of how to assist those at the centre. And every now and again she could write them all under the table. A unique woman.

Introduction to
PRIVATE WORDS
Letters and Diaries from the Second World War

ed. Ronald Blythe, 1993

The more able to be clearly viewed in retrospect, the more astonishing so much Second World War activity appears. It was a time of firsts and lasts. The Battle of Britain was a first and last, for it is surely most unlikely that armies of small aeroplanes will clash decisively on a blue field again. Equally unlikely, unless somebody manages to destroy today's world wide telecommunications system, is it that millions of people will keep in touch via the written and not the spoken word as they did during the 1940s. The letter reached its peak of private importance then. It was a desolation not to receive them. Parted for as many as three years at a time, and more if one was an early prisoner of war, one lived for them. Watching his fellow sailors all busily writing home in the YMCA, the poet Roy Fuller observed:

305

Aftermath

> *The letters are permanent*
> *And written with our hands*
> *Which crease into their lines*
>
> *And breathe, but are not so*
> *Living as these letters.*
> *Our hands are seas apart.*

These letters – and diaries – are now half a century old and lie behind ageing lives in huge quantities. Many, each one so private, provide social history in public libraries. Letters from sons and daughters, letters from parents and lovers, letters from best friends, letters about being hurt and frightened, and about new lands, dutiful letters and letters of genius. Journals too. The authorities were none too keen on the latter, but it took more than a regulation to stop the natural diarist. This last great avalanche of private correspondence and of expressing oneself on the page generally while the earth rocked is a vast enough subject for myriad interpretations. Here is one look at it and one assessment of it. 'Just a few lines' from Keith Douglas's journal as he went into battle suggest the twin sources of the literacy which helped to create not only the brilliant achievement of writers such as himself, but also the good minor one of almost everybody who wrote home – and from home. These sources were the convention of writing a letter whenever there was something important to say, and the need to have a book to read.

I had that feeling of almost unstable lightness which is felt physically immediately after putting down a heavy weight. All my mental inquiries and arguments about the future were shelved, perhaps permanently. I got out my writing paper and wrote two letters, one to my Mother and one to David Hicks in Cairo. Although in writing these letters (which, of course, got lost, and were never posted) I felt very dramatic, the tone of them was not particularly theatrical . . . I had asked Andrew one or two questions in the hope of not showing myself too ignorant in my first action [in the Battle of Alamein, which opened on 23 October 1942]. But it was fairly plain that he knew nothing himself. 'I shouldn't worry, old boy,' was all he would say . . .

When I had written my letters I got into the turret [of his Mark III Crusader tank] with Evan and tried to learn its geography. My place as tank commander was on the right of the six pounder. I had a seat, from which I could look out through a periscope. . . On the shelf, when we were in action, we usually kept some Penguin books, chocolate or boiled sweets.

Always letters and Penguin books, or indeed any old books: these were among the necessities of existence for serviceman and civilian at the time. That there were letters and letters, and books and trash made little difference. Everyone needed to write and loved to read. Education had been strongly formal whether it was elementary, grammar or public school, and if people could write little else, it was expected of all classes that they could put a letter together correctly. Not to be able to spell was as disgraceful as having a hole in one's sock. For millions, not to be able to read during the Depression would have blocked the only affordable means of escape. Many people had had much time on their hands between the wars and had read the penurious years away. Rural society retained the last habits of the ancient story-telling tradition. When the war came every kind of fresh experience – unprepared-for emotion, travel, violence, homesickness, the intensification of friendship, incredible boredom – discovered an often well-trained literary outlet. Had the war not happened, very few of its letter-writers and diarists would have dreamed of communicating as they did. The expression of the self through letters by men and women long-parted was often disconcerting. Things were written which would never have been said. Sometimes a stranger would begin to emerge from the post. Reunion was a constant theme but also one containing an underlying dread. After the war the self so nakedly displayed in the letters would lie at the back of the drawer, at the back of the mind.

Censorship inhibited some correspondents, others totally ignored the fact that their private lives were left open for a stranger to read. Fellow officers belonging to a mess would censor each other's letters rather like priests hearing each other's confessions, making an effort to obliterate with professionalism what they were learning about a friend. The future novelist Barbara Pym, censoring in London, pretended to be comically exasperated: 'Oh these are dull people,' said the Censor in a low dragging tone. 'They do not seem to realize that we are at war. They write only of trivialities and the young woman does not know her own mind. All these quotations, too, it is not natural.' The poet Arthur Waley was satirical:

I have been a censor for fifteen weeks,
The building where I work has four times been bombed.
Glass, boards and paper, each in turn,
Have been blasted from the windows.

It is not easy to wash, keep warm and eat;
At times we lack gas, water or light.
The rules for censors are difficult to keep.

The Air Raid Bible alters from day to day;
Official orders are not clearly expressed.
One may mention Harrod's but not Derry and Toms;
One may write of mist but may not write of rain.

Witty posters by Fougasse, showing Hitler and other Nazis eavesdropping on the Underground, in the pub, in the kitchen, were everywhere – 'Be like Dad, keep Mum.'

While an impressive public reticence was maintained regarding troop and ship movements, the last especially, private lives soon learned to ignore the blue pencil. Although the literary and social convention of the period forbade explicitness, letters and diaries held very little back. They were written in Stephen's ink or Rowney's HB pencil on flimsy paper or aerograms, the letters often numbered to tell the recipient which had been lost on the way. Considering the nightmare conditions of delivery, the postal service was very near a miracle of trustworthiness. Writing materials were an essential item of any parcel sent to the war zones. It was the zenith of the fountain pen. Parker pens and wrist-watches vied in popularity as twenty-first birthday presents. In 1942 Penguin Books were advertising the Penguin Pen, price 5s. 6d. It had an ebony streamlined holder with an iridium-tipped fourteen carat gold nib, fine, medium or broad.

Guaranteed five years. Paper was precious and often filled to the edge. British handwriting was still dominated by the old copperplate 'thick and thin', American was open and rounded. One reason for the immense amount of letter-writing in the services was having so much unfilled time. Long stretches of the war were, for those actually fighting in it, spent in semi-idleness. It was like film-making, with an almost intolerable inaction between shootings. It was also spent in crowds and a dual boredom of wasteful days and hugger-mugger propinquity caused the writing of a letter to be seen as both a sane task and an acceptable retreat into privacy.

The continuous discipline of letter-writing and diary-keeping, and the solace of reading, proved to many people that they could 'write' stories, maybe, poems, an autobiography. A novel. This phenomenon began to reveal itself early in the war when editors and publishers began to receive a flow of new work which lay outside any of the literary beginnings with which they were familiar. It was sharp, colourful and often political. The more established literary world regarded it with enthusiasm. It appeared in paperback collections like *Penguin New Writing* and *Poetry London*, and was much encouraged. Stephen Spender dedicated his *Life and the Poet*, a Searchlight Books paperback, 'to the young writers in the Armed Forces, Civil Defence and the Pacifist Organizations of Democracy, in the hope that this tribute may encourage them to write'. Similarly, the poet R. N. Currey, serving as a gunner officer, brought together in his anthology *Poems from India* a wonderful collection of work written for the most part by men (and one woman) who would not have written had not the war given them its powerful literary training. There were many forces' anthologies of prose and poetry by mainly young people who had discovered how to write through the regular practice of letters.

Letters from home could be in danger of carrying to some poor chap struggling with the realities of the Western Desert or a convoy *en route* to Russia the insufferable cheerfulness propagated by radio comedians, the tabloids and some films, while those from the front, anxious not to cause worry, could be bland. The contrast between what the soldier saw and what women, mainly, were prevented from seeing bore no comparison to the situation during 1914-18, when men on leave from

the trenches entered a madhouse of smiling patriotism. Robert Graves
wrote of staggering around a euphoric London gradually realising that
there was no way of talking about what was actually happening in
Flanders to a lady. Not so John Masefield, working in a field hospital;
his letters to his wife concealed nothing, softened nothing. If the
Second World War soldier-airman-sailor left out the horrors, it was
because he knew there were horrors enough back home with the raids
and the hardships. Illness was different. The private writing of these
years reveals much illness in the forces due to stress, climate and
epidemics. Death too is a frequent subject. One day the letters would
stop coming – it could happen. Correspondents would dwell quite
luxuriously on this probability. It was often among the calmest themes
of their letters and of the poetry which sometimes extended from them.
Gunner R. A. George found a body so shallowly buried that the hands
stretched out of the earth, so he knelt down and covered them up.

> *It seems so strange, the unexpected things,*
> *That one is called to do, in times like these.*

The principal concern of this writing, however, is how to hold a
fragmented existence together until, until . . . Not ever knowing when
the war would end was agony. Could a family or a friendship, or plans
to change the scheme of things entirely, ever last out? By mid-war the
writing becomes very political and determined. It is 'get rid of Hitler
and the Japs, and then!' A future other than that being arranged by the
establishment is being incubated. The pre-war conditions in which
millions of Britons lived, looked at from distant reaches of the Empire,
or a prison, or from an ack-ack gunsite on Muswell Hill, are seen as
not only evil but pointless. The act of thinking things out week by
week on a writing-pad brought self-confidence and understanding.
Accompanying snapshots tumbled from the envelopes showing the
same face, and yet a different face. Women carried fat wodges of air
letters in their handbags, men in the breast pockets of their uniforms.
Letters went on travelling. The poets found them especially poignant.
Keith Douglas, on leave in Cairo, wonders whether to 'cut myself a
piece of cake' with Marcelle,

> *Parisienne*
> *always preoccupied with her dull dead lover;*
> *she has all the photographs and his letters*
> *tied in a bundle and stamped Décédé.*

But this was never their purpose. Those who wrote them stamped them 'Life'.

Stranded from the normal, taken-for-granted usefulness of their lives, people often felt that they would go mad if they could not occupy themselves in what was logical, rational and wholly personal. At a time when no one was left alone, there had to be an activity which required an aloneness which could not be criticised. During these years a book, for countless individuals, became the cell into which they could withdraw from the wearing enforced sociability the times demanded. Throughout the war the call for books to be sent to ships, camps and prisoners grew ever more urgent as those who once may have just amused themselves with a tale or two now longed for that most effective escape from the boredom of their situation, the printed word. There were book drives – often abused by householders who saw a way of getting rid of otherwise indestructibly well-bound rubbish – and there was the thoughtful passing on of books, fiction mostly, which guaranteed pleasure. The paper shortage and the massive destruction of publishers' pre-war stocks during the blitz combined in making titles rare or flimsily produced. On the other hand, the great nineteenth century novelists, sets of whose works had formed part of the circulation struggle in Fleet Street and which languished glossily in many a front room, came into their own. Their serialisation on the wireless, Anthony Trollope especially, was so widely enjoyed that current notions of popular taste had to be revised.

Before the war the hopeful notion of bringing the masses 'up' was accepted as an ideal. Reading good books was the surest way to rise. That people might be well-read in different ways was disallowed. In 1934 the preface to the *Authors and Writers Who's Who* could lament:

The trend of both literature and journalism as a whole is still towards the masses. Newspapers with a common or sensational appeal continue to gain ground and it is sensational books of a 'thriller' nature which are selling by the thousand. But it is incorrect to assume that the literary class of reader is disappearing entirely. Rather it is that the more general and superficial class of reader, spoonfed by the popular press and the circulating libraries, is growing in numbers every year.

Nearly all the weeklies, monthlies and quarterlies carried short stories and serialised novels, most of which were illustrated. The most popular 'literary' weekly was *John O'London's*, which unaffectedly propagated an emotion well known then, the love of books. But it was the public library and the commercial circulating library, such as Mudie's and Boot's (there were many others), which created a wide novel-reading public which was unconscious of being lowbrow or middlebrow because it revered and believed in its favourite authors. Life for so many was penurious and cramped, but the novel – and the cinema – brought riches and space. Reading was cheap, absorbing, consoling and exciting. Successful popular novelists were expected to maintain a steady flow. The customary price of an 80,000-word novel was 7s. 6d. – 8s. 6d. if it was 'long' – and there would be a 3s. 6d. edition once the demand for the full price edition slackened. A number of publishers produced their own distinctive 'libraries', inexpensive, often well-bound volumes which encouraged people to build up an excellent private collection. J. M. Dent's Everyman's Library, Jonathan Cape's Travellers' Library, Nelson Classics, Oxford University Press's World's Classics and Collins's Library of Classics were among the most distinguished of these. In 1936 a young publisher named Allen Lane began issuing unbound books which he called paperbacks at 6d. each from the basement of a London church. By 1939 Penguin and Pelican Books had become the most admired and loved of all publications. For the writer it was a mark of distinction either to be reprinted by Penguin or to be commissioned to write one of their 'Specials'. By the first year of the war Penguin and Pelican were set on a course to become a formidable part of the new adult education process which would alter so much of Britain's thinking and moribund attitudes. Few publications could have been as treasured as were these extremely light and elegant books – you could pack half a dozen in a kit bag and hardly notice their weight – and they were read to shreds from Scapa Flow to Malaya, and their influence upon the letters and diaries of these years was considerable.

During the thirties the whodunit, the best as now usually written by women, became the most boasted about leisure reading of the great. These murder puzzles set in strong class-observing situations, with their well-bred or outsider sleuths, and only just enough violence to produce a corpse or six, got a bit roughed up as a genre by the James Hadley Chase school of sex and guns. What readers wanted was the recurring hero. If a writer could invent a Captain Hornblower, a Saint, a Topper, a Whiteoaks family or a world (P G Wodehouse) of characters who would never run out of pages, he or she was made. The recurring hero or family or place in fiction became a comfort and reassurance, and the mores and sayings of these novels had an effect on letter-writing. Women read Ethel Mannin (romance, common sense and liberation), Sheila Kaye-Smith (romance in faithfully observed Sussex countryside), Angela Thirkell (romance and unapologetic snobbery – she was famous for describing Australia as a 'country for warrant officers'), Mills and Boon, E. M. Delafield (still very funny fictitious diary of a middle class lady) and Naomi Jacob (romance and fighting spirit). The erotic was nearly always a big let-down. Novels such as *Lady Chatterley's Lover, The Well of Loneliness* by Radclyffe Hall, *Boy* by James Hanley and Joyce's *Ulysses* remained banned, while *Forever Amber*, Kathleen Winsor's sub-Defoe blockbuster, promised far more than it could give. Favourite permissible naughty reading was the pocket magazine *Men Only*. Women's magazine reading was less passionate in substance than wildly melodramatic. Or else just cosy. Many letters and diaries sternly repudiated the pictures given of foreign countries by writers such as Rosita Forbes, H. M. E. Clamp – even W. Somerset Maugham. But three novels, *The Good Earth* by Pearl S. Buck and the translations of Mikhail Sholokhov's *And Quiet Flows the Don* (1934) and *The Don Flows Home to the Sea* (1941), were to have quite a profound meaning for those British readers who were beginning to see beyond the bounds of Empire. The book clubs of the thirties also began to introduce American writers like Steinbeck, Thurber and Runyon, whose work helped to loosen the stiff style of some wartime diarists, though the chief easer in this respect was more likely to be radio shows such as *ITMA* and *Much Binding in the Marsh*. There was certainly a flood of language to carry along those obliged to write home or to communicate with themselves. It got into their descriptions and confessions, giving them extra scope for what they had to say.

If a single multifarious reason for so much wartime writing had to be chosen, it would be travel. The somewhat static boardgame which was life for the majority of people had been tipped over and the pieces thrown in all directions. Or directed to billets which had to be described to be believed. It was not just the impact of Africa or the Far East, and particularly India, but of a Nissen hut on Orkney or some blacked-out Midlands station. Journeys were drab and difficult yet absorbing, or at least something to write home about. Considering that no mention could be made of where one was going when one was on the way, or where one was when one reached a destination, the traveller in wartime had a method of showing very fully the effects of so much helpless moving about. For, unlike the regular serviceman and servicewoman, the called-up civilian could never wholly submit to being sent here, there and everywhere. Their letters and diaries thus record a struggle between necessity and resistance. But this enforced going places and its endless variety of scene – a Catterick to Arakan spectrum – drove the pen as did no other stimulus. Belonging mainly to a generation which had been brought up on the journeys of the Great War – the brief, so often one way trip to France or the memorably beautiful voyage to Mesopotamia and Gallipoli – and on the emotion-choked embarkations from English ports of troops for the Empire wars, one of the first things which the Second World War travellers felt in their bones was that theirs were journeys without precedent. That they were not going where their fathers had gone before, even where the place bore the same name. And shifting about in Britain itself was not a homely business, not even to where one may have spent a holiday. A discomforting, hostile element had crept in. At the same time travel of any kind sprang adventures and stripped away background. One could feel excitingly free while being virtually imprisoned on a slow cold train to Inverness, or on a slow hot liner to Suez.

Travel proper had been confined to a very small group before the war. This group was chiefly made up of the officials who administrated the Empire, and included great numbers of soldiers and sailors ('Join the Navy and see the world') and the better-off who, for pleasure or health, took cruises. The only way the average young man could go abroad was to join up or emigrate to one of the colonies. For most people travel had to be a vicarious activity undertaken through novels, films and songs. To sail on a liner especially or to visit New York or the pyramids was such an impossibility that common sense kept it firmly among the stuff of dreams. They had one week's paid holiday a year and spent it traditionally at a local coastal resort or having what were called 'days out' on a 10s. rail-card which allowed a week's travelling about. During the Depression great numbers of the unemployed had virtually saved their sanity as well as their bodies by walking and cycling, camping and rambling, especially in the north. These became true travellers. They were educated by Dutt's guides, Bartholomew's maps and by Arthur Mee and H. V. Morton, and by a whole library of open road literature. Writers like J. B. Priestley would celebrate this claiming of England as of birthright by walking it. Such travellers were rightly convinced that their explorations were as valid as those of the people who could afford to get themselves to Africa. All the same, foreign parts were never more alluring, more frustratingly unreachable. In the classroom framed prints of the Empire inculcated a global Britain. In the cinema, films such as *The Lives of a Bengal Lancer* (Gary Cooper, Franchot Tone and C. Aubrey Smith) and *Sanders of the River*, in which one sensible white man deals out *Boy's Own Paper* justice to the childish natives, made on location, became doubly thrilling because of their scenery. All the churches supported missionaries, whose infrequent furloughs laid emphasis on distance.

The Empire was both old and brazenly new, at its peak and near collapse. Less than forty years before the war Joseph Chamberlain was justifying its acquisition by declaring, 'We, as fast as we acquire new territory and develop it, develop it as trustees of civilization in the interests of the world.' And the youthful Churchill had written that, in seizing fresh lands for the Crown, 'The act is virtuous, the exercise invigorating and the result often profitable.' Empire travel, via rhetoric,

315

fiction, film and a tremendous amount of storytelling by returned 'builders' of all kinds, created a non-parochial and, on the whole, a non-European concept of travel. Hollywood, of course, became the single, irresistible guide to the United States, where nobody expected to wander except through celluloid. Perhaps the part of the world in which people who had never travelled outside their own country best knew their way about was the Middle East. Christianity as well as the British Arabists, most notably T. E. Lawrence between the wars, had made it as familiar to them as their own backyard. Or so they thought. Wartime letters from the Holy Land to the Home Counties reveal some conflict. The highest and lowest matters have to be reconciled.

Air travel was minimal. Delta Air Lines and Pan American Airways had begun to run passenger services in the United States in 1929 and during the following decade all kinds of civil airways were functioning in Britain and elsewhere, but the principal means of getting about the world was still by liner. During the thirties the liner reached its glorious apogee in the streamlined forms of the *Bremen*, the *Normandie* and the *Queen Mary*; never before or since has travel been so luxurious. 'Liners' because they belonged to various shipping lines, the most celebrated of which was the P & O, founded by two Scots in 1837, the initials standing for the Peninsular and Oriental Steam Navigation Company. These evocative ships, shed of all their rich furnishings and packed to the gunwales with soldiers, carried armies to the battlefields. To be sailing across the Mediterranean, or in the Indian Ocean, even under such austere conditions, was for many an individual who had never before been afloat, like being admitted to take part in a legend. Minus their mock baronial halls, Versailles ballrooms, cabins like satin caves and, most of all, their hordes of servants, though not entirely their elaborate rituals, these liners managed to preserve much of their romance while on their war footing. They confirmed Kipling's claim, 'The Liner she's a lady.' Blacked out, soundlessly as possible, zigzagging and protected by their convoys, they became one of the most potent images for the wartime travellers. They may not have been 'posh' – going out to India port side to avoid the blast of Red Sea heat and returning starboard for the same reason – but they were routed where the climate would turn from winter to summer in a week or two, and where they would smell

Morocco. Few in the 1940s believed that liners would not sail for ever. In peacetime they left harbour in a rain of streamers; thousands of paper umbilical cords tore to let them part from the land as the band played 'A Life on the Ocean Wave'. Now the vast shapes sneaked out furtively, led by minesweepers and dreading U-boats.

The Empire itself had to be unsinkable, too much emotion had been invested in it for it to be imperilled. But on 15 February 1942 Singapore, its major Far East bastion, fell easily to the Japanese. Sixty million pounds had been lavished on it to make it safe and formidable, with tiers of guns pointing out to sea to deter the mightiest aggressor. The Japanese took it from behind. With the loss of Singapore the whole attitude to travel altered. In a nutshell, the certainties and probabilities of starboard-side home vanished. Letters from Burma and Malaya often reveal a sense of the writer being somehow stranded or unable to make the old connections. The landscapes, instead of colouring the prose, seem to clog and engulf it. For those at home a son or husband was, for anything they could comprehend in geographical terms, nerve-rackingly off the map. Rudyard Kipling knew the feeling when it only applied to coffee and rubber planters, and their wives.

How runs the old indictment? 'Dear and slow',
So much and twice so much. We gird but go.
For all the soul of our sad East is there,
Beneath the house flag of the P & O.

Introduction to
COMPONENTS OF THE SCENE
An Anthology of the Prose and Poetry of the Second World War

ed. Ronald Blythe, 1966

We in our haste can only see the small components of the scene
We cannot tell what incidents will focus on the final screen.

> *A barrage of disruptive sound, a petal on a sleeping face,*
> *Both must be noted, both must have their place;*
> *It may be that our later selves or else our unborn sons*
> *Will search for meaning in the dust of long deserted guns,*
> *We only watch, and indicate and make our scribbled pencil notes.*
> *We do not wish to moralize, only to ease our dusty throats.*
>
> Donald Bain

This anthology seeks to capture the special precision of the poetry of the Second World War and to evoke the deliberate mixture of realism and sensibility which dominated the prose of those violent years. It was, in France and Britain particularly, a highly literary war; if everybody did not burst out writing (and reading), it often seemed that they did. Writers generally believed that they were witnessing a dissolution of the old civilised scene and that they had a duty to preserve the great basic values which had created this scene. They also felt that they must resist the new facelessness forced upon Europe by fascist politics and military expediency; that salvation and hope began with the discovery of one's own identity and its maintenance against all the pressures of the emergency.

The war demanded a temporary suspension of personal identity but, as all wars do, it inevitably offered a great profusion of those experiences by which identity is fed: foreign travel, sexual freedom, bereavement, pain, separation, comradeship and those close groupings which, far from turning many individuals into a regiment or a ship's company or a bomber's crew, brings each man face to face with his own essential solitude. The writers of 1939-45 fully accepted engagement in the struggle but rejected the suspension of private life advocated by the various propaganda machines. This was the condition by which their conscience permitted them to fight, as well as forsake the indignation of the poets of 1916-18. Their work was not addressed to great audiences or to the nation, but to another individual. Eventually, as the war intensified and its strangely fragmented pattern added to the impression of world insanity, the quiet urbanity of its literature provided a climate in which the urgent dialogue of the human condition could take place. These writers saw themselves, and with considerable modesty, as healthy cells in a rotting tissue. Their duty was to create other such cells.

Although there was a so-called 'boom' in poetry, with the thirties poets' new work being eagerly read for both moral and technical guidance, and many new writers finding print under the cryptic shelter of a movement called the New Apocalypse, for a considerable period after the war had ended there was only a hazy assessment of its real poetic statement. It was a statement which was awaited with some impatience when the war began. 'Where are the war-poets?' asked the *Times Literary Supplement* in 1940. The popular press asked the same question, only with patriotic indignation. Soon there were accusations; it was implied that while everybody else had taken up their action stations, the poets had not – and they who had been so noisy about Spain! Yet even people like Cyril Connolly, who was so near to the literary heart of the war, became apprehensive about a hush which continued until after the fall of France, when everything pointed to the abyss. Had the poets, like Gide, taken a vow of silence until the war was over? If they had, commented Connolly bitterly, 'they will disappear and their disappearance provide further evidence that the human race has outstayed its welcome.' He urged them to 'flower like the almond blossom'.

Some writers had already decided that almond blossom might stand a better chance in a less gloomy climate and had transplanted themselves to New York and California, most notably W. H. Auden. Their apparent flight to what Connolly called 'a land rich in incident' gave great offence. This was not purged by the shocking logic of E .M. Forster's remark that it was better to be a swimming rat than a sinking ship. Auden himself had no reason to apologise. He had been fighting his war against the fascists – at home and abroad – a whole decade before Mr Chamberlain came to the microphone on 3 September 1939, and he was to leave behind for the war-poets proper invaluable techniques for the expression of their faith. And T.S.Eliot also recognised during the blackest months of the war the absolute priority of the Word in a gobbledegook universe and could tell Stephen Spender at this time that 'it is very important that as many writers as possible should remain detached, and not have any official position'.

Spender's official position was in the Auxiliary Fire Service. From it he looked back in grief and disillusionment to the brief Apollonian Germany of the late twenties which had so terribly given way to the Dionysian Germany of Hitler. What was it which allowed nations to accept the convention of the war- time, peace-time cycle?

> *Why cannot the one good*
> *Benevolent feasible*
> *Final dove descend?*

he asked.

It was a rhetorical question for Sidney Keyes, Alun Lewis, Keith Douglas, Richard Spender, Herbert Corby, G. S. Fraser, Henry Reed, R. N. Currey, F. T. Prince, Rayner Heppenstall and the many other young writers in uniform. They had by the very fact of accepting a uniform made a choice which Alex Comfort summed up as 'refusal or death'. Their brief adult experiences had been circumscribed by corrupt politics. Sidney Keyes, one of the most important and prolific of the Second World War poets, was not quite twenty-one when he died in North Africa. The thirties poets had left their 'singing feasts' in order to practise what they preached – in Spain. The forties poets refused to preach at all and thus, beyond the normal duties of the fighting man, they felt they had few obligations beyond those governing their relationship with another human being, and that they were free to use the little time at their disposal in discovering themselves. The great thing was not to pretend, or proffer solutions, or to be histrionic. Each poet spoke as wholly and truthfully as he could from out of the one inviolate spot of an otherwise violated order, his own identity. This he found more threatened by the inanities of the barracks, war-time bureaucrats and those countless inroads upon the dignity of the person which a national emergency prescribes, than by the terrible etiquette of the battlefield. There he could only marvel at the way military primitivism worked afresh for every new generation of victims.

> *How can I live among this gentle*
> *obsolescent breed of heroes, and not weep?*

320

asks Keith Douglas.

There's no prescribed or easy word
For dissolution in the Army books . . .

says Sidney Keyes.

Softly the civilized
Centuries fall,
Paper on paper,
Peter on Paul . . .

notes Alun Lewis in a poem of such feathery valediction that it is like the leave-taking of ghosts. F. T. Prince, watching soldiers bathing, sees two great Renaissance pictures come to life before his eyes, Michelangelo's mercenaries being called away suddenly from their innocent splashings to kill or be killed, and Pollaiuolo's 'brother naked' warriors hacking at each other. Here, as recurring as its heroism, is 'war's sorrow and disgrace'.

Sidney Keyes particularly, and most of the Second World War poets to a degree, accepted Rilke's belief that each man carries his own death within him. It was of Keyes that R. N. Currey said that he went 'further than any poet of the First War in his realization that mankind was at war because it was not yet ready for peace, because men were proud and greedy and destructive at heart'.

The other great influence on these identity-claiming poets was Hölderlin, born the same year as Wordsworth but spiritually if not physically killed by the *mal de siècle* which followed the moment of hopefulness released over Europe by the French Revolution. Hölderlin's disillusionment sprang from what his translator J. B. Leishman describes as the 'vast gulf between the actual and the ideal'. Vulgarians, particularly nationalists, were soon to smudge these two states together and call them 'destiny', a pretty word for action and power. 'Sacred Destiny' was what Hölderlin called it in 1796 but five years later he is forced to realise that life and art are only seen in their true fullness when destiny, that claptrap term so convenient for

321

national leaders, is 'suspended'. Hölderlin's tragic life presented to the poets of 1939-45 a romantic analogy of their own bitterly realistic position. They had to make swift decisions as to what was politically genuine and what was part of the corrosive ritual, and on the whole they felt they had to do this without cynicism. Hölderlin's *Menon's Laments For Diotima*, one of the world's great elegies, and a defence of the personal life, taught them, in the words of his translator, how poetry in becoming more personal also becomes more universal.

Shortly after writing his *Laments* Hölderlin went mad and wandered abstractly through a Europe where glory was rapidly giving place to something called '*la gloire*'. A century and a half of ardent nationalism and militarism faced the world. One day the poet was discovered in the grounds of a château near the Loire and was questioned by the owner.

'You are a Greek, perhaps?'
'No! – on the contrary, I am a German!'
'On the contrary? – Is the German the opposite of the Greek?'
'Yes – We all are! You, the Frenchman, are too; the Englishman, your enemy, is too – we all are!'

The Second World War poets recognised the difference with humility. The sublime heritage was in the gutter and each and all were culpable. All they could do in the short time which was left was individually to repudiate the state myths and, as Hölderlin requested,

. . . proffer their hands to each other
Before the sociable light has yet
Quite gone and the night is upon them.

A strict privacy, though a witty one, also marked William Empson's reaction to the war. While refusing to be stampeded by the quake, natural or national, he equally refused to be shaken to bits by it – 'It seemed the best thing to be up and go'. The mannerisms curl off into essentials, just like Chinese Chippendale.

For T. S. Eliot, in his early fifties when the war began, it was a time of assessment. Three hundred years of English Christianity separate him from the ancestor who left East Coker for New England. What now?

> *So here I am, in the middle way, having had twenty years –*
> *Twenty years largely wasted, the years of l'entre deux guerres*
> *Trying to learn to use words . . .*

He also says that 'Home is where one starts from', a reminder of origins and that each man bears a unique responsibility for the then and now. The magnificent *Four Quartets* appeared during the darkest years of the war: with *Little Gidding* in 1942 comes a very different kind of patriotism.

> *We die with the dying:*
> *See, they depart, and we go with them.*
> *We are born with the dead;*
> *See, they return, and bring us with them.*
> *The moment of the rose and the moment of the yew-tree*
> *Are of equal duration. A people without history*
> *Is not redeemed from time, for history is a pattern*
> *Of timeless moments. So, while the light fails*
> *On a winter's afternoon, in a secluded chapel*
> *History is now and England.*

David Gascoyne, the only important surrealist poet of the thirties, also used Christian themes for his war poetry, and Edith Sitwell's profoundly moving *Still Falls the Rain* sees her as a mourner at the crucifixion of cities during air-raids. But it was Dylan Thomas who translated statistics into loss by offering the poor insignificant victims of the bombings – 'A child of a few hours', 'A man aged a hundred' – a similar rich and sonorous devotion to their earthly existence as that offered by the seventeenth-century Henry King to his dead wife in the *Exequy*. Henry Moore was to complement this poetry with his *Shelter Sketchbook* (1943) in which his hieratic treatment of the citizens of mid-twentieth-century London repeats over and over again the profound outline of the entombed. A majesty emanates from these

323

classic cocoons as, in Dylan Thomas's words, they await 'the incendiary eve of deaths and entrances'. Countless other human beings reduced to war's bundles in the sealed trains criss-crossing Europe to the final solution schedules, and on the Eastern Front and in the fetid depths of ships, awaited it too.

Dylan Thomas was twenty-four when the war began. His biographer, Constantine FitzGibbon, has described how he found it a personal affront. He had a premonition of a short life, that he would die before he was forty, and now this little span, so essential to his art, was to be interfered with by 'them' – meaning not the Nazis but the various government departments. It was vaguely from this detestation of state meddling in private lives that the idea of *Milk Wood* began to take shape. Thomas's fabulous voice, reading poems and giving talks on the B.B.C., and encrusting the uproar in numerous dismal blacked-out Fitzrovian pubs, was a key sound of these years, while his work released some poets from the precise conditions which Eliot, Auden and their followers had laid upon the language. The singing note returned. There was a fresh lyricism; and the heady love affair with words soon produced prose variants in the stories of Glyn Jones, V. S. Pritchett and Fred Urquhart. The Irish W. R. Rodgers, with his *Awake! and other poems* (1941), was to add to this exultation of language, rich words which contrasted so vividly with the war's special poverty. This word-spree was to continue throughout the forties, feeding itself on austerity in some paradoxical fashion, to reach its apogee in the lively twentieth- century-Jacobean of Christopher Fry's plays and his translations of Anouilh and Giraudoux.

*

In January 1940 the first number of *Horizon* appeared and was greeted with groans of disappointment. 'A magazine should be the reflection of its time and one that ceases to reflect this should come to an end,' declared its editor. Then let it die, wept its subscribers who had bought up every copy, and who had asked for bread and had been given H. E. Bates. Not that he was negligible by any means but his glassily finished stories could be read everywhere. Yet the germ of *Horizon's* future importance was present in this otherwise cautious issue, buried in a little travel-essay by Cyril Connolly and only to be observed in retrospect. This essay, *The Ant Lion*, is ostensibly about Albi, the little Provençal town which was the centre of the Albigensian heresy and the home of Toulouse-Lautrec. In essence it is a statement of *Horizon's* non-parochial intention. Modern wars choke the lines of communication between writers, national literature is inflated and the validity of enemy art denied. While Britain waited for Hitler to invade, Connolly had his own warning to give – 'An island fortress must always be on its guard against provincialism!' His readers – probably the most enthusiastic any magazine has ever had – took due note of this and soon *Horizon*, with its indulgent baroque retrospection following it like an expertly stocked baggage-train, and its international high-table atmosphere, came to epitomise for them a Europe really worth saving. They were pleasantly seduced by its editor's notoriously skilful lament for the lost *douceur de vivre*. Constant mention of painters, poets, architects and musicians working away 'above' the war, as it were, reminded them of the unity of real civilisation. *Horizon* regularly infiltrated the smug Home Front by letting in the ideas of Aragon, Moravia, Cavafy, Barea, Croce, Mallarmé, Eluard, Malraux, Pasternak, Miro, Camus, Bartók, Gide, Sartre, Picasso and others.

Connolly celebrated the dingy months of victory with an introspective masterpiece, *The Unquiet Grave*. The book is a private distillation of melancholy which, exuded drop by aphoristic drop, gets the reader wonderfully drunk; it is a Brocks' Benefit Night of the 1939-45 soul, with the great darkness fitfully illuminated by a fine display of adroit scholarship and high imagination, and at the heart it reveals Connolly's celebrated analysis of *Angst*, its causes and its cures. With this anthology-autobiography the forties search of the self achieved full circle.

A profusion of other little magazines shared the scene – in spite of every discouragement, niggardly paper rations, bombed offices, breakdowns in distribution and, above all, the fact that nearly everybody connected with their production had full-time national work as well. The most popular was *Penguin New Writing*, which began publication in 1936, but which established itself in a much broader sense after 1940. While lacking the curious glamour of *Horizon*, under the editorship of John Lehmann it maintained a distinguished and inimitable climate of its own with stories, essays and poems, as well as film, ballet, art and theatrical criticism of a high level. To be published in *New Writing* was to have arrived. Copies of it travelled the world in small-packs and kit-bags, along with its subsidiary *Penguin Parade*. The most exotic of the little magazines was undoubtedly J. M. Tambimuttu's *Poetry London*, with its glowing lyre-bird covers by Graham Sutherland, Henry Moore and John Craxton, its lavish menu-size format and lucky-dip contents. Tambi's descent on London and his subsequent reign over a large collection of poets and pubs were not the least wonders of the war. A grimly comic description of him is given by the late Julian Maclaren-Ross in *Memoirs of the Forties* (1965). Other magazines included Reginald Moore's *Modern Reading*, Alex Comfort's *New Road*, Robert Herring's *Life and Letters Today*, Geoffrey Grigson's *New Verse*, Wrey Gardiner's *Poetry Quarterly* and Neville Braybrooke's *Wind and the Rain*.

Another group of editors, notably Patricia Ledward, Keidrych Rhys and R. N. Currey, made periodical collections of war poetry. These often included a single fine poem by an unknown writer never to be heard of again in the literary sense. Excellent but isolated short stories and essays would frequently appear in this way from one or other of the ironically named 'theatres' of war, an imaginative fragment struck from some otherwise non-creative hand by a collision in unique circumstances.

*

The fiction of these years only really takes on some vaguely cohesive pattern in the development of the novel if the dates are stretched from *Brighton Rock* (1938) to *Lucky Jim* (1953). It is only in this way that it is possible to trace the progress of the anti-hero and eventually to see the mannered climate of Christian guilt swept away by an ill-mannered gale of social protest. Journalists dubbed the protestants Angry Young Men. The real note was one of deliberately graceless laughter at the bloodless niceties of British life. Some sharp reaction to the now infamous romanticism of the forties was inevitable. This romanticism had grown out of a valid anxiety during the early war years for novelists to conserve traditional liberal values. In 1941 Walter Allen observed a halt amongst artists of all kinds in associating themselves with the thirties idea of art and action. A period of reflection had set in. Allen recommended a fresh consideration of Flaubert's withdrawal doctrine. Flaubert was a most unfashionable writer just then, and he made the important point that the much ridiculed Flaubertian ivory tower was not a shelter from the world, but a quiet eminence from which the writer could view his world.

The artist should be in his work, like God in creation, invisible and all-powerful; he should be felt everywhere and seen nowhere (wrote Flaubert). And the art should be raised above personal affections and nervous susceptibilities. It is time to give it the precision of the physical sciences by means of pitiless method.

But when one looks back on the results of these four or so years of creative dedication and, so far as could be claimed from war work and war pressures, the novelists' vocational position, it is to see them not so much as en-towered observers as a group of literary Simeon Stylites, each aloft on his pillar above the revolution, and able to convey very little of the tumult below.

Graham Greene, in *The Power and the Glory* (1940), became the first and eventually the foremost novelist of the last twenty-five years to draw elaborate moral conclusions from lives ruined by sin-consciousness. His Mexican whisky priest and his seedy Scobie from *The Heart of the Matter* (1948) could hardly be called sinners at all in a world which contained Himmler and Josef Kramer or – in a different sense – the airmen who dropped the bomb on Hiroshima. Yet each of these novels was immediately seen to contain a direct relevance to what was happening in national spheres of evil. Greene sees both heaven and the jungle as man's natural states, and man's tragedy that he has to fluctuate between both.

Henry Green, too, was a writer who offered an accurate vision of the war existence in microcosmic terms. His novels did what nobody else's did, they moved from class to class with a new kind of conviction. They had brief meaningful titles which told one exactly what the story was about, *Caught, Loving, Party Going*; but the characters constantly

327

act out of character. Henry Green defied the neat pigeon-holing of humanity and challenged surface judgements. His novels have something of the oriental subtlety and refinement of William Empson's poetry. *Caught* (1943) is about the Fire Service and is remarkable for its accurate use of working-class dialogue.

1940 saw Dylan Thomas's *Portrait of the Artist as a Young Dog*, C. P. Snow's *Strangers and Brothers*, Charles Morgan's *The Voyage* as well as Graham Greene's *The Power and the Glory*, but saved its top honours for Arthur Koestler's *Darkness at Noon*, perhaps the greatest novel to have come out of the war. Both 1941 and 1942 were lean years for fiction, although one brilliant dialogue continued as imperturbably as ever with Ivy Compton Burnett's *Parents and Children* (1941). This was also the year of Rex Warner's Kafkaesque study *The Aerodrome*, and of Elizabeth Bowen's stories, *Look At All Those Roses*. In 1942 came the famous novel which turned Gerald Kersh into a barrack-room myth, *They Die With Their Boots Clean*. 1942 also witnessed the beginning of the American 'Deep South School' influence on British fiction with Carson McCullers' *Reflections in a Golden Eye*, followed a few months later by her *The Heart is a Lonely Hunter*. Further American stories arrived on the scene, all full of extraordinary emotional material, vivid dialogue and colour, Eudora Welty's *A Curtain of Green* (1943), *The Robber Bridegroom* (1944), *The Wide Net* (1945); the first stories of J. D. Salinger and, most potent of all though not Deep South, Edmund Wilson's *Memoirs Of Hecate County* (1945).

At the time the really good short story seemed to be a rare event. Critics – including George Orwell and Stephen Spender constantly attacked the form, declared that it was tepid and too concerned with tidiness, and looked back longingly to Lawrence and Turgenev. But hindsight shows the war years unusually rich in first-rate short stories, and that it is these, rather than the novels, which retain their spell. The work of James Hanley, Frank Sargeson, William Sansom, Elizabeth Bowen, Glyn Jones, V. S. Pritchett, Alun Lewis, Fred Urquhart and Julian Maclaren-Ross touches the nerve of the period with an exactitude which often escapes the novel.

The most distinguished fiction of the second half of the war includes

Rayner Heppenstall's *Saturnine* (1943), C. S. Forester's *The Ship* (1943), L. P. Hartley's *The Shrimp and the Anemone* (1943), Nigel Balchin's *The Small Back Room* (1943), Rosamund Lehmann's *The Ballad and the Source* (1944), Joyce Cary's *The Horse's Mouth* (1944), Mervyn Peake's *Titus Groan* (1945), Aldous Huxley's *Time Must Have A Stop* (1945) and George Orwell's terrible fairy-tale, *Animal Farm* (1945). Not one of these books, or any lesser novel of these times, attempted to offer some really great answer to what was happening; there is also a general avoidance of the 'great description' of events. Among the victim heroes there is no Good Soldier Schweik – although 1939-45 was a Schweik Age if ever there was one – and among the novelists there was no Mottram, no Remarque or Jules Romains. Perhaps World War One had set a precedent of poetry during battle and fiction afterwards. Perhaps the uniquely barbarous way in which World War Two ended – Belsen and the atom bomb – suddenly drove the whole subject beyond what were believed to be up until this point in human conduct, the barrierless limits of the artist's comment. But whatever it was which caused so many of the best novelists to occupy themselves as they did while hell gaped, it is significant that the best-known attempt to produce a 'great' Second World War novel was made by Norman Mailer with *The Naked And The Dead*. Walter Allen, considering this question at the time, wrote that 'The brands of liberalism and rationalization held by the bulk of present day writers are incapable of assimilating large-scale evil'. But in France Jean-Paul Sartre's 'Immortality is a dreadful alibi' was the accusation made about writers who neglected the crucial debates of their day for art and the private vision.

At the end of the war, British writers hurried to liberated Paris to see for themselves the superior literary landscape which was rumoured to exist there, and they were overwhelmed by what they found. Guido de Ruggiero's definition of *Angst* – 'the flashing spark of shock between two unknowns, the individual and God' – had to face Sartre's definition of Existentialism. It was the old melancholy versus the new hell. The flourishing state of French writing as well as giving pleasure to the liberators gave cause for heart-searching too. It was immediately observed that although the French were undernourished and made tense by the risk of torture, they did not suffer from the crushing fatigue which afflicted the British writer, who was worn-out by having to double the essentially lonely terms of his vocation with the various forms of gregariousness demanded by what the newspapers called 'a nation in arms'. Paulhan, the distinguished French poetry critic, and an anti-Puritan, could look at the Paris scene just before the victors arrived and say that 'art benefits by being clandestine and subversive'. In the work of British writers during the Second World War it is possible to see a continuous – and emotionally exhausting – effort to subvert the immanence of their artist-nature from the demands made on it, not only by the state, but by unique appeals to their conscience.

IN ANGER
Culture in the Cold War, 1945-60

Robert Hewison, 1981

Reading the cultural history of a day which one has lived through is rather like having mirrors arranged in order to study something as undeniable and yet as unfamiliar, as one's face in profile. Here is the passed-down outline, and here, there and everywhere are the marks made by various kinds of deliberate acquisition or rejection over the years. And here most of all, if rather askew, is the uncomfortable self-regarding eye.

When the events here began their progress, I was a youthful socialist and poet in the Suffolk countryside; when they reached their climacteric, as Robert Hewison calls 1956, I was writing novels and stories on the Suffolk coast and working for Benjamin Britten. I was also contributing essays to the *Observer* and *New Statesman* which seemed at the time like being allowed to add to holy writ. But in the light of Robert Hewison's breakaway separatism of Movement goats and Bloomsbury sheep, I must admit that it was literature, art and music, not messages, that I was after, and that I never did this sorting-out business myself. The Movement was exciting because it hustled life into a fresh, robust territory, but it in no way made all the former paths stale and suspect.

In Anger is the second volume of what is eventually intended to be a trilogy on the cultural life of Britain from the outbreak of the last war to the present. The first volume, *Under Siege: Literary Life in London, 1939-45*, showed Robert Hewison as an impressive marshaller of facts and sorter-out of telling detail. His final book intends to bring 'what at times appears to be the decline and fall of English literature even closer' to the fearful Eighties. But now, we have the lead-up to this still startling phenomenon of 1956, when the work of a number of disparate playwrights and novelists who had no contact with each other, and certain crises in international affairs coincided, half accidentally, half intentionally. For this was the year that British writers 'took a hard look at the form of society they had inherited and, in destroying the conventional acceptance of an ordered homogenous Mandarin culture, at least opened up the possibilities of future change. Anger, however, confused, is a more positive response than nostalgia or despair.'

What occurred, of course, was the rage we all felt about Suez and Hungary meeting head-on the anti-Establishment values of Amis, Osborne, Wain and Colin Wilson, and immediately turning these greatly surprised young men into Daniels come to judgement and generational oracles. Soon there was a steadier, more widely-spread and dull kind of anger which was to feed the class of '68, a final trickling away of postwar optimism and faith, as the power of the old guard was seen to have been scarcely dented by the revolution of 1945, and the deathly facts of life for a yawning future were nuclear weapons and a ferocious polarisation of East and West.

This ordering of politics and art, the picking up of its myriad interconnections, many of them not at all apparent when they were happening even to those in the thick of them, is where Robert Hewison excels. He gives not only the full facts but his own shrewd reactions to them. He is concise and accurate, if sometimes a bit sweeping in his assessment of a writer or artist, though usually just. He knows too how to work into his calendar of creativity such things as publishing economics, the disaster caused to the British film industry by monopolist distributors, BBC politics and the effect of the Butler Education Act.

But to outline his Cold War culture. He starts with the arrival in London in the spring of 1945 of Edmund Wilson, and his admiration of our cultural achievement in spite of everything. There was a worrying question, however. Why was everybody, though often most sensitively and beautifully, forking over the cultural past? Priestley, also staring around, though after the 'revolution', declared that 'We are revolutionaries who have not swept away anything . . . We have probably the best children and the dullest adults in Europe. We are a Socialist-Monarchy that is really the last monument of Liberalism.' Regression, regression is the theme of these regrets. The wartime book boom ended around 1947, Hewison puts it down to publishing difficulties and paper shortages, but there was another factor. Strangely enough, there is a vast amount of non-duty time during a war which drove the most unlikely people to reading. But now many established writers of high reputation, whose work was still being printed, found themselves earning the merest pittance. In 1951, the BBC invented the Third Programme, its object to be the dispensation of artistic excellence. But it commissioned comparatively little new work. In 1951, too, Gerald Barry, formerly of the *News Chronicle*, managed to get the authorities fascinated by a commemoration of the Great Exhibition of 1851 which turned out to be the very happy but touchingly flimsy Festival of Britain.

The state's patronage of the arts could be seen growing in many other directions also, and the sixteen prewar universities were rapidly being added to. There were twelve new arts festivals and the foundation-stone of the National Theatre had been laid. On the surface, the ways things were going was not too bad.

The collator of this hopefulness, however, is not deceived. The new coffee bars are a sham bohemianism, new magazines such as *Encounter* (1953) are 'born middle-aged', the Lord Chamberlain hangs over the theatre like a loony and C. P. Snow's new men 'nonetheless operate in the old places'. Sociology hadn't as yet found its feet and Hewison finds it symptomatic that the two most important works of the period were cultural studies produced by literary critics, not sociologists: Richard Hoggart's *The Uses of Literacy* (1957) and Raymond Williams's *Culture and Society* (1958). In the same year and about to burst through was the 'shining barbarism' (Hoggart) of pop and pulp to take aim at the lowest common denominator, 'the ceaseless exploitation of a hollow brightness'.

Then the tanks, plays and novels of that *annus mirabilis*, 1956. 'It is the first moment of history after the Second World War about which there is anything like a persistent myth, and like the myths of wartime, it is a combination of historical truths and popular distortion.' *In Anger* justifies some of the claims of both truth and myth, actuality and legend. During the Fifties television licences went up from a quarter of a million to ten millions. In 1958 CND was born. Even more important for British culture, whether for its makers or partakers, 'the effect of 1956 was to end the automatic connection between being a Marxist, and being a member of the Communist Party.'

AUSTERITY / BINGE
The Decorative Arts of the Forties and Fifties
Bevis Hillier, 1975

'I believe that the decorative arts of any period are worth considering, however barren of talent they may seem to be,' writes Bevis Hillier at the beginning of what Sir John Betjeman calls his 'alarming selection' of graphics, fashion furniture, artefacts and amusements which engulfed us during the Forties and Fifties. As one who closed *Brideshead* to jive for an hour or two during the first decade, and whose blankets carried the authentic Utility mark through to the next, I gazed for the most part at this lively resurrection work with anything but nostalgia; although every now and then, some still-potent bauble, learnedly described as it bobbed past on time's trash-choked stream, made me blink a bit. Demob and New Look suits jostling in the Regency-striped bar. Brylcreem and Soir-de-Paris affrighting the lambent air as some talked of Sartre. Our knowing author makes it clear that, where he is concerned, it is research, not memory, which holds the door, by including a photo of himself, at five, in victory year.

The first half of Hillier's book, *Austerity*, is dominated by firm orders, mystic national oratory and personal whimsy. Love of country is symbolised by farm-fresh images of it. Whether digging for victory or parting at Paddington, we tended to stay well-groomed. The abstractions of camouflage, and laboratory models of molecular structure, produced designs for tables and fabrics. Votive Churchilliana began early in the decade with V-sign vases and dreadful pottery images of a Buddha in a hard hat. The arrival of the Americans brought a touch of gabardine svelteness which gave us all a sartorial inferiority complex. Some of the serious things, as Bevis Hillier rightly says, remained irredeemably comic. Gas masks, for instance . . .'with their weird chrysalis-green snouts . . . emblems of anticlimax on a grand scale'. A woman I knew carried hers in a smart leatherette case with 'Mrs E. Smith, OBE' inscribed on it in fluorescent paint. There was a boom in photograph frames – 'many women saw more of their husbands in photograph frames than in bed' – and, for husbands, a boom in pin-ups.

Bevis Hillier's detached view is at an advantage when it comes to the recurring motif. The repetition of the disembodied hand, for example, in high-class advertising. Their elegant surrealistic pleading probably had its artistic impetus in the paintings of Chirico, Paul Nash and John Armstrong, but, looking at them afresh, they seem touched by saluting hands, parting hands, drowning hands and hands stretching out of Belsen. The winged horse, Pegasus, became another motif for film posters, brooches and porcelain. In the late Forties, Glynis Johns in *Miranda* looked as though she had founded the mermaid motif, but Hillier takes this back to Paul Delvaux's *Sirènes* paintings of some years earlier. Although mermaid jewellery, weaves, etc., looked decidedly more Johns than Delvaux, the surfacing of the fish-lady as a fabulous symbol really owed most to the rediscovery of the Swiss artist, Arnold Böcklin (1827-1901). The Böcklinian mermaid, wrote Robin Ironside (*World Review*, November 1951), 'is a beast brimming with hilarious desires' in a scene 'in which man and beast participate without distinction or hindrance'.

The occult looms high on the list of Forties escapism. So does ballet, Disney, romantic historical fiction and the out-of-doors Elysia of gypsies, canalmen, balloonists and circuses appeared to offer a world fit for heroes to float off in. Even the authorities recognised that men did not live by rations alone and entirely reconstituted the glories of Brighton Pavilion – 'the Kama Sutra of architecture' – and, yet more wonderfully, launched the Festival of Britain. Its symbol was Britannia spiked on a star from which bunting was strung in a sunny loop. All its optimism and some of its inventiveness spread to every town hall and village green.

The Festival opened the 'Binge', as Bevis Hillier calls the Fifties, a time of 'aggressive whimsy, frothy fashions and Rock culture, when ornament seemed to take a revenge on the inhuman times through which men had just passed'. In the latter part he is quoting what Bouilhet said of the Twenties. So, after the Second World War, we postponed the carnival in order to have a quiet revolution. Carnival broke out anew with the Coronation, which was stage-managed by the architects of the Festival, as well as by the superb Duke of Norfolk. After this – 'the last flowering of the old establishment culture in Britain' – the working class began to muscle in. The young ganged up against the aged (twenty-five-plus) and sang loud and rude. Many middle-class people missed a lump of Rock culture because they had become hypnotised by the Ross-Mitford U-turn, which Bevis Hillier does not mention. It was jolly sinister, as Evelyn Waugh pointed out (*Encounter*, December 1955) – Miss Mitford was playing with fire in explaining class argot to Tom, Dick and Marlene. Waugh wrote:

Have you heard of the Butler Education Act? It was one of the things which politicians did when no one was looking . . . the name derives from Mr Butler who, at the time of writing, has just knocked something off the price of my clothes. Clearly he is a generous fellow. In his Education Act he provided for the free distribution of University degrees for the deserving poor – very handy for splitting the atom, you will say. But quite a lot for Mr Butler's protégés choose, or are directed into, 'Literature'. I could make your flesh creep by telling you about the new wave of philistinism with which we are threatened by these grim young people who are coming off the assembly lines . . . L'Ecole de Butler are the primal man and woman of the classless society.

A pretty virulent class-consciousness prevailed throughout Mr Hillier's picture-book period and he has gleaned some telling glimpses of it. The immense issues which preoccupied us – Hiroshima, genocide, Marxism versus Stalinism, dissolution of Empire, the implications of Fulton, etc. – are not blamed for the look on our neat faces. Basically, what is amusingly and occasionally profoundly achieved here is a record of the flights of fancy which we made over wartime functionalism. Charming flights at first, then sulkier and noisier escapades as the new pop sub-culture tried its wings.

TELLING TALES

HENRY JAMES AND THE KNOWING GIRL

Introduction to *The Awkward Age*, 1987

Disappointment can harass the confidence necessary for creation but it can also do the reverse and act as a stimulant. For it to revitalise and not crush there has to be a swift abandonment of what brought it about, a candid recognition of having thrust along the wrong path. It was not hubris or even experiment which led Henry James to stray from fiction to plays during the early nineties. Far less sensitive ears than his had detected the shift of social comment from the story to the stage, and for him at that moment it seemed no more than a natural progression that his dialogue should advance from being read to being spoken. All he was certain of, and this only in his kind, humble way, was that his art was singularly capable of picking up the nuances of a darkly altering scene. The wits and the moralists, Wilde, Ibsen and others, saw the old veneer cracking and were far from tentative in their exposure of what lay beneath it. James, the recognized master of surfaces and what they concealed, believed that he had a role among the playwrights who were transforming the turgid Victorian theatre. It was an error and it took him five years and four unproduced comedies, plus the disaster of *Guy Domville*, to recognise it as such. When he did there was elation rather than despair – 'It has been a great relief to feel that one of the most detestable incidents in my life has closed.' He was injured and bewildered as people are when they have, very roughly in his case, been forced to recognise that they have laid claim to what can never be theirs, then healed and renewed. There was pain but no sense of waste. If the novel could not extend itself via the theatre, then the conditions of the play would be employed to carry the talk in fiction to hitherto unsuspected depths. The novel was his unchallengeable ground and no one would dispute his right to strike fresh routes through it.

339

For all the quickness of recovery, it took Henry James a fair while to fully come to terms with his 1890-95 years of hurt and failure, and label them as his 'strange sacred time', as he realised that without all the true creativity which had gone into them and ensured the magnitude of his defeat, there would have been little development in his writing. The experience had virtually hounded him into another 'originality', and at fifty-two, when he was so elaborately set in his old ways! He was ageing, the century was ageing, and yet he was beginning! The latent possibilities of his new play-inspired style, made him visionary and alert. He changed all his ways. The countryside instead of Kensington, a typist taking down his spoken words instead of the silence of his pen, bicycle rides instead of pavement walks, provincial values and entertainments instead of sophistication. He had retired in order to start again. Rye would provide his perspective for what was occurring in London, Lamb House might well be seen as his retreat by his friends but to him it would be his observatory. Society had reached one of its moments of flux and corruption, and because of what the stage had taught him he would be able to devise a means by which his readers would have to participate in his tale of it if they wanted to know what was happening.

Such a way of writing fiction was all right for Gyp, he said in his Preface to *The Awkward Age*, but far from all right for a novelist with his reputation. Gyp was the *nom-de-plume* of Marie Antoinette de Riquetti de Mirabeau, comtesse de Martel de Janville, a delightful satirical entertainer who wrote almost entirely in dialogue highly readable pieces such as *Mademoiselle Loulou* and *Le Manage de Chiffon*, and who struck James 'as mistress, in her levity, of one of the happiest of forms'. But, as the sales of *The Awkward Age* proved, it was not a happy form for Anglo-Saxons who might consume it when it came in the shape of speeches across the footlights, but who would 'flagrantly reject it when served, so to speak, *au naturel*'. So accustomed to densely descriptive pages was the novel-reading public that 'an English, an American Gyp would typographically offend, and that would be the end of her'. The publishers, it was true, had always clamoured for plenty of dialogue of a sort, but they found 'dialogue organic and dramatic, speaking for itself, representing and embodying

340

substance and form . . . an uncanny and abhorrent thing . . .' Long-running plays made few people want to *read* what was being declaimed. Perhaps, James thought, he should have allowed the Gyp influence to show. While not pretending that she had no influence, he had kept the fact rather hidden. But although he read her light sketches with enjoyment she was too like the author of the French novel which Lord Petherton and Little Aggie romp over in Tishy Grendon's tainted house for his readers to think of her in the same breath as himself. Great writers can surprise their admirers by their occasional respect for what the latter would call trash.

The concept of a play-novel began to spin in his imagination even before it became necessary to find a project sufficiently engrossing to obliterate the first night jeers of *Guy Domville*. But so much had happened to him during this bewildering last decade of the century that he knew he would have to prepare himself like a writer at the start of his career before he could carry it through. It was not the time to bravely 'go on', it was the moment to begin anew. Mortality was everywhere. The theatre venture had run parallel with his young sister's long illness and death. Alice James had arrived from Massachusetts in 1884 (when he was writing *The Bostonians*) and had died from cancer of the breast ten years later. Unknown to Henry she kept a diary which, when they later received copies, shocked her brothers. Henry destroyed his, William made no mention of having ever received it. It was courageous about death and caustic about the British. Alice and Henry were devoted and close to each other during these London- Leamington years, and she – and after her death the diary – caused him to reflect on her fate, not as a middle-aged spinster, but as a young woman in a well-to-do family. '. . . in our family group girls seem scarcely to have had a chance . . . tragic health was, in a manner, the only solution for her of the practical problem of life.' He had written in his notebook, 'Youth, the most beautiful word in the language.' But what happened in youth? If one was a girl either nothing, or the ritual disposal of her purity to a husband.

Turning back the clock for himself, about to try his hand as 'another' writer, James began to look at human thresholds. Girls are growing up in his 1896-9 tales and are knowing. Maisie in *What Maisie Knew* is

341

an aware child who is too young for her brilliant inner life to be darkened by what she knows about the adults who surround her. Leon Edel recognises Maisie as the little Henry James, precocious, endangered, yet whose innocence is made safe by art. After Maisie comes *The Turn of the Screw* with Flora and Miles (a dead, seventeen year old Miles is briefly recollected by his brother in *The Awkward Age*). Whether they are polluted or not has long been a matter of necessary speculation. His 'little book' is how James described it, for unlike so many of the tales he now intended for the magazines, it hadn't galloped away with him. A story of similar length was offered to *Harper's Weekly* for $3,000, but it burst all bounds before he was a fraction of the path through it and he was obliged to tell the editor that 'I can't do the very little thing any more', and promised to try again. This intended 'very little thing' was *The Awkward Age*, and the reason why it wouldn't stay little was because he had switched from the pen to the reckless joys of dictation.

Just before leaving London for Rye his right wrist had grown painful. It was while he was working on *What Maisie Knew*. His brother William prescribed rest for the rheumatic arm and suggested that he should employ somebody to take-down his fiction. Thus, in 1897, there came the purchase which was to bring about an historic development in the English novel, Henry James's typewriter. Plus, and of equivalent importance, a typist to work it. Play it, one might almost say. There was also the all important fact that rarely again would the master be alone in a silent room during the hours of creation. From henceforth his mornings would be filled with the sounds of his own voice and the machine. The decided fatigue of long spells of pen and ink vanished, to be replaced by zest as his sentences rolled effortlessly on, or could be made to wander obliquely or fold back into parentheses. Most fascinatingly, this talking-down the tale made it possible for him to weave together the 'literary' and the vernacular with an otherwise impossible precision. Slang itself could appear as the *mot juste*. Dictation soon had a marked effect on Henry James's conversation which, from the time of *The Awkward Age* onwards, began to awe, puzzle and dazzle his friends with its circumlocutions. Not nearly enough praise has gone to that key figure of this period, his typist, a young Scot named William MacAlpine, who toiled part time as a shorthand-reporter and part-time as the near-miraculous person capable of taking-down the master's 'late manner'. It enabled James to be 'Proustian before Proust', as Edel put it.

But while for the novelist himself it was a swift, undrudging fashion in which to work, for his now long-established readership it was a very different story. *The Awkward Age* and subsequent novels for them meant getting down to work, and not having the old easy access to a favourite author's latest delights. In today's terms there could be an analogy with a good radio play in which the listener has to fill out all kinds of spaces by his own creative processes. James's public, accustomed to receiving every written action, inflection and description, blanched at this novel minimalism and was equally loath, on the other hand, to make the effort which was necessary to 'hear' talk set down with all the complexity and beauty of spoken music. And without any proper understanding of which there was simply no book.

The Awkward Age is approached via a welcomed upheaval in Henry James's life. With London exhibiting its hollowness, he had a craving for some pretty spot where he could be sociable outside his sacred working hours but out of reach of Society itself. Strong feelings for both cities and the countryside had always run in parallel with him. Cities had their areas of pollution when it was wise to forsake them. Under so many ugly pressures – gross display of wealth, the manipulation of the conventions for every kind of self-protection or advancement, the hypocrisies released by the Wilde trial, and much else – the decent surface had fissured and exposed what lay beneath. It was a sight to force his retreat so as to take stock of what was happening. The for so long toyed-with notion of a house of innocence far from the West End and what it represented was now a matter of urgency. The house would stand for the old values and dignity, and would be as unlike that in *The Spoils of Poynton* as it would be possible to imagine. Poynton is the temple to the god of acquiring, collecting and amassment. This short novel about a mother who values her *objets d'art* more than her son's happiness is James's preparation for the devastating criticism of society which would be given full expression in *What Maisie Knew* and *The Awkward Age*. In these stories it would not be an ageing moralist who condemned the loss of standards and the new vulgarity, but uncomfortably observant adolescents, young girls who were conventionally supposed not to see or hear what was going on.

During the summer of 1897 one of those little avalanches of coincidence which, though not uncommon in life, are best kept out of fiction, occurred to Henry James during a visit to Bournemouth. One day, immediately after reading a volume of the letters of Edward FitzGerald which W. Aldis Wright had edited, James went for a stroll and met and talked with the brother of 'Posh' Fletcher, the poet's fisherman friend. As if this were not coincidence enough, a letter inviting him to FitzGerald's Suffolk coastline awaited him on his return. It was from an American cousin holidaying at Dunwich. He went, and soon the five of them – the cousin had brought her three daughters with her – were exploring the neighbourhood. Two things had particularly struck James as he read FitzGerald's letters: the ancient resonance of place-names like Saxmundham, and the constant by-play made by the poet of his forsaking of society for cosy rural seclusion, his reluctance to come up to town, and his comically extravagant preference for being out of things. Although Fitz had been dead for fourteen years his presence seemed to pervade the little east Suffolk towns which Henry James was now seeing in all their remoteness. Extraordinarily remote to him was Beccles.

Soon after his return from Suffolk, James sealed his own withdrawn future by signing a twenty-one years' lease for Lamb House, Rye, at £70 per annum. The rusticated die was cast. It was there a year later that, now with full mastery of his new 'spoken' story telling art, he poured out to his stenographer MacAlpine *The Awkward Age*. Ignoring the limits set by magazine editors, he let the long novel flow on until all was said. The creation was swift and was completed between September and December 1898. It opens with Mr Longdon, an elderly bachelor from Beccles (he is fifty-five, the same age as the writer), waking up to the perils threatening society, and closes with his rescuing of a girl from a milieu which has long since made it impossible for her to know the meaning of innocence. The girl is

Fernanda Brookenham and she is the grand-daughter of Lady Julia, a woman who was the epitome of the old social virtues, and whom the youthful Longdon hopelessly loved. Fernanda – Nanda – will encounter the not too fustian remnants of these virtues at old, quiet, warm-bricked Lamb House which, in the novel, like the Santa Casa, has been wafted, lock, stock and gardens, from Rye to Beccles. Mr Longdon has to visit London after an absence of thirty-years to gain first-hand knowledge of its moral decline. Henry James has to abandon it after almost as long being part of its intricate social culture to gain a perspective on its failings. *The Awkward Age* is about the desertion of principle, about being young and growing old, and about what happens to young and old alike when they are caught up in one of society's periodic ethical scene shifts.

But as others have pointed out it isn't just Nanda's and Mr Longdon's generations which are at the 'awkward age'. With the nineteenth century nearly over and the twentieth almost upon them, all the characters are ill at ease and are without the poise of Lady Julia or the certainties of Mr Longdon. Mrs Brookenham, Nanda's mother, is exquisitely awkward and James's description of her helplessly running into obstacles, instead of being protected from all danger by her birthright, is just one aspect of the magnificent portrait he has drawn of a woman who is both captivating – and nothing. Her son Harold, light fingered and runtish, is decidedly awkward to have around. Her husband doesn't care enough to be awkward about her lover – which is subtly awkward for their friends. The lover, Vanderbank, is made awkward by his own attractiveness which is openly commented upon by both men and women. Mitchy is the awkward creature of the times, the millionaire tradesman's son who is too rich to be excluded from society. Lord Petherton sponges on him, as does Harold for trifling amounts, and as will the Duchess, in effect, when she captures him and his fortune for her niece Agnesina. The Duchess's relentless duenna-ship has kept every awkwardness from her Little Aggie, presenting her, immaculate at the altar, to Mitchy, who is not supposed to find Petherton's subsequent interest in her awkward at all. Only the servants reveal a complete absence of awkwardness as they announce entrances and effect exits, are sharply ordered about, and abide their time. 'Mrs

345

Brook' and her set, knowing that they see all, are cold and peremptory with them. James has taken them straight from a drawing-room stage drama of much door-opening.

The complexity into which Mrs Brook and her set, and most of all Mr Longdon, are thrown is as much the result of dawning freedoms as disobedience towards the old restraints. While underhandedly breaking the old rules they have no longing for change. Threatened by it, their response is either cruel and vulgar or, in one of the group's in-phrases, 'too beautiful'. (The handsome but invalid Jonathan Sturges, like Vanderbank aged thirty four, had been James's guest during the writing of *The Awkward Age* and had called the Rye fishermen's 'What Ho!' 'too beautiful'.) Too beautiful intentionally was the talk in Mrs Brook's salon in fashionable Buckingham Crescent, too deliberately clever and lovely for what lay behind it to show, at least not too realistically. 'There are more things [to talk about] in London . . . than anywhere else in the world; hence the charm of the dramatic struggle reflected in my book, the struggle somehow to fit propriety into a smooth general case which is really all the while bristling and crumbling into fierce particular ones,' said Henry James in his later Preface to the novel. Certainly a 'fierce particular' issue which was struggling from the 'smooth general case' at this time was that of the New Woman. Vivien Jones has drawn attention to the fact that *The Awkward Age* appeared at a moment when women's freedom and education were being hotly debated, and not long after the feminist Mrs Crackanthorpe had instigated in the press a series of articles on female emancipation under the title 'The Revolt of the Daughters'. James's sister Alice too had a very radical tongue on such matters, and while his Nanda must not be at all closely connected with a *fin de siècle* women's movement, her having her own sitting-room, latch-key, servant, her freedom to visit friends or receive them on her own, smoke, etc., and especially to decide her own future, do point to something stronger than lack of supervision. Though the last thing that she herself wants to be is liberated by such behaviour. Having the terribly unwanted knowledge of the free goings-on all around her, she would far rather be her grandmother Lady Julia than any woman of her own day. Mr Longdon saves her by taking her back with him to the ideals which her contemporaries are challenging. It is these, not he, that she weds.

And then there is the question of money, on the personality-distorting effects of which Henry James is as astute as Jane Austen. Mitchy the shoemaker's son has £40,000 a year, but the aristocratic Brookenhams, with their town house and their apparently modest place in Gloucestershire (they call it 'The Hovel'), have had to obtain a modest £1,200 a year to stay afloat. The rich but modest-living Mr Longdon pumps Van hard on the Brookenhams' means. Van is evasive. It is not that he thinks it strange or tasteless that such inquiries should be made on the very first night of their acquaintance but that, as somebody who himself contrives to exist in society on a small salary for which, unlike anyone else in the novel, he works hard, he wants to show Mr Longdon how they forget money at Mrs Brook's. 'She must have had something,' persists the old man, who of course remembers her background. 'Yes, indeed, she had something – and she always has her intense cleverness. She knows thoroughly how. They do it tremendously well . . . Oh, they're all right,' says Van evasively. Mitchy, much later on, more accurately reflects the group's hard interest in wealth when he describes Mr Longdon as 'bloated'.

By then the latter has made up his mind to '*doter*' Nanda, as the Duchess frankly puts it, and he would similarly *doter* Van if lack of money restrained him from proposing to her and making her happy. But Van has no intention of marrying his lover's daughter because she has been sullied by the too-free conduct of the Buckingham Crescent set of which he is the Apollo. Knowing that charmers must charm before the charmed begin to smell a rat, James allows us to like and even admire Van very much, until mounting evidence of his astute self-protection undermines our pleasure in him. Only part of his leisure is spent talking at Mrs Brook's; there are regular weekends at country houses where her son has witnessed his less cerebral diversions. His sitting-room is crammed with photographic trophies in rich frames, the pin-ups of the age. He doesn't love Mrs Brook, who is six years his senior though still very beautiful. Intimacy is achieved by the very free stylised talk for which her salon is famous.

347

But she loves him, and so does her daughter Nanda, needless to add. So would any woman. Van exists to receive the kind of love which he cannot return. But Nanda is not 'any woman'. Her mother knows this and it embarrasses her. Long before Nanda knows that Van will reject her, she has made up her mind to reject him because she recognises that, ungiving though he is, he is all that her mother possesses, all that she has. Such a profound understanding is further evidence of her undesirable maturity. Nanda has certainly acquired something during her unfortunate wanderings betwixt schoolroom and drawingroom – kindness and wisdom. There is the question of her plainness. Mr Longdon finds it incomprehensible. As she is the image of Lady Julia, how can she be plain? In this, as in every other matter to do with ageing men having to come to terms with changing values, Henry James is speaking highly personally via his *alter ego* from Beccles.

As he approached his fifties James became more and more preoccupied, not so much with lost youth, as with the varying measurements of childhood's comprehension of what it was witnessing. Nanda's was to be the ultimate degree of such comprehension to be placed beneath his microscope. The asexuality of children was part of the preferred Victorian dream and he was then more than ever before drawn to frequent explorations of this fantasy. Neither he nor his sister Alice had been able to refrain from the comparison of English and American girlhoods in particular, with their very differently set standards of freedom, education and protection. The novelist had long observed that in Britain these standards had been so ritualised that an adolescent girl was often neither free, taught nor safe. In much of Europe there was severity under the ritual, and a virgin could still be delivered ignorant to her husband-to-be. That she should be so was indeed the major duty of her mother. English mothers tended towards a conventional acceptance of the rites but did not press the rules. A woman who had been married from the schoolroom might well resent the sudden ageing which could occur when, still under forty, a replica of herself at eighteen, her hair up for the first time and ravishing in her first adult finery, descended to the drawing room. It was a piquant situation which attracted many writers. It is the opening dilemma of Ouida's novel *Moths* when Lady Dolly, aged thirty-four and the toast of the French Riviera, is unable to prevent her sixteen year old daughter from joining her. 'What on earth shall I do with her?' – meaning, 'How can I hide her?' English girls, coming out, were credited with the strengths of innocence, yet it was in ignorance that they were married-off, swiftly to give birth and thus set the entire guarded process in motion once again.

Mrs Brook, Henry James's most brilliant creation in *The Awkward Age*, was married-off in her teens, knowing nothing, to a nobody. They had four children, two of whom are kept well out of the story, two of whom provide its threats. Now forty, she sees all too clearly the wastes ahead of her 'lovely, silly eyes'. Whether the Duchess, her husband's cousin, was married-off to her Italian duke, we are not told. Certainly there appear to have been no wastes either before or during her widowhood. One feels that she made a career out of being a wife and is now making a second one out of being an aunt, a duenna in the grand continental tradition. Henry James is intensely interested in precocity, his Duchess dreads it. 'Don't understand, my darling – don't understand!' But when Mr Longdon is shown Aggie's photograph, one of the many in Van's bachelor rooms, he destroys the artifice by saying, 'She's very beautiful – but she's not a little girl.' Van then reveals his own sexual sophistication by lightly explaining that Italian girls develop early and, anyway, he never had been able to tell how old or how young girls are. However, he is quite inexperienced in the kind of relationship which is now rushing ahead over cigarettes in his rooms, after rain had forced him and Mr Longdon to leave Mrs Brook's in a four-wheeler. Their question and answer session leaves them mutually spellbound. What is admitted at this first meeting lays down the ground plan of all that is to follow. Opening the story by means of the beginning of a friendship between two men so ethically distant that they have to build all kinds of bridges in order to communicate is one of James's most fascinating devices. Here the old commonplace of fiction – the dramatic conflict ensuing from the injustice of there being one law for men and quite another law for women – is used to bring a startling new impetus to the subject: and this via the creaky old business of chaperonage.

Van's many affairs cannot impair his eligibility or make him impure. For sixteen-year-old Aggie even to have heard (and understood) about affairs could fatally compromise her as a marriage prize. For nineteen-year-old Nanda, a naturally intelligent young grown-up who can truthfully say, as any person her age surely must be able to say, 'there was never a time when I didn't know *something* or other and that I became more and more aware as I grew older, of a hundred little chinks of daylight', there is no eligibility at all. It has long vanished. Her mother knows it; it is why she no longer makes any semblance of constraint.

Leon Edel suggests that we may see in Nanda and Aggie a double projection of Henry James himself in late adolescence, that part of him which was continentalised by travel and nourished with the forbidden fruit of French novels, and that other side of him which was the serious young literary novice making what he could of his native New England environment when he was Nanda's age. The young are violated most by conventional forms of social protection, and by the not-so-young's erotic interest in the stages of their maturing. The manner in which the Duchess promotes a sensual interest in Aggie's purity, though expert and socially admirable, comes close to that of a bawd. Nanda, on the other hand, with no 'purity' to display, emancipated from all this little-girl whiteness, has access to the many shades of existence. This is what terrifies her mother and her circle. Aggie and Nanda, says Henry James in his Preface, 'were projected as small things, yet finally had to be provided for as comparative monsters'. One of them had been removed 'from the sphere of the play of her mind' by early marriage, the other had not.

The Awkward Age is fitted together in ten books or sections which are made to span Mr Longdon's remembrance of his past and Nanda's contemplation of her future. His history determines her fate. Although Book One is entitled 'Lady Julia', it is really about her unsuccessful lover's sudden wish to follow up the careers of her descendants after many years. He expects their London to be very unlike his, but is bewildered by the changes. Like Edward FitzGerald, he exaggerates his Suffolk provinciality as he catechises Van. 'You do put one through!' says the young man who finds that although his elderly new friend has no presence, he had 'somehow an effect'. Mr Longdon pumps him shamelessly for facts. Blatant questions on his income and habits are put in order to loosen him up for the real information required, that on Nanda. It leads Van to a denunciation of London's vulgarity and corruption which is Henry James's own criticism of the life he has fled from.

'But beauty, in London . . . staring, glaring, obvious, knock-down beauty, as plain as a poster on a wall, an advertisement of soap or whisky, something that speaks to the crowd and crosses the foot-lights, fetches such a price in the market that the absence of it, for a woman with a girl to marry, inspires endless terrors and constitutes for the wretched pair – to speak of mother and daughter alone – a sort of social bankruptcy. London doesn't love the latent or the lurking, has neither time, nor taste, nor sense for anything less discernible than the red flag in front of the steamroller. It wants cash over the counter and letters ten feet high. Therefore, you see, it's all as yet rather a dark question for poor Nanda – a question that, in a way, quite occupies the foreground of her mother's earnest little life.'

This is the ferocious London which jeered at the first night of *Guy Domville*. Van, who is more part of it than he would wish, and who has already privately likened Mr Longdon to a priest, opens his worldly heart to this probing visitor. 'You see we don't in the least know where we are. We're lost – and you find us.' It is Mr Longdon's intention to do more than just find Nanda, he means to save her, to free her from the smart cant which masquerades as high culture and emotion at Buckingham Crescent.

The florid Anglo-Italian Duchess with her loud and certain pronouncements is the foil to Mrs Brookenham and her now fearful uncertainties. The Duchess has 'bloomed in the hothouse of her widowhood', as Van cattily puts it, and now she is exclusively and entirely engaged in damping down the slightest sexual fire in or around her niece. Fanned by marriage, let them rage as they will. 'Mr Longdon's impenetrability crashed like glass at the elbow-touch of this large, handsome, practised woman who walked for him, like some brazen pagan goddess, in a cloud of queer legend.' We hear of her 'acquired Calabrian sonorities, from her voluminous title down' and can see her as the perfect Edith Evans role. The Duchess urges Mrs Brook to marry Nanda off . . . 'soon . . . and while you *can*'. Men won't marry girls who have been 'pitchforked into everything'. Mrs Brook defends her failure to prevent Nanda from discovering about life by saying, 'The sort of men *I* know anything about. . . . are not looking for mechanical dolls. They're looking for smart, safe, sensible, English girls.' Unconsciously she gives herself away. Nanda is not safe. But neither has she been 'pitchforked' anywhere; she has gone where she has gone by her own free will – even to Tishy Grendon's unrespectable house – and as a natural part of growing up. The verbal battles between Mrs Brook and the Duchess are comic and serious, the dialogue sparkling and tender by turn. Mrs Brook's pitiful situation is seen in all its vulnerability as troubles beset her from every side, to her bewilderment more than anything else. Why is she, Lady Julia's child, in this position? How did it happen? In her beloved salon is she talking her way into relationships which are superior to affairs, or talking her way out of a disaster? Her helplessness and her wit are entrancing. They make her desirable to the reader but not to her family and friends, not really. She is spellbound by their disenchantment, and alone when they are present. Her predicament is great, but no Mr Longdon comes to save *her*. She would like her daughter and herself to live together like two intelligent women, neither concerned with what the other does. What is happening to them is happening throughout society – 'We're all in the troupe now . . . and we must travel with the show.' Nanda 'has her little place with the circus – it's the way we earn our living.' The Duchess is impatient with Buckingham Crescent's art-form conversations. She has returned to find that 'most English talk is like a quadrille in a sentry-box'. Like Mr Longdon, she has been away from London long enough to find nothing as it once was. She booms forth on vanished values, not comprehending that she is giving them too foreign an emphasis. She is a monument from Henry James's wanderings in Italy, and he delights in her stage worthiness, giving her plenty of good lines.

Her opposite is Mitchy, the boot-manufacturer's son. He has no pretensions, which is just as well in that circle. He is young, pleasantly ugly, badly dressed and enormously rich. At the beginning of the novel the Duchess insultingly suggests that he might do for Nanda – 'We must take what we can get, and I shall be the first to take it.' Not many pages pass before the Duchess takes him for Aggie, he with his tolerance, awkwardness and his 'little deep-down delicious niceness, and sweet sensibility', plus, of course, his barnacle-like friend Lord Petherton to bring Aggie out. Nanda does not blame her; it is her way of discovering her identity, and she has a right, at sixteen, to behave badly. James spares the reader not a jot of the coarseness of the Victorian marriage mart, and through Mr Longdon and Nanda he makes a plea for the virtues of the single state. Mr Longdon's wealth is used, not to catch her but to free her. Asked about marriage, Nanda says, 'I shall be one of the people who don't. I shall be at the end one of those who haven't.' She goes to live with Mr Longdon, the man who should have been her grandfather, at Beccles in all the serenity of Lamb House. Nanda's independence is awesome. She has not come out, she has stepped out from all the trammels with which society confines and restricts women, and will do as she likes. It is, if one may be allowed a pun, a wry ending.

Leon Edel sums up this conclusion with characteristic percipience:

Mr Longdon achieved what Henry James had done all his life – harbour within his house, the house of the novelist's inner world, the spirit of a young adult female, worldly-wise and curious, possessing a treasure of unassailable virginity and innocence and able to yield to the masculine active world-searching side of James an ever-fresh and exquisite vision of feminine youth and innocence. For this was the androgynous nature of the creator and the drama of his novels; innocence and worldliness, the paradisial America and the cruel and corrupt Europe – or in other variations, youthful ignorant America and wise and civilized Europe.

In no earlier novel had James called British society so to account. *The Awkward Age* records his complete disenchantment.

Just as at a party or gathering one makes a stab at what is actually occurring, what is really being said, below or beyond the flood of talk and sociability, so one must make an effort to see and hear beyond the quicksilver talk and very slow movement of *The Awkward Age*. It is the surface alone which leads one to the story's depths, this shimmering surface which rises without warning to glitteringly dangerous points, or lurches into blackness and vulgarity. Mrs Brook's own talk attracts multiple conclusions which, drawn as they are from the conversation of a woman who uses her own drawing-room as a confessional, make one apprehensive and questioning. The action is sparse, the talk torrential. The diarist Ivy Jacquier, after reading *Portrait of a Lady*, commented, 'He writes no novels, it is one long frieze and he depicts a part, and what he does not depict goes on, before and after, like life of which one can only know one part.' In *The Awkward Age* it is customary to see only Nanda, Aggie and perhaps Mr Longdon as innocents who are, in their different ignorances, getting to know what is going on. But what of those who think they know, like Mitchy, or are sure they know, like Van and the Duchess, or who cannot bear to know, like Mrs Brookenham? Or, more crucially, the reader himself? The curtain has gone up and will, in Chapter XXXVIII, come down on something perfectly dramatically begun and ended, but with nobody knowing all they should, the reader included. Self-knowledge can be obtained only at a cost, at being defiled by 'knowing'. A conventional marriage alone permits a young woman to 'know', and thus proceed to self-knowledge. Aggie is thrust through the convention by her old-fashioned aunt so that she can break out, not settle down. Nanda, self-aware, dismisses marriage.

DICKENS TAKING NOTES

The Observer, 1960

In the early 1830s the *Morning Chronicle* sent its lively young representative, Mr Charles Dickens, upon tortuous journeys into the political bad-lands of East Anglia. His duties were to edge his way from the inn to the market-place and, amidst the shrieking mob which rocked the hustings, to obtain first-hand news of William IV's legislators. The coaches were freezing, the roads cruel, and the boroughs, as is well known, rotten. But the elegant Dickens loved it all, and particularly those warrened halls of hospitality, the coaching inns, where beef and beer made the climate, and in whose buried snugs the best conversation, as well as the oddest humanity, could be found. There he saw Tupman and Winkle in the flesh, gathered in femaleless conclave around Mr Norfor – or, if you will, Pickwick himself. The stag of stags.

Every town had these conversation-pieces, gossipy winelogged meetings of persons of substance rather than gentlemen of means. Mr Glasspool the grocer, Mr Moon the chandler, Mr Absolam whose lady maintained a seminary, and, of course, Mr Norfor/Pickwick their secretary, honourable, benevolent; the amiable totem around which they revolved.

How often we had imagined those evenings, the candles polishing the faces of those to whom the town, its streets, gardens, houses and inns, belonged long before we were thought of. Then one day it was all revealed to us, softly, like a cottage interior when the wicks are turned up. There before us were Mr Norfor's minutes impossibly spiralling in what to the Society was a fair hand, but to us is a miracle; the full gamut of quillmanship. Here for us are the goings-on of the Great Yarmouth Society of Friends, instituted on October 29, 1769.

None of the fourteen rules tells us why the Society was formed. Just that thirty-one gentlemen were to meet every Tuesday evening at the Old Half Moon; which injunction, perhaps, was reason enough. The madeira has certainly got into the minutes. What did they talk about? Mr Norfor doesn't say, but their actions receive all his attention, and we know that the junior member snuffed out the candles and that, of the original thirty-one, eight members were expelled for bandying the Society's affairs about the streets of Yarmouth. Mr Norfor called it contumacy. There were sharp raps, too, for social failings. 'The manner in which you left the Society was not with that politeness as might have been expected.'

Distinguished strangers peregrinating Yarmouth were entertained. There was Mr Waddy of the Theatre Royal, Norwich; Captain Steward the Wandering Piper: Mr Miles, miniature painter to Queen Charlotte and Mr Scraggs the Comedian. We feel that Mr Scragg's visit was providential, for in August, just two months before he arrived, an event of truly Pagliaccian tragedy had occurred. In calligraphy which grief compelled to be exquisite is this entry:-

August 1793. The Society met to pay the last tribute of Friendship to their late Secretary (Mr Norfor), who was unfortunately killed by the Gaff of the Wherry falling on him . . . when on a party of pleasure the 8th inst., being the annual water-frolic. . . .

The festive barque falters at the estuary, its great sails slack. Fiddlers consort in the bows. Over the decks clamber the Society, already wondering about the wine, the cold partridge. Pleasantly detached, intangible as Mr Richard Wilson's Carthage, dips Great Yarmouth in the August heat. All is gaiety. All is friendly. Mr Norfor smiles beneath the fatal gaff. And then the homecoming with the fiddlers silent and the hock unregarded and Great Yarmouth no longer opalescent, but a very dull town indeed.

But life goes on, and if mortality and contumacy should reduce their numbers there were always fresh young apothecaries and dusty old captains to come forward and bring up their strength. Romance, too, is given a place:-

This evening Mr Martin complimented the Society with a five pint bottle of wine upon his embracing the connubial Rites.

What would be more Tupmanesque, more Snodgrassian, even?

And then it was not all piping captains and queen-painters. Sometimes it was the very great who visited them:-

Lord Nelson arrived this day in Yarmouth. Many of the members of this Society spent the evening at the Wrestlers and were honoured with his company.

That is all. Not a word of what the great admiral said, his pale face made paler in the ham-hung gloom, his patch dark as a void above his cheek. Was he cold or convivial? Did he hug the fire as slender people do, or because it was warmer in Naples? And what on earth did he say to Mr Glasspool the grocer and to Mr Moon? We suspect he ate little and drank less, but was happy because he was home in Norfolk again.

And so it continued until the 1830s, when Mr Norfor's successor noticed a youthful reporter lolling in the public rooms of the Wrestlers (or the Rose and Crown or the Great White Horse) and, because he seemed a droll lad with something to say of the world outside, he invited him into the snug, where a good deal more of the ways of Yarmouth (or of Ipswich or St Edmundsbury) might be learned than those apparent in the High Street. So Dickens nodded and noted, ripening for the splendid betrayal.

MUCH OBLIGED JEEVES

P. G. Wodehouse, 1971

The reason for the learned valet's choice of employment, mysterious even to the experts who have now been on his trail for fifty years, remains comfortingly opaque in Wodehouse's new novel. When Bertie bursts into Jeeves's 'lair' to engage in a descending scale of asininity one might marvel at Jeeve's patience, but one never expects anything less. Once only in the latest helping is Jeeves excused by his master from rising when he enters the room and this, not because he is deep in Spinoza, 'Bertie's Christmas present', but because he is nursing the cat. Cats for Bertie, as for Pelham, are holy beasts.

Jeeves's basic function of seeing that Bertie is properly turned-out in the right togs has certainly been somewhat eroded. Jeeves's once unflagging determination to get his gentleman in and out of quiet suits all day has flagged considerably. But the sartorial eye, like that of King George V, and that of his militarists, is still pretty unswerving. In the early novels Jeeves's constant overriding of Bertie's doggedness in the matter is both a demonstration of power and, presumably, the keeping alight of the frail flame of civilisation. 'There is no time when ties do not matter, sir.' But Bertie has not lived for fifty intimate years with his servile guru without picking up a scrap or two of fashion philosophy. 'Turtle-neck sweaters,' he declares 'are a royal raiment when they're worn for virtue's sake.' He is defending some 'probably frightfully good chaps' who had chucked eggs at the Conservative candidate for Market Snodsbury. Jeeves, who has never attempted to hide his own humble origins – which would have been impossible anyway as his family network wields a sort of supra-domestic power throughout England – refuses to know anything about these jerseyed protestants. A strange admission for one who is frequently up to his dickie in 'the poet Burns'.

The action takes place in Aunt Dahlia's country house in Worcestershire during an 'election, when all and sundry have been called to the aid of the Party. Ginger Winship has to be winkled into a far from safe seat. Aunt Dahlia's bait for the apolitical is gouts of *Suprême de foie gras au champagne* cooked by Anatole, her chef. The house and park are fairly thick with pests on account of this. Bertie's sole attempt at canvassing falls flat, his victim all unbeknown to him being the rival candidate. Ginger Winship is just as foxed and would have been sunk had it not been for the support of that deplorable old spellbinder, Lord Sidcup, whose mesmeric Tory hwyls are famous for starting landslides.

The election needless to say, is merely the trivial front to conceal the serious business of settling Sidcup's hash, restoring the stolen register of employers to the Junior Ganymede Club and a bit of stolen silver to Aunt Dahlia. Also to rearrange the courting pattern of various platinum blondes so that marriages are staved off. In the confusion of the hustings Jeeves's first name – Reggie – slips out into full view, which is no end of a leg-up, and also oddly reminiscent in terms of literary restraint of the single instant when we hear what Mr Knightley was christened.

Bertie, born aged about twenty-five during World War One, and Jeeves, who shimmered into view a year or two later, are amongst our most sublime anachronisms. They are denizens of the idyll and, as such, the prey of valet-snatchers, hag aunts, bounders and matrimony. It is significant that they made their debut in America. They have been kept afloat on the Pals' Code laid down in letters of vanilla during Wodehouse's own public school days. Bertie possesses only one gift (like Lord Havershot in *Laughing Gas*, 1936), which is 'for getting things out of people's eyes'. Motes, maybe. Jeeves has enough gifts to take him to All Souls. If there is a moral, then it is certainly against the rules to mention it. Wodehouse's apotheosis of British innocence is, like the 'Choirboys' Bicycle Handicap', open to all those whose voices had not broken before the first Sunday in Epiphany and it offers the longest free-run of comic pleasure paced on a typewriter this century. While Jeeves mutters *Medio de fonte leporum surgit amari aliquid in ipsis floribus angat* as he is serving breakfast, Bertie mangles a kipper and observes: 'Yes, I think we may say everything's more or less oojah-cum-spiff.' And so it is.

DARKNESS VISIBLE

William Golding, 1979

The new Golding is a chiefly malign work which, in spite of the presence of the charred saint who wanders through it, gives few directions for recovery. One is thrown back and forth by the constantly alternating brilliance and obscurities in the writing, as well as being brought to a critical standstill by a sequence of great scenes, such as that with which the bitter tale begins.

It all starts during the London blitz, and with the borrowing of two of the most celebrated literary images drawn from that conflagration: the collapse of a vast building whose hollow window aperture mercifully coincides with the spot of ground on which the firemen are standing (William Sansom's 'The Wall'), and a pentecostalist vision of the burning city, out of which strides a boy, naked but for his 'intolerable shirt of flame' ('Little Gidding'). One of the boy's firemen-rescuers is a bookseller, appropriately enough, for this maimed and nameless East End child is to become a man of the Book, a bible mystic, a Blakeian innocent who believes himself to be so near to the Word that ordinary speech is like the ejection of stones. Isolated by disfigurement, to some degree sheltered by it, he communicates via a journal which he writes somewhat in the style of a follower of George Fox. In this scarred *inconnu*, dubbed Matty by the skingraft nurses, who constitutes a kind of one-man travelling enclosed order in a wicked world, Golding has invented one of his most compelling characters.

Virtue on the scale which Matty so guilelessly practises is essential, for the rest of the action involves first, that peculiarly British form of furtiveness and retribution which is still profitably maintained by the popular Sundays; and second, current trends in socio-sexual amorality among the young, as well as a completely new brand of heartlessness. It reveals the allure, moral ignorance – rather than innocence – and treachery of children being carried forward into a maturity that now constitutes an entirely fresh type of behavioural squalor. Look around you, Golding is saying, and see what is being condoned. Not fluttery old boy-lovers like Mr Pedigree, of course; see, rather, the pitiless faces of beautiful and cruel young adults who operate their lives outside all the understood affiliations, particularly that of fellow-feeling. The latter is understandable; how can you join in a sensation you have never had? Golding's punkish people are not youngsters passing through a stage, as they say, but the anarchic phenomenon of our times. The smilers with the knife, pad-bred and outrageous. A middle-aged novelist's pronouncement of anathema upon the nastier extremes of our subculture? Partly – and partly, also, a transference of his compulsive watching of the ill-will of children to that of these dreadful new adults, only to find how similar it is. Except that as it is now fired (if this is the word) by sex and politics, it could all go a lot further than we care to imagine. Golding himself imagines what makes Sophy and her friends tick with a fascination which puts him in danger of moral disgust. He is deeply involved in the actions of the immature, and in seeing just how far they can go.

The story leads off in various directions which ultimately converge.

There is Matty's direction, which is heavenward; Mr Pedigree's, which is to the dogs; Sophy's, which is towards being a moors-murderer; and there are the traditional directions followed by most of the men and women they encounter during their strange odysseys. Matty travels as far as Australia, where an Abo, who has never been the same since taking part in a wildlife film, nearly does for Matty's manhood – an incident which is the trailer for the revolting climax to Sophy's search for a thrill. The analysis of the personalities of Matty as the mutilated being who carries salvation within him, and Sophy as the mutilator who echoes with all the vacuities and self-centredness of the Seventies, is extraordinarily powerful. In outline, such a tract is familiar enough; but Golding fills it in with ancient symbols and modern frightfulness until it rocks our reason, like the Book of Revelations itself. His getting into Sophy's head is a remarkable achievement. As for Mr Pedigree, classical scholar, pederast and old silly, his is the classic English cropper. Here Golding shows a man being made to loiter and fumble in marionette-like obedience to the role to which society has degraded him.

Holding the strands together are what might be called the trans-generationists, the people who carry over-page the manners and hopes and notions which belong to a Fifties or Thirties concept of life. Fido, the narcissistic athlete, is one of these naive old souls who although young in years, are so handsomely encased in jolly decent attitudes that they are incapable of seeing what is creeping up on them through the multinational high streets, the nihilism of pop music and the tabloids – and out of a hole hacked through civilisation itself. Greenfield is the provincial town where all these paths meet. It contains a public school, and some charming remnants of its recent past that are in the process of being vividly transformed by African and Asian enterprise. Oil princelings worth a ransom attend the school. Sim and his friends at the bookshop vaguely deplore these developments, and hark back to the days when those perfect little ladies, the Misses Stanhope (Sophy and her twin), epitomised the perfect Englishness of the place.

Thus it falls to Sophy to put her bomb under the town. It misfires, and creates infinitely more horror than even she could have hoped for.

Matty makes one last blazing, saving gesture, Pedigree, one last pass before the insistent gaze of his detractors, and Sophy her first infant victim. For the next few days, Greenfield is all headlines about terrorist kidnappers. It is this shorthand of our hour which Golding spells out, telling us about it in a narrative which is much convoluted by his need to drive home his own tortured vision of a society which is becoming more and more at the mercy of the infantile. For it is they who are best able to invent, and then act upon, extreme solutions, for everything from the mystery of God to the riddle of pain – and they now do so daily.

Sophy's ghastly moronic 'truth' appeared as the dictum: 'The way towards simplicity is through outrage.' 'Honest to God, Sophy,' says her boyfriend, 'I don't know what you're on about.' But we, listening to almost any news bulletin, can gather the gist of it. Not even Matty's incandescence can do much to lighten this murky story.

THE PORNOGRAPHER

John McGahern, 1979

Towards the close of this life-affirming novel which rides full pelt into the wall of cant that we have erected around some of the unavoidable human experiences, John McGahern makes one of his characters, the porn-broker Maloney, ask why the Irish are so keen on coffins, fantasist and wildly permissive about them in fact, and so repressive about sex. 'We master the darkness with ceremonies,' remarks another character as he puts the lid on Mrs O'Doherty, boxing-in the heroic flesh which has at long last conceded the victory to cancer, twisting down the silver screws shaped like crosses. Everybody who wanted to have taken their fill of her mortality, have glutted themselves with its excitements, giving themselves up to God knows what sensations, and all of them perfectly legal, of course. To gloat by the grave is a very respectable thing to do. But to have glimpsed that act which brought the admirable Mrs O'Doherty into being – what shock, what revulsion!

This is a lively tale about the cult of two national morbidities, that which treats sexual joy as the final obscenity, and that which surrounds death with emotions which have little to do with grief. John McGahern isn't against mourning, indeed he approaches it in the noblest of terms. Neither is he anti-marriage and legitimate ecstasies – in spite of his nonconformist hero. What rattles him is how slow Ireland is to examine and throw out most of its death customs, and to replace them with life customs which aren't smutted all over with superstitious guilt. Those who cannot face up to either morbidity he allows to hurry off to the bar – 'I have nothing but praise for drink. It is like a change of country.'

The handsome young hero describes how there is another escape route to more interesting territory than that which is mapped out for one by the conventions, a land of erotic possibility and absurd impossibility where, guided by Mavis and the Colonel, they can achieve bliss, or at least a good laugh. Mavis and her friend are the lovers in a pornographic serial which the young man scribbles for cash, detachedly at first, or so he believes, but soon with the realisation that one cannot provide sexual pleasure for others without providing some for oneself. He is a village boy doing well (doing ill, the repressionists would say) in Dublin. His family thinks that he is getting on as a journalist. They too have been drawn into the city because of sickness and the novel's more bizarre and randy lessons are backed with the poignancy of Mrs O'Doherty's sufferings in the hospital. She is his aunt and he blunts her pain with brandy (purchased with funds from Mr Maloney, his poet porn-broker who retails the adventures of Mavis and the Colonel).

As so often with illness and death – yet one more of Mr McGahern's percipient realisations – those who are most closely in contact with disease and departure frequently discover a strong vitality and sexual restlessness within themselves. His daily dose of porn on the page and his affectionate and deeply understanding visit to the hospital ward completed, the hero takes himself off to the dance hall to find a woman. 'We met much like we met – like most of Ireland meets – at a dance.' The woman is husband-hunting with all the artfulness of a thirty-eight-year-old and the young man needs to exert all his skill and sexual honesty not to be trapped by her. She writes for a magazine for river and canal enthusiasts and is more bewildered than horrified when she reads what he writes. He narrates an entrancingly funny-sad account of her desirability, hypocrisy, wildness and astounded recognition that nothing she can do, including getting pregnant, is going to get him to the altar. He is telling her that if she is going to play these antiquated tricks she must take the consequences. Fortunately for her, a booby takes pity on her and makes her an honest woman. The affair allows McGahern to explore a mating game which cannot be won by honest rules. She has convinced herself that she will have got her beautiful boy for keeps by the oldest ruse in the courtship book, by not taking precautions and then registering moral concern. It says everything for McGahern's art that he is able to present this banal affair and its predictable and vulgar consequences with wit and taste. Hoist on her own petard, if that is not too apt a position in the circumstances, the woman at once calls for all the traditions of religion to assist her. But who has seduced whom? Her final disaster, except it isn't quite that, is to find that her liking for his body has deepened into a love for him in his far from admirable entirety, whilst he feels nothing at all. Anyway, the pretty nurse on the cancer ward offers happiness without such complications.

The question of the pornographer's amorality and cruelty would loom large were it not for his attitude to his dying aunt. In it the reader sees what the women he sleeps with could never see, the compassion and tenderness which are somehow divorced from his sexuality. The hospital visits and the gradual coming to the end of Mrs O'Doherty and the coming to birth of his child, each process as slow-moving and dark as a river, also bring together the strong currents of countryside and city, winding them in and out, yet proving their essential separateness. The scenes with the sawyer uncle are masterly, with their delicate clashing of rural wisdom and integrity against the brittle notions of the town.

What will be immediately asked, of course, is, 'Can we believe in the pornographer as such? Does he know his trade?' Some lengthy and comically thrilling extracts from Mavis and the Colonel present very convincing credentials. They also present the entire and ubiquitous subject of modern pornography in terms which demand a scrupulously honest and personal reaction. It is this, rather than the hero's pale imitations of his fictional exploits, which gives one such a jolt. This and the marvellous writing which is so sharp and at the same time so soft that it is hard to make up one's mind whether one's prejudices are being spiked or simply spirited away.

WATERLAND

Graham Swift, 1983

This book is yet further proof that something very remarkable is happening to fiction, although exactly what it is, is too early to say. It is as if, after decades of doing everything imaginable to catch the reader's eye, the novelists have recently captured his total attention.

A handful of writers, Graham Swift now among them, have set a new pace. His *Waterland* is written in what might be called the first-person-instructive. It is the teacher's tale. And what a story. A freshly redundant teacher, to be exact, a plight which provides him with the necessary incentive to view all that has occurred to him with irony and circumlocution.

Country people who find themselves in sole possession of some key facts see little point in surrendering them without going through a lot of narrative twistings and turnings. Swift emulates the eel, the creature whose coiling progress most influences the Fen folk in their 'land of Nothing' in his storytelling. He knows how to hold crucial information back in order to make the reader crane forward, and how to do that fascinating old thing, visit the sins of the fathers upon their children.

It is dangerous territory, this basic rural one of sexual melodrama and preferred indigenous darkness but Swift winds his way through it with enormous skill. Because so few have dared to set foot in it for quite a long time, he has the advantage of being able to treat it like new ground. To have created the wrong kind of interest, or a smile, would have been disastrous – but no fear of such hazards. The novel is perfectly controlled, superbly written, and, as they used to say, riveting.

It explores the paradox of the wide-open Fens and the shut-in people who inhabit them. Place and its dwellers are seen indivisibly; the human blood system and Vermuyden's sluices and dykes course along fretfully together. An historic isolation drains through the Crick family and it isn't quite natural to find Tom Crick washed up at a Lewisham school.

But Swift makes it a dull urban prominence from which to survey those black and glittering flats sprawling from Cambridge to the sea. His history master has come to see reality as uneventfulness, flatness; and history as the drama which obscures it. He describes how each of us raises 'in the flatness of his own unsung existence . . . his own props and scenery – for there are very few of us who can be, for any length of time, merely realistic.'

Thus these sensational goings-on in the dead-level stage of the Fens. The initial tragedy is caused more by first sex than first love. The lock-keeper's sons, one bright, the other a potato-head, vie with their friends for the favours of Mary. The potato-head is not actually the lock-keeper's son, but a child of his wife's by her father. This boy can swim like a fish but is otherwise a zombie. When another lad gets drowned and Mary pregnant, the children, for they are little more, cope with these huge disasters as best they can.

For years they lie, like the dreadful evidence of false starts, deep beneath the surface, before rising and bobbing about, and threatening what everybody involved has come to see as their history. Who killed Freddie Farr and who impregnated the saintly Mary? Dick the wanting eel-boy, too daft to know his own strength? But who in reality created all this drama by the River Leem in 1943? Ancestors? The Fens themselves? But, listen, listen. Your history teacher wishes to give you the complete and final version

And so Swift traces the watery roots of middle-aged Mary's action when she steals another woman's baby in the supermarket, trailing them all the way back to the village abortionist (hideously memorable), and those of her husband back even further to the madness of the first World War, and the madness to be found in a particular Coronation Ale, and again the need for men to do an act because they can't bear the flat Nothing in which God has placed them.

The conventional sights of this countryside, Hereward the Wake, the Newport Riots, and (wonderfully well written) Dutch engineering, flap behind Freddie's murder and Mary's teenage pregnancy like posters. *Waterland* is original, compelling and narration of the highest order.

WATSON'S APOLOGY

Beryl Bainbridge, 1984

When they abolished the death penalty, they cut off one of the main supplies of sensation required by the British soul. Shorn of the ghastly etiquette which handed a hitherto respectable person, preferably middle-class, from his home to the public hangman, murder has lost all its old frisson. Repetitive attempts to rebuild the gallows might be seen as part of the conservation movement, a national plea for those nosey old shivers without which life cannot be lived to the full.

Beryl Bainbridge restores us to a Britain at the zenith of its morbidity, to a land where poring over the fate of the accused was as unapologetically enjoyable as poring over anything from a menu to the Scriptures. There were heaps of homicides and executions to glut on, but the really thrilling ones were those involving the solid bourgeoisie. She tops the list with the Reverend J.S.Watson, headmaster and classical scholar, who on an October afternoon in 1871, after church and luncheon, battered his wife's skull to a pulp with a pistol butt. She was 64 and he was 67. There was no glamour, no money, no mistress, nothing except that most intriguing of all façades, a conventional house in a residential road saying nothing to nobody, and with a servant to open its door.

Novelising murder is often the only way of comprehending it. Where a murderer is concerned, the legal, medical and prison reports are frequently like a huge pile of rubble so far as his person and personality are concerned. Only an artist can make them into a recognisable human being, and this, rather than a search for motives, or for further terrors, as Mrs Belloc Lowndes offered in *The Lodger*, has been Beryl Bainbridge's task: to give us John and Anne Watson in reasonably good nick before they fragmented all over the newspapers. There has been much research, but the Bainbridge genius has not been restrained by it, and the telling pages are not those of her careful documentation, but where she darts free to give vignette after vignette its due as only she knows how. Harbours, schools, the dentist's, the prison cell, the Clapham streets, but most of all the various rooms in which the Watsons find themselves. 'Remember I have always been a private man,' he implores the police when they come for him. The intention here is not to invade such a privacy but to present it.

Watson's Apology, as well as being a wonderfully sad entertainment based on a popular form of Victorian crime, is a rare study of the compulsive literary drudgery of the period. Watson was more upset by Longman the publisher calling him an unsuccessful author during the trial, than by anything. Beryl Bainbridge doesn't try to prove that his biographies of Porson and Warburton, his translations of the classics for Bohn's library and his monumental history of the Papacy are fit for anything but oblivion; what she understands is the absorption of the work, the impossibility for a man like the Reverend J. S. Watson of not constantly writing, and the frowstily pleasant atmosphere which the regular toil created. It gave him poise and protection until he was ceremoniously sacked (a fine silver salver) from the headship of the Grammar School, then no protection at all. It was one thing to return daily to the barely educated Irish Anne who tippled, walked about in her petticoat, had the deplorable Mrs Tulley for croney, and ran after the Clapham funerals, and another never to be shot of her for an hour. People noticed Mrs Watson's 'searing glances of calculated insolence' and felt sorry for her learned husband, who never complained. Mrs Watson was bold and odd, Mr Watson hoped to write an essay explaining why there had to be an Established Church. He went in for near-lunatic acts of Christian charity, she savoured with Mrs Tulley 'the ruthlessness of Irish humour'. Incessant erudition on his part only just kept her at bay. A dreadfully memorable picture emerges of a woman who is like a large, untrained pet for whom it is too late to learn to act reasonably.

Their thirty-year-old initial correspondence is produced in court and forms the first chapter. Beryl Bainbridge's method is to write a novel between different groupings of such papers and not fictionalise them. Their facts launch her imagination. The wedding-night scene on the packet bringing the Reverend Mr Watson and his bride to England from Dublin is masterly, he craving, she both ladylike and uncouth. The real investigation starts here, and it is not of a murder but of a marriage – of the enigma of many marriages, and of murder in certain circumstances as a marriage rite. For a long time the slight disgust which overcame Watson when he first touched Anne Armstrong kept them tolerably close. But when his world fell apart and he was left with nothing but her, he bludgeoned his way out of the mess. After being sentenced to death, reprieved and imprisoned for many years, he asked for a Greek New Testament, Seneca, etc. He would study and write again. The Directors of Convict Prisons thought that he would use such books to encode messages, and escape. He was eighty. He died from erysipelas of the ear contracted when he tumbled from his hammock on to his tin pot. This is Bainbridgian domestic melodrama of the deepest dye and artistry.

A MAGGOT
John Fowles, 1985

LAST LETTERS FROM HAV
Jan Morris, 1985

If there are still those who need convincing of the novel's unique ability to explore and explain what often history itself cannot, they should without delay read *A Maggot*. It is about the power and purpose of dissent in Christianity, and the real reason why orthodoxy has feared and repressed this element, crucial though it is to what Christ taught.

By means of a quite astonishing ability to re-create the colloquial language of early-18th-century England, itself a sufficient reason for grappling with this complex tale, and by his grasp of its moral, sexual and political climate – in itself an amazing imaginative feat – John Fowles allows the reader to become part of a present, rather than to stare into the past. It is here that the drama lies, in our being made to share the very air of the months which followed 'the late and last afternoon of an April long ago', or the spring-to-autumn of 1736. As though conscious of our difficulty in breathing such strong gusts of it, Fowles every now and then breaks into his own clever time trap with schoolmasterly facts. The device works well. It also permits him to put his own philosophy into the action, so to speak.

The story gradually emerged from a recurring dream of travellers riding through a deserted landscape (to where?) and the acquisition of a watercolour portrait of a young woman dated 1683. The dream and the picture provided the irritants which, in the pearl-making process, have to be coated with substance, interest and worth. Three men and a woman are journeying through the West Country, which according to the thinking of the day is all so much desert. They are respectively a young peer, an actor, a celebrated London prostitute and the peer's manservant. The girl has made her reputation at a St James's bordello by playing Virtue being overcome – a peculiarly exciting sexual role. Her face is pure and she looks like a great saint. At the inns en route to Bideford, their alleged destination, the little party causes comment.

The questions for the reader are, is it on some ordinary business, or on a quest for something which might cure his Lordship's impotence? Why are the peer and the handsome, halfwit servant so close? Why doesn't the girl suffer corruption in spite of what has, and is happening to her? Gradually it is she who begins to dominate the pages, not as flesh but as spirit.

The novel then moves towards its series of alarming interrogations. The servant has been found hanged on a tree, a suicide. The peer has vanished. All who saw the travellers on the western journey are in the dock, the girl last of all. She is pregnant with the servant's child, but married to a Manchester blacksmith. She is born again, though not in today's Madison Avenue terms, which Fowles despises. She is to become the mother of Ann Lee, founder of the United Society of Believers in Christ's Second Coming, or the Shakers. His interrogation chapters are masterly question and answer exercises on those aspects of Christianity which the Church has always done its best to withhold, far preferring instruction to letting in light. Fowles has a genius for spinning things out and holding things back, for enticing and teaching. *A Maggot* is sensuous, learned and wholly original. It is also a formidable addition towards an historic understanding of feminism.

A delectable hitherto obscured city announces itself in the gazetteer – Hav. If you are still longing, one way or another, to set foot in Hare Hatch House or maybe Xanadu, you will certainly want to get to Hav, if only for a week. Jan Morris sustains her journeying jeu d'esprit to the very last page, striking just the right note and being just sufficiently relaxed to avoid farce. Part of the fun is to recognise that, if you have done your share of Mediterranean wanderings, you will have already met with more or less everything that Hav has to offer. This wonderfully boring place is founded on the clichés of the Med's literary circuit. Its seedy architecture and torpid rule, its predictable sins and its familiar inhabitants are as comforting as the favourite decidedly un-grand Grand Hotel into which we tumble in preference to some Hilton.

Hav is that minuscule state which no scribbling traveller from Lady

Hester to Robert Byron could ignore. Its name appears in a thousand memoirs and histories, poems and novels, and no doubt in *Mein Kampf* and all such works of philosophy. And so it was inevitable that Jan Morris, that constant visitor to its region and excellent guide to the glories of the eastern European coast, should add her tribute.

Alas, we may need to postpone our package tour to a city which can include Noel Coward, Herr Hitler, Lenin and Njinsky (of course) among its short-stay guests, because no sooner had Miss Morris gathered her notes than warships gathered in the harbour. So not for us the thrills of the Roof Race, the Levantine langour and the cabarets still echoing with the Hot Club of France. Until Her Majesty's po-faced agent, Ronald, gives us the all-clear we shall have to console ourselves with Jan Morris's authoritatively funny book.

THE NEWS FROM IRELAND
And Other Stories
William Trevor, 1986

THE FISHER KING
Anthony Powell, 1986

News not only from Ireland, but from England and Italy too, that special Trevor intelligence which here gathers up a triple-stranded look at life. This dozen of his latest stories is beautifully fleshed-out in both senses of the term as bodies carry on their hopeless battle against souls. He is a master of disengagement, disappointment and just making-do. His characters, mercifully, are not quite up to fully comprehending the extent of their particular tragedy. This is for the reader's eye alone.

What Trevor himself sees, and predominantly in pubs, cafés and restaurants, where very private arrangements are momentarily exposed, are degrees of lack of judgement, lack of taste and lack of capability. Solitaries make one error of not remaining solitary, that far from regrettable estate to which God has called them, dreamers the mistake of attempting to realise that some realities are insubstantial. Just a few of his folk live and learn, as it were, and make sensible if heartless breaks with anyone or anything holding them back from what they recognise as the direction which their common sense tells them they have to go.

But these tales, for all their sad themes, are never bleak, and never less than tremendously enjoyable. Trevor is the kind of storyteller who appeals to a kind of fiction-seeking glutton, on account of his generous hand when it comes to setting the scene and introducing its inhabitants. Such unstinted rich detail, such a frequent feeling for us of often imagining that we are well into some spacious novel. This deceptive leisureliness – for the writing is actually economical – is Trevor's hallmark, his purely Irish artistry, and is derived from his knowing that the storyteller's skill involves a mixture of good manners, perfect timing and an exact amount of information, plus of course whatever is required to provide pleasure.

He structures the humdrum, the ordinary. While quite merciless with his people, the middle-aged in particular, he never produces a grotesque, and he has a wonderful way of showing a man or woman with their bodies and minds marked by all that they have heard, seen and done since the 1940s, say.

The title story is about an English family's intrusion on Irish grief during the potato famine. The Pulvertafts from Suffolk have inherited a country house, and their reaction to a national disaster is on the face of it charitable. Starving villagers are made to build an unwanted road in order to be paid a subsistence. Entire communities die, or sail away to America, despite the soup. The English governess adds what is really an unconscious condemnation of what is happening by keeping a diary. Trevor himself keeps all these Irish-English attitudes within hungry '40s' limits.

The rest of the stories are modern but with long roots. They are about people who have either lost their sexual and emotional confidence, and thus unable to take an opportunity or chance when it is presented to them once or twice on a plate, as it were, or who have become over the years coarse-grained and undesirable without

373

knowing it. The 57-year-old travel-brochure writer picked up in Florence by the beautiful Mrs Faraday, a nice American in search of a holiday companion, belongs to the former category. She can never know what he can never forget, those few humiliating attempts of his in the past to be a lover.

He extricates himself from her advances, she presumably takes a chance with a man who knows all about rich ladies who are more in search of passion than of paintings, and is murdered. The nervous writer continues to wait for her in a cocktail bar, listening 'to the music she'd said she liked, and mourned her as a lover might'.

In *Bodily Secrets* a handsome widow who knows that her figure is far from being as attractive as her face weds the kind of man who will never want to see her without her elegant clothes, and escapes from her ruthless son and her dead husband's fat and sweaty pals. *On the Zattere* is about a father and daughter's relationship coming to grief because he lacks the dignity and restraint necessary for a man of his age.

Lunch in Winter has much the same theme, except that here it is a woman who chats up those young enough to be her children. Trevor is marvellous at evoking the manners and style of what might be called the immediate pre-pop era, with its different innocence, and he has a vivid understanding of the little quirks of behaviour which, as much as anything historically profound, define a generation. The invalid boy who writes with the kind of delicate amorousness which alters the existence of those who receive such letters is an example of how accurately Trevor can touch a nerve of the recent past. He also refuses to allow the breaks to show: life just runs on whether one is watching Linda Darnell or *Dynasty*.

Anthony Powell's new novel sets a group of today's power-wielders acting out an Arthurian myth. A tough Fleet Street editor, a pair of avant-garde musicologists, a bestselling historical novelist of the kind who sells millions of copies without ever being reviewed, an industrialist and his formidable doctor daughter are part of a group on a culture cruise to Orkney, or Ultima Thule, the end of the world. But the entire ship is mesmerised by the presence of Henchman, the celebrated photographer, and his ravishing girlfriend Barberina, a ballet-dancer who abandoned her career for him. He is an ageing cripple, impotent yet devastatingly attractive to women.

The voyage encloses these fretful passengers, and they are seen having to cope with their outsize egos in a confined situation. Although they are thrusting creatures from the contemporary free-market society, they are also trapped by some kind of mystical requirements. They are playing ancient roles, and are not free at all. Among them are a few individuals who, had it not been for the etiquette of life aboard ship, would have had no access to people such as Henchman and his fashionable colour-supplement circle.

The celebrities and the non-celebrities are shaken together by the sea and by the laws of the myth which has engulfed them. All the gossip and speculation are centred on the famous photographer and his mistress. When they split, as they must, where will she go? How can he exist? *The Fisher King* is vintage Powell, original; memorable.

CLOSE QUARTERS

William Golding, 1987

As *Rites of Passage* draws to its close with the burial at sea of poor Mr Colley, the Anglican clergyman who died of shame, Captain Anderson tells Mr Talbot not to forget to include in his journal 'that whatever may be said of the passengers, as far as the people and my officers are concerned this is a happy ship'.

Seven years on finds Golding's ancient Australia-bound man-o'war-turned emigrant carrier running into weed. Should they push on for Sydney Cove or make for the river Plate? It is Tarpaulin (sailors' talk) and Millinery (ladies talk) which impede Mr Talbot's cheerfulness. However, he has managed to purchase a new folio manuscript book from the purser and is filling it with the events described here.

When *Close Quarters* ends he is 'envisaging with gusto the three splendid volumes of Talbot's Voyage, or The Ends of the Earth!'

Talbot's first diary was written for the eyes of his noble godfather, and thus with an eye to the main chance, but his second is written for himself.

The novel which contains it opens with a disaster which can only remind the reader of recent happenings. Lt Deverel leaves an inexperienced midshipman at the wheel in order to go to his cabin and have a drink. A sudden squall tilts the ship and brings the masts and rigging down. No souls lost but smithereens aloft.

A splendid farce follows. A sail is sighted and the wildest patriotic hysteria sweeps through crew and emigrants alike. Boney is about to conquer the Antipodes and has sent out a flyer. Mr Talbot begs for a cutlass as the Captain declares, 'I shall fight!' However the flyer turns out to be HM Frigate *Alcyone* under Captain Sir Henry Somerset. Boney is beat, he announces, so huzza for King Louis XVIII.

The emigrant ship and the frigate are then lashed together for the purpose of a celebration ball. Finery is dragged from trunks, music (a bit Tarpaulin) is made and a grand dance is held on a Coleridgean ocean. It is a glittering Golding episode. Sir Henry is accompanied by his frumpish wife and she by Miss Chumley, who is too young to be anything other than pure and lovely. Mr Talbot loses his heart to her even as he considers whether he might do better than a parson's daughter.

Somewhere during the festivities the careless Lt Deverel is exchanged for the *Alcyone's* Lt Benet, a stunning beauty. Mr Talbot's heart sinks every time he sees him. What with his looks and what with his energy and ability what chance would he have with a girl who had been twenty-seven days out of Plymouth with such a god?

Yes, the new officer tells Talbot, he had a good time on the frigate, but with Lady Somerset, not her companion. She had simply kept *cave*. Talbot is as appalled by Benet's wanting an ageing woman as he is by knowing what Miss Chumley has seen.

He is now beginning also to have a bit of trouble with his status. When he first came aboard his manner and his astute references to having a peer for a godfather brought him the sobriquet 'Lord Talbot', to which he gradually found himself becoming entitled. But a necessary friendship made in the interest of having someone in his journal to be a feed for his observations undermines this fantasy. The friend is Lt Summers, a plain man with no pretensions. Summers calls him 'Edmund,' which is both comforting and disturbing of rank.

But then we are nearing Australia, Summers lectures 'Lord Talbot' and the god-like Benet – 'Those who go down to the sea in ships can sometimes find themselves in a combination of circumstances which produce an appearance of malevolence! I do not refer to storms and flat calms . . . but to small events and minor characteristics, to odd exceptions and unstatistical behaviours'.

Golding's trilogy is turning out to be a great sentimental journey of the naval kind. The grasp of what travellers thought, knew, or were ignorant of in 1815 is uncanny. As in *Rites of Passage*, the huge, cumbrous old fighting ship reeks and creaks on the page.

He is the poet of male conceit and of young men's uncertainties. The women are a kind of precious luggage being hauled down under with as little damage as could be expected in their situation. Now and then they break all hearts in this lurching wooden capsule, bound really for God knows where, by a movement or a look straight from some decent London drawing-room or from the shires. When Mrs East, who has been ill, sings a country folk song, for instance.

This is how it must have been. Something is being kept from these ladies, and from the seamen for that matter. It is that they are not aboard what the intelligent Lt Summers would regard as a ship any longer but trapped in a floating hulk. There can be no help. The party over, the *Alcyone* is far away, people fall about and hurt their heads. Dragropes are used to release the weed. Why on earth did the Captain agree to sail such a hulk? Because officers who refuse a ship never get another.

The final chapters dealing with the cutting away of weed and coral to free the ship are as good and strange as Conrad at his finest. There are soldiers as well as a good mix of emigrants on board, a marine artist and fast learners like young Mr Talbot, but all must give way to the seamen.

The crisis is cathartic. It leaves the journalising hero buoyant and able to take a wonderfully sentimental farewell of Mr Summers after the latter hears that he has been immortalised in the journal. Golding flicks comedy into the tale simply by means of letting men attempt to put their sincerities into words. 'Edmund, I adjure you! Be a writer!' the hero tells himself as he opens the purser's clean pages, and this vast maiden voyage may well be that of a Georgian novelist learning his trade.

Cocky as Baron Boswell, vulnerable as the likes of him must always be in proto-New South Wales, reticent when it comes to who and what he really is, we shall await his conclusion with interest. This is the trip to maturity which only a few of us make.

THE MASKED FISHERMAN
And Other Stories

George Mackay Brown, 1989

Here are twenty-one winter's tales by someone who, uniquely now, spans the gulf between short-story writing and story-telling. This collection shows the Orcadian master at his peak. They are tales of all times, from the distant past to the immediate future, with the characters and their islands maintained in a continuum. Whether Norse or twenty-first century, people do not progress, do not get any better or any worse, but fall into the categories which make up a working community and its culture. The chief divisions are sea work and land work, youth and age, saintliness and savagery. The style is hard and sharp, like the monoliths at Stenness. There is a ruthless narrational pull of the reader's full attention. Real storytellers do not have to hope for a listening ear; they simply begin.

A popular novelist of no true merit goes back to the wrecked croft from which his grandparents migrated and discovers his soul. A pair of actual poets who lived hundreds of years apart, Bjarni Kolbeinson and Edwin Muir, are seen as having sat by the same hearth of Wyre. The White Horse Inn at Hamnavoe, today's Stromness, and George Mackay Brown's epicentre, is visited by its regulars, and they are made to personify today's Orkney, farmers and fishermen, townsmen and crofters.

Women are briefly lovely then a long time cantankerous and clacking. Men are briefly angelic then a long time disappointed and toil-battered. There is a staggering story about a bright boy who got himself to the university and then came home to write a never-ending book which would have taken him to the grave had he not regained his wits and gone to the fair. The stories are crowded with children, all trapped on their home islands, all coming to grief before they can come to joy.

The descriptive writing, especially that dealing with landscape and with rooms, is honed and spare. The dialogue is full of easily used archaisms given with a 'find out the meaning for yourself' nerve. While nobody talks like this in Orkney, nor ever did, we are made to hear its permanent ancient language. Mackay Brown uses it liturgically, forcing it to carry great meaning. Place, people and action, and time itself, are all made to struggle against the wind, for whether it is AD 700 or AD 2050 it is mostly December, though summer gets a look in here and there.

The islands' history contains just a handful of great names, a few earls, a saint or two, some legendary poets. These celebrities are wanderers. They loot Ireland, Byzantium, Norway, Rome and Jerusalem, not of the usual treasure but of verse forms, music and dances, carrying them back to Orkney, there to be hardened for local consumption. The one big omission is the wartime history of the twentieth century and the naval graveyards, prisoner-of-war camps and the defensive litter of concrete on a heroic scale. The Viking saga-line cuts its way through all this recent and alien junk like a laser, ignoring it completely.

George Mackay Brown has a habit of prefacing his books with a note of regret at the storyteller's fireside stool having to give way to the television set, but his own stories are then made to prove the opposite. He works within the old tradition, yet everything he writes is bright and new, and displaces the normal sequence of historical events. The reader is made to feel contemporary with its islanders, whether they are medieval or modern. He is very good on Orkney's loners, on its shipping and ecology, on the rough stateliness of its inhabitants and on the benefits and drawbacks of an isolated world.

The observation is exact. How deep-sea sailors always have a 'cosmopolitan accent', how at Easter it is 'difficult to tell whether a grey lump in a field was a sheep or old lingering snow', how 'young men and women from different villages, occasionally, looked at each other with enchanted eyes' and how during summer storms 'last night, for hours lanterns thronged clifftops and shore' as the wreckers fall on a 'chartless ship', only to discover that its passengers are frightened actors and its cargo harps, flutes and masks. A travelling theatre en route from Galway to the Low Countries. George Mackay Brown's Orkney is a country where a workaday people are always running into art and revelation, and where toil and climate tear them to bits.

THE NASH CATS' STORY

Ronald Blythe, 2003

These cats were named Queenie, Mad Doll and Wewak. Queenie was orange, Mad Doll was a tabby and Wewak was a brindled tom. Wewak was named after the Japanese garrison on the New Guinea coast which General MacArthur by-passed during his sweep to the Philippines during the spring and summer of 1944.

The three cats lived together at Bottengoms Farm, Wormingford, which was a sloping kind of place on the banks of the Stour. In summer they baked under gooseberry bushes and in winter they singed in fenders. Queenie was one for putting on airs and graces, Mad Doll was given to unexpected leaps and turns, and Wewak knew his place, which was on anyone's lap. Mr Nash regarded them all with weary affection, and his wife with her brisk form of love.

Their origins were virtually untraceable but they liked to think of themselves respectively as a Cedric cat, a Pearce cat and a Hairy-

Knees cat. Sir Cedric was a gardener who painted in his spare time, the Pearces lived nearby at the Old Vicarage, and Hairy-Knees was of course Mr Algernon Gibbs, the famous weaver who wore the kilt.

Mr Nash could be capricious when it came to entertaining cats in his studio, or so they thought. Should he glimpse a mouse or hear a rat it would be: 'Wewak! Wewak!' But should Queenie or Mad Doll make up a nice bed on some old watercolours and lie there peacefully sniffing the turpentine, it was a very different story: 'Out! Out!' And with military oaths.

When December came, Mrs Nash, who felt the cold most cruelly, would gather up a cat or two for creature warmth. Often all three could be found spread over her, their toes tangling in hanks of silk as she embroidered under her Aladdin lamp. And she would amaze her husband by begging him to bring her 'the tiniest little drink, darling, because I don't like to disturb the cats'.

Mr Nash, his 'art-work', as he called it, finished for the day, was probably playing Schumann on the Steinway. There were evenings when he sat down and the keys went *thunk, thunk*. Mad Doll was in the piano along with mislaid invitations to private views and cigarette ash, soft pencils and a lost page of *Träumerei*. Curses and entreaties, and then a flying emergence. Mrs Nash would then run after Mad Doll to soothe her fractured nerves. Later, to show that there was no lasting hard feeling, Mr Nash would draw Mad Doll's portrait. All three cats were passionately fond of music and could never get close enough to it.

The cats knew that the Farm was better than anywhere else on earth. It had a broken-backed barn, pigsties full of tall nettles, a granary full of mouldy canvases, some of them masterpieces, a garage filled with junk, a pump-room filled with martins, a cracked greenhouse, a track filled with holes, a horsepond filled with newts and a garden full of surprises.

And yet Mr Nash would abandon it – and always during the best weather. It had to be done, else they would all starve. Dorset had to be painted, Skye even. 'What is going to happen to us?' mewed Queenie, Mad Doll and Wewak, and they looked up the number of the local RSPCA. Then they remembered! The young Poet would take care of them!

Like all young poets he was beautiful and indolent, lying in the sun and reading novels all day, but with pen and paper handy just in case he became inspired. Queenie, Mad Doll and Wewak found him restful. And how innocent he was! For it was no great difficulty to con him into believing that they must have four meals a day. And there was that memorable day when cat four arrived, or rather slunk about on the fringe of things. He was feral and black and almost as beautiful in his way as the Poet, with lustrous green eyes and a tail to die for. Mr and Mrs Nash's final words to the Poet before setting off to Cornwall were, '*Do not approach him.*' They advised the Poet to chuck Blackie his grub and steer clear of him. Their very words. The Poet, a naturally obedient boy, did as he was told, but after his friends had driven off to paint Cornwall, each day Blackie and he faced each other across a strip of lawn, and each day the distance between them grew less until, on the fifth hot morning, the feral cat was within touch of his bare feet. It is impossible to describe the courage of the Poet at this crucial moment. Did he run away? Did he shout 'Shoo!'? No, he put out his hand so that Blackie could give it a lick and a promise. Soon they were in each other's arms. Later, when the artist and his wife returned to find the Poet and the feral cat curled up on the sofa, they said that it made them think of Isaiah 65 v. 25.

With another little mouth to feed and all four cats in cahoots regarding four square meals a day, the Poet was in and out of Mr Kerridge the butcher's and Mr Green the fishmonger's twice a week. He went to their shops on his bike and was received politely but unenthusiastically, for it was scarcely a profitable business. '*More* lights?' '*More* cods' heads?' They laughed. 'I reckon he's tuckin' into them hisself', said Mr Kerridge to his lady assistant, causing the Poet to blush.

Recipe for Lights
Peel bloody paper from the lights and place them in the lights saucepan. Cover with water and boil. Leave the kitchen or if necessary the house. Cool. Strain.

382

Lights = sheep's lungs, which are light. You learn something every day.

Keep juice. Cut the lights up with the kitchen scissors, splash with juice, which should be grey, and serve on tin plates.

Recipe for Cods' Heads
Ditto, except bone.

A further bike ride was to Sir Cedric's house, Queenie's ancestral home, or so she liked to think. The baronet's cook Lett would be reading Elizabeth David, his feet in cats. Art students were everywhere, lolling out of windows, up trees, drawing each other, clinging to easels, showing off in the Life Class, lost in flowers, and all kept busy. For Art was the best thing there ever was next to Love and Food. Sir Cedric and his cook were delighted to see the Poet and would spoil him. They would place him next to their friend Kathleen 'Moggie' Hale at dinner who wrote scandalous books about cats and she would enquire about 'the Bottengoms mob'. She had a little fringe and a little Roman nose, and she would tell him all about her tom-cat Orlando who had brought her notoriety and wealth beyond the dreams of average. She had a charming voice, the Poet decided. Both Sir Cedric and his cook had appeared in her books (the cook as a fiend called the Katnapper) which caused them to be half flattered and half riled. Everyone hoped that the Poet was working and not skiving at Bottengoms, for there was nothing like toil. The art students sighed.

Sir Cedric read the Orlando books in a somewhat mystified manner, remarking to Moggie Hale, 'Do you mean to tell me, Kathleen, that you have hung your slender reputation on the broad shoulders of a eunuch cat?'.

Since it has been brought up, it should be explained that the 'doctoring' of cats in those days could be a hit-or-miss affair, and love would often find a way. Which is why so many Nash, Pearce, Cedric and Hairy-Knees kittens changed hands.

These Nash and Cedric cats were immortalised by their artist friends, usually of an evening during chat or the radio, as they dozed on chairs and sills. Their somnolent fur and closed eyes would draw from their owners looks of profound affection. Home was not complete without them. At Bottengoms the poet read Henry James or L. P. Hartley to Mr and Mrs Nash, to background purr, and until they dropped off. It was then that Queenie, Mad Doll, Wewak and now Blackie, would become suddenly wide awake and flee into the adventurous night.

DIVINE LANDSCAPES

PLACES OF INSPIRATION

James Pipkin, 1990

A grand concept. Those who made it possible for the author-photographer to carry it out – journeys to thirteen countries and all five continents – were clearly men of faith. James Pipkin is a young Washington attorney and this handsome book is the fruit of a sabbatical spent wandering round the globe visiting the places where God or the gods spoke, or where even today's shallowly motivated tourism is brought up, if only momentarily, to a thoughtful halt.

Such a list of holy sites must necessarily include some of the world's most familiar scenes, such as the Taj Mahal, Ayers Rock, Standing Stones, the Alhambra gardens, the Swiss Alps, the Ganges, Lascaux, for long the subjects of many picture-books. But the charm of this book, and it is charm rather than anything in the way of fresh revelation, is that Pipkin has the kind of innocence which somehow persuades us that what is new to him is new to us. His text is no more than extended captions but it is personal, and it includes some memorable lines – 'A quiet place does not ensure a quiet mind'.

There are five sections: Deserts, Caves, Mountains, Seacoasts and Gardens. One of the difficulties was finding that a place renowned for centuries for its silence was now loud with packaged trippers. In this respect the Taj Mahal just scraped home. But then he was anxious not to limit his choice to places beyond the reach of the average traveller, which was courteous and sensible, for in a somewhat extravagant sense *Places of Inspiration* is a good elementary textbook for those who recognise that the ordinary guide with its dates and scientific facts is low on immanence. What is this height called Sinai, or Horeb, or Gabal Musa all about?

Sinai provides some of his best pictures and observations. It is much climbed, unlike so many holy mountains, which frown on impious feet. The inclusion of Mont Blanc and the Matterhorn should have been accompanied by a mention of Matthew Arnold and those half-mystical Victorian climbers and reading-parties. But Pipkin did find a group of Americans singing 'Nearer, my God, to thee' at 10,000 feet, which showed how basic theology can be.

Pipkin's own spiritual journey seems to have been achieved when he had to get up early to catch the dawn light, or else when he captured sunsets. Now and then one gets the impression that he is trying to photograph Awe, which is a mistake. And, as with so much contemporary photo-journalism, there is a great dominance of matt-blue sky, and of the use of silhouette. Fearing that I could be wrong in finding the sheer expertise of some of the hard-edged pictures so uninteresting, I glanced at Fay Godwin's *Land* (matchless black and white, of course) and knew why. It is simply that for me the wonder has vanished from the results of technical perfection.

But Pipkin too has his magic camera. There are some ravishing photographs of ritual cleansing in the Ganges, the courts of the Alhambra and some English woodland gardens which he sees as the 'descendants of the sacred grove'. One of the latter is not a garden at all, but Wiston's Wood on Dartmoor, which he describes in non-ecological language, rather like an apprehensive traveller from another century. He notes our appreciation 'of the benefits of solitude among trees' and quotes Edmund Waller. He is full of surprises.

Books such as this, and Tony Hiss's startling *The Experience of Place*, are essentially questioning today's easy mass travel. Devoid of all elements of pilgrimage, sacred or secular, how can these site-seeings inform or refresh? The beaten track now leads anywhere you fancy in the brochure and is smoothed out by the tour operators. But, as the Lord asked in another context, 'What did you go into the wilderness to see?'

James Pipkin wants us to go where he feels the spirit still lives, in painted caves, among the megaliths of Scottish islands, in certain sublime buildings, in Japanese Zen gardens, in Cappadocia, the home of the Early Fathers, in Monument Valley in the American south-west, on the Balinese coast and in California. Getting around on this scale – he grouses about the weight of his cameras, having to wash his socks and having to spend 'more than a hundred nights by myself in anonymous hotels' – drove him to meditation, as indeed it would anyone. Having briefly encountered every race and clime he wisely, if not originally, concludes that 'we are all in it together'.

THE ATLAS OF SACRED PLACES
Meeting Points of Heaven and Earth

James Harpur, 1996

Off we go once more with our scallop-shell of quiet and a volume such as this to the tombs and the shrines, to those monuments which still have something to say to us, and to those which are silent and enigmatic. James Harpur is a lucid guide with an intelligent approach, and he brings fresh views to the most trodden of destinations. There are plenty of simple picture-maps and a vast spread of bright photos from a hundred picture-libraries. But the text is the thing. It is eloquent and thoughtful, and often we do not feel that we have been here before, or if we have that we missed something of crucial importance.

We are on our way to hopeful graves, to profound temples, to where miracles challenge medicine, to serene domes which are full of prayer, to sublime follies such as the pyramids of Giza and to once bloody corners like that in the north aisle of Canterbury Cathedral. Harpur gives the correct archaeological facts but adds his own lively asides. He is a sensitive traveller who realises that he would be doing no more than covering familiar ground if he did not give his own strong views of it. He is philosophical and contemplative, and he writes well. Who could ask more of a guide? So here is a good glossy map, but with an absence of smoothness in what it covers.

The chair-borne or air-borne traveller has in 1996 to ask himself where he is going, and why. And does he arrive too easily and too soon? Even kings once did the last mile barefoot. Re-visiting these enduring monuments via this *Atlas* one realises that there should be more preparation than going to the travel agency or getting the car out – more uncertainty in the actual approach to them. 'What went ye into the wilderness to see?' might be the big question, for in some ways, where great numbers of tourists are concerned, all these sacred places are sited in religious and cultural 'deserts'. These centres of ancient enlightenment do not just stand there like abandoned arenas, they continue to beckon. They teach and they defy. Thus to stand in the theatre at Ephesus, or upon the holy mountain, Kailas or Sinai, or to creep through the stone corridors of Megalithic princes, the 'preliterates', as Harpur calls them, is marvellously unsettling.

His tour begins with the restlessness of the world's spiritual leaders. God-filled men who themselves found it necessary to put down markers in the landscape so that the rest of us could halt in our life's journey and hear and see things which the rest of the natural landscape and its artefacts were unable to reveal to us. Jews and Christians, Buddhists and Muslims have all laid great stress on their geography. Each faith has its holy land. Now and then the saints attempted to escape the demands made on them by a country. They longed to be nowhere. St Columba's reason for going to Iona was that he could live there without seeing Ireland. Harpur tells the story of this famous settlement, as he does all the other well-known tales of spiritual movement, with a choice of words which avoid the travelogue, and with no fear of sounding at times awed and halted in his tracks.

The hopeful graves include barrows and ship-burials, pyramids and that of the first Emperor of China, Shi Huangdi, a man absolutely terrified of dying. So much so that he had drawn up round his tomb six thousand terracotta soldiers, none facially alike, and all with swords and spears at the ready. Time has taken their arms from them and their hands clutch air. Rather like Hitler, Shi Huangdi believed that his dynasty would last ten thousand generations when it collapsed after only fifteen years.

There is something majestic still about the Megalithic bone-holes, the noble barrows on their hills, whereas the immense tombs of the pharaohs reflect a monumental and, to us, crazy self-concern. Harpur's description of Karnak manages to sweep away the indignation and bafflement which the visitor to Egypt often experiences when he is regaled with the tonnage of the pyramids. Karnak was to the Nile kingdom what a medieval cathedral still is to us. From the many sublime cathedrals which Western Europe has to offer he chooses Cologne, and from among the mosques, Isfahan 'shimmering above the horizon through the glassy distortions of the liquid air'.

It seems that humanity has always required a temple and a public space, some spot where an individual listened to God, and an heroic tomb. These four basic requirements have created what we still all search for – what we all continue to travel towards – on the sacred atlas. Our pilgrimages are now practically effortless and because of this it is likely that we return with more architecture and art in our heads than numinosity. Harpur does his best to put first things first. He is scholarly and is himself often inspired by what he has come to, and he often makes the point, though not in so many words, that pilgrimage and a trip are not the same journey.

FOOTPRINTS OF THE NORTHERN SAINTS

Basil Hume, 1996

And who trod in those footprints from boyhood on? The author himself. It makes this little book, modestly presented by him as a tie-in to a television programme on Channel 4, so much more. The simplicity of its learning and the insistent autobiographical element remind one of another tie-in-book – to a mission he held in Oxford in 1960 – by Michael Ramsey, *Introducing the Christian Faith*. The rich ingredients of great scholarship and personal faith have, in the culinary sense, been 'reduced' to their essentials. What occurred on the Northumbrian coast during the seventh century not long after St Augustine's mission to Kent has affected British Christianity to this day. Had it not done so the eleven-year-old child at Ampleforth might not have become a monk. Officially, Celtic Christianity was short-lived, being absorbed into the Roman tradition at the Synod of Whitby in 664. Spiritually, it touches the heart and the imagination still, and is too much alive to be seen purely historically. *Vide* the Cardinal's own life.

Getting the saints in the right order and rescuing the clan kings from obscurity is necessary if we are to come into close human contact with Lindisfarne, Durham and that immense seascape where the wild prayers were said and the poetry was made. This is the land of England's most enthralling monk-bishops and their Irish ways. 'I want you to join me, and follow me, in this pilgrimage to meet these great personalities . . . In spite of the difficulties of their time, they managed to create what was in many ways a Golden age within the Christian story . . .'

The immortal characters in this particular history were/are St Augustine's assistant St Paulinus, King Oswald, St Aidan ('to my way of thinking, the perfect pastor'), the formidable St Hilda, that exquisite cowman-composer Caedmon, St Theodore of Tarsus, St Bede, showy St Wilfrid and matchless St Cuthbert. The latter's constant striving to be a hermit, when the local church insisted that he should be its bishop, reminds the Cardinal how, when he was Abbot of Ampleforth, he refused to allow one of his monks to become a hermit, and how wrong he was. When at last he let the monk withdraw to the Yorkshire moors to be with God, he remembered St Cuthbert's giving up his bishopric after only two years, and sailing away to where he knew he should be, lonely Inner Farne.

There are many saints and territories which can no longer communicate with us, so much have they been obscured by time and development. But nothing at all stands between us and the Celtic vision of Christ. Given the kind of map which Basil Hume offers, and this not from books but from his own loving experience of Northumbria and its holy people, we can travel easily to this sacred place. Just to stand by Cuthbert's tomb in Durham Cathedral, with its one-word inscription *Cuthbertus*, clears the dense ecclesiastical air. The nippy gales of Oswald's shore blow away whatever cultural or other barriers there may be which keep us from making contact with a thrilling aspect of the faith.

The virtue of Northumbria is that it is sparsely furnished, so to speak. But what artefacts Christian hands have made, and what prayers Christian hearts have uttered in that otherwise glorious coastal emptiness just happen to be sublime. Take *Footprints of the Northern Saints* with you whenever you drive north of Scarborough or look out of the window of the coast-hugging train to Edinburgh. You and I, as the Cardinal reminds his readers, are the journeymen of the post-Christian age and we need to see more than perp. and dec. and dates. Something as well as ecology.

STRANGE LANDSCAPE
A Journey through the Middle Ages

Christopher Frayling, 1995

And what a journey – a tour de force. Finding one's way to and through the cathedrals sans Baedeker and Pevsner is a necessity if we are to see what those who built them saw. The very term 'Gothic' (barbarous) was one of abuse and, like most of our current perceptions of the faith and artistry of these years, has to be ditched before we set out. The notion of there having been a 'middle time' of European history which held up Graeco-Roman civilisation until the Renaissance managed to release it, and the Enlightment to sanctify it, has allowed us to view these centuries as non-progressive. Even their mighty saints, poets and artists have been confined by their times and recognised as victims of the medieval mind. Worse, this mind has been made to serve later fantasists and provided stuff for many a dark tale. Even to politely call this period the Age of Faith implies that it possessed a credulity from which later ages would have freed themselves.

Christopher Frayling will have none of this. Strange country though it is, his map of it is not the quaint and curious one of 'here be dragons' etc. On the contrary, it guides us through a glorious territory equal to any which stretches before and after it. It is a racy look-around, slangy even at times. But we get there. Its Christian philosophers speak with a fresh coherence, its famous lovers breathe, its ideas are a revelation. The only mystery or 'darkness' lies in why or how it happened – the brilliant interlude dubbed the Middle Ages. It was a star-burst of human achievement and, far from being limited by what could only be known then, this long pause between the fall of Rome and the rise of modernity was filled with an intellectual and spiritual light which, when it is permitted to blaze upon us as it does here, leaves us gasping.

This dazzling of us by using an easy though still learned language, a kind of Schoolmen for Beginners, makes it plain from the start that we are to be at ease with men and women such as St Francis, Abelard, Heloise, Bernard of Clairvaux, Dante, Beatrice, Suger, various twelfth and thirteenth century popes, Hildegard of Bingen, Anselm of Leon and a whole host of voices from a witty, sacred society which, until essays such as this, spoke in an impacted way which was hard to hear. Frayling's central dialogue between Bernard of Clairvaux and Peter Abelard forms the heart of this interesting book. He calls it 'The Saint and the Scholar'. Bernard's knowledge of God is mystically arrived at, Peter's intellectually. Each of them is enormously famous and listened to. Bernard is rustic, Peter urban. The Christ of the countryside and the Christ of the city are seen in some conflict. Meanwhile the cult of His Mother flowers in both places, though differently. Frayling shows Cimabue's elegant *Virgin and Child Enthroned* and contrasts it with the earthy wooden sculpture before which Bernard prayed, and which can still be seen in the chapel of St Vorles at Chatillon-sur-Seine. Both concepts of Mary, one as court lady, the other as peasant, would dominate Christendom. Frayling then examines Bernard's and Peter's credentials for the immense roles they played at a time when rhetoric, or gesture, was itself an accepted part of spiritual or intellectual integrity. Best of all – and this in all his chapters – he quotes from well-translated writings, and one finds oneself taken aback by the directness, for example, of the personal letters which Heloise wrote to Peter Abelard after the atrocity which should have ended their love and ruined his reputation, but which did neither.

And of course the puzzling, glorious business of cathedral-building has to further be examined. Here Frayling is influenced by Jean Gimpel, maybe, whose radical and disturbing enquiry *The Cathedral Builders* lays the foundations, as it were, of a far more realistic view of this divine craze. Though thank God for it. Canterbury, Chartres, Beauvais . . . what can we do eight hundred years on but stare up in silence, dumb with wonder '. . . works of art achieved significance or meaning, only insofar as they managed to reveal the *splendor veritatis*, of the light of Truth, by becoming shadow-versions of the Creator's work. The great medieval cathedrals of the twelfth and thirteenth centuries were more than anything else a new architectural light . . . They were encyclopaedias of the latest thought, art and engineering; experimental laboratories where geometry plus craft techniques could be tested out; facsimiles of the Heavenly City itself . . . [Places] almost literally out of this world.'

Strange Landscape is well illustrated. The Church appears in picture and text as both Christ-like and Devil-like (its hideous massacres). At the close one ponders yet again on its piling of such mountains of requirements upon the simplicity of the Gospel.

THE CATHEDRAL BUILDERS

Jean Gimpel, 1993

There can have been few religions which escaped being entangled in architecture. Since neolithic times faith has spelt stone. In Christian Europe the heights of faith were expressed in the building of vast churches. Visiting them, awed by their glory, we now know a great deal about their dates and style, etc. but very little about the motive behind their existence. We say that they are the product of the Age of Faith, equating them, maybe, with the faith which could move mountains. But on earth could a society with some of our precision-tools and only fragments of our science build Beauvais, or St Denis, or Canterbury? More important, why did the followers of one who advocated 'a temple not made with hands' expend their brief lives and endless ingenuity, not to mention every penny they possessed, on buildings? Not even Jean Gimpel can answer this question in full, for nobody can. But in his new deservedly-famous little book, first published five years ago, he manages to wed the spiritual and practical impetus which created the cathedrals in a language which is an eye-opener. After all, the whole of Europe for close on two centuries could not have erected cathedral after cathedral – not to mention thousands of parish churches and abbeys – in a kind of sacred numinosity. It had all to begin with a deep digging into pockets and quarries, and it had all to end with a workmanlike attempt to achieve the everlasting.

Gimpel proves that there have always been plenty of facts about the cathedral-builders and thus no need for the fog of legend into which we seem to have preferred to plunge them. He places the dynamic of their constructions between the years 1150-1300, and contemporary with 'the greatest spirits of the Western world, St Bernard, Abelard, St Francis, St Thomas Aquinas, Roger Bacon and St Louis. Gimpel's is a French view of the architectural Middle Ages and his Gallic earthiness provides a strong antidote to mystic, not to say misty, craftsmanship, He tells how the 'cathedral crusade' took shape and how, after the energies required for the military crusades began to falter, the entire hierarchy of the church, from pope to parish priest, spiritually and financially, took to building. This was not the universal single-minded activity we like to think it was. Many Christians looked on askance at what they saw as an expensive, pride-filled and irrational activity. 'Pious men in important positions were profoundly shocked by these great works. Pierre le Chantre, a highly placed cathedral dignitary in Paris, wrote vehemently in 1180: 'It is a sin to build the kind of churches which are being built nowadays.' He said it was a 'sickness' and that 'Monastic churches and cathedrals are being built by usury and avarice, by cunning and lies, and by the deception of preachers.'

Sens marked the beginning, says Gimpel, and from then on for close on two centuries there was to be no end to the glories fashioned from stone, glass, wood and paint. Churches were made so huge that great crowds enter their sanctuaries – something previously unknown – and whole multitudes could swarm through their dizzy naves on feast days. The vastness of the cathedrals and the communal toil and artistry required for their completion turned them into the medieval equivalent of peoples' palaces. They were the ante-rooms of Paradise. As for our notion of the ordinary man of the Middle Ages being put to a perpetual grind, Gimpel reminds us that no civilisation other than Christianity's has ever given so many holidays to its peasantry. He destroys the popular concept of the anonymous, faceless artisan and labourer putting up God's house whilst their betters take the credit, and gives working hours, wages – even names. Most importantly, he remembers 'the forgotten quarryman', he who chopped and heaved amazing masses of stone from the pits at Caen, Barnack, etc. and humped it to the construction sites. Women were a major force and they specialised as plasterers. Lives were brief and few of those who saw a cathedral's foundations dug would have witnessed the cross being placed on its spire.

Gimpel insists that the title of 'cathedral builders' belongs more justly to the canons than to the bishops. It was the chapter which organised and carried on the tremendous enterprise and that, indeed, which continued to build cathedrals long after the general passion for them had waned. Because so much is owed to them, and because bishops, like kings, tend to be credited with the architectural achievements of their times, Gimpel offers an illuminating look at canons and chapters. It is here, rather than among the artisans, that an undeserved anonymity exists. There was, human nature being what it is, competitiveness and over-striving, usually for what was highest. The cathedral builders' reach did sometimes exceed their grasp. The vault of Beauvais, the highest in the world, fell down. Whereas the humblest cathedral workman could soar to the top of his near-miraculous trade if he was specially gifted, and a feudal system which kept folk in their place on the land seemed to vanish once a mason got his foot on one of those dizzy tied-together ladders. Abbot Suger, the splendiferous creator of St Denis was the son of a serf.

Gimpel moans that it was fashionable 'taste' which wrecked, altered or destroyed France's gothic glories during the 17th and 18th centuries. Our iconoclasts may have purified the medieval churches by hacking out works of art which have left us mourning ever since, but at least their motives were theological, whereas in France the motives were crass. *The Cathedral Builders* is a must, a sensible foundation for all the facts and figures of the guides.

CHARTRES AND THE BIRTH OF THE CATHEDRAL
Titus Burckhardt, 1996

This is a noble and self-denying essay, for the distinguished art historian Titus Burckhardt allows his own profession to be no more than a handmaid to what he has to say about Chartres. Ably translated all these years since it first appeared in 1962, it takes us back to the philosophical origins of the 'cathedral'. Its aesthetic origins were simply by the way. Countless men and women – and children – few of them named – quarried stone, dragged carts, roasted colours into glass, tied together cat's cradles of scaffolding, dug, carved, painted, plastered and built. The result was an incomparable work of art made up of thousands of invididual yet unified masterpieces. Burckhardt quotes from Wren's tomb in St Paul's: 'If you want to know who these builders were, look around you.'

In their clockless world, time was no more than a rhythm, a pulse. And what so obsesses us, our individualism, was a human concept unknown to them. No one signed a thing. No *fecit* anywhere. But the geometry, the cosmology, the intellectual foundations, as well as the architectural basis of this peerless church are everywhere, and they would have been as much surprised by our not being capable of 'reading' them as they would be by our chief reason for visiting Chartres – simply to look at it. They looked at Christ and his Mother through it. To them its blue windows were walls which had been penetrated by the history of our redemption. They were walls as light, and not windows at all. The famous rose window, an Islamic idea, symbolised the world wheel, the turning of all seasons and generations.

Burckhardt goes further back than most cathedral historians, or at least he gives a sharper and more compelling account of the well-known development of the Christian basilica from the pagan temple. The temple had to house a god or goddess, not a congregation. The first churches, says Burckhardt, were like covered streets leading to a destination and their forecourts were beautiful gardens which represented paradise. Wherever possible, they were like cities, villages and parish boundaries, orientated according to the cosmic cross seen in the night sky.

During the twelfth century a miraculous form of cathedral architecture sprang up to accommodate relics and their devout armies of venerators. Previously, relics lay in caves and holes below church floors, sanctifying the foundations of the building. It was inevitable that when they were brought up where people could see them they would attract the crowds. As their cults grew, so did the walkways – ambulatories – of the pilgrims.

At Chartres this holy indoor journey was uniquely beautiful and instructive. It guided Christians through all the territories of their neo-platonic and Eden-to-Bethlehem universe. It was a symbolic route which two centuries later would be mapped by Dante in *The Divine Comedy*. Today, symbols are harder to read than words and Burckhardt's particular gift is for de-misting them, as it were. He wants us to see them not simply as art but as the Christ-following man of the Middle Ages saw them, and he wants us to see *him* as a person (it can also be her) who could turn his hand, quite naturally when it was required, to high art.

Chartres began building in 1145, shortly after Abbot Suger had inscribed on the door of his sublimely restored Saint-Denis, 'Wonder not at the gold, nor at the cost, but at the work.' His friend St Bernard of Clairvaux did, of course, wonder at all three. He was busy preaching the second crusade and was utterly against the introduction of splendid ornaments, especially to monastic communities.

Abbot Suger and he were opposites. Suger saw the Creator as the father of creators. His mentor was Dionysius the Areopagite, master of symbolism. He believed that the bones of Dionysius lay at Saint-Denis – just as the townsfolk of Chartres believed that their church sheltered the *sancta camisia*, the Virgin's tunic. For Suger, they were blessed fragments of Heaven and he intended that all such sacred left-behind things should be given as much Heaven as was earthly possible. He spoke of being drawn away from worries and cares by the beauty of the House of God, and of how meditation transposed the material into the spiritual.

As the tall Gothic cathedrals sprang up all over France and then across Europe, Abbot Suger's apology for their divine extravagance, genius and nerve could have been that of any priest or layman as he

399

stood before them.

It seems to me as if I dwelt in a strange part of the universe, such as exists neither in the mire of the earth nor in the purity of Heaven, and then, with God's grace, it may happen that in anagogical [mystically interpretive] manner, I am raised up from this lower to that higher world.

In building their wondrous house of the Lord, the people of Chartres also meant it to be the paradisal palace on earth for Mary. It is said that it was courteous, austere St Bernard who first addressed her as *Notre Dame*. His text was, 'Hard labour for God'. The way in which everybody at Chartres, from peers to ploughmen, from great ladies to peasant girls, hacked and carted and toiled year in, year out, to make their cathedral certainly does require both social and analogical interpretation. The age of faith could not have had much time to spend on its knees.

Titus Burckhardt's study of the phenomenon of the cathedral builders is learned, very readable and ultimately staggering. Suger was right, of course. Whether at Saint-Denis, Ely – or simply your own parish church, c.1350: 'Wonder not at the cost, but at the work.'

ENGLISH CATHEDRALS

Edwin Smith & Olive Cook, 1989

This is not another handbook for an already laden shelf, but many other things. First it is a summation of a writing-photographing partnership between man and wife which ceased in 1971, when Edwin Smith died leaving his widow with an archive of some of the finest pictures of architecture taken in the twentieth century. Secondly, it is the antithesis of today's sleek guide which whisks the reader through the familiar arcades with glossy ease. Smith, who worked with a half-plate bellows camera made by Thomas Pickard in 1904, and called

'The Ruby', was once all set up in Lincoln Cathedral when the bell announced Matins. 'I have come to worship with the eye', he explained, 'and to offer the praise of my humble craft'.

Similarly, Olive Cook his wife is in many ways an historian at prayer as she investigates and explains these peerless creations of the medieval mind, this anticipation of heaven in stone and wood and glass. Although she and Edwin collaborated on so many books, their *English Cathedrals* could be said to state all that they stood for, learning, taste and vision. No tourist-speak in this black and white album, no mercy either for those who today would 'market' this spiritual inheritance. And no patience in it for those who lack the nous to recognise that cathedral-visiting is worship via sightseeing.

The vast buildings appear chronologically from Norman Durham to Basil Spence's Coventry, their impetus always that of their time. Gigantean drums of rubble cased in dressed stone and thin windows in thick walls, barbaric chevrons and gaudy paint produced interiors of might and awe. These first cathedrals were the work of artists from far afield, for the Norman empire reached to Sicily. Olive Cook describes 'the furious energy which is both contained and enhanced by the stately unhurried measure of Norman bays.' Descriptively alone her essay is remarkable for the Ruskin-like way in which her sentences are able to carry an intertwined mixture of hard facts and imaginative impressions. It must be one of the most difficult things possible to write about Canterbury or Ely with originality, or with the freshness with which one might write about some newly-excavated Romano-British temple, yet hers is a cathedral guide without clichés and without echoes. The subject is too immense, too crammed with furniture, music, literature and craftsmanship of every sort, not to mention liturgy, to be more than touched upon in a work such as this, though what a correctly selecting touch she has.

Crypts, for instance. Why does England have so many and the Continent so few? These stumpy churches beneath a church are strange places which drew the photographer and his sharp-eyed wife over many years. Some are the furtive holy places of the Anglo-Saxons, sacred caves over which the conquerors spread their immense naves. Some seem to trap the very air which their makers breathed.

Olive Cook is at her best with memorials, knowing just which among so many need her personal introduction. She says striking things about them and points out what few must have noticed here. She knows all about what the effigies are wearing, or their nakedness, and why they stand or sit or lie. She mentions their funerals and who took them. William Longespee, the son of Henry II and Fair Rosamund, and Lord Pembroke, buried respectively in Salisbury Cathedral and the Temple Church, London, are the first 'representations of relaxed recumbency'. Her favourite effigy is that of Edward II – 'unforgettable beauty – like Marlowe's masterpiece it invests the tragic tale of the king's incompetence, weakness and dreadful death with universal significance.' This image at Gloucester was one of the first alabaster portraits. She leads one to a succession of tomb glories, reaching from the intricate chantries of the late Middle Ages to the engraved slate stones of Leicestershire during the eighteenth century, with their dazzling calligraphy.

Like the cathedral architecture itself, the photographs and text reach their peak in the sections dealing with the Gothic miracle, and here one must commend the extraordinary quality of the pictures when compared with that of the colour plates in the brochures which the cathedrals themselves sell on their bookstalls. Fan-vaulting aisles, galilees, choirs, and most of all the usually not easily seen triforium and spandrel sculpture – Smith's camera not only captures the greatness of this but declares its essence. There is a haunting photograph of the angel expelling Adam and Eve from Eden, a triforium sculpture at Lincoln, the sinners with hard, knowing faces, the angel hard and implacable in another way. Reading what Olive Cook says about it, one realises how this husband and wife, over many years of marriage and wandering across Britain, must have stood side by side at such discoveries as this, their reactions and impressions coming together. Almost twenty years after Edwin's death Olive has still been able to put together this truly 'joint' book.

The present appals her, and she does not hide the fact. After listing the hazards and destruction, the alterations (her *bête noire* is Wyatt), the neglect and the vandalism of the ages – and still the cathedrals stand – she freezes when it comes to the triteness into which contemporary vulgarity and materialism have lured them, and is indeed scathing.

In her final chapter, called 'In a Secular Age', she deplores the abandonment of the Authorized Version and the Book of Common Prayer and says:

The visual accompaniments of the Alternative Service Book are the glass front doors, the postcard, book and souvenir shops, the cafeterias, coffee areas, sinks and toilets, the ugly pile-up of cars and coaches in the precincts and the destruction of the fabric by a deadlier agent than either time or weather – pollution which more than anything else reflects the fanatical preoccupation of the age with the pursuit of profit and material wealth. This is the background against which the history and meaning of cathedrals in the present century must be seen.

THE HOLY GRAIL
Its Origins, Secrets and Meaning Revealed
Malcolm Godwin, 1994

The Grail, says Malcolm Godwin, is the ultimate quest for all and everything. This being so, it must never be found. It comes into the category of Browning's.

> *Ah, but a man's reach should exceed his grasp.*
> *Or what's a heaven for?*

But to track down the tales behind the quest is less frustrating. Begin at the generally acknowledged literary source, the French poet Chretien de Troyes, and then go backwards and forwards. Chretien flourished – the word is especially fitting – during the late twelfth century and in his story *Perceval* or *Conte del Graal* introduces a mysterious dish into what had until then been a popular folktale about a boy who gets to court, becomes a brave knight, rescues and marries a damsel, and takes care of his poor old mother. Perceval glimpsed this dish in a castle, along with a bleeding lance, and would have spent the rest of his life finding what they really were, except that Chretien left his poem unfinished.

And then, says Godwin, in less than twenty-five years, everyone in Christendom was searching for the castle and its dish (now the cup in which Joseph of Arimathea caught the blood of Christ during the Crucifixion and brought to Britain). So far, so familiar. Malory and a host of subsequent writers and artists have left us with such a recognisable chalice that we 'see' it on every altar. Godwin denies this Arthurian-cum-pre-Raphaelite version of the Cup of the Lord's Blood and returns to Chretien's 'dish', which is none other than the Celtic 'grail', or caldron of plenty – a cornucopia of nature's providence. He is wonderfully erudite about all this and the reader must make up his mind whether he is indeed on the latest Grail quest, or on a wild-goose chase through some staggeringly interesting material.

Did the medieval Church christianise the Grail quest? If Grail was originally Graal, which is likely, then it did. Godwin blames this on, or attributes it to, the Cistercians. He describes the extraordinary religious climate in which the Grail legend was born, one dominated by the enormous mythology which supported the Crusades; and by the exquisite truth which St Francis embodied – Godwin thinks him to have been 'perhaps the greatest spiritual figure in the West since Christ himself'. Then there were the Courts of Love reigned over by the English intellectual Queen Eleanor, and the noble Sufi doctrines and poetry which turned many a French or English Jerusalem-farer into an undeliberate heretic, and Islamic architectural ideas, and countless cross-fertilisations of culture and faith, so causing the Church to lay down the law with a cruel hand.

All this Godwin explores, often indignantly, usually learnedly, now and then dottily. But questers have to have a bee in their bonnet. Godwin's leads him on and on, and us with him. He is often eloquent – 'History and myth seldom make promising bedfellows. History is doggedly linear . . . myth is cyclic.' He throws in many a thought-provoking scrap of information. The Nazaritish word *Najjar* means both carpenter and Holy Man.

404

A good part of his grail quest is to find the eternal Woman. In some ways Godwin's book is feminist theology, with the Magdalene rediscovered as the Great Goddess. It follows the magic cup in three directions, the Celtic, the Chymical and the Christian.

'But what is the grail exactly, and what is it supposed to do?' Wolfram, the poet of the Chymical direction, asks. 'There was a Thing that was called the Grail, the crown of all earthly wishes, fair fullness that ne'er shall fail'. Godwin says that the quest is as varied as the vessel sought. It is seen as the search for the Cauldron of Rebirth, the Fountain of Everlasting Youth, Direct Communion with God through the Body of Christ . . .

So now read on, Godwin offers maps but in effect he draws one into his own labyrinthine pleasures, with one path leading to another so that one knows from the start that one is never going to get anywhere for certain. It is a radical journey, with many a swipe at the Church and its confiscations from the pagan ages.

The Holy Grail is as embellished as a Pugin chancel. Photographs, paintings and engravings fight for supremacy through the text. It becomes obvious that our pilgrimage to this sacred Thing, as Wolfram calls it, is brilliantly Victorian, with Tennyson and Burne-Jones (and Wagner) leading. But to prove that the old journey is still in progress, there is a full-page photograph of the Anglican ordination of a woman. Esoteric, mystical, even cranky though Godwin may be seen to be, he sees himself as one not interested in ornate religious by-paths, but as keen as Sir Gawaine to dedicate his life to the Quest.

THE QUEST FOR MERLIN

Nikolai Tolstoy, 1985

It has long been all too easy, and too convenient, for us to write off those strange years between Rome's retreat from these islands, and Christ's advance into them, as 'dark'. Archaeology alone has been proving otherwise. If they have appeared barbarous and unenlightened it is because it has suited our religious culture to have them so. There is a sense of national spiritual achievement in starting from scratch against black odds. But with today's slow recognition that myth – certainly the great myths marking this period – is a form of truth that incorporates imagination, actuality and the human need constantly to re-hear certain stories, we are gradually finding it possible to penetrate these notorious mists. Writers of genius from Geoffrey of Monmouth and Thomas Malory to T. H. White and J. R. R. Tolkien have run wild in this early land, with glorious results. But who and what were its priests, prophets and kingdoms? Was it possible, for example, to go in search of a man named Merlin as one would of a man named Alfred the Great?

Yes, says Nikolai Tolstoy, and proves the possibility. But one has to begin young. Figures like Merlin have to catch the eye and heart in childhood and then become such a part of one's life that there is no option but to seek them out and re-adjust the world's false notion of them. Count Tolstoy is evangelical on our supreme wizard's behalf, but excitingly learned too. Good scholarship and hunches have taken him all the way from the little boy blissfully lost in his illustrated *Morte D'Arthur* above Bideford to the determined explorer who at last steps into the Lothian gulley above the Roman road where, in the late 6th century AD, a magnificent druidical prophet had retreated and from where he inspired a pocket of northern paganism. Merlin. Tolstoy gives some 1,400 years chapter and verse, plus some recent photographs. His descriptions of the virtually unaltered geography of mountainous regions with their springs and river courses are most moving. Tennyson could be said to have rehabilitated Merlin in this grand setting after the seer had been turned into a grotesque by two centuries of writers, and this book adds a rich cairn of facts to stand beside the poetry.

Tolstoy does not claim to be the first to become engrossed with the likelihood of the historical Merlin, and he acknowledges that the similarly obsessed W. F. Skene came this way in the 1860s. 'We can see that, concealed under these extravagant fables, are the outlines of one of those great historical struggles which altered the fate of a country,' the latter told the Society of Antiquaries of Scotland, describing the battle from which Merlin fled into exile. But Tolstoy possesses exceptional gifts for running a huge mass of translation, findings too simple to have attracted previous Merlin-hunters and brilliant interpretation into a handsome piece of straightforward narrative. Given such convincing flesh and blood, Merlin the legendary enchanter and King Arthur's friend often seems like druidical Britain's Isaiah, a sublime patriot inspiring his people from the wilderness.

In his famous order to St Augustine, Pope Gregory said 'Don't destroy the heathen temples but replace the gods with Christ', thus creating duel devotions for a long time to come, for Merlin's deities hung around in the religious sub-conscious, and his magic became encrusted with Christian magic. Eventually that part of his mystery which had been symbolically caught up with the ordinary creatures of his countryside, particularly pigs and the stags of Hartfell, made him the model for the horned devil of the Church. While it is not Count Tolstoy's intention to say 'Will the real druid philosopher and British hero named Merlin stand up', he does leave us with a compelling person whom in future we will need to balance against the portraits and libels of superstition and first-rate literature alike. Merlin disciple of the god of light – Lug. Romans left, 'There was no returning, there never had been any darkness foreshadowing of the light'.

BEFORE THE KING'S MAJESTY
Lancelot Andrewes and his Writings
ed. Raymond Chapman, 2009

HAPPINESS AND HOLINESS
Thomas Traherne and his Writings
ed. Denise Inge, 2009

Lancelot Andrewes and Thomas Traherne produced matchless works of early Anglican devotional literature, yet their writing was differently hidden from general view for ages, one in the realm of academic theology, the other on book barrows and bonfires. Their essence has been presented in the two books under review. New readers will not be the only group to benefit: Andrewes and Traherne scholars will also be pleased and startled by the findings and presentations of Raymond Chapman and Denise Inge.

Anglicanism's linguistic heritage is so beguiling as to be worshipful in itself. It is said that James I shivered when Andrewes, as Bishop of Ely, came to court, in spite of the Bishop's belief in the King's divinity. Regularly, year after year, on Good Friday, Whit-Sunday, Easter, Christmas Day and Gunpowder Day, James quaked before this son of an Essex mariner whose keen East Anglian radicalism drove like a wind through his huge learning. The Gunpowder sermons on November 5 were delivered with special feeling as the preacher himself would have perished if the plot had succeeded. He believed that God had preserved him. James and his Court were told, often in a mixture of magnificent oratory and irresistible word play, that Christ was present in the Eucharist but that the bread and wine did not become his body, that the Jews alone were not guilty of the crucifixion but the entire human race, and a host of reassuring and discomforting things which they could never forget. Raymond Chapman's choice of material in *Before the King's Majesty* seats us below the Whitehall pulpit. Similarly, Denise Inge's selection of Thomas Traherne's writings in *Happiness and Holiness* is an important addition to Traherne studies in itself, even for those who think they know him.

Lancelot Andrewes and Thomas Traherne were born some three generations apart. Their boyhoods should have been scarred by the cruelties of the Counter-Reformation and the Civil War, but they were not. Their religion itself, including their literal beliefs about hell, can hardly be said to match that of modern believers in an obvious way. But then comes their Jesus, the figure with whom George Herbert went on walks in the water-meadows, and for whom his mother laid a place at dinner – that companionable Christ of the Caroline poets who speaks to us so lucidly today. It is worthwhile becoming acquainted with the logjam of early Anglican theology if only to see Jesus rise above it. Great writers are of their time, and we must 'read' their time to comprehend them. Both these collections must be praised for showing two religious times so readably.

Like most seeds which lie dormant until some great disturbance brings them up to where the sun can warm them, Traherne's books disappeared from sight for hundreds of years: it is a famous bookman's tale. Denise Inge says, 'the story of the discovery of his manuscripts, largely unnamed and some untitled, lying in deep obscurity, reads like a novel, with astonishing twists and surprises, moments of serendipity, hazard, happenstance, resolve – volumes rescued from book barrows, from misattribution, from a burning rubbish heap, the flames batted out, the leather smouldering'. He is a writer of luck if luck were anything to go by, and should have disappeared altogether. He so nearly did. There is little chance now that he will.

C. S. Lewis thought that Traherne's *Centuries of Meditations* was almost the most beautiful book in English. When more of his scattered pages were discovered in the Lambeth Palace library in 1958, a seventeenth-century hand had written on the flyleaf, 'Why is this so long detained in a dark manuscript, that if it were printed would be a Light to the World & a Universal Blessing'.

When W.T.Brooke bought a rough bundle of pages entitled *Centuries*, plus a folio volume of poems and a Commonplace Book for a few pence from a London stall on a winter's day in 1896-7, be cried, 'Henry Vaughan!'. Vaughan's exultation of the cosmos and his tender recognition of the visionary powers of childhood fitted so well. But detective work by the antiquarian bookseller Bertram Dobell led him to the chaplain of Sir Orlando Bridgeman. Dobell published *The Poetical Works of Thomas Traherne* in 1903 and *Centuries* in 1908. A new master had entered the Anglican devotional field.

The Church had never much liked the exuberance (technically known as the Affirmative Way) that is Traherne's trademark. Happiness is what heaven was for, it believed. The ecclesiastical establishment particularly disliked the kind of happiness that had strong links with nature. It had stood back from Richard Rolle's *Fire of Love* and it would certainly have put the dampers on Julian of Norwich's *Revelations of Divine Love*, had it known about this spiritual classic. 'Of all the things we may do for God and the most honouring to him is to live gladly', Traherne wrote. He was much taken with Edmund Spenser's 'felicity', the basis of happiness, in his view. As we discover in Inge's wideranging discussion, Traherne was a gregarious, talkative, sensuous young man who had to praise God through his body as well as his soul. George Herbert thought it sin not to be happy on earth. Traherne shows a familiarity with *The Temple* volume. And it is likely that he had read Herbert's *A Priest to the Temple*, or, *The Country Parson* (1652), for the report on him at Credenhill, the Herefordshire living where he ministered for many years, shows a Herbert-like care for a little rural parish. Traherne's only living was at Credenhill. Hereford Puritans appointed him to it. The surrounding countryside appeared contemplative during his youthful ministry. There was a prayer group at nearby Kington led by Mrs Susannah Hopton, to whom he sent some of his work. Further along the Welsh Border, about thirty miles away, lived his contemporary Henry Vaughan, a medical doctor. It is not known whether the two great poets ever met. To Thomas Traherne his four-hearth rectory was 'the House of Paradise'. His handful of parishioners lived in rural slums, for he wrote, 'And when I enter into Houses, let me remember the Glory I saw in the fields'. Herbert ordered his country parson into every dwelling, no matter how great the stench. Traherne had £50 a year. In his day, parish churches all over the land were being patched up after the second 'cleansing' or iconoclasm of the Cromwellian era. Traherne loved them and wrote something about them which might be in today's guidebooks.

When I see a Little Church Environed with Trees, how many Things are there which mine Eye discerneth not. The Labor of them which in Ancient Ages Builded it; the conversion of a Kingdom to God from Paganism, its protection to Law, its subjection to Kings, its relation to Bishops, usefulness and convenience for the Entertainment of Christians, the Divine Service, office of the ministry, Solemn Assemblies, Prayers and Thanksgivings, for the sake of which it was permitted, it Governed, standeth and flourisheth . . . the Services are such as that He should Delight in . . . Especially I who have been nourished at universities in Beautiful Streets & famous Colledges & am sent hither from God Almighty to teach Immortal Souls the way to Heaven . . .

Thomas and his younger brother Philip were the sons of John Traherne, a Hereford shoemaker. Nothing is known of their mother. Their father had fought as a Royalist officer during the Civil War. Later the city maintained a Parliamentary garrison and the Cathedral was staffed by Puritan ministers. Both brothers were ordained and remained close all their lives. Thomas gives a vivid glimpse of Philip in a poem entitled 'On Leaping over the Moon':

> *To the same purpose, he, not long before*
> *Brought home from Nurse, going to the door*
> *To do some little thing*
> *He must not do within*
> *With Wonder cries,*
> *As in the Skies*
> *He saw the Moon, "O yonder is the Moon*
> *Newly com after me to Town,*
> *That shin'd at Lugwardin but yesternight,*
> *Where I enjoy'd the self-same Light".*

At first the Trahernes were very poor, but soon John prospered sufficiently to buy property in Hereford – those same dwellings that Thomas would leave in his will as an almshouse, and which still stand in Widemarsh Street. He wrote of 'rags and cottages', but also of his childhood possessions, a rare inventory.

The Glass of Imagination was the only Mirror, wherein anything was represented or appeared to me. All Things were absent which they talk not of. So I began among my Playfellows to prize a Drum, a fine Coat, a Peny, a Gilded Book &c. Who before never dreamed of any such Wealth. Goodly Objects to drown all the Knowledge of Heaven and Earth. As for the Heavens, the Sun and the Stars they disappeared, and were no more unto me than the bare walls. So that the Strange Riches of Men's Invention quite overcame the Riches of Nature.

Though not for long. In 1653, aged fifteen, Traherne went up to Brasenose College, Oxford, where he found 'Glorious Secrets and

Glorious Persons past Imagination'. But there were shortcomings. No one taught 'Felicity'. Four years later and still in his teens, he was at Credenhill and there, 'having all my Time in my own Hands', he resolved to spend it, 'Whatever it cost me, in Search of Happiness'. And a more entrancingly described search was never written.

Happiness and Holiness is now the finest guide into Traherne that we have. It shows how his sometimes ecstatic, sometimes earthy prose-poetry grew out of his formidable learning. The style might well have produced some overworked Caroline necklace of words, some conceit of the period. The actual result is a lovely string of Anglican prayer-beads, something meditative for today, its very repetitions an added blessing. Attempts to modernise Traherne's English (evidenced in a work such as Margaret Bottrell's *The Way of Blessedness*) are not a success. Something strange is lost. Denise Inge is so at home with him that she is able to talk through his eccentricities in a way which makes them almost colloquial for us. She adds her account of Traherne's life and her critical information in a series of small, acute essays. For example:

Richard Hooker the country parson and Lancelot Andrewes the urbane bishop and court preacher were both models of a kind for Traherne . . . like Hooker, he worked among his people while writing theology. Like Andrewes, he knew what it was to find favour with eminent men, move to London, enjoy for a time the company of those not far from the King. Traherne uses the Easter Sermons of Andrewes in his meditations after Easter, and both Hooker and Andrewes on the subject of angels in his Michaelmas meditations. From Andrewes he took a model of prayerfulness, modelling *The Thanksgiving* after Andrewes's *Preces Privatao* from Hooker he gleaned among other things, a desire to communicate with laity as well as clergy . . . No matter is too small for his attention . . . How should we live? Traherne says to ministers: be among your people. He says to all . . . know what you are inside, where your life comes from and where it is headed . . . be not a bubble; be solid.

He found that there were Christians who desire Happiness now and Christians who defer it. He thought that men were angels of a sort and that 'an Angel will be Happy anywhere'. He said that 'A Christian is an Oak flourishing in Winter', and that 'Eternity is a Mysterious Absence of Times and Ages'. And it is in no time at all that we, the twenty-first-century readers, tumble into his statements, casting off our restraints. He writes approvingly of 'Nakedness'. He could be seeing our role in the universe when he writes, 'Infinity of Space is like a Painter's Table, prepared for the Ground and Field of those Colours that are to be laid thereon.' He asked God to 'Turn my Retirements into Songs' – and was convinced that his prayers were answered.

In *Before the King's Majesty*, Raymond Chapman follows Denise Inge in making a fascinating Anglican writer accessible to a new readership. Not the least attractive aspect of Lancelot Andrewes to us is that, like Traherne, he was an outdoors man and a dedicated walker. As a student his walks from Cambridge to London, where his father now lived, were part of his spiritual progress; and when he became Dean of Westminster in 1601, he would lead the schoolboys along the Thames path as far as Chelsea, teaching en route. One of the boys was George Herbert.

Peeping into Andrewes's chapel, Herbert saw what the Victorians would call 'the beauty of holiness'. A three-and-a-quarter-foot-high altar lit by two tapers, a service book on a velvet cushion, a silver basket lined with cambric lace for the bread, a chalice covered with a pure linen 'aire', an incense boat – and a great stillness. Years later, he would carry these requirements to his church at Bemerton, near Salisbury. The Westminster boys called their teacher their *Stella Predicantum* and Herbert would write; 'I know the ways of Learning: both the head/And pipes that feed the press, and make it run.'

James I, too, knew the ways of learning, and it was Bishop Andrewes who fed the pipes which, every few months, brought severe rushes of moral purpose to the King's wayward court. A few months after his arrival in England from Scotland, James had attended the Hampton Court Conference in bitter January. Although the matter was not high on the agenda, it was suggested that a fresh translation of the Bible might be useful. Andrewes headed the 'company' of six which was allotted Genesis to 2 Kings. Although a large part of this new Bible was based on William Tyndale's magnificent translation, there is no acknowledgement, only a preface which would immortalise James. Indirectly it has immortalised Lancelot Andrewes as well. Such a voice could hardly be kept out of these early biblical passages, and we no doubt catch echoes of it when Abraham speaks. But *Before the King's Majesty* helps to isolate Andrewes's contribution from the hubbub of history. Here he is at court on Christmas Day, 1618, talking about Bethlehem:

Every word here is a wonder. An infant; the infant Word, the Word, without a word; the eternal Word not able to speak a word; a wonder sure. And swaddled; and that a wonder too. He that . . . taketh the vast body of the main seam turns it to and fro, as a little child, and rolls it about with the swaddling bands of darkness . . . There lieth He, the Lord of glory without all glory. Instead of a palace, a poor stable; of a cradle of state, a beast's cratch; no pillow but a lock of hay; no hangings but dust and cobwebs; no attendants, but 'in the midst of animals', as the Fathers read the [prophet] Habakkuk . . . So low. Well may this be said a sign . . . to wonder at. If it be well looked into, it is able to strike any man into an ecstasy.

Although Andrewes's sermons relate him to the Stuarts, Raymond Chapman reminds us that he was an Elizabethan. His writings create a grand bridge between Shakespeare and the later Metaphysical poets. The Queen's court was robust, the King's unsavoury for such a priest. Chapman sees him as totally devoted to the emerging Church of England, and finds his thought 'mystical rather than speculative'. Andrewes died in 1626 and his sermons were published three years later and dedicated to Charles I, who was told, 'Though they could not live with all the elegancy which they had upon his tongue, yet you were graciously pleased to think a paper-life better than none'.

Well, here is a renewed paper-life. Andrewes had what they said was a jerkiness of style compared with, say, Jeremy Taylor and his flowing periods, but it is this intimate finding the right word and then building upon it, and the rusticity which creeps through his enormous scholarship, that bring him close to us, and never more so than in the famous Nativity sermons. He is one of the Anglican 'Fathers', a

Jerome for a Reformed belief. When he admonishes, he does so in homely terms. When he teaches, we are the young in faith trailing in his wake along the river bank. He lies in effigy in Southwark Cathedral with his sermons in his hand, a few paces from Shakespeare's actor brother. Andrewes himself had no gestures. He occupied a series of high positions with an indifference to their grandeur, lived spartanly, venerated kingship and was masterly in his ability to apply the imagery of Scripture to the humdrum business of life. We are not told what his voice sounded like. Chapman divides the sermons under the rubrics of Incarnation, Passion, Resurrection and Ascension, Sacraments, Law and Government, etc. adding Andrewes's intense Prayers.

One Easter sermon is on the colour red – 'My beloved is white and Red'. When he says that 'we must not slip the collar' our thoughts travel to Herbert, who did slip it to be 'Loose as the winde', only to hear above his ravings 'one calling, *Child*'.

Chapman says that Andrewes's style went out of fashion in the late seventeenth century, and quotes John Evelyn's *Diary*, which describes a clergyman who 'preached much after Bish. Andrewes' method, full of logical divisions, in short and broken periods, and Latin sentences . . . now quite out of fashion in the pulpit'. But T.S.Eliot found Andrewes still vigorous and memorable. 'When Andrewes begins his sermon, from beginning to end you are sure that he is wholly in his subject, unaware of anything else, that his emotion grows as he penetrates more deeply into his subject, that he is finally "alone with the Alone", with the mystery which he is trying to grasp more and more firmly.' One of the Gunpowder Plot homilies would not be out of place in the mouth of an American preacher in the aftermath of September 11, 2001. The sermon is now the least-known literary form, and *Before the King's Majesty* provides a fine means by which to recover it.

PILGRIM'S PROGRESS
from *Divine Landscapes*, 1986

It is ironic that the landscape which provided the features for this country's finest spiritual allegory should be that of one of its least regarded counties where scenery is concerned. More, that Britain's most popular journey of the soul should have been made among views that have mostly been passing ones for earth-bound travellers, both ancient and modern. In the old days, the great roads running north and south tended to hurry everyone through Bedfordshire with a minimum account of its existence, and in our own time it offers the kind of motorway and main-line panorama which streams past the retina like a green Nowhere. And yet this is where John Bunyan's pilgrims walked and in their footsteps, for the better part of three centuries, walked all the English-reading world. Generations, millions walking in what they sensed was 'a vain shadow', followed the sacred map which he transposed on his native fields in order to reach the City of God. Never before or since has the geography of heaven and earth received so direct a literary integration. Except in the Scriptures themselves, of course. It was the newly published Authorized Version of these which took total charge of Bunyan's existence. They told him that he and his Midland contemporaries had no option but to set out for Christ or for Apollyon the Destroyer from their own flat lands. They insisted that no man living could avoid taking some path or other. Bunyan spun these options out – 'Still as I pulled it came' – in *The Pilgrim's Progress*, plainly and vigorously, and for a vast public, even in his own day. Indeed it was the runaway success of his Christian (*The Pilgrim's Progress* is two linked novels) that seems to have decided him on his Christiana – this and his need to honour women. The preface to the sequel shows Bunyan's unconcealed delight in the wholly unexpected popularity of the first volume.

> *My pilgrim's book has travelled sea and land . . .*
> *In France and Flanders where men kill each other*
> *My pilgrim is esteemed a friend, a brother.*
> *In Holland too, 'tis said, as I am told,*

My pilgrim is with some, worth more than gold.
Highlanders, and wild-Irish can agree,
My pilgrim should familiar with them be.
'Tis in New England under such advance . . .
As to be trimmed, new clothed and decked with gems,
That it might show its features, and its limbs,
Yet more; so comely doth my pilgrim walk,
That of him thousands daily sing and talk.

Already, in his own lifetime, Bunyan's Bedfordshire-turned-Holy Land had become the territory of an international Puritan quest. It is a prison book and a dream book. For years denied his wanderings across country to village meetings or to repair household utensils, prevented from preaching, cooped up, Bunyan's reaction to Bedford Gaol became that of an unstoppable river which, dammed in its natural course, floods its banks. All prison writing, from St Paul's to Breytenbach's, does this. There is little that could be called a longing for his local haunts in Bunyan's prison books. All his longing is for the Celestial City and he merely routes a way to it for others through the most familiar territory he knows. Did not Christ do the same? Roger Sharrock, the modern authority on Bunyan, sees him illuminating or recasting traditional symbols to some extent. 'The figure of the lonely wayfaring man, the simple honest foot-traveller with his pack on his back, goes back to the middle ages: Langland's Piers Plowman sets out thus on pilgrimage to find Truth after he had ploughed his half-acre. The modern imagination perhaps tends to see man more as a prisoner than as a traveller, but the image of the purposeful journey through life still has great evocative power . . .' Where Bunyan differed from both the medieval pilgrimage-writer and from ourselves was in what Sharrock calls 'the psychological dynamic' of his Calvinism. 'Puritanism has been misconceived as restrictive moral prohibitions, weighed down by sexual guilt; in the mid-seventeenth century it was a fiery religious and social dynamic resembling contemporary Marxism more than modern Fundamentalism.' Bunyan's advantage, he says, was that as a convert to Puritanism from a reformed earlier faith (which he adored when a boy), he was able to draw on the spirit of both in his writing.

That he did so unreservedly in *The Pilgrim's Progress* is the reason why he hesitated to publish a book which simply ran away with him. As the author of a number of profoundly serious works, including *Grace Abounding to the Chief of Sinners*, a spiritual autobiography which ranks with those by St Augustine and St Teresa, and as leader of the Bedford congregation, it has an enchanting, entertaining aspect to it which clearly bothered some of his friends. His preface to it in the form of a poem admits everything, how he was at work on another book when he 'fell' into this one – a dilemma which has overtaken many writers – how he wrote it for self-gratification, his literary genius getting the better of his moralising, and then his delightful offering it for the approval of his fellow Christians.

> *Some said, 'John, print it'; others said, 'not so';*
> *Some said, 'it might do good'; others said 'no'.*

He concludes, no author offering his new work more truthfully, that,

> *This book will make a traveller of thee,*
> *If by its counsel thou wilt ruled be;*
> *It will direct thee to the Holy Land,*
> *If thou wilt its directions understand . . .*

And it does. So does Bunyan-Christian's entire life in far from dull Bedfordshire. It is safe to say that it is best to know nothing of Bunyan if you want to tour this county under the usual topographical conditions. If not, it is the land of Last Things, of a sublime metaphor, of paths to paradise, of everything you couldn't see on the Inter City or M1 rush through the whole length of it. Bedfordshire needs a special exploration. But give it its earthly dimensions first, although not before adding that there is something to be said for those consistently passed-over places on the tourist route, for, not always being pressed and recommended, they are able to speak up for themselves when visited. Bedfordshire says many an unexpected thing. It is at first glance a wide open swoop of land which descends from the chalky barrier of the Chilterns (880ft/268m) to below sea level as it runs into Huntingdonshire and its black peats. Bunyan's quags and plats and bottoms have been called to order by modern agriculture and engineering, but are clearly only just below its tidy surface. Although a broad country, it is well hemmed in. The London Brick Company's works, once the largest in the world, fume away to the south of Bedford, whilst the Ouse, a big, handsome river, winds right across the central plain on its way to King's Lynn. Bunyan once accompanied his father on the long boat trip to Lynn to fetch metal for their trade. They were skilled pewterers and ironmongers, and of more superior stock than either of them ever realised, descending from yeomen who had lived in the district for centuries. Tinkers, they were called, and Bunyan made no attempt to improve this description. Similarly, the real facts of his native countryside, natural or historical, rarely got into his writing. For him, Bedfordshire's ecology was a series of hallowed or unhallowed places, its every feature telling a heavenly or a hellish tale. Born on the North Beds clayey mud, for him the chalk hills became infinitely preferable, not because they offered an easier working environment for a villager, but simply because they were white. He thought that the chalk which constituted the Chiltern ranges which stretched from Totternhoe to Barton and from Warden Hill to Dunstable Downs was like 'the Child of God . . . White in his life, easily wrought upon'. Exquisitely carved clunch from the Chiltern quarries was everywhere. It was a material which gave itself up completely to a creative hand. He wrote,

This stone is white, yea, warm, and also soft,
Easy to work upon, unless 'tis naught.
It leaves a white impression upon those
Whom it doth touch, be they Friends or Foes.

Gradually, this milky escarpment beyond the huge and, in his time, ill-drained vale of clay, blue with distance and with an unseeable world behind it, became the mountains carrying the soul of man upward to the level at which it could dwell with God. The peaks of the world have always been the seats of the Holy Ones, whether they be Kilimanjaro, Olympus or Cader Idris, but the blessed heights of Bunyan's landscape

419

are different. It is their modest ascendance at the limits of all that was familiar to him which gives his sublime story its human scale. Men are pilgrims and, as such, must encounter experiences ranging from happiness to terror in their journey to the divine presence. But they do not make this journey outside their own country. The universal success of *The Pilgrim's Progress* was due to its routing countless readers past all the strongest image-bearing geographical delights and hazards of their personal localities, reliable stretches of straight old road, meandering footpaths, the marketplace, the rectory, the welcoming inn, the low-lying spots full of the horrors, the warm, flowery meadows, those places which enlighten you and those which half-kill you. Everyone, from the unlettered peasant listening to it being read by the hearth, to the sophisticated person, knew exactly what it meant and how it applied privately to him. In order to live, he had to lift up his eyes unto the hills. Allegory, having made an extremely popular twentieth-century bow in terms of Tolkien and C. S. Lewis, is not the academic thing it was until recently. All the same, veiled moralisings are not the literary adventures they were, and those who read Bunyan now, do so differently to their grandparents. What was the most urgent and profound traveller's tale in the world to them, is just an astounding piece of prose to us. How was it done (we could ask)? By knowing that it had to be done, in the same way as a great rescue operation has to be done. John Bunyan, pot-mender, itinerant preacher and prisoner of conscience, who first tried his hand at popularising his own spiritual autobiography, eventually succeeded in producing a superb novelised Rule for Puritans. Roger Sharrock puts it most faithfully: 'A seventeenth-century Calvinist sat down to write a tract and produced a folk-epic of the universal religious imagination.'

Before entering some of the scenes which lent their contours to this folk-epic, and most surprisingly extant and little altered they are, we should perhaps glance at Elstow, where Bunyan was born and brought up, and at Bedford, a mile or two away, where he wrote. Although the road which links the two places is now built along – that same road in which, during his twenties, the tormented young man asked God to perform miracles through him by altering the position of its puddles – both town and village have managed to keep their distance. Bunyan

420

saw Elstow as the scene of his early degeneracy and Bedford, although it was the scene of his salvation, as the 'City of Destruction'. For him it was a town of very mixed blessings. Although it locked him up for many years, it could truly, with hindsight, say that it did so for his own good. For had it let him preach there would have been no need for him to write. He was a brilliant speaker and at first in the gaol all he tried to do was to put his silenced sermons on to paper. His pen then ran away with him into realms of natural literary expression. The quality of his writing was instantly recognisable to his contemporaries, and whatever else may have happened to him under the Clarendon Acts by way of humiliation and privation, he was never a prophet without honour in Bedfordshire. He was 'Bishop Bunyan', the spiritual father of his people, and the author of some sixty books, two of them masterpieces, and, from the moment of his arrest, a revered local man.

Briefly lumped by the conventional clergy with the ranters, Bunyan rapidly moved to a position in which he wrote for Englishmen of all classes. He was a phenomenon, a map-maker of Everyman's spiritual terrain. After so much confusing theological direction, here was a tough but sensible way of getting to Heaven set out in a language which everybody could understand. In order to live for ever more a man had to lift his sights from what normally elevated him, including church steeples, and take in his real prospect, which was nothing less than Christ's Kingdom itself. It beckoned on the edge of the home scenery. The journey to it was to be via the local track, not the stars. 'Have you never a hill Mizar to remember? Have you forgot the close, the milk house, the stable, the barn, and the like, where God did visit your soul?' *Grace Abounding*, a book which Bunyan intended to be no more than his own private traveller's tale of finding the way into the Kingdom, is full of precise Bedfordshire locations. We can see them feeding his imagination and his terror, but eventually nourishing his conviction that he was on the right road. We can see too that the fields and architecture of his boyhood were more than sufficient for all that a great writer needed during his childhood as founding facts and images for later creativity. As a Calvinist Bunyan would have abandoned all that belonged to his unredeemed self, but since it was traditional for such a convert to make a complete inventory of what he had turned from, *Grace Abounding* contains as intimate an account of a young man's view of the early seventeenth-century countryside as can be found anywhere. We know that although one's early life can be turned from, it does not go away. Bunyan's old and new lives rest one upon the other in *Grace Abounding* as the young man of merry England searches for the turning which will take him to immortality. When he discovered it, his eagerness to travel along it led to a coarsely rich simile which his contemporaries would have appreciated. 'My mind was now so turned, that it lay like a horse leech at the vein, still crying out, Give, give . . .' But had he a permit to enter the divine realm? This was his dilemma.

The mile or two of lanes and fields between Bedford and Elstow are both John Bunyan's playground and his *via dolorosa*. Here he ran wild with his friend Harry ('I now shook him off'), danced, rang all the bells, exploited his strength and good looks, and got a roaring boy's reputation. And here, in exactly the same place, he got the sudden urge to find the redemption which produced his breakdown. At first, amidst buildings and paths that exist to this day, it was, 'Oh these temptations were suitable for my flesh, I being a young man, and my nature in its prime', then it was deep spiritual crisis and envying laughing old women of Bedford because they 'were set on the sunny side of some high mountain . . . while I was shivering and shrinking in the cold'. Here, somewhere between the roads running out of Bedford to Ampthill and Hitchin he 'moped in the fields', desperately repeating over and over again, 'Thou art my love, thou art my love, thou art my love', his eyes full of tears and his conscience telling him, 'God hath been weary of you these several years . . . your bawlings in his ears hath been no pleasant voice to him.' Terrifyingly he came to believe that he had committed a special sin which was *outside* those for which Christ died, and he wished that he had been born a fish or a bird. And then, wandering once more in the Elstow fields – the reprieve! 'Christ! Christ! there was nothing but Christ that was before mine eyes . . .' Later, sitting by the fire with his newly married wife, and realising that, if there *was* a way to God, one would naturally have to travel along it, he asked her if she knew a text which said, 'I must go to Jesus'. She said she would see, but, two or three minutes later, a verse from Hebrews 12 'came bolting in upon me'. It was verse 22,

But ye are come unto mount Sion, and unto the city of the living God, the heavenly Jerusalem, and to an innumerable company of angels.

Bunyan had hit upon his Way, as well as, though some years hence, the journeying theme of *The Pilgrim's Progress*. 'That night was a good night to me, I never had but few better!' It was both natural and supernatural for a man to struggle out of his home clay towards those distant white heights and cerulean pinnacles. One can see how the Chilterns had attracted his upward stares as a child.

His actual birthplace is now no more than a corner of an empty field. The house site itself is a rough little copse by the side of a rivulet which supplied water for his family for centuries. The house, like the family, was originally more substantial than Bunyan ever understood. 'For my descent then, it was, as is well known by many, of a low and inconsiderable generation, my father's house being of that rank that is meanest and most despised of all the families in the land.' The Bunyans were in fact yeomen reduced to itinerant whitesmiths and John himself was a tall, well-built and impressive man whose education, if at Bedford Grammar School, would have been similar to that of Shakespeare. The total disappearance of his house excepted, Bunyan's home fields must be among the least changed surrounding the home of any major British writer, for they still can only be reached by the footpaths which he used, one of which follows the stream from Harrowden road and the other of which leads to Elstow. This little bit of country is soaked in association, Tinker's Hill, Bunyan's Field, Bunyan's Farm, and with references such as that written by the vicar of the neighbouring parish of Houghton Conquest: 'Memorandum – That in Anno 1625 one Bonion of Elsto clyminge of Rookes nests in the Bery wood found 3 Rookes in a nest, all as white as milke and not a black feather in them.' It lies on the Bedford side of a curiously large almost roadless rectangle which stretches from the town's suburbs to Wilshamstead, and with still more than a hint of the unenclosed ploughlands which the writer would have seen. But delectable (an adjective which Milton liked to use for trees) additions to what must always have been an unadorned native situation fill the horizon; Ampthill Heights and the mixture of a little palace and a parish church which post-Reformation builders created at Elstow. Artistry and Hebron shone across these flats. Coming to the isolated spot, marked now just by sloes, scraps of tile and a recent memorial, one is pressed between wheat and blackberries with unusually large flowers which edge the brook. This ditch runs into Cardington Brook, which is a tributary of the Ouse. Thus Bunyan can be said to have drunk for the whole of his youth the water in which he was baptised and through which he passed, metaphorically, in death. Also, to be less symbolic, twice nearly to natural death by drowning, once at Lynn.

The church of St Mary and St Helen at Elstow whose Laudian services Bunyan once so much enjoyed, and in which he was christened, stands at the top of a fine green. Its history is a witty and worldly one, and his account of his early life reflects a tradition of colourful goings-on in the neighbourhood. For the church, the ruined mansion beside it and the curious separate tower nearby are all part of what was until the Reformation a magnificent Benedictine abbey founded by William 1's niece Judith and ruled over for centuries by a succession of litigious and elegant ladies. An extravagant secularisation of the abbey had taken place just before Bunyan's birth, when the nuns' cathedral-like church had been mutilated to suit ordinary parish requirements and all the rest of their fine architecture demolished to provide stone for a glorious Inigo-Jones-like house for a local magnate, Sir Thomas Hillersdon. Throughout Bunyan's writing there is the alluring concept of the place of domestic ease, hospitality, earthly refinements and love being *en route* to the dwelling of God. Inside Elstow Church, amidst drastic 1880 changes, there is still much that Bunyan saw and touched. In the south aisle are the altar and rails at which he received the Sacraments, and in the north aisle the huge Perpendicular font to which his parents carried him from their poor old house across the meadows on 13 November 1628 to be named after his father. Here too his daughters, one of them the blind Mary who daily brought him hot soup during his long imprisonment, were baptised. Although Bunyan underwent adult baptism by immersion, he never forced it on his family or on others as a condition of faith. 'It is Love,' he said, 'not Baptism that discovereth us to the world to be Christ's Disciples.' All around the church are the medieval carvings which haunted him as a boy and which filled his dreams. Here among the corbels and trefoils reprieved by the Victorian rebuilder are the art forms which first pressed themselves on the imagination of one of the world's most influential dream-writers. William James, in his *The Varieties of Religious Experience* (1902), said that Bunyan's 'was a typical case of the psychopathic temperament, sensitive of conscience to a diseased degree, beset by doubts, fears, insistent ideas, and a victim of verbal automatisms, both motor and sensory. These were usually texts of Scripture which, sometimes damnatory and sometimes favourable, would come in half-hallucinatory form as if they were voices, and fasten on his mind and buffet it between them like a shuttlecock. Added to this were a fearful melancholy, self-contempt and despair.'

This game analogy is an apt one. Bunyan, like many village men, was mad about sport and recreation generally. When we wonder over his guilt concerning dancing and bellringing, we have to realise that it is the anxiety felt by a mature person at the hold which play continued to have on them. Bunyan possessed an outsized gift for enjoying himself, a zest for amusement. The time given up to watching, discussing and following games in the twentieth century is enormous but on the whole self-guiltless. Not so for the Puritan, for whom it was a trivialisation of his mortal existence. What Bunyan was unable to comprehend was that for him recreation, playing, spilled over into art, into music, and into nourishing his fantasies. To appreciate how a sermon against playing games on Sunday, which was about the most hackneyed rebuke which could come from a seventeenth-century village pulpit, could have put Bunyan into such a state of spiritual turbulence as to allow him to see 'the Lord Jesus looking down upon me, as being very hotly displeased with me', we have to understand that it was an overwhelming criticism and affront to his natural light-heartedness and artistry combined. What was he, if he was not of what he excelled at?

The landscape of this divine criticism remains little altered. At one end stands the parish church whose north door (now blocked up!) is the Wicket through which Christian passed to the House of the Interpreter, and nearby the tempting belfry, the castle from which Beelzebub shoots arrows at all who dare to approach the Straight Gate.

Now, you must know, that before this I had taken much delight in ringing, but my conscience beginning to be tender, I thought such practice was but vain, and therefore forced myself to leave it, yet my mind hankered . . . I began to think, how, if one of the bells should fall. Then I chose to stand under a main beam, that I might stand sure, but then I should think again, should the bell fall with a swing, it might first hit the wall, and then rebounding upon me, might kill me for all this beam, This made me stand in the steeple door; and now, thought I, I am safe enough; for if a bell should fall, I can slip out behind these thick walls, and so be preserved notwithstanding . . . Another thing was my dancing; I was a full year before I could quite leave that.

Below stretches the green where Bunyan danced and played games and attended the May fairs, the medieval Green House, now called the Moot Hall, with its arcaded shops, and West End Lane leading to Ampthill and the 'stately palace named Beautiful'. It was on Elstow Green, surrounded by all kinds of buildings and paths which he was to weave into his allegory, and which survive to this day, that, about to strike the 'cat' in the game of tip-cat, he heard God ask him the direct and dreadful question, 'Wilt thou leave thy sins and go to heaven, or have thy sins and go to hell?' His first reaction was that of a man who decides that he may as well be hanged for a sheep as for a lamb. He had, he says, 'a great desire to take my fill of sin, still studying what sin was yet to be committed, that I might taste the sweetness of it; and I made as much haste as I could to fill my belly with its delicates, lest I should die before I had my desires.' This sensuous craving Bunyan confesses in the opening pages of *Grace Abounding* because, he declares, it is 'more usual amongst poor creatures than many are aware of'. And so he fed on his pleasures 'with great greediness' and 'playing the madman', so much so that a woman shopkeeper let fly at him, telling him to his face that he was a source of corruption in the village. This coming from a person known locally for her own looseness shook him and he began to pull himself together, only to hate and despise what he was now seen as, a primly respectable young man.

Salvation may have uttered itself in the wilderness of the Bedford-Elstow fields and during lonely walks along their pot-holed lanes, but its language was that of books. Immense books like the newly translated Bible, a ragged, falling to pieces book called *A Commentary on Galatians* by Martin Luther which astounded Bunyan because, he said, it seemed to 'have been written out of my heart', and a couple of pious homilies which, although 'they did not reach my heart' can now be seen as part of his literary awakening; one was called *The Plain Man's Pathway to Heaven*. Even as he stumbled about, alternating between wild and sedate behaviour, we can see that details of his own immortal contribution to the literature of human life as an essentially solitary passage through a physical universe to a perfect spiritual destination were creeping into his subconscious. Although much later on, as a celebrated local preacher and popular author, Bunyan rode to engagements all over the East Midlands, and occasionally to London, the landscape experience which fills his poetry and prose is that of the walker. As a walking craftsman summoned by householders living within a twelve-mile radius of Bedford to repair their precious copper, brass and pewter, he would naturally have taken all the short-cuts possible to the farms, halls and cottages, unconsciously absorbing their privacy and intimacy, and, as Kim Taplin says in her study, *The English Path* (the best explanation of a neglected subject), equally unconsciously sorting out his ideas.

The image of life as a journey is so old and so persuasive that it is easy to forget it is one; but there is yet great emotional power in the contrast between a grim journeying and a state of house-keeping, settled content towards which, or out from which the traveller goes. English rural writers have often visualized the road of life as a country footpath . . . *Solvitur ambulando* – the old Latin tag means something like, 'You can sort it out by walking.' Working out, finding out, unknotting and freeing are all possible connotations of the word *solvitur* . . . A companionable path was more apt for a curative release than a road, since solitude, peace, and close contact with nature, as well as the action of walking, are all important ingredients. Problems unravel as the feet cover the miles, but through the body's surroundings, as well as the body's action.

She quotes the country priest-poet Andrew Young in his *A Traveller in Time*:

Where was I? What was I about to see?
Solvitur ambulando.
A path offered its company.

In his *Silver Ley*, the novelised autobiography of a young man farming in Suffolk, Adrian Bell supports the concept of the footpath, or 'narrow way', as the true thoroughfare, as it were, to where one must, at all cost, get. It is the snowy Christmas of 1928 and the main transport of the village, the bicycle, has been made obsolete overnight. Staring out of his window at the quiet white scene, he notes 'the reason for the dying away of footpaths in this our land. For now people are seen plodding straight for their object across the fields, whether it is the church spire, snow-encrusted, or the smoke of a cottage chimney. Who are they? Not travellers from far, for they would not venture out today – in fact the travelling area is suddenly restricted in time as it was a century ago. These are those parish workers who, when times are normal, take the serpentine routes of by-roads on bicycles.' 'Take the gentle path,' advises George Herbert in his poem *Discipline*. Although Bedford and Elstow between them are able to muster an extraordinary number of sites and associations connected with Bunyan and have few equals where a writer of his genius is concerned, still the closest one can come to him is via the little tracks criss-crossing the entire area. These are what stimulated both his rich introspection and his vision of the blue and high horizon as a sacred view. A simple way to become a 'heavenly footman' is to walk this earth.

So tread in his steps along the footpath running from Old Harrowden Lane to his birthplace, taking in all that is close at hand and all that is most distant. Find a good map and pick out its ancient cross- country ways to Haynes, Flitton, Pulloxhill, Marston Moretaine, Astwood, Oakley, Clapham, Mogerhanger, Old Warden, Wootton, Steppingley,

Ridgmont, Ravensden and old isolated farms and mills, secret reaches of the Ouse, ancient protective woods and especially any path leading up to an eminence which would allow the eyes to feast on the Chilterns, for these are where, walking between customers and congregations, Bunyan recognised himself and his God. 'Where was I? What was I about to see?' Any of us following him around should go on asking these questions. For it is a country whose answers do not lie on the Ordnance Survey, help though it is.

But we cannot drive off without touring the Bedfordshire basis of Christian's progress. Even in an age which knows little of the book, it is still a profoundly affecting experience, this visiting the actual geography out of which was created a religious metaphor which served a worldwide Protestant philosophy for three centuries. 'These are the words of the Lord,' wrote the prophet Jeremiah. 'Stop at the crossroads, look for the ancient paths; ask, "Where is the way that leads to what is good?" Then take that way, and you will find rest for yourselves. But they said, "We will not" Then I will appoint watchmen to direct you, listen to their trumpet call.' Bunyan doesn't mention this text but it seems to contain the very plot and inspiration of *The Pilgrim's Progress*. It fits across his Bedfordshire like a template, and one can still stop at a particular crossroads, trace certain ancient paths, see the house from which the writer's own trusted watchman set him right, as country people say when they have given a traveller information, and stand by a wide river across which nightly he heard a trumpet-call. The tracing of that most famous of all English journeys from despair to bliss via both the busy main roads and silent lanes which lead from the centre of Bedford to the Chiltern Hills is one of Britain's major literary landscape adventures.

One of the most compelling aspects of the Gospels for the Puritan reader was their restlessness. The age itself, radical and seeking, roaming and energetic, thrust its way past all kinds of things which previous centuries had regarded as ends in themselves. Obedience to old institutions became of no consequence in comparison with obedience to Scripture. Reading the stupendous new translation of the life of Jesus, the Puritan encountered a perfectly rational human intelligence as well as the Christ. The Gospels were so full of action and movement that they became a dynamic which began to drive the whole social fabric. The most appalling question for many, and for Bunyan and the saints of his Bedfordshire plain, was, were they a predestined part of this sacred vitality, or were they just being dragged along in its wake with no guarantee that they would ever reach its blessed destination? Individually, and with intense relief, he and countless others decided that although they were indeed predestined for God's presence at the last, they had no right to believe that they could arrive in it without following his Son's instructions to the letter. It was then that they recognized the human as well as the divine scale of Christ's law – 'For the Son of Man is as a man taking a far journey, who left his house, and gave authority to his servants, and to every man his work, and commanded the porter to watch.' What could be clearer? He had left them with his commission and their task, but as he had also said, 'Follow me', they had to carry them out while making a lifelong progress to where he waited for them in the Celestial City.

Bunyan's feat was to correlate the long walk which Jesus made through Palestine with the typical walk through life made by a seventeenth-century Englishman. *The Pilgrim's Progress* inaugurated a whole new love and understanding of Christ, because men found that there were long stretches of the way where they could keep step with him. But the conditions for going Christ's way were severe; Bunyan-Christian, the vulnerable hero of the story, gets lost, gets terrified, gets into every kind of predicament before he and his friend Hopeful cross the River, enter the Gate and are able to 'look their Redeemer in the face with joy'. Jesus's walk through this world was both touchingly natural and wondrously supernatural. Its natural progression took in sights and experiences which were often very little removed from those of Bunyan's rural contemporaries. Although born into an ancient civilisation of settled temples and courts, Christ remained from birth to death a being of passage. His birth was crowded with journeys and his death followed a long walk to the scaffold. In between, the references to his unsettled state are ceaseless, and unsettlement is what he commanded of his followers. The Saviour walks on and on through villages, towns, fields, meadows, past wells and pools and the great lake, and in his human exhaustion envies the foxes and birds their cosy homes. He travels to the wilderness for self examination and climbs the mountains to be near his Father in prayer. He sees wheat, thistles, figs, trees, mustard, brambles, colts, pigs, fish, grapes, barns, friends' houses, inns, shepherds, beggars, soldiers, prostitutes, children, disease, beauty, everything of the best, everything unmentionable. It is a life of endless encounters and withdrawals. He loves Palestine and when he prays he always gives thanks to the Father of heaven and earth. He talks of cleansed men walking through dry places, seeking rest. 'Nevertheless,' he tells his companions, 'I must walk today, and tomorrow, and the day following . . .' He urges them to 'Walk while ye have the light, that ye may be the children of light . . . Whither I go ye know, and the way ye know . . . *I am the way.*' His direction is the ultimate one. 'He that doesn't take his cross and follow me, isn't worthy of me.' On this journey a man must leave behind his stave, scrip, food, money and spare coat, must leave his wife and children if necessary.

Christian did. Bunyan too was accused of making his family suffer for the sake of refusing to promise not to preach and thus having to stay in prison instead of looking after them. Bedford became his Nazareth, the Ouse his Jordan-Lethe, the Chilterns the high road to the New Jerusalem, the Elstow fields his wilderness, Stevington his Calvary and the homes of his friends his Bethany. Soon, in his own lifetime, huge numbers of the Gospel-absorbed world would be reading his allegory and translating it into their native scenery. Sion would lie beyond Snowdon or Brown Willy, or just the blue of any distant rise; ploughmen squelching and struggling through the undrained bottom of a field were powerfully reminded of the sin of despair. Fine new Tudor houses, many of them constructed from old abbeys and priories, rather than churches, foretold the 'many mansions' which awaited the people of God. Rivers became sacred again for the first time since the days of the ancient nature gods, due to their secret use for baptism by immersion. Twice in a lifetime their waters had to be braved, once when the Christian symbolically died to the 'world', once when he departed from the earthly scene. All over the country, whether they were modest streams like Suffolk's river Box and

Shropshire's river Teme, or the broad Thames and Severn, they now spoke of inescapable tests and of eternity. No single work of English literature has so 're-symbolised' a local landscape as *The Pilgrim's Progress*.

The Puritan cosmos claimed each man's home ground, and caused him to be confined to the limits of a moral and spiritual map. 'For the Kingdom of Heaven is as a man travelling into a far country.' *A* man – not generations, not populations, not generalised humanity – this was the accent on Bunyan's traveller, an individuality through which each separate reader could see his own progress, or lack of it. As in a great novel, the reader becomes one with the central character. Where Bunyan shows his genius is in seeing that his heaven-bound man, woman or child, although guaranteed a safe eternal lodging at the last, never wanders away from their earthliness into realms of fantasy. If Bedfordshire and its inhabitants are one's earthly lot, then it will be they, not some tempting Elfland and its creatures, which will provide life's ups and downs until the struggle is over. Roger Sharrock points out that it is not the landscape and characters of *The Pilgrim's Progress* which have reached a position where we can no longer easily identify with them, but its theology. For generations of his readers the life-cycle rolled on, in or out of obedience, with a doctrine of Redemption which even the ignorant intuitively recognized and accepted but which today few know anything about. The grandeur of the book, in popular terms, is thus lost.

But a tour of its setting is still an incomparable spiritual experience. The country of those folk we still know so well, Pliable, Obstinate, Worldly-Wiseman, Talkative, Faithful, Hopeful, Madam Bubble, Mr Honest, Mr Stand-fast, Mr Great-heart, Giant Despair and all the rest of them (and us), lies open to anyone with a copy of the allegory and a copy of Sheet 147 of the Ordnance Survey. Some of its sites, Stevington, for example, are as moving to discover as those of martyrdom. Others, like Houghton House, charge the sightseeing imagination. But there are too Bunyan's witty generalisations throughout the book, such as when Christian runs into a fellow traveller called Mr By-ends of Fair-speech, a gentleman of rank *en route* to Paradise, who loves to walk with religion in the street if the sun shines. Which one of us, who, after reading Mr By-ends's airy description of his pedigree will ever be able to take the average claims of local magnates without a pinch of Leveller's salt? – 'to tell you the truth, I am become a gentleman of good quality; yet my great grandfather was but a waterman, looking one way and rowing another: and I got most of my estate by the same occupation . . . my wife is a very virtuous woman, the daughter of a virtuous woman. She was my Lady Faining's daughter, therefore she came of a very honourable family, and is arrived to such a pitch of breeding that she knows how to carry it to all . . .' These are lines which wouldn't come amiss on the Restoration stage. Although some people in his book called Christian 'Fool and Noddy', Bunyan's remains an often painfully sharp English intelligence.

Begin then in Bedford itself, where the book began 'in the similitude of a dream', and in the town gaol which stood at the corner of High Street and Silver Street, and where the dreamer beheld 'a man clothed with rags, standing in a certain place, with his face from his own house [Bunyan's was only five minutes away in St Cuthbert's Street], a book in his hand, and a great burden on his back'. There in a little town of then no more than two thousand inhabitants, which in his allegory he has unified with his birthplace Elstow, we can follow the anxious Bunyan-Christian about, and see why he was terrified that he would be pressed down into Tophet (Hell) by the weight of evil that he was carrying. Here are scores of houses which he would have known, but most importantly that of his friend John Gifford, St John's Rectory, south of the river. Here Gifford explained and taught an entirely Bible-bound faith to the worried young tradesman who immortalised it as 'the House of the Interpreter'. The two of them talked in the main room which was once a medieval refectory and, according to legend, under the cedar and mulberry trees which still thrive in the garden. When at the Restoration Gifford was ejected from the living as an 'intruder', he and his friends were unceremoniously described as 'one Bunnion, a tincker, Burton a coachsmith, and one Gifford, all schismatics'. A few steps from St John's flows the Ouse and the Duck Mill backwater where, late at night, Bunyan received baptism from his 'Interpreter'. From the small religious community which was formed under John

Gifford in 1650 there has sprung one of the most celebrated independent Christian churches in the world, the Bunyan Meeting. Its home in Mill Street contains relics of the writer so intimate and so clearly invested with his presence still, that all the rationality of Calvinism fails to rid them entirely of their relic-like power. His meeting-house chair, his iron violin, his anvil, probably the very one he lugged with him all the way to Ampthill and his 'House Beautiful'; the door of his prison cell, his walking-stick, the table he wrote on in the gaol, and the table at which he presided during Communion, the warrant for his arrest and scraps of wood from his various pulpits, the latter in particular proving the persistence of relicry even to the emancipated, all are here. Bedford produced a great saint and has always known it. The doors of the Meeting reveal a further example of Puritanism's ability to accept what it is popularly believed to detest, ecclesiastical imagery of the highest order in the form of a pair of bronze doors by the Victorian artist Frederick Thrupp on which, inspired by Ghiberti, ten high-relief panels picture *The Pilgrim's Progress*. Given by the 9th Duke of Bedford in 1876 and hung to the singing of Handel's Hallelujah Chorus, their magnificence is only now being comprehended. If anything, these lovely doors witness more than anything else to the generally unsuspected ecumenicity of the Bedford faithful, who from the start have always allowed both infant and adult baptism, with all that these two concepts imply. Bunyan, who received the interpretation of Christ which he could accept at St John the Baptist's Rectory, would have enjoyed the coincidence that an English work of art based on *The Pilgrim's Progress* should have evolved from the youthful Thrupp's contemplation of Ghiberti's 'Paradise Doors' which opened on to the Baptistry of St John in Florence.

Tracing *The Pilgrim's Progress* makes a memorable beginning to the discovery of Bedfordshire. Easily the most startling halt by the way is Stevington, a cruciform village five miles from Bedford along the Sharnbrook road. A medieval market cross rises from its hub and below, down a dipping lane which peters out into water-meadows, stands the parish church with its Saxon tower. Both church and houses are built on rocky lime outcrops. From the one which supports the church a limestone spring with an immemorial reputation for curing blindness gushes. A holy well. When I was there, little girls were splashing its water against their bright eyes 'to see better'. The valley-descending lane becomes a muddy track at this point and half lost under the butterbur (*Petasites hybridus*). Neither the ubiquitous flower festival taking place in the church, nor its architectural guide, had the faintest reference to the fact that Stevington was the scene of a salvation experience which, next to those in the Bible itself, had more influence on post-Reformation England than any other. For it is believed that this village, to which the young Bunyan frequently walked to preach to the Independents at their secret meetings in the Holmes Wood, crossing over as he did so, and ironically for him, Dancing Meadow ('and then there was my dancing . . .'), was the place where Christian lost his burden. It is the incident in the allegory, next to that in which Mr Valiant-for-Truth passes over the river of death and has 'the trumpets sounded for him on the other side' (Bunyan heard a trumpeter sound the curfew each night by Bedford bridge), which most thrilled countless readers, and at Stevington one can walk through its imagery from beginning to end.

Christian, having been told by the Interpreter the road he has to go, and accompanied as all Celestial City-bound travellers are by the Comforter, ran with difficulty, because of his heavy load of sin, up the highway. 'He ran thus until he came at a place somewhat ascending [the lane leading from Stevington church]; and upon that place stood a Cross [the present market cross, and the one which Bunyan probably had in mind when, in his tract *The Heavenly Footman*, he writes that 'the cross is the standing way mark by which all they that go to glory must pass by'], and a little below in the bottom, a sepulchre [the holy well]. So I saw in my dream, that just as Christian came up with the Cross, his burden loosed from off his shoulders, and fell from off his back; and began to tumble, and so continued to do till it came to the mouth of the sepulchre, where it fell in, and I saw it no more. Then was Christian glad and lightsome, and said with a merry heart, "He hath given me rest, by his sorrow, and life, by his death." Then he stood still a while, to look and wonder; for it was very surprising to him that the sight of the Cross should thus ease him of his burden. He looked therefore, and looked again, even till the springs that were in his head sent the waters down his cheeks.' Later, it is by the wall of Stevington church that Christian encounters Simple, Sloth, Presumption, Formalist and Hypocrisy.

For John Bunyan, the village of Stevington was associated with intense personal meaning and emotion. The notorious Five Mile Act which forbad nonconforming Christians to assemble in Bedford had swelled its open-air meeting and the record kept of the services gives a vivid picture of what it was like to worship late at night in the soaking meadows below the church 'when the females screened their minister's head from the damps of the night with their aprons'. In many parts of England nonconformists, especially Quakers, were being hunted; breaking up their assemblies and routing them from their hiding place had become a loutish sport. The Holmes Wood at Stevington is a potent mark on the Bedfordshire map for it is where Bunyan began to understand himself, and discovered that he possessed a power with words, spoken ones first and then, when these were silenced, words on a page. His discreet and threatened walks, there and to other secluded spots, contained a drama and excitement which fed his literary imagination – 'hedges have eyes' – and helped to lay the foundations of his masterpiece. Vera Brittain in her biography says that 'Bunyan made Bedfordshire's homely villages and peaceful streams shine with the light of Heaven itself and turned the life of an ordinary man struggling to overcome his daily temptations into a journey as heroic as Jason's quest for the Golden Fleece.' She adds that it was a supreme example of unconscious achievement, 'for he neither knew nor cared that at a single step he had created the English novel'. She saw him as a naturally tolerant man existing amidst national intolerance and that 'he wrought an unrecognized miracle in his cell above the gateway of the county gaol'. Kipling called Bunyan 'The Father of the Novel/Salvation's first Defoe', and Disraeli, 'the Spenser of the people'.

The essence of this divine peregrination is to realise always that wherever his hero went, whether they were the heights and depths of the spirit or of Bedfordshire, its author had gone before. *The Pilgrim's Progress* has sanctified an English county in a manner which no other book has done before or since. Christian was never made to travel beyond the bounds of a Bedford Meeting saint, literally or figuratively, and ever since his life has remained an astonishing lesson on how an ordinary person can intensify the home scene. Don't get bogged down in it, as Bunyan's contemporaries frequently were in both senses as they grasped for money and social standing on their ill-drained, swampy plain. Get up and go to the visible heights of love. He took stock of this prospect from the window of a palace whilst mending a bath, his 'House Beautiful', Lord Ailesbury's seat on Ampthill Heights (Hill Difficulty), for two centuries now a soaring, empty shell called Houghton House. It was a view which loomed large when, many years of imprisonment and twenty-two books later, he gave in to an urge 'to use those metaphysical descriptions which Hosea called "similitudes"' (Vera Brittain) in a tale which would make millions look up from the daily round to a transcendance which, with 'a little grace, a little love, a little true fear of God', could be theirs.

Other *Pilgrim's Progress* places are Milibrook on its hill, below which lies 'The Valley of the Shadow of Death'; Cardington Brook, 'the Slough of Despond'; the Vale of Flit, 'the Valley of Humiliation', and Watling Street and the Baldock-Biggleswade stretches of Roman road, the 'strait' path. John Bunyan's allegory supplanted in popularity in the Protestant esteem John Foxe's *Book of Martyrs*, a work which he knew backwards. In the latter the Italian martyr Algerius is quoted as saying, 'In this world there is no mansion firm to me, and therefore I will travel up to the New Jerusalem, which is in Heaven, and which offereth itself to me without paying any fine or income. Behold, I have entered already on my journey, where my house standeth for me prepared, and where I shall have riches, kinsfolk, delights, honours, never failing.'

Bunyan defended his superb allegory from accusations of its being a frivolous version of the faith by citing Christ himself who 'in olden times held forth by types, shadows and metaphors'. In August 1688, a wild, wet month, he set out yet again towards the Delectable Mountains, this time on horseback, riding below them across the Aylesbury Plain to Marlow, Henley and Reading to London, where he had promised to preach for a friend. He was sixty and the burly strength which both he and his followers had for so long taken for

437

granted was failing him. He arrived in the capital soaked and exhausted, and died a few days later from pneumonia. Thus it was that instead of a resurrection-awaiting grave by the wide Ouse, he was taken to what Southey called 'the Campo Santo of the Dissenters', Bunhill Fields, where he lies beneath a blitzed memorial near William Blake, Susannah Wesley, Daniel Defoe, Isaac Watts and thousands more who, it is no exaggeration to say, would have known his book by heart. There was to be a further suitability, for just west of Bunhill Fields is Bunhill Row, where John Milton completed *Paradise Lost*, England's major Christian epic. These two extraordinary instances of Puritan genius were published within a year of each other.

Among the lines of *Paradise Lost*, which Milton wrote only a short walk from Bunyan's grave, are these. Michael is reconciling Adam to the next best thing to Eden. Having been brought 'To dwell on even ground' because of his sin, he is not to despair, for

> . . . *doubt not for in Vallie and in Plaine*
> *God is as here, and will be found alike*
> *Present, and of his presence many a signe*
> *Still following thee, still compassing thee round*
> *With goodness and paternal love, his Face*
> *Express, and of his steps the track Divine.*

And did that face see and those feet walk England's green and pleasant land, Blake was to ask. Humanity usually searches for its deity on the home ground.

Elstow, the epicentre of Bunyan's spiritual disturbance and the heart of *The Pilgrim's Progress*, has now been designated a suitable place to deposit nuclear waste.

THE VIEW IN WINTER

Introduction to
THE VIEW IN WINTER
Reflections on Old Age

Ronald Blythe, 1979

Our earthly time allowance has rapidly shot up from an average of forty years to an average of seventy years plus within the experience of all the old people alive at present. Nothing comparable to it has been known before. Although it was accepted that the body had been programmed to last for the classic three- score-years-and-ten, until now there was an all too eloquent proof that very few bodies ever did, and for a man to 'see his time out', as they used to say, was exceptional. We counter this fact by declaring that one was old at forty in those days. Yet one was not, at least not in the sense of cumulative time, which is what defines actual old age. A vast number of men and women became toil-worn and disease-marked in middle age to a degree no longer seen in Western society, but however exhausted and unhygienic their flesh, it was unlikely to have been senescent when the grave claimed it. Apart from the minority whose mortal clock – the workings of which are still a mystery – went the full round, most were not involved in the ageing process and seemed to have lived without thought or preparation for it.

It is one of the essential ways in which our forebears differ from us. Their knowledge of the destruction of the physical self was quite unlike anything we understand by hospital visits or by simply walking down the street. If a Renaissance or Georgian man could return he would be as much astonished by the sight of two or three thousand septuagenarians and octogenarians lining a south-coast resort on a summer's day in their preponderantly white and palely coloured clothes, as he would by a television-set. Astonished and maybe shocked. His was a world where it was the exception to go grey, to

441

reach the menopause, to retire, to become senile and to acquire that subtle blend of voice, skin and behavioural changes which features so largely in our long-lived times. Because of its customary incompletion, life for him operated from a quite different premise. For one thing, it contained a precariousness which we, for all our nuclear hazards, no longer feel. For another, it conditioned a man to accept his cut-down or halved time-scale as that against which he would need to plan his education or craft training, his work and his children's future, and to think of reaching seventy in quasi-religious terms. To be seventy or eighty was to be as 'full of years' as a multicentenarian Old Testament prophet.

Another contrast between old age then and old age now is that we place dying in what we take to be its logical position, which is at the close of a long life – when our ancestors accepted the futility of placing it in any position at all. In the midst of life we are in death, they said, and they meant it. To them it was a fact, to us it is a metaphor. It secretly disturbs us to see old people talking and behaving as if they were in the midst of life. We ask ourselves, 'How can they . . . with so little time to go?' But to love and travel and fight and bluster in the face of death, as it once confronted the early middle-aged, was thought brave and admirable. It meant that people were once, for all their fatal illnesses, vital, capable and very much alive up to the edge of their graves. It was said of the seventy-year-old Elizabeth I, when death came to her, that she was a lady surprised by time. But she was old and this was gallantry.

The manner in which death suddenly announced itself to the average mortal was indeed a surprise and the subject of a poignant literature. The common fate of a brief life bred apprehension, swift-moving ambition or piety, according to one's character, but because the majority of men knew no other life it had a normality which is now outside our comprehension. So altered are we that it sometimes seems that we are reaching the stage when we may have to announce ourselves to death, and may find its avoidance of us hurtful and neglectful. In hospitals up and down the land lie the finished lives which appear, as it were, to have been 'cut dead' by death. It is as though one needs a special strength to die, and not a final weakness.

Yet weakness is what characterises the old most of all. And so, in its less extreme state, is there a power in this unique weakness which sustains age and makes it as positive a time as youth or maturity? One of the reasons why the old suffer is because the non-old dislike the notion that they are vital still. 'How well old people come to know that peculiar look of suppressed disgust which their obstinate concentration on some restricted sensual pleasure excites in the feverish idealism of the young and in the impatient pragmatism of the middle-aged! What is their wisest method of mental defence against the shameful discomfort caused by this look?' wrote John Cowper Powys when he was seventy-two.

We talk and think and generally preoccupy ourselves with this new fate of an old age for everybody. But we never say, as we might with any other general advancement, 'How wonderful it is that by the year 2000 everybody will be more or less guaranteed of a full life!' Instead we mutter, our faces thickened with anxiety, 'Just think, in twenty years' time half the population will be over sixty.' We rarely add that any blame for an imbalance must be shared by the young for not having babies or that when *we* reach sixty our energies and hopes and intentions are as likely to carry us forward into the welcome decades to come as much as the next old man's.

The economics of national longevity apart, the ordinariness of living to be old is too novel a thing at the moment to appreciate. The old have been made to feel that they have been sentenced to life and turned into a matter for public concern. They are the first generations of the full-timers and thus the first generations of old people for whom the state, experimentally, grudgingly and uncertainly, is having to make special supportive conditions. This book listens to them talking. Except for a few spiritual travellers – and the most heroic of these confess to weeks and months and years when the static element in old age makes it impossible for them to advance an inch in the heavenly direction – all movement in the talk is backward to youth and childhood. The skill and determination with which the aged are able to return to their first memories is only equalled by the world's eels slipping back to the Sargasso Sea. They find peace in childhood but none in maturity remembered and little in the present. So they embark, along with any

443

willing ear, for the beginning, where things still move fast and are bright and clearly defined.

The most irreconcilable aspect of agedness is the destruction of progressive movement, that hard fact of having come to the end of the journey when custom and instinct still insist that one can, and should, go on. When the old say, as they so often do, 'I simply can't go on,' they are stating their major frustration, not announcing a coming to terms with death. Few are nervous about the nearness of death, although what time remains often becomes very precious and sweet in spite of the harassment by disease and arthritic pain, unhealing skin and multiplying discomforts. Many old people, talking within months or weeks of their deaths, became exceptionally alive and were greedy for every sight and touch. Some were full of arrangements about the disposal of possessions. A few dropped the mask by which the world – and this could include their families – had known them and confessed to what they really were. These masks were primarily those of orthodoxy hiding the married homosexual, the church-going unbeliever and the heretic in the political party. More of a conspiratorial than a cowardly attitude was revealed in the reasons for wearing masks; all the world being a stage, it appears that there are far more people who get their dramatic kicks by operating its conventions than is suspected. The old, too, revealed conversions to a host of well-nigh forgotten causes and loyalty towards vanished concepts. These ideas lie about in their natures and in their thinking, an ineradicable tincture acquired half a century or more ago in the Empire, on some grim farm, in the ritualistic Mess, via Douglas Credit or early Hollywood, Toc-H, the Left Book Club, the British Union of Fascists ('Ah,' said the eighty-year-old Henry Williamson gently, going through his snapshots, 'the S.S. . . .') and never quite disappear. Men are usually converted to notions and creeds for which they have an innate disposition. Listening to the nonagenarian who had opened her heart and mind to the teachings of Maria Montessori, one saw the highest example of such a predisposition.

Many of today's old people had such rough starts, such small scraps of education, wages and possessions generally, that they feel they are ending their days in clover. 'Manage' is a word they much use and having 'managed' then, they manage now. They describe penurious and exhausting working lives without rancour. They are proud if they never cheated, and they are proud if they did and got away with it. But some find that now is the deprived time. They are aware of ceaseless depredation and of everything being snatched from them or placed out of reach, and of being narrowed and lessened and ground-out of their very personality. They are shaken by the extent of their impoverishment, both spiritually and materially, and are disturbed when such guardians of their riches as a loving family or a good doctor are powerless to prevent it happening. Tolstoy dealt with this terrible dismantling of the ego in his story *The Death of Ivan Ilyich*, in which a middle-aged man who has acquired everything necessary for his social identification among the successful and the conventional, has to watch himself stripped down by cancer until all that is left of him is a scream. Constantly, as one talked to the aged, one felt this struggle to say who they are, not just who and what they have been.

And then there are the relinquishers and abdicators who drop the reins of their own accord, who sometimes acquire new friends because they don't insist on close relationships, and whose main action seems to be stretching out an irreverent arm and sweeping the clutter off the board. This category of old person often welcomes solitude, which is thought perverse and awkward of them by the family and by the welfare authorities. Many old people, however, simply want what they have had. They want it badly, and there is never much diminution in the strength of their hankering for what has been, for all the convenient talk about the merciful failing of desire. Old age is not an emancipation from desire for most of us; that is a large part of its tragedy. The old want (but their sensible refusal to put such wants into words suggests to us that they have given up wanting) their professional status back, or their looks, or their circle which is now a lot of crossed-off names in the address-book, or sex, or just a normal future-orientated existence. Most of all they want to be wanted. It crashes on them like a nightmare, the leaden fact that they are eighty, and that now it is often not so much a matter of their being incapable of having some of the things they want, as there being laws and conventions preventing their access to them.

445

Perhaps, as the young begin to realise that they are likely to be 'old' for twenty or more years, radical changes will effect what the aged want and could still have. Certainly, we are likely to see retirement-refusal, and a lifting of one of the last big sexual taboos, that placed on sex in old age.

The hope that sexuality itself would wither away and not add its desperate frustrations to agedness has long since been turned into the quite unfounded assurance that with age we naturally become asexual. What evidence we have to the contrary we manipulate to prove the social desirability of a sexless old age and to advocate the controls needed to achieve it. We tell the old, if you do not conform to this negative ideal you will be either ludicrous or indecent, that people will be frightened of you and think of you as pitiful or as a nuisance, for you are engaging in what is next to impossible or unthinkable. Thus the wistful legend and the rules of convenience which it has spawned. These rules and attitudes are among the very last to be overturned by our society in its urgent need to understand the realities of ageing. But the notion that the old are beyond sex still governs most public and private systems to house them and, outside, in countless ordinary situations such as going to the pub, the cinema or on holiday, the elderly man or woman finds it prudent to conceal any interest in what takes his or her fancy. We approve of this and are grateful to old relatives, friends, neighbours and even old strangers for this disciplined concealment. But we prefer not to know that among the most important reasons why the old guard their eroticism from the risk of having it mocked or judged is not because they believe it to be shameful or unnatural at their time of life, but to protect something which has in the past brought them so much love and delight from contempt. For all our new caring and planning, to be old today is to be contemptible. Why? Because to be old is to be part of a huge and ordinary multitude, a section of society so fast-growing in its needs and demands as to create another kind of helplessness in the young and middle-aged, making them feel guilty and resentful. The reason why old age was venerated in the past was because it was extraordinary. Among the few ways an aged individual can escape from a vast problematical category into his own distinctive personality is via his genital primacy, even if it means little more at this stage than living in what has been called 'a kind of after image'.

Proof that overt sexuality in the aged is all part of the sexual legitimacy which accompanies us from the cradle to the grave, so to speak, lies in its ability to disturb society as it does. We may prohibit it or ridicule it, but when we become involved with it, however peripherally, it is always a bit of a shock to find in it something neither old nor age-defying. As was said at the first symposium of the Boston Society for Gerontologic Psychiatry nearly twenty years ago, when the whole subject began to be demythologised, 'The conflicts concerning sexual thought and behaviour that are so clearly seen in younger people survive in the old. In many of the aged, conflicts concerning sexual expression are longstanding. However, many people who during their youth and middle years were able to achieve relative comfort about sexuality became uncomfortable with their erotic desire in a culture that either forbids or denies it its reality.'

'The fact that the idealized sexual standard of the culture emphasizes the firm bodies of youth may also reactivate oedipal conflicts in the aged,' it was pointed out by two of the delegates, Dr Zinberg and Dr Kaufman. 'The passage of years has not made forbidden sexual interests any easier for the person to tolerate [and] we know full well from our patients that it is not only the children, but also the parents, whose sexual interests and defenses against them are activated by the processes of development. This *ronde* does not stop until death. The shame experienced by the old man as the result of a forbidden sexual impulse that may or may not be repressed sets up reverberations in his younger physician and family . . . This rondelay of point and counterpoint is complicated by the cultural attitude which makes it extremely necessary for both sides to deny that it is taking place. When feelings are so urgently repressed, the result is often more rather than less activity . . .'

However, the aged are not only expected to continue to suppress what they were obliged to suppress most of their lives but also that conventional sexuality which, until they became old, was an acceptable or even a welcome aspect of their personalities. It could include a permissible and admired sexual display on the dance-floor and the beach, the wearing of attractive clothes and hair-styles, and the playful sensuality which doesn't feel obliged to conceal itself in the conventional body-contacts of hugs, handshakes, kisses, etc. All this, should it still exist, has to be subject to a new discretion. Not the least tragic aspect of old age is learning how to provide false evidence in such matters. Old men and women will continue to do so for their own safety's sake until society rids itself of its inhibitions on the subject.

Modern geriatric psychiatry speaks of the old being wounded in their narcissism, a poignant term and one which eloquently compresses the whole business of what we once were, and what we must inevitably become, should we see our time out. To be sexually prohibited, even if it is only in some ignorant, unwritten and folk-belief sense, is a gratuitous addition to this hurt. The natural checks of old age lie in sublimations and in the slowly dying organism itself, not in such repressions. In any case, they are only a surface thing, for the old learn how to prevent too great a wounding of their narcissism by healing forays into the past, where there can still be found much of what is necessary to maintain a self-acceptable image of themselves. Such an image is bound to have its bright sexual facets, for, as A.L.Vischer says, 'It is difficult to renounce a thing when we know its value and the delight which it affords and when our memory of it does not fade but even calls for repetition.' He adds that in a period in which youth, physical beauty and the achievement of sexual ecstasy are the standard grist of every popular newspaper, glossy magazine, song, film and advertisement, 'it is not surprising that the subject of sexuality is not so easily exhausted by the older generation'.

At present there is much in our treatment of the old and our attitudes towards them which is scandalously similar to that which governed nineteenth-century attempts to solve the 'intractable' problem of the poor. They are not *us*, is what we are often saying (politely and humanely, of course), and there are so many of them! Such a situation can only alter when it becomes natural to say that the old *are* us – and to believe it.

The inescapability of old age is now secretly for many the new predicament. And even those who pray, and save, for a long life have the feeling that by eating and behaving in the way which they believe

448

will encourage longevity, they are tempting fate. Some comfort is gained by seeing 'old Mr Smith, who is wonderful' at eighty-two, and by avoiding the sight of old Mrs Everard, who *was* wonderful at eighty but who now lies, year after year, under a tidy white hump of hospital quilt which is almost as still as her little green mound will be – though when? That is her quandary, the slow motion departure.

To be a potential candidate for the Tithonus situation is the great dread of the aged. The possibility haunts the latter years of retirement. Tithonus was a beautiful young man who so delighted in being alive that he asked Aurora, goddess of morning, to make him immortal. She did, but as it had not occurred to him to request perpetual youthfulness as well, he simply became an old man who could not die. Eventually, taking pity on him after listening to his repeated prayer that he should be freed from his never-ending dissolution, the goddess turned him into a grasshopper. Not, presumably, the burdensome insect of Ecclesiastes, which some have interpreted as an image of the withered, useless genitals of an old man, nor yet the swollen-paunched locust of the modern translators of the same passage, but the leaping, chirping creature whose alacrity is the antithesis of fixed senility.

Tennyson's finest poem is based on this legend. In his 'Tithonus' we hear the voice of all those old people who have long passed 'the goal of ordinance' and who yet are cursed to open their drugged gaze on morning after new morning. The poem is the most eloquent case made for those whose last fate it is to be toyed with by time, to be mutilated and mocked by it. If the Mrs Everards of the proliferating geriatric wards could utter, it would be against every new morning. Nor is this longing to depart confined to advanced senility in its tragically comprehending moments; old men who still appear to be enjoying life will suddenly chill the talk by inquiring the way to death as matter-of-factly as they might ask the way to Totnes. A man of eighty-four, widowed and with more pain and difficulties than might have been supposed from his delightful conversation, turned to a contemporary as they were leaving a party and said, 'I'll tell you what I *really* want to know. I want to know how one gets off the hook . . .'

In today's Tithonian situation, the request is for the longest possible spell of the conditions we enjoy during the early years of retirement.

449

Life is good and buoyant then, and we want it to last. With a new house in a new place and, subsequently, a new circle, there can come a new energy which breaks into new interests, often with more forcefulness than that which inaugurated our working days, for we still retain the poise given us by the seniority of the work from which we have just retired. Under modern conditions, too, the sixties to the early seventies are often very healthy years. As Montaigne observed, 'The greatest vice the sages see in us is, that our desires incessantly grow young again; we are always beginning again to live. Our studies and desires should sometimes be sensible of old age; we have one foot in the grave, and yet our appetites and pursuits spring up every day.' We now take this perennial resurgence of appetite and pursuit to be a blessing, though the fact that it drives us along with some of the same zest as that which sent us on our travels when we were young, or prospecting for fresh jobs, experiences, etc., has to be reckoned with. If, as seems likely, chronic unemployment brings increasingly reduced working lives for the employed, retirement will begin so early that men will enter it without being toil worn, and possessing latent energies which are going to demand from a very long 'old age' an expression which is at present not catered for at all by society in its planning for the superannuated community. As for the workless – or even the under-worked-man, how does he 'retire'?

It is now increasingly accepted that the first decade of retirement is not old age. Senescence, though visible enough during these years, is not devastatingly apparent. People often live with it very comfortably. They put their feet up intellectually as well as physically and turn the worries of the world off. They promote a heightened sense of well-being with 'little treats' and exude stability and permanency. They do a vast amount of unpaid voluntary work and are always 'on the go' in directions which do not tire them in the deep psychic way in which bringing up children and the exacting demands of a career once tired them. The Tithonus of retirement, though so near to him, cannot conceive the Tithonus of the geriatric ward. His prayer is that he will live long but not *that* long. He says, quite often, 'I told my doctor – he's become such a friend – "Doctor, don't let me become a cabbage. Whatever you do, you will tell me, won't you, if you see it beginning

450

to happen, if I do funny things?" I don't mind what happens to me now so long as I don't become a cabbage.' A cabbage? Why not a rose or an apple? Because a cabbage has come to symbolise the most tightly furled and withdrawn member of that vegetable kingdom which the medieval mind placed lowest in the hierarchy of organic things. However, a man cannot become a cabbage. What he becomes – sometimes – is a very slow dying man.

None of the talkers in this book displayed cabbageness although most confessed to the horror that they one day might. It is clearly modern man's ultimate dread. The voices speak for that sprawling new commonwealth of the aged which is here to stay and whose citizenship we are all likely to take. They are a mixture of villagers, scholars, craftsmen, city-dwellers, priests, miners, rich and poor who, while in the process of telling how it was *then*, drop the curtain to reveal a little of how it is for them now. Has any previous group lived to witness such an outmoding and abolition of the social and moral tenets of its youth, such immense advances, such losses and such a transformation of the common scene? Is it any wonder that with so many contemporaries dead and so many signposts obliterated, a lot of thought and energy goes in to repeating who you are, both to the young and to yourself? 'You need only claim the events of your life to make yourself yours,' wrote Florida Scott-Maxwell at eighty. Small events tend to have the greatest claim to be remembered. Seldom do the very old deal in the epic. They specialise in flakes of colourful minutiae, as if they know that, when they are dead, it is not great deeds from their maturity which will recall their individual tones but the way they described a day on the river long ago. What they are saying in essence is, 'There are records to tell you when I was demobbed, married, honoured/disgraced, sacked, promoted; but *I* want to tell you what I now want to hear about myself. Those matters which haven't been entered on my passport, in the school register, on the call-up papers, because I *must* be more than I am officially!'

When people are old it isn't just egotism and a senescent liberation of the libido which speeds them down the autobiographical routes at such a determined pace. It is the compulsion to piece together a true self from all the fragments which have no place in the official file. 'So

451

you see why I had to leave Cardiff that September,' concludes the old woman. 'So you see, I was quite a boy!' says the old man with satisfaction. You don't see – not exactly – but the talkers do. They see themselves as no one sees them any more. But if not seeing very clearly, you feel, and that is important. To be able to arouse more than that solicitous feeling which we reserve for the over-eighties is a triumph for the old. A breakthrough. It causes them to hope against hope that the next step can be taken, the step which leads to some aspect of them which can be loved, for, as that eloquent Swiss geriatric apologist Paul Tournier flatly declares:

I have come to the conclusion that there is one essential, profound, underlying problem, and it is that the old are not loved. They do not feel themselves to be loved, and too many people treat them with indifference and seek no contact with them. . . . I think of the multitudes of retired people who hold aloof, who do know that people are concerned that they should have, as we say, decent living conditions, but who know that no personal interest is being taken in them.

Staring directly at the new bureaucracy which is taking more and more charge of his expanding needs (the average cost of looking after a seventy-five-year-old is seven times that of the state treatment for a worker), fixing his unfooled eye on the professionally kind rest-home entrepreneur, and even on the dutiful middle-aged daughter, the aged man or woman can repeat with Jean-Jacques Rousseau, 'These people do not love me.'

Unable to love the old, we approach them via sentiment, duty and an eye to our own eventual decline. We make sure that they are housed, fed, medicated and facing their favourite channel. We see ourselves in them and they see – what is it that the aged see? Down on a young arm? God in majesty? The world's superstructure collapsing? We care for them without real interest and believe that they must be unhappy because we would not be happy to be old. Yet a recent Age Concern survey proved that old people are far happier than their image suggests. This survey says that only seven per cent of them feel lonely most of the time and that only eight per cent feel that they have nothing to look forward to. What half the old people interviewed had to admit was that no one relied upon them any more, and that a third would have gone on working if they had been allowed to. At the moment their annual cost to the main social welfare programmes is, £10,000m, or a third of this budget. So far we have given the old both what we believe is good for them and what will keep them apart from the rest of us, but in 1979 the Government is taking the unusual step of publishing a White Paper on what the aged say *they* want. It could be the beginning of a revolution as the number of the old increases – twenty-four per cent more seventy-five year olds plus in 1986 than now – and it demands a more participatory role. It has to be remembered that the old have votes.

It is surprising how many post-war gerontological studies, both European and American, examine the ageing process as if it had no previous literary or even scientific history. As though ageing had to reach today's proportions before it was sufficiently intriguing to stand alongside love, death, sex, adventure, faith, art, work, war, etc. in the gamut of written human experience. Simone de Beauvoir decries most literary conceptions of old age up to the nineteenth century because they leave out the old age of the majority, the common people, and only describe that of the privileged classes, thus giving a false idea of its personal and social effects at any period. She writes:

The picture is blurred, uncertain and contradictory. It is important to realize that the expression 'old age' has two very different meanings throughout the various pieces of evidence that we possess. It is either a certain social category which has greater or lesser value according to circumstances. Or for each person it is one particular fate: his own. The first point of view is that of the lawgivers and moralists; the second that of the poets; and for the most part they are radically opposed. Lawyers and poets always belong to the privileged classes, which is one of the reasons that their words have no great value. They never say anything but part-truths and very often they lie. The poets are the more sincere, however, since they express themselves more spontaneously. The ideologists produce conceptions of old age that fit in with the interests of their class.

453

All this is most questionable. The fact is that if centuries of poets, playwrights and novelists have not gone to the subject of old age as often as they have to those of love, adventure, crime, power, etc., they certainly have not dodged it. If one includes journals, autobiography and biography, the literature of old age will be seen to be immense. But somehow, perhaps because we care less to think of it existing as a collective comment than we do about the assembled knowledge we possess on every other aspect of the human condition, there is a feeling that it has been ignored or avoided. Or that it is fresh ground which we have got to brace ourselves to explore. And while we know that the mass of the people do live and die with the minimal reference to their ever having existed, what is said in the literature of old age is as generally applicable to them as to the privileged classes. Shakespeare, Shirley, Gray, Hardy and many other writers use the ultimate sameness of the fate of rich and poor like a repeating clock in their work. The fate of Lear was the archetypal fate of many an old peasant whose children were greedy for his farm. His abdication of all that he was in the interests of the young was only different in degree to that of the clerk giving up his desk, the craftsman his bench and the miner his lamp to pressing successors:

> *To shake all cares and business from our age,*
> *Conferring them on younger strengths, while we*
> *Unburden'd crawl towards death.*

Lear, too, makes the most ignored of all human requests, that one should be allowed to remain within the circle until the very end:

> *If you do love old men, if your sweet sway*
> *Allow obedience, if you yourselves are old,*
> *Make it your cause ...*

It is Lear also who connects an emancipated libido with geriatric collapse – 'When the mind's free the body's delicate.' In these and in statements throughout the play four centuries of every condition of men can see their final selves. When they look up now to the eyes running the bank, the shop, the pub, the church, the daughter's home, what is it that they repeatedly read in them but,

> *O, sir, you are old;*
> *Nature in you stands on the very verge*
> *Of her confine.*

Or, if the old dare to show that they can still keep up with things which are strictly preserved for the young, is the sharp reminder given to Falstaff any different from that given by society today?

Do you set down your name in the scroll of youth, that are written down old with all the characters of age? Have you not a moist eye, a dry hand, a yellow cheek, a white beard, a decreasing leg, and increasing belly? Is not your voice broken, your wind short, your chin double, your wit single, and every part of you blasted with antiquity? And will you yet call yourself young? Fie, fie, fie, Sir John!

To know one's place is now the chief duty of the aged, to refuse the placing a crime.

Chaucer would have none of this. He probably wrote *The Canterbury Tales* when in his forties. In this masterpiece, which the critic Stephen Medcalf has called the humour of the sublime, a rollicking picture is given of the old participating in anything they fancied, with beneficial or farcical results. If one was like the old woman in 'The Nun's Priest's Tale' who reared chickens – including Chanticleer and Pertelote – and was content with her lot, her diet kept healthy by a narrow purse, her body exercised by hard work and, now and then, a jolly dance, there was little to fear. No gout, no apoplexy and nothing ridiculous or repellent for the world to condemn. But if one was self-deceiving, like two of the five husbands of the Wife of Bath, old men who tell themselves that she has married them for their passion, then one was simply unrealistic. Both old husbands had plenty of opportunity to discover that she 'never had much for old bacon' yet were unable to see themselves in this category, and so the Wife gives them belltinker, more for their vanity than their inadequacies. As she

455

ages, she is scandalously honest about her passion for a boy named Jankin, the sight of whose legs at her fifth husband's funeral besots her. She weds Jankin and enjoys him, once she has managed to stop him reading books, which are his real lust. But soon he dies like the rest, this being an instance of ripeness annihilating greenness. The Wife adores living and gets better and better at it, storing up experiences on which to nourish her old age:

But, Lord Christ! When it all comes back to me, and I recall my youth and gaiety, it tickles me to the roots of my heart. To this day it does my heart good that in my time I've had my fling. But age, alas! that cankers everything, has stripped me of my beauty and go. Goodbye, let them go, and the devil go with them! What's left to say? The flour's all gone, and now I must sell the bran as best I may. Even so I mean to rejoice!

'The Merchant's Tale' tells a very different old age story. It is about a bachelor knight named January who, at sixty, the same age as that when Chaucer himself died repudiating his genius for what he called 'lascivious lay' and repenting his *Troilus and Cressida* and all the delights which trespassed against the purity of Christ, decides to get married. Unlike the impotent old men of the other Tales, January is sexually vigorous and has woken to the realisation that it is now or never. His only worry is that his old age may turn out to be so blissful and successful that Purgatory won't provide its traditional 'happy release'. His bride is a teenager named May, and January is immensely kind to her and is as active in bed as a lad. But as Chaucer, with his deep understanding of the life cycle, shows, the performances of age, however sturdy, are not the performances of youth. For one thing, they are unaesthetic – 'God knows what May thought in her heart when she saw him sitting up in his shirt with his nightcap on and the slack skin round his neck ashake.' Also, when January wants May he cannot wait and when January takes May, it is at a price. Something snaps in a body which should be past this compulsion and the old husband becomes blind. Enter, unseen, the inevitable cuckold, Damien the young squire. At first the shocked realisation of what Damien is doing to May makes January very clear-sighted, but soon his wife is able to convince him, in the way in which the old are always finally manipulated by those who still care for them but who are no longer able to regard them as whole people, that in future he might often imagine such foolishness. Thus, having sown the seeds of uncertainty in the old, she is free to carry on as she likes. Her moral reasoning behind her adultery is that it is more unnatural for January and May to be bedded together than it is for young lovers to seize their chance. 'The Merchant's Tale' is psychologically fascinating because in it Chaucer allows that often the old do possess the capabilities of youth and a zest for living, also tenderness and warmth, but that none of these things are of value when youth itself is there to supply them.

Some old people are so entirely absorbed in an interest which unites the intellectual and the sensual that time ceases to threaten, question or mock their actions. When Gilbert White made the last entry in his Journal in June 1793 – 'the ground is as hard as iron' – there isn't the faintest forewarning of what was to happen a few days later, when he would be lowered into it. He was just continuing what he had begun twenty-five years earlier with 'Horses are still falling with the general disorder. It freezes under people's beds.' He is an example of those who pay scant attention to ageing. Other than a mention of his getting a bit deaf in his fifties and, on the day before his last entry, that he had been 'pulled down' by the 'wandering gout', there is no indication of his going on to be seventy-three, a great age for that time. His final letter concludes, 'The season with us is unhealthy,' and somehow the sentence does suggest that he could have been thinking of something other than the weather, which was bitter, or that he had just heard of Louis XVI's execution.

White had integrated himself with the movements of two calendars, the simple movement of a rural parish and the infinitely complex movement of the natural year. Because he had to act on the movements of both calendars daily he became a philosopher of the present, which is why he is so satisfying. We read him less for his science than for his daily-ness. The rising sap, the state of the cucumbers and endive, the flash of the blue hawk across the wheat stubble and the sound of the nightingale in the 'harsh evening' are steadiers. If we learn to look like this that spinning yearly-ness of old age is kept in some check.

457

Knowing that White is in his seventies when he writes such sentences as, 'My weeding-woman swept-up on the grass-plot a bushel-basket of blossoms from the white apple-tree' or 'Finished piling my wood', we are more affected than if he had confessed all the particulars of his physical and mental change as his life ebbed. He died in great pain which was a little relieved by laudanum, though only after a last week of being quite normally active and death-free. White's old age was that of the man who is too busy to dwell on it and who, outside a good deal, riding, walking, digging, often wet-through and becoming one with plants and birds and climate, gets too tired in the usual way to feel its special weariness.

Age-consciousness comes very early to some men. John Middleton Murry, when he was sixty, told a friend, 'It's very nice to be old.' He was not being facetious. He saw alterations in himself which made him decide to 'acquiesce gracefully in the beginning of the declining curve'. The first half of his life had been so emotionally strenuous, so work-stacked and so idealistically committed to this cause and that, as to leave insufficient energy for the latter half. But he welcomed this running-down of his strength and used it for purposes which would have been outside his range in his heyday. The first half of his life, the deaths of two wives from tuberculosis, a disastrous third marriage, a vast output of critical literary studies, philosophy and journalism compounded with intense relationships, such as that with D.H. Lawrence, the editorship of magazines and an active commitment to many of the important moral issues of the Fascist decades, had burnt him out. But he enjoyed making something from the ashes, and in this he shared one of the most subtle pleasures of the very old, which is the utilisation of one's frailty and slightness, the knowing how short a distance one can go – and then going it. And the knowing that one need not do more because it is impossible to do more. Ever again.

Frank Lea, Middleton Murry's biographer, draws an intriguing picture of this premature and not unwelcome senescence. At twenty-five, he says, Murry had been young for his age, at fifty, old for his years. 'Even physically he appeared to have shrunk, to have turned small and hard-drawn, like a mummy.' The Second World War had punctured many of his hopes and his third wife had wrecked all he understood by what he called 'the true man-woman relation'. Where publishers were concerned, he was an outmoded prophet and he himself, though only middle-aged, continuously dwelt in the past. He believed that he was a literary failure because he had put more of his imagination into the man-woman relation idea than into his books, and he saw the careers of certain contemporaries, such as T. S. Eliot and Joyce Cary, as instances of the success of single-mindedness. And then at a time when most writers would have been driven by habit and the need to rehabilitate themselves to go on working, Murry retreated to a Suffolk village with a girl who was the antithesis of all his wives to lead a life dominated by St Benedict's motto *laborare est orare*, to work is to pray, which for Murry did not mean literature. He told the world that his farm was 'nothing less than the Monte Cassino of a new Christian civilization' and a 'winning back of the waste lands of the modern world', two images which proved how stuck he was with a recent past. Like some octogenarians he wants to leave the record straight, and he has to nurse both head and hand in order not to go to the grave without making a final statement, *Love, Freedom and Society*. With this book he said that his 'thought adventure' had come to an end, and his biographer speaks of his extraordinary state of gladness that he could draw such a premature conclusion. 'I have a hunch – nothing more – that this feeling of mine [that he and Eliot had something important to say to each other] is connected with my conviction that my strange and weary pilgrimage . . . is over,' he wrote to the poet.

At sixty his face aged so much that it began to closely resemble that of his father in his eighties. At sixty-six he said he was 'completely unable to remember as a living fact the hydrogen bomb'. Gardening brought on an attack of angina pectoris and he died saying, 'I should not have asked Katherine [Mansfield, his first wife] to go on, I should not have asked Lawrence to go on . . .' as though he had been guilty of wishing a long life on others. D. H. Lawrence had died at forty-five and Katherine Mansfield at thirty-five, so, comparatively speaking, the years had carried Murry quite a distance from the sources of his vitality and by their terms he was aged.

Coleridge, too, experienced an early ageing, though his was exacerbated by abuse (drugs) of his mind and neglect (sloth) of his

body. When he died at sixty-two he was a sorry wreck. In his poetry
the old terrify the young. They accost strangers and spoil their day, like
Death in medieval experience, who links arms with youth or maiden in
broad sunshine. In his The Old Man of the Alps an aged father stops a
traveller to pour out a tale of personal grief just to be pitied – it is
'sweet to pity an aged breast'. In The Three Graves, a poem which
enthralled Thomas Hardy, another old man, a sexton, tells a traveller a
dreadful story of a thwarted marriage, and in The Rime of the Ancient
Mariner the wedding guest, a man about to participate in one of the
major celebrations of human joy, is waylaid by age and its blighting
confessions. But in his Limbo Coleridge insists that even the most
vacant senility is preferable to death and the 'mere horror of blank
Naught-at-all'. Better a moonfaced old man, 'his eyeless face all eye',
conscious only of light, his head turned to the moon in order 'to gaze
at that which seems to gaze on him!' for at least he is still in 'human
time'. In Youth and Age, written when he was fifty, he reads the signs
and dreads them. He sees 'this drooping gait, this altered size' which
tell him that 'Youth's no longer here' and that soon, if he wants to catch
its attention, he can only bring it to a standstill with the terrible
information which only old men can give. Coleridge's old men are
Gribouillists, the term given in modern geriatric psychiatry to those
who embrace the hideousness of old age and who use it to plague the
rest of society.

A writer who is interested in the full range of human activity will not
omit old age and even where this theme is not used explicitly for a
novel or a poem, there will be pointers throughout his work to how he
sees it. Sir Zachary Cope was able to diagnose that Jane Austen's last
illness was the then undiscovered Addison's Disease from the fleeting
yet intensely truthful and percipient descriptions of what was
happening to her which began to run through her letters. And a
similarly individual trail of change can be traced in the ageing writer,
or in the young writer brought up against the ageing of his parents or
friends. So, while Old Age as a principal theme makes up a short list
when we compare it with Childhood, its existence as a literary aside is
endless. And even the short list is much longer than is generally
supposed and repudiates the odd idea, so often expressed, that up until

now, when the cost of gerontology has forced us to face it, the whole subject has been avoided. For as well as the acknowledged masterpieces, *King Lear*, Cicero's *De Senectute*, Sophocles' *Oedipus at Colonus* and Swift's appalling tirade, written when he was fifty-five and the most hate-bearing statement on ageing that we possess, there is a range of comment upon and experience of the last years of life which, when we add it up, omits nothing.

In his *Acharnians*, Aristophanes shocks his age-despising, youth-adoring audience by siding with the old. Brecht in his *The Unworthy Old Lady* takes a similar theme to V. Sackville-West's *All Passion Spent* and describes an aged woman refusing to fit into the role which society has created for her and causing consternation by what the world regards as her waywardness – i.e., an insistence on experiment, change and lack of supervision. In *Endgame, Krapp's Last Tape* and *Happy Days*, Beckett sees the impotence and helplessness of the old as part of that half-appalling, half-comic individual solitude and ineffectuality which can enclose a man at any age. In Dante's *Il Convivio*, the old are weary ocean-worn barks making harbour, in Yeats's poems they are incorrigible – 'Why should not old men be mad?' – or they have strange remembrancers such as grave diggers 'who thrust their buried men back in the human mind again'. Philip Larkin sees an old woman discovering some sheet-music (just as today's young will come across some pop album sixty years hence) and finding that 'The glare of that much-mentioned brilliance, love' had not fulfilled its promise when she felt the 'certainty of time laid up in store' and that it 'could not now'. Larkin, in a number of poems, says be your age. Don't look forward because,

Always too eager for the future, we
Pick up bad habits of expectancy.

And don't look backwards because it is futile:

You cannot always keep
That unfakable young surface.
You must learn your lines ... .

R. S. Thomas finds the old often undeserving of the kindness and consideration with which it has become the social ideal to surround them:

Here; every farm has its
Grandfather or grandmother, gnarled hands
On the cheque book, a long, slow
Pull on the placenta about the neck.
Old lips monopolise the talk
When a friend calls. The children listen
From the kitchen; the children march
With angry patience against the dawn.
They are waiting for someone to die . . .

A truth which can nowadays only be whispered about the old is that they can be boring, cruel or disgusting, and that they can make the middle-aged ill.

Almost as tentative and unexamined a subject as old age and sexuality, is that of the octogenarian and the emotional effect he – or more likely she – has on their child. If there is a taboo on old age and sex, there is certainly a very strong natural and social stricture on what middle-aged sons and daughters can say when confronted, maybe, with a decade of geriatric care and nursing. The dread that this may happen is often so overwhelming that it begins to eat away at the respect and affection which the children have for their parents long before, or if, they show signs of senility. It is not just a reluctance to take on a burden which causes this corrosion but the emotional shock and resentment at the reversal of the roles. Many people suffer from a kind of indignation when they see what looks like an abdication of parental care in their mother. No longer capable of exercising it, she becomes in effect not entirely their mother. It feels as though she has freed herself from them but they, in contrast, are imprisoned by her. Even if a parent enters an old people's home (where, though it is hard to accept, there is often greater happiness and affection than can be found in the family) the middle-aged children can still suffer from this strange sense of imprisonment. On the other hand, a son or daughter will care for their aged parents with the utmost devotion and even find pleasure and fulfilment in this duty, dreading the day of release. But whatever the direction such a relationship takes, it is one of the most difficult to discuss, and we still know too little of the effect of longevity on younger people who are now having to spend years in close contact with it.

Even 'angry patience' is achieved at a cost. In Prosper Mérimée's *Lettres à une Inconnue* the correspondent is frank about her dutiful visits to an aged godmother who is 'a cross-grained old woman who ought to die'. It is to make certain that she inherits an exquisite service of Sèvres china. So she puts up with 'a querulous, selfish old creature who has not a lovable quality in her whole disposition' only to find that when this 'useless tyrannical life ends' her godmother hasn't made a will and all her possessions go to a distant relation who has never so much as called on her. But the young will endure the vulgarity of the old because they are vulnerable as well as powerful, though this does not prevent a mounting distaste, and perhaps, with full-span lives having become the norm, people may need to learn how to be aged as they once had to learn how to be adult. It may soon be necessary and legitimate to criticise the long years of vapidity in which a well, elderly person does little more than eat and play Bingo, or consumes excessive amounts of drugs, or expects a self-indulgent stupidity to go unchecked. Just as the old should be convinced that, whatever happens during senescence, they will never suffer exclusion, so they should understand that age does not exempt them from being despicable. To fall into purposelessness is to fall out of all real consideration. Many old people reduce life to such trifling routines that they cause the rest of us to turn away in revulsion. Sometimes we should say to them, 'How can you expect us to be interested in this minimal you, with your mean days and little grumbles?' This slide into purposelessness must not be confused with the ability of the old not to take life all that seriously, for this has its virtues and assets. To appreciate the transience of all things is one matter, to narrow the last years - and they can be numerous – down to a dreary thread is another. One of the most dreadful sights in the country of the old is that of the long rows of women playing the Las Vegas fruit machines. Had Dante heard of it he would have cleared a space for it in Hell. It is symbolic of that specially self-indulgent mindlessness of old age which is its most intolerable aspect.

Proust illustrated how even the limited movement and interests of extreme old age could enliven the day. Few dramas can be as minuscule as Aunt Léonie's in *Swann's Way*, yet hers remains tiny without being trivial. This ancient woman has turned her small obsessions to good account and has made some of the less admirable foibles of old age, hypochondria, domestic tyranny, nosiness, etc., into something which is life-supporting not only for herself but for her family and the neighbours. Aunt Léonie is a trial but she isn't a bore. She sits behind a curtain and spies on the town, sips Vichy water and uses her prayer- book like a drill manual. She is beadily absorbed in life and her personality is so unfractured that those who know her don't have to adopt charitable attitudes when they discuss her. On the contrary, her sayings and doings are collected and prized, like the first words of a baby: '"I do not ask to live to a hundred," my aunt would say, for she preferred to have no definite limit to the number of her days.' No one, whether doctor, daughter, grandchild, priest or friend, thought of her as a problem or as anything less than she had been at any other stage of her life. Age had added comedy to her attributes, that was all. She was allowed the amusing notion 'that there was something broken in her head and floating loose there, which she might displace by talking too loud' and her little lies about never 'sleeping a wink', her tedious rituals and avid gossip. Her amnesia is respected and when she apologises for it to her maid, saying that she is wasting her time, Françoise replies that her time 'is not so precious; whoever made our time didn't sell it to us.' Nobody thinks that it is a pity that Aunt Léonie isn't either younger or dead. She is as much enfranchised to make what she can of life in her eighties as she was when she was eighteen, and she doesn't need to conceal her eccentricities any more than a child does. A child will badger, will fantasise and will demand special assistance, and so will the aged. In Aunt Léonie's family first and last words are significant and are reported. Similarly, just as her parents entered into her childhood games, so do her relations enter into the spirit of her final playtime, her 'little jog-trot', as she calls it. The marked difference in pace entertains them. They relate it without damaging her integrity for, like the poet W. J. Turner, they discover that

The young are serious but the old are not frivolous,
They see what they saw in the days of their youth,
Yet all things appear to them in different proportion.
The young are impatient, but the old are not desperate,
Though they see in the distance the rock which divides.

One of the reasons why old people make so many journeys into the past is to satisfy themselves that it is still there. In his seventies, Thomas Hardy returned emotionally and geographically to convince himself that he was once in love with his wife. And he was eighty-eight when he published *Winter Words*, which opens with a Tithonus-like demand to Dawn to explain what she is 'doing outside my walls', and which includes a number of 'look back' poems. Sandwiched between a poem in which he tells the Dawn that he must no longer look back on love or attempt to love again, and one which attempts to get inside the mind of his best friend at the moment of his suicide, Hardy has placed his reflection on his eighty-sixth birthday, 'He Never Expected Much'. In it he accepts a certain colourlessness in his life and a certain injustice. Finally, in 'He Resolves To Say No More', Hardy refuses to let Time roll backward or forward in his poetry. What he has seen and what he sees ahead he'll keep to himself. He has spent a long life revealing past and future, now he will be silent. The silence of old age is unnerving. We expect the aged to speak and when they do not we are devastated.

Sometimes the old check on the marks they made when they were young. Even a signature on a tree, or like the name which a boy carved inside a Suffolk belfry when he was eighteen and which he climbed the stairs to look at when he was ninety and near to having it repeated on a stone below. Often there is an intensely resurgent interest in the long journey just when it looks like coming to an end. It is reminiscent of Rousseau's 'I only began to live when I looked upon myself as dead.' He was a young man recovering from Ménière's disease, from which

465

Swift also suffered. Rousseau's *Confessions*, written in late middle age, were as accurate a retracement of his steps as he could manage. He is more truthful than most men about their ability to say what actually happened to them, and says that

memory often failed me or furnished but imperfect recollections, and I filled up space by details supplied by imagination to supplement those recollections . . . I loved to expatiate on the happy moments of my life, and I sometimes embellished them with ornaments supplied by tender regrets. I said things I had forgotten as it seemed to me they ought to have been, and as perhaps in fact they were . . . I sometimes lent strange charms to truth.

Restif de la Bretonne, a literary ancestor of Genet and known in his own day as 'the Gutter Rousseau' – *le Rousseau du ruisseau* – both because he had as great a passion for pavements as his nick-namesake had for wild nature and because of the candour of his writing, carved every important happening of his life on the walls of the *Ile Saint-Louis*. He carved the record of an event immediately after it occurred, symbolically using a key to scratch the paragraph of personal history to which he added a Latin commentary. Havelock Ellis says that Restif turned this beautiful Parisian district into his personal temple, incising his life into its stone parapets. This was one version. The other lay embedded in his quasi-autobiography *Monsieur Nicolas* which Schiller placed alongside Cellini's *Life* as a masterpiece of self-statement. But when Restif was a filthy old man, thought by some to be the greatest writer of the eighteenth century and by others its major pornographer, it was not to the printed but to the carved word that he made pilgrimages to see what really had happened to him. After the Revolution, he would be glimpsed, late at night, making the rounds of his carvings, knowing that the energy which had produced them was part of that same force which had produced the events which they described.

Wells, Dickens, Tolstoy, Ionesco, Colette, Michelangelo, Gide, Maugham, Hemingway, Milton, Eliot, Amis, Spark – the list is present wherever and at whatever period one looks in literature – have all said something about age. But the subject has a way of being fugitive, of being little seen even where it is profusely represented, as it is in Larkin's *Oxford Book of Twentieth Century English Verse*, for example, where there is a startling range of old-age poetry.

Few writers in the past needed to consider the dangers and blessings of being pensioned off, or its effect on a previously work regulated life, because such things hardly ever occurred. Charles Lamb in *The Superannuated Man* is able to deal with such a subject as a novelty. Even so, his picture has an accuracy which is relevant to contemporary retirement. He tells of a fifty year-old clerk who has worked in a Mincing Lane counting house since he was fourteen and who is beginning to show signs of physical collapse. This clerk has averaged a ten-hour day, six days a week, for thirty-six years, working mostly in candlelight and, like 'animals in cages', had grown doggedly content. It is only when he starts to disintegrate that the clerk realises that the routine breaks from this dim tread-mill, Sundays, Christmas and an annual week in the country, have neither refreshed nor re-created him. On the contrary, Sabbatarianism has introduced a repressive 'weight in the air' which has actually stopped him from enjoying himself. As for the week in Hertfordshire, no sooner has he begun to relax there than it is time to get back to the City. The reader can contrast a future prospect of excessive leisure with a time when it was minimal.

One day the clerk's employers summon him for what he thinks is the sack, being conscious that his work is not what it used to be and that, try as he will, he cannot get back to his old standards. Instead, to his amazement, he is retired on two-thirds of his wages out of gratitude for his past achievements. His feelings are mixed. He is 'stunned, overwhelmed' and he wanders about idly 'thinking I was happy and knowing that I was not' and realises that 'I had more time on my hands than I could ever manage.' He warns others of his fate and tells them not to retire all at once as the strict switch from a work routine to no routine is dangerous. He sees a young man at his desk and using his hat-peg, and it is a kind of death. Although he knows that walking the City in work-time and feeling the sun and not candles should be paradisial, he uncomfortably compares 'the change in my condition to passing into another world'. Soon, the fifty-year-old clerk turns into the un-needed, unnecessary man we see on the public seats in parks and libraries today. 'I am no longer clerk to the Firm of, etc. I am Retired Leisure. I am to be met with in trim gardens. I am already come to be known by my vacant face and careless gesture, perambulating at no fixed pace, nor with any settled purpose. I walk about; not to and from . . .' This chilling Beckett-like confession comes only after the work-denied man has paid his conventional tribute to the retired state. It includes the ironic statement that 'had I a little son, I would christen him Nothing-To-Do; he should do nothing. Man, I verily believe, is out his element as long as he is operative.' Charles Lamb, an office-worker all his life, is listening to the corporate sigh of that vast army of nineteenth-century clerks, chained from school to grave to their ledgers, who cannot imagine drawing a line on employment.

Literature is also full of examples of old people who are the victims of transience. A. L. Vischer, describing our experience of transience, says that

the desire to stay where we are and the desire to press forward are two distinct categories of human life. We participate in both and both are capable of proving a source of good or evil for old people, depending on the attitude which they adopt and on how they put their attitude into effect. A positive experience of transience can release powerful forces which may act as an incentive for us to make the most of our remaining days.

But many people stay where they were, long years ago, not because they have made up their minds to do so, but because what happened then was seismic, turbulent and thrilling. Having been part of a great political or artistic or scientific upheaval, they only realise that they are no longer in the avant-garde when, in advancing years, they sense a solitude and a silence and, looking around, see that they are alone. These old men are the victims of transience. Biography is full of examples of their plight. It is a strange thing to be left behind by later generations whose moral or material advance is due to the heart -and-soul battles of one's own youth. And stranger still to be battling on when the cause has been won and forgotten. Worse, to find that although the cause was a correct one, and of benefit to oneself and to the world, it is now slotted into the general orthodoxy with no very great addition to the sum of human happiness.

Edward Clodd, the folklorist and disseminator of Darwinism, was in his twenties when the great debate on evolution began and forty when he abandoned Christianity for the Rationalists. At this period he was a kind of scientific Theist who was constantly ill. In fact, such was his continuous stress and exhaustion that he did not expect to see his fortieth birthday. On the day he was able to convince himself that God did not exist he began to grow well and happy. At fifty, while admitting that 'the future has not the potency of the past', he was transformed into the robust figure who, to his huge circle of intellectual friends, epitomised man released from his superstitious chains. He exuded well-being and joy and, like many Victorians, he did three people's work, managing a joint stock bank, churning out a stream of books and articles, and maintaining a complex social life. His friends included Thomas Hardy, Edward Whymper, George Meredith, George Gissing and Holman-Hunt. As he got to know them, and scores of other intellectuals besides, he discovered that most of them far from shared his total emancipation from religion. Huxley still retained some theology in his library, Hardy was seen in church, one of his guests was caught praying and Gissing had a priest present when he was dying. It seemed never to have occurred to Clodd that while most of his friends were artists, he was fundamentally a propagandist. That, in Jacquetta Hawkes's phrase, he lived in flatland while they retained some of the vision of creatures who could not live without symbol and ceremony. In *Boon* H. G. Wells said that Clodd ('Dodd') had banished God from the universe but he hadn't actually got rid of him, and thus he had constituted himself a sort of alert customs officer of a materialistic age . . . and slept with a large revolver under his pillow for fear of revelation.

As he aged Clodd's sense of purpose faded, chiefly because it required a tough response from the leaders of those who did not share it. Neither could his mid-nineteenth-century mind comprehend twentieth-century mathematics and scientific theory. At eighty he wrote, 'I am like Milton's angels, "in wandering mazes lost. . ." How one sighs for Huxley to make the thing luminous!' The reference to Huxley throws up another complication for the kind of old person 'who has known everybody' – his constant bereavement. Also, Clodd's faith in human progress had been battered by the casualties and political cruelties of the First World War. Yet at seventy-four he could not bring himself to think that life was over and had married a second wife, a young scientist who, when she was in her eighties, was to kill herself rather than further endure old age. At the time of this marriage, Clodd read Havelock Ellis's *Psychology of Sex* and wished 'that it had been published when I was a younger man when so much that one would have been the better for knowing was not talked about'. At this period he felt that 'man must be his own Redeemer' and that the only place for Jesus, should he be on this planet during the twentieth century, would be 'on the Committee of the Fabian Society'.

He was eighty when he published his last book, *Magic in Names and Other Things*. A year later, condemning Wells's belief in the moral advance of society, Clodd declared, 'Today all the forces of disintegration are in full play.' At eighty-three the deaths of friends and acquaintances were so multitudinous that they poured into his little house by the North Sea like an icy storm. He had eczema, was less able to walk but still read omnivorously, though he found himself disturbed by the new explicitness regarding both sex and spiritual philosophy in the learned journals. When he was eighty-seven he had a slight stroke followed by aphasia. At eighty-eight his eyes and speech began to fail and he became bed-ridden, and then just a few months before his death in his ninetieth year, he began to walk once more. A few days before his death he read and re-read Arnold's 'Dover Beach' and 'Empedocles on Etna', and noted how all values alter when one is ill. During the final period he returned to the scientists of his youth and was delighted and relieved to find a critic condemning Freud as 'a dangerous lunatic'. In March 1930 his bronchial asthma returned, brought on, he believed, by the dreaded Suffolk coast east winds. He remained fully conscious to the end, repeating, 'I die, I die.' Edward Clodd retained intelligence and appetite for life into extreme old age but neither could cope with the amazing new fare which they had helped to initiate, and it was as a victim of transience that he matched the thud of the sea on the Aldeburgh shingle a few yards from his death-bed with Matthew Arnold's 'melancholy, long, withdrawing roar'.

It is the nature of old men and women to become their own confessors, poets, philosophers, apologists and story-tellers. My method, if method it can be called, in listening to a few of them, some friends, some strangers, was to hear what they had to say with an ear which had been mostly informed by what someone called 'the low-lying literature of old age'. No single conclusion can be deduced from them or it. Old age is full of death and full of life. It is a tolerable achievement and it is a disaster. It transcends desire and it taunts it. It is long enough and it is far from being long enough, as the poet Ruth Fainlight says in 'Losers':

Assume nothing at all.
Even to hope you might live for ever
Brings the end too close.

WHAT DOES IT MEAN TO GROW OLD?
Reflections from the Humanities
eds. Thomas R. Cole & Sally Gadow, 1986

OUR AGEING SOCIETY
Paradox and Promise
eds. Alan Pifer & Lydia Bronte, 1986

Not so very long ago, the possibility of living *all* our human allotted time-span would have seemed as unlikely as entering the earthly paradise. We would not have counted on it. Many did make it to their sixties and seventies, and a few to their eighties and nineties, but the majority of us did not. However, due to all sorts of factors (including some evidence that a revolution in our domestic habits, rather than a revolution in medicine, could be the main cause), our once brief life portion has lengthened. In the West, it is now quite difficult, even aberrant, to die in the early middle age, except from AIDS. Nor has the extension settled for the classic three score years and ten (and a few extra if you have the strength to bear them). Today's ordinarily attainable life-spans would have seemed like encroachments upon eternity to our great-grandparents.

So, hurrah? Jubilation? Celebration? Far from it read our 1950s onwards gerontologists, sociologists, and economists. The arrival of old age for everybody is a blessing some of them can do without, some find incalculable, and some have settled down to make a living from. Judging from the library shelves, old age drives its explainers and managers to ink. A vast literature has emerged, most of it unfit for the elderly. But during the last decade or so there has been a marked change in its drift, and thus in its literary style. Philosophy, the single most important element in the experience of, or the explanation of, ageing has come to the fore and is greatly altering our attitudes.

As we now live a long time, we must grow old. If such is to be the common fate, we have to accept it. There is no alternative. To read some of today's old age writing – its sudden proliferation is as challenging in its way as certain aspects of the sixties' youth culture explosion – one would think that we are all being forced to face up to an unnatural dilemma thrust upon us by modern social conditions.

The old and non-old (the latter are not necessarily young) alike exhibit an underlying guilt and embarrassment about what the politicians call 'limited resources.' A primitive thinking, ever more politely expressed, argues that those who no longer produce can no longer expect to receive more than what is required for their most basic needs. The implication is that although they may have as much as thirty more years of life, as social contributory they are in large part dead. What little remains of them has to be honoured, of course. No civilised state could do otherwise, no son or daughter either. The aged are highly sensitive to being a burden – how could they not be in today's bothered climate? – but have no way of escape. A character in Anthony Powell's novel *Temporary Kings* says, 'Growing old is like being increasingly penalized for a crime you haven't committed.'

In *What Does It Mean to Grow Old?* and *Our Ageing Society* some two dozen essayists come to grips as best they can with the phenomenon of an America that is about to become the Old Country. They have been drawn from every kind of relevant discipline – gerontology, social medicine, finance, politics, education, health, demography, anthropology, ethics, law – and asked to speak their mind. Or rather they have been asked to express themselves readably for a non-specialist public as well as for their academic peers. Most of them write extremely well and the abandonment of nearly all the jargon, which made so much fifties' old age literature awful, not to say frightening for the old themselves, shows how far we have come in humanity and taste. There is some repetition, usually in the opening statements about the astonishing turnabout in the life-expectancy figures for Americans in the twentieth century, but the contributors' own sharply individual voices are heard. We learn a lot.

If a best had to be chosen it would be Harry R Moody's 'The Meaning of Life and the Meaning of Old Age,' the opening chapter of *What Does It Mean to Grow Old?* and a truly wonderful statement of the fresh values and recognitions now required in the United States. Moody attacks a culture dominated by both a therapeutic outlook and a hostility toward its old people. In his view, placing life in the three boxes of education, work, and retirement; the cult of activity; and neglect of contemplation won't do for any of us, let alone the new old. He is stern, 'Cultivate your garden,' has always been the recipe for a happy retirement. But, Moody asks, what if when you are old, your garden is no more than a window-box?

Other contributors to this anthology speak about investing for the future. Stock your mind as well as your pension scheme, for the tolerability and even the triumphs of old age are utterly dependent upon inner resources. Moody reminds us how relentlessly today's world projects meaning into the future – 'thus, savings, and deferred gratification are all strivings for a goal located in – old age.' But upon arriving at old age, many would agree with Yeats's comment, 'Life is a preparation for something that never happens.' We live, he adds, 'in a society in which the denial of aging and death is deeply rooted.'

This remarkable book reinstates many an old-fashioned reality, which the 'new priesthood of professionals' who are now managing the aged have weeded out: the need to be contemplative, to be stoical,

473

to be able to read with enjoyment, not to be rude or nasty or trying or a nuisance, and (one contributor dares to add) to be courageous. The horrors of senile decay apart (and comparatively few of us will suffer from the dreaded Alzheimer's disease and its like), all the writers agree that old age should be a time of high civilisation and spirituality.

They argue that, as it has become the common fate to live a very long time and to work for quite a short time, all the logistical aid imaginable by governments, doctors, and the army of old age caretakers which is now on the march cannot 'save' us. We save ourselves by accepting that the boy or girl, man or woman we were is now in the last protracted stage of life, which falls into its own natural divisions; just as children must be supported without being deprived of their individual freedom, so the aged need a few props. Those whose profession it is to provide these props have no right to take us over or even intrude upon our privacy. Bizarre though it may seem, the old often harbour a greater fear of the new 'caring' than of death. The new caring needs to watch its language. Is it fit for the old to hear?

Our Ageing Society shows us the social prospects of ageing, which are so enormous and transforming that they will certainly lead to increasing control by America's old people, and a politics based on their power as the largest of the age groups. An ageing populace is not at all the same as an ageing person and the realisation that the United States, the New World, the land of youth, is about to become a country of the old could prove traumatic. Hence this volume of essays, this breaking of the bad news – and the suggestion that, after the initial shock, the future isn't necessarily threatened.

At the moment some fifty million Americans are in the third quarter of their lives, or over sixty-five. While the 'greening' of America was celebrated in the late 1960s, the country's 'graying' causes alarm. But should it? This is what these writers are asking in essays that reflect the sad and fascinating business of human ageing, its splendours and difficulties.

For an Englishman, the ageing of a country at the pinnacle of world power is more intriguing than fearful, and *Our Ageing Society's* twenty-four or so contributors are careful not to sensationalise the matter. Instead, they use it as an opportunity to preach and extend the

474

enlightened ideas of Thomas R. Cole, Sally Gadow, and other humanists. They warn, 'American culture encourages people to make the problems of old age invisible.' They shake up present platitudes: 'There has already begun a blurring of what have long been accepted as the three main life periods.'

They remind us, if this is necessary, that 'the world of the very old is a world of women,' and that 'the concepts of obligation, loyalty, and reverence for tradition and for the elderly are relatively alien to American values.' And they write, inelegantly though vividly, about 'youth creep' in the healthy old. They also offer some of the best authoritative comment on the politics of retirement, 'a roleless role' and on how the old themselves, being so numerous and powerful, must inevitably legislate in their own favour.

As in *What Does It Mean to Grow Old?*, *Our Ageing Society* jettisons the ugly non-English of earlier old-age writing – although I shall treasure the term 'kin-keepers' as a funny horror – and wisely and successfully attempts to make its findings public in words that are often eloquent and always impressive. It offers an original approach to an enormously written about subject, by viewing old age in national rather than individual terms.

Both books make clear that the guiltlessness and innocence of old age have to be recognised, felt, stressed. Never mind what has brought about this mass ageing, which shakes the plans that the non-old have in store for the world. Never mind what has stimulated the analyses of ageing that appear in these books. Let us all, before we write or say another word, see how pointless it is to be accusative or apologetic about any period of a person's life, be it five or ninety-five. The aged should not be made, as so many of them are, to toy with the notion that they should not be here, anymore than a youth should think that he isn't worth the space he takes up. Economists and demographers may 'cost out' the generation groups and the costs for the oldest generation may be staggering, but the aged are as guiltless of their expense as children.

The various methods of budgeting for the elderly since the early pension schemes of this century have in some respects been absurd and insulting, although governments have always given themselves huge

475

pats on the back for any legislation that takes care of the old. This 'concern' needs to be recognised for what it is, an attitude that decides that those over seventy are no longer entirely *us* and have to be reminded. This attitude lays down in us the foundations of that diminished self, which we are encouraged to believe arrives with retirement and then shrinks its way to the grave.

Old age could be like this, or it could be like a thousand other progressions through the years. For in the final third of life, like the other two-thirds, an old individual will make highly personal paths across the common framework. Living from sixty-five to eighty-five is an extremely interesting business. Even some young people, like the Irish writer John Stewart Collis, claimed they couldn't wait to get there. He wrote the following when he was about thirty:

I constantly think how delightful it will be to be a *vigorous* old man. I wait impatiently for old age. For how marvellous it will be to walk down the street unburdened by the problem of money, the problem of sex, the problem of housing, the problem of the literary battle; all these, including the problem of marriage, will have worked themselves out into solutions . . .

Collis did live to be a vigorous old man, although he could not bear to be spoken of as old, by way of self-apology. Collis was an imaginative writer who had the nerve to intrude on matters that are usually the preserve of scientists and specialists. And so, I suppose, have I, although I have the highest respect for the disciplines and never deliberately set out to offer a counter view.

I came to old age as a child, mystified, enthralled and made fanciful and questioning by its existence. Being a country boy I witnessed the last of the ancient sit-by-the-fires, my grandmother included, nearly a century old when she died, and born in 1860. Looking back, I realise that from the start I was a voyeur of what they now euphemistically call the Third Age. And so indeed have been poets, storytellers, philosophers, artists, and recorders from time immemorial. A few always get mentioned in gerontological studies, Seneca and Beckett, for example. But although there exists almost as much art about old age as about war or love, our eyes slide away from the subject. On the whole, death has made a more tolerable drama than old age.

Both these books altered my thinking on old age. But they also confirmed what I had always believed, that if you don't lay in some philosophy as well as some pension funds in the days of thy youth, you are likely to be a great trial to yourself as well as everybody else, not in the evening, but in the very long late afternoon of thy life.

IN THE HOUR OF DEATH

from *Akenfield*, Ronald Blythe, 1969

'Tender' Russ is a widower and lives by himself in a severe brick cottage called Malyons. The cottage is built endways to the road and into a bank so high that blackberries can hang away from their roots and trail on the slates. The garden is planted but rank. Rows of sprouts have rotted until they have become yellow pustulate sticks; potatoes have reached up as far as they could go and fallen back into faded tangles. Tender sows but apparently doesn't reap. He has retreated to one room in the cottage and closed all the others up. It is a Charles Spenserlahye room, a jackdaw's nest of saved matchsticks, preserved newspapers, clung-to coronation mugs and every kind of clutter. In a corner a bakelite radio gives every news bulletin there ever was. Tender's two budgies, Boy and Girl, drown announcements of famine, war, murder and sport with an incessant chatter. He is short but strongly built. Vivid blue eyes strain and flash to add meaning and explanation to what he feels are inadequate words.

Tender is a monopolist and a pluralist. He amalgamates graveyards and pounces on cemeteries. Although there has been little or no competition for this great accumulation of burial grounds, Tender has a right to feel unique and powerful, privileged and indispensable. He has buried 608 people in thirty different churchyards since 1961 and keeps his own records of 'where they lie and *how* they lie'. And this is only the work of his maturity. Before this mortuary climax there were decades of interrings. Tender has never had a day's holiday, never missed a church service on a Sunday and also never missed an opportunity to carry on his rancorous love-hate debate with his God, the clergy and the quick. The dead are exempt from his fury and he is on their side against the living. He has all their names in an address book contrived out of shelf-paper and a bulldog-clip. The young and the old, the rich and the poor are listed in violet pencil at first, and in biro later.

He works incredibly hard and with great independence, travelling from village to village on a moped to the carrier of which is tied a gleaming spade and fork. He drives well out towards the centre of the road and the Anglo-American traffic has to swerve and swear to avoid him. Quite a lot of people recognise him, however, for he is a famous person, and give him a wide berth. They know they are seeing Time's winged chariot with a two-stroke.

When people need Tender they need him badly, and will make much of him because of this. The need over, they avoid him. Or is it that he avoids them? His eloquence is enormous and violent, and seems to be only indirectly aimed at God and man. He is arguing with the mindless knife-bearing wind which carries the ice of the sea to the vulnerable flesh and fields of the inhabited places. He is a religious man who is listening for God in a hurricane. There used to be certainties but now the parsons say they aren't so certain after all. The Bible itself has whirled past him – a mocking paper-chase of discarded views. Almost every day he hears about the 'resurrection of the body' as he waits tactfully behind a tree, filling-in spade covered with a sack. Most days he is left alone with the new dead. The pity of it all! The muddle of it all! Automatic bird-scarers go off in the pea-fields like minute guns. Something has gone wrong – very wrong.

'Why "Tender"?'
'Oh, that's not *his* name,' said the woman at the pub. 'He inherited it from his father. We call him Tender because of his father, but that's not his name.'

I started digging graves when I was twelve years old and before I left school. I began by helping an old man and by the time I was thirteen I could do the job as well as I can now. I dug graves before my voice broke – there now! People would look down into the hole and see a child. The work didn't upset me; I took it in my stride. Right from a little boy – if Mother was alive she'd be able to tell you – I used to bury guinea pigs, rabbits, all sorts of things. I had about fifty rabbits and when one died I would make a coffin for it, get my choir surplice from the church vestry and read the Burial Service over it. So burying has been in my blood from a child. I never wanted to do anything else; graves are my vocation.

I've been at the church, official-like, since 1918. I was the legal sexton when I was thirteen and I've buried damn near the whole of the old village, everyone of them. I remember the first grave I dug. It was for a man named Hayman. I've got all my burials down since the day I started, men, women and children.

So far as funerals are concerned, we've gone from one extreme to the other. Bodies used to be kept in the house for twelve days. Everyone kept the body at home for as long as they could then; they didn't care to part with it, you see. Now they can't get it out quick enough. They didn't like hurrying about anything when I was young, particularly about death. They were afraid that the corpse might still be alive – that was the real reason for hanging on to it. People have a post mortem now and it's all settled in a minute, but there's no doubt that years ago there were a rare lot of folk who got buried alive. When a sick man passed on the doctor was told, but he never came to look at the corpse. He just wrote out the death certificate. People always made a point of leaving an instruction in their wills to have a vein cut. Just to be on the safe side.

There was an old man near Framlingham, old Micah Hibble, he was laid out for dead three times. The last time he was actually in his coffin and waiting for the funeral to begin. When I asked, 'Anymore for a last look before he's screwed down?' there was the usual nuisance pushing his way through the mourners and saying, 'Yes, I do!' Trust somebody to get you fiddling about and making the funeral late. The bell was going, so you know how late it was. Anyway, when this man looked in the coffin he saw that Micah had moved. Well do you know, he recovered! And what's more, he is supposed to have written a book

479

about what he saw, although I've never set eyes on it. He reckoned he saw Heaven and Hell but he wouldn't say what he saw in Hell; he thought it would be too much for Framlingham. He lived for years after this.

And there was this old lady at Wickham Market and she was in three different coffins. They called her Cheat-the-grave at last. All these things happened because people will insist on checking on death with a mirror, which isn't a mite of good. The only way is to stick a shred of cotton wool where the lips part and if there's the least little wind of life it will flutter. I can always tell if a person is dead by looking at the eyes. I never make a mistake about dead eyes. I see at once when the seeing has gone.

Village folk have been buried over and over again in the same little bits of churchyard. You have to throw somebody out to get somebody in – three or four sometimes. I always put all the bones back so that they lie tidy like just under the new person. They're soon all one. The parson said to me, 'How is it that you get so many in one grave?' and I always tell him that I must have disturbed a plague pit. Parsons will believe anything.

The rich people are buried in vaults, you know. I had to open a vault the other day and put a woman in. She joined six or seven others and I had to shove 'em over and say, 'Come you together now, make room for a little 'un!' Vaults are sweet places. Everybody lies in lead first, then wood, so there's no smell. I went into the vault at Stanton when Lord Eastham's wife died. It was full and I had to lay her on the floor because her relations had all the shelves. It was first come, first served. The coffins were all made of panelled oak, great black things as black as a fireplace. Good God, they last for generations!

I've dug for all denominations, from Catholic to Plymouth Brethren. The chapel people are the worst. First of all they're a good three-quarters of an hour in the chapel while the preacher spouts about the dead man and estimates whether he's saved, and then, when they get to the grave, on it goes again. There's no end to it. They forget we all knew the corpse. And then, when they're none too sure about the saving, you should hear them then! There was Jed's funeral – well we don't need any telling about Jed! Well Jed might have been a bad lot but he wasn't a bad sort. You know. I mean he was Jed, wasn't he? Well, this chapel preacher stood there by the hole I had got ready for Jed and was as near as damn it saying that Jed wasn't saved although he *hoped* he was. So after the funeral I went up to him and said, 'My God, you've had some talk about Jed, haven't you? I know you're here to say a few words – but you've said too much!' I said, 'Do you reckon that you are saved?' He said, 'I hope so'. 'Very well then,' I said, 'but do you remember when you get in front of your Maker he won't ask you what Jed has done – he'll ask what you've been up to.' You could see he didn't like it.

The parsons aren't much better. But there, you don't find many *parsons* now. Only men who have done their life's work serving as a colonel or a schoolmaster and then get themselves ordained. I don't really call these people parsons. I don't mince my words with them. When you bury between 180-200 people a year you can afford to be honest.

Dust to dust they say. It makes me laugh. Mud to mud, more like. Half the graves round here are water-logged. Foxton is a terrible wet place; the moment you get the grass off, you're in the water. I float grass on the water so the mourners can't see it but when the coffin is lowered it has to be held under with a pole until you can get a bit of heavy soil on top of it. At Dearburgh the graves fill up to within eight inches of the top. I've drawn as much as fifty pails of water out of a grave at Dearburgh, the last when the funeral was coming up the path. And still the coffin had to be held under three feet of it. It all comes down from the cricket pitch.

The bodies are washed and dressed in shrouds. Except for a parson, and he's buried in his robes. When you bury a parson you always bury him 're incumbent' – the opposite way to everybody else. Everybody lies with their feet to the east so that when they rise they face the Lord. But a parson, you see, you bury him with his feet to the west, so that when he rises he faces his flock. And serve him right, I say. I had a bit of bother about this once.

An old canon had died and was cremated, and the ashes were kept until his wife passed on. I put the jar of ashes on the wife's coffin and lowered the two together. Well, of course, as everybody knows, all that family, particularly the daughters, were over-educated. They were old maids. They weren't cranky because they hadn't had a man but because they'd had too many old books. Their brains were strained. Well, a month after I had buried her mother's corpse and her father's ashes, along comes Miss Bolt to my house to kick up hell. 'You haven't buried Father right,' she says. 'Oh?' I says. 'You knew he should have been buried re incumbent,' she says. 'What *are* you talking about, Miss Bolt?' I say. 'I put your Father's urn on your Mother's coffin, and if you can tell me the difference between the way I put him and the way you want him, I'll dig him up and turn him round.' So then she says that I should have turned her mother the other way round as the reverend was on top of her! I mean if parsons' wives are going to get themselves buried re incumbent, where's it going to stop?

We've got a man in the churchyard named Tyler. He used to be secretary to the golf club. When he died he was buried facing south so that when he rises he can see the links. And it was done! I told the parson, 'If a person of my walk of life expressed a wish like that, you'd say I was qualified for the tall chimney' [St Audrey's Mental Hospital].

I never had any qualms about my work. When I was young I delighted in death. The funerals were big and grand and slow. You learnt a lot about everybody. They crept about in the deepest black – now they come to a funeral in all the colours of the rainbow. And afterwards they don't even walk up to the churchyard to cart the dead flowers away. They have one word for the dead when they have got them into the ground, and that is 'forgotten'. I tell them, too. They're upset, but it's the truth. They'll put a stone up with a 'There you are, we've done all we can for you, now bugger you!' They'll even put crazy paving on top of the grave so they don't have to pay me to clip the grass. And the price of it all! When I started you could get coffin, wreaths and everything for £5 – you could actually get a coffin for 30s. Now you wouldn't buy a coffin for a stillborn for under three quid. As for an adult's, it will cost you between £40-50.

And talking of money, I must mention the Table of Fees. Each church has got a Table of Fees which says where the money should go at a funeral. There is the incumbent with his price, there is the clerk with his price and there is the sexton with his price. You would think it was plain enough but I have to read the damn thing aloud to half the parsons or they'd diddle me out of a mint of money. When I do a funeral I'm entitled to 10s. for the service in the church – any church. I don't often get this because the parson takes it. Of course you could argue around this because the Table of Fees says, 'Where no clerk or sexton is employed the incumbent can take the money' – which of course is fair enough up to a point. But believe me when it comes to *little* money matters, parsons are the biggest swindlers on earth. They are. They're that quick on the small change you don't see the passing of it. The burial fees are terrible. It costs a £10 church fee for a parishioner to be buried at Weston – in his own churchyard!

Every parson you come into contact with will have different ways about death. You can't keep 'em in order, you know, these damned parsons! They'll all think different if they can. They'll either cut things out of the Burial Service or stuff things in. It's no use giving the mourners a book so they can follow what is going on. Now old Canon Watson, he'd give you the Service, no more and no less. But the majority of parsons use the 1928 version – which, I agree, is much more cheerful. There's nothing in it like that bit of Job where it talks about the skin worms destroying the body, for instance. Nor that bit about corruption from Corinthians. They say these things are morbid. Well they are morbid. It is what people need when they are staring down at the grave-dirt.

It's the same with the Litany. I said to the old Bishop, 'How often could you walk into a church now and hear the Litany read? Or the Athanasian Creed – and that should be said at least three times a year!' 'Ho! ho!' says he, 'it's all out of date.' I said, 'What was good enough for your forefathers should be good enough for you.' 'Ho! ho!' he says.

The clergy don't stick to religion as we knew it. They do things that are forbidden. They are pulling the Bible to pieces. Altering, altering. . . . I said to the Bishop, 'What do you think of parsons, my lord?' He said, 'What do you?' I said, 'Well they don't preach hellfire. They used to, why don't they now?' He said, 'What, are you blaming the parsons?' 'Certainly,' I said. 'All these parsons preach is the love of God. But they leave out the wrath. What is the use of love without wrath? Tell me that.' I said, 'You are told what will happen to you if you obey His will, so it is only fair that you should know what will happen to you if you don't.' People aren't frightened any more, that is the trouble. If they had to do my work they would know that life is a frightening business. I had a parson say to me the other day, as I was digging a grave, 'Do you think these people will ever come out there again, Tender?' I said, 'They'll have a damned job after I've finished with them!' He said, seriously, 'Once you're in there, you're finished'. 'Never!' I said. But we don't know, do we? We've just got to leave the body after it has been covered up. The people I've accidentally smashed to pieces in my time, they're going to have a rum time of it.

I'll tell you what I think. In the Burial Service it tells you that when you are dead you go into the earth like a grain but it doesn't say anything about your coming out in the same form as you went in. You might come back as a cat! I love cats. I have a family of ten cats in the churchyard. They used to sleep cold among the tombs but I've made a little hole in the charnel door and now they're very comfortable indeed. They cost me 10s. a week to feed and they don't even belong to me. They don't belong to anybody. They watch the funerals from afar off. It's a healthy life for them. There are worse things than coming back as a cat.

I'm not a Christian. I do a lot of things I shouldn't do, so I can't count myself as one. Life isn't as comfortable as it used to be. Nobody wants to know you. I have been widowed for ten years. I go to church every Sunday but nobody speaks to me unless they want something. Snobbish. They're all snobs now. I'm not blowing my own trumpet, but almost ever since I was born I have been at everybody's beck and call. I have no family, none at all. No one in all the world is my relation. I never did read a lot. I never could give my mind to it. I talk too much, that is my failing. I come into contact with many people at a serious time, so I have picked up serious conversation. What most folk have once or twice in a lifetime, I have every day. I want to be cremated and my ashes thrown in the air. Straight from the flames to the winds, and let that be that.

THE CHURCHYARD HANDBOOK

Peter Burman & Henry Stapleton, 1988

Trenchant, bossy even, and entirely admirable, this is one of the most interesting books anybody could read. Originally published a quarter of a century ago, it has been entirely re-ordered to come down like a ton of old tombs on those who during this period have been wrecking our ancient churchyards with their mowers and bad taste. Incumbents have been much to blame, for in most instances they are the legal owners of the churchyard, and they should not have allowed such things as lining-up old, and often beautiful gravestones along the walls of the church, like visiting-cards, or garish flower-beds, or the destruction of wild flowers in areas no longer in use for burials, they and their PCCs. Burman and Stapleton recommend acts of retribution. If you have mown your, often rich, local plant life, as it uniquely exists in a country churchyard, out of existence, then re-introduce it. John Stevens' wild flower nursery at Little Cornard, Suffolk, will provide the species. If some fool has lined-up tombstones, then why not put them back where they rightly belong – over the bodies of those they commemorate?

Mercifully, we are witnessing a new intolerance of such things as banal inscriptions, marble fenders filled with chippings and excessive tidiness. An old graveyard is most likely to contain a thousand years of burials, almost none of them until the 18th century memorialised. The liturgy, the poets, each one of us as we pensively wander through them, for they often contain things which are every bit as enthralling as in the sacred building they surround, recognise churchyards as ideal places for mature reflection. Also as places for seeing the best work of provincial sculptors and letter-cutters, and for finding an acre or two of the local botany as it was before the chemicals arrived. Sheep were the traditional churchyard mowers. I saw them in a Sussex churchyard as late as the mid-Sixties. The authors see no reason why they should not be re-introduced. Such pastorality would carry one of the most generally understood and loved Christian promises. They see the current cult of the lawn as more destructive than 'neglect', and advocate widely-mown path edges which are cut against the rich and various flower-filled meadow grasses which still thrive around countless parish churches. They also give magisterial advice on tree-planting and say that the yew and the cedar of Lebanon are the glories of churchyard silviculture. If the great gale has left you with tree space, think generations ahead and of a towering dark cedar of Lebanon, the ultimate botanical complement to the (usually) lovely architecture nearby.

We are going through something of a funerary revolution. Death-talk is more acceptable than it was a decade or two ago, more people are being cremated than buried, and our churchyards are beginning to show rather too much rationality where our mourning habits are concerned. We have gone from the excess of full-black, and marble angels, to what the authors call 'the pets' cemetery slabs of the average cremation corner. What makes us see ashes as a diminishment which allows us to commemorate a man so meanly? There are no such thing as ashes, as a matter of fact. What we bury is purified calcined bone. It should be placed in the earth without a container, the place marked but not memorialised. Instead, churches are recommended to carve or paint the names of these dead on a board, or to letter them in a book of remembrance which is kept open in the church.

The authors stress all the recent rules and regulations about what one can and cannot do where memorials are concerned. Although these policies have removed much ugliness from our churchyards, they have also inadvertently let in much triteness. Many texts, if they can be described as such, are dreadful, and the clergy should direct mourners to the old tried sources, words from which provide dignified conclusions for believer and non-believer alike. It is salutary to remember that nearly all of us vanish from recollection in a surprisingly short time and that, after this, should our gravestones survive, all they will bring to the churchyard wanderer is a kind of poetry, history and meditation. And who but the most egotistical could ask for more.

Every parishioner has the right to lie in the churchyard whether he is atheist, Muslim, Christian or whatever. But he has no right to have a memorial. Old local families who happen to have lived away, are usually allowed to come home to a grave. Old tombs are frequently works of genius and should be cared for as expertly as the sculpture on the church itself. In spite of the fact that this book has existed for years, parishioner and church authority alike can still display crass and ignorant thinking where it comes to churchyards, and Peter Burman's and Dean Stapleton's witty and uncompromising message is that although the dead are indifferent to what may happen to them there, the living have to encounter an inescapable reality when they enter them. Amiably pottering about in a Cotswold churchyard, reading names like Amariah and Tobit, and deft epitaphs, I suddenly thought of a thousand years of grief on this humpy, stone-strewn meadow.